PRIVACY AND MEDIA FREEDOM

PRIVACY
AND MEDIA
FREEDOM

RAYMOND WACKS

BA, LLB, LLM, LLD, MLitt, PhD

*Emeritus Professor of Law
and Legal Theory*

OXFORD
UNIVERSITY PRESS

OXFORD
UNIVERSITY PRESS

Great Clarendon Street, Oxford, OX2 6DP,
United Kingdom

Oxford University Press is a department of the University of Oxford.
It furthers the University's objective of excellence in research, scholarship,
and education by publishing worldwide. Oxford is a registered trade mark of
Oxford University Press in the UK and in certain other countries

First Edition published in 2013

Impression: 1

British Library Cataloguing in Publication Data

Data available

ISBN 978–0–19–966865–6
ISBN 978–0–19–966866–3 (Pbk.)

Printed and bound in Great Britain by
CPI Group (UK) Ltd, Croydon, CR0 4YY

Preface

The convulsions sparked by the Great British telephone hacking scandal revived the perennial debate about privacy and media freedom. Unable—or reluctant—to resist the public uproar, the government established a judge-led inquiry into 'the culture, practices, and ethics of the press'. Its terms of reference extended well beyond the specific issue of intercepted voicemail; they imposed upon its chairman, Lord Justice Leveson, the onerous task of investigating a host of associated matters, including the relationship between newspapers and politicians, the press and the police, and the extent to which the existing regulatory framework has failed.

Although charting the frontiers between privacy and freedom of expression did not fall explicitly within the inquiry's purview, it permeates many of the rigorous report's 2,000 pages. Predictably perhaps, the preponderance of the ensuing debate has been fixated by the recommendation that the current regime of media self-regulation—widely acknowledged as ineffective—be replaced by a system with 'statutory underpinning'. This proposal has, unsurprisingly, been greeted with considerable media disquiet, bordering, in some quarters, on hysteria. The question of how best to strike a just equilibrium between privacy and free speech has been almost entirely overlooked. Yet it is fundamental to any conscientious assessment of the constitutional status, and future, of these ostensibly competing rights.

Apprehension concerning the United Kingdom's position within the European Union, and unease about the jurisdiction of the European Court of Human Rights, has generated a campaign to replace the Human Rights Act 1998 with a home-grown bill of rights. Little has been said about how any such prospective document might advance the prevailing privacy jurisprudence which, as I attempt to show in the pages that follow, provides inadequate analytical clarity—and, hence, uncertain safeguards—to both rights. One can only hope that, in post-Levesonian tranquillity, the obsession with media regulation will yield to a sober deliberation of these more elemental issues.

Though I consider the specific problem of telephone hacking and other forms of intrusion, especially in Chapter 6, the focus of this work is on the *publication* of personal information and its bearing on freedom of expression, or, in the context of the Human Rights Act, the conflict between Articles 8 and 10 of the European Convention on Human Rights. My objective in this book is to examine the manner in which, and extent to which, the law seeks to reconcile individual privacy and freedom of expression when exercised by the media. This entails, of course, a description of the law both before and after the enactment of the Human Rights Act. And, as one whose privacy odyssey spans four decades of critically observing the vicissitudes of privacy protection, my analysis is unashamedly critical, though, I hope, constructive. My principal qualms and quibbles are marshalled in the final chapter; they—and my general approach—have as their main rationale to fortify the ramparts of both privacy and media freedom.

It is no hyperbole to assert that in the nearly eighteen years since I published *Privacy and Press Freedom*, the legal landscape has altered almost beyond recognition. There are, nevertheless, certain features that have undergone only partial modification or adjustment. Most conspicuously, the action for breach of confidence still pervades the terrain; its ancient doctrines continue to apply both in their own right and, albeit in an attenuated form, in the protection of personal information. Also, of course, the democratic values that lie at the heart of free speech and privacy endure, if anything, more cogently.

I have been fortunate periodically to descend the ivory tower to serve on law reform and other committees dedicated to illuminating the protean nature of privacy, and formulating measures by which this crucial right might be better protected. The experience gained from these opportunities has exerted a powerful influence on my understanding of, and judgment about, privacy and data protection. I am indebted to the members of the Law Reform Commission of Hong Kong privacy sub-committee from whom I learned so much.

A contingent of colleagues, commissioners, and other cognoscenti has, over many years, provided encouragement, advice, and assistance in miscellaneous forms. My gratitude is owed to Michelle Ainsworth, John Bacon-Shone, Eric Barendt, Colin Bennett, Mark Berthold, Jon Bing, the late Peter Birks, Michael Bryan, Ann Cavoukian, the late 'Con' Conway, David Flaherty, Graham Greenleaf, Godfrey Kan, Justice Michael Kirby, Stephen Lau, Robin McLeish, Mr Justice Barry Mortimer, James O'Neil, Charles Raab, Megan

Richardson, Geoffrey Robertson QC, Stefano Rodotà, Jamie Smith, and Nigel Waters. Naturally, none is answerable for the offences I have committed here or elsewhere. As always, members of Oxford University Press have been congenial collaborators in this enterprise. I am especially grateful to Alex Flach, Natasha Flemming, Joy Ruskin-Tompkins, Barath Rajasekaran, and Julie Stone.

I have endeavoured to state the law as at 1 March 2013.

Raymond Wacks

Contents

Table of Cases

Tables of Legislation

I

The pursuit of privacy

Hardly a day passes without yet another onslaught on our privacy.[1] Most conspicuous, of course, is the susceptibility of personal information online to myriad forms of misuse. Other threats generated by the digital world abound. Innovations in biometrics, CCTV surveillance, Radio Frequency Identification (RFID) systems, GPS, smart identity cards, 'Big Data', and the manifold anti-terrorist measures all pose threats to this fundamental value—even in democratic societies. At the same time, however, the disconcerting explosion of private data through the growth of blogs, social media, and other contrivances of our information age render simple generalities about the significance of privacy problematic.[2] And the hunger for gossip continues to fuel sensationalist media that frequently degrade the notion of a private domain to which we reasonably lay claim. Celebrity is treated as a licence to intrude.

We seem to have come full circle. Journalistic infractions, of the kind that stirred Warren and Brandeis to sound their celebrated alarm, is yet again—particularly in Britain—the principal source of public unease. The advent of computers supplanted this ostensibly quaint apprehension; the fear began to shift toward a new Orwellian enterprise: the collection and use of personal data. This panic, when I began my research more than forty years ago,

---

1. I draw in this chapter on some of my previous attempts to consider this question, especially R Wacks, *Personal Information: Privacy and the Law* (Oxford: Clarendon Press, 1989), R Wacks, *The Protection of Privacy* (London: Sweet & Maxwell, 1980); R Wacks, 'The Right to Privacy' in *Human Rights in Hong Kong* (Hong Kong: Oxford University Press, 1992), R Wacks, *Law, Morality, and the Private Domain* (Hong Kong: Hong Kong University Press, 2000), and R Wacks, *Privacy: A Very Short Introduction* (Oxford: Oxford University Press, 2010). Many of the articles discussed or cited in this book may be found in R Wacks (ed), *Privacy*, The International Library of Essays in Law and Legal Theory (London/Dartmouth/New York: New York University Press, 1993), vol I: *The Concept of Privacy*; vol II: *Privacy and the Law*.
2. See Chapter 6.

seemed a neurotic indulgence by anxious German and Scandinavian law-makers. The misuse of personal data was an embryonic, mildly exotic, incu-bus whose ramifications were remote to all but these—prescient—prophets of doom. Those days of innocence have long gone; the seismic shifts in technology have over the past four decades radically transformed the land-scape. The Internet generates risks, unimagined even twenty years ago, to the security and integrity of information in all its forms. It is astonishing to recall that Facebook was launched as recently as 2004, and Twitter in 2006. The manner in which information is collected, stored, exchanged, and used has changed forever—and with it, the character of the threats to individual privacy. But while the electronic revolution touches almost every part of our lives, it is not, of course, technology itself that is the villain, but the uses to which it is put. Do we remain a free society when we surrender our right to be unobserved—even when the ends are beneficial?

My foray into the field originated as an academic venture to clarify the elusive notion of privacy. But the practical dimensions of this increasingly vulnerable right were never far away. Change was looming. The binary uni-verse and its manifold digital incarnations along with new, sophisticated electronic surveillance devices and an audaciously invasive media rendered any complacency about the security of personal information rash.[3] The law—the principal focus of this book—has, breathlessly, attempted to play catch-up. I concentrate on the common law, particularly the English law, but I refer also to the law of other jurisdictions including the United States, Australia, New Zealand, Europe, and the progenitor of much of its law in this area, the European Court of Human Rights.[4]

---

3. It is important to stress that I use the term 'intrusion' throughout these pages to describe those acts (as yet unrecognized as tortious per se) that intrude upon an individual's seclusion or solitude, or private affairs. They include activities such as auditory or visual surveillance by any means, including eavesdropping, watching, spying, computer and telephone hacking or interception, bugging, and so on. (See Chapter 6.) Where, on the other hand, the wrongful act consists in the public disclosure of private facts (whether or not obtained by intrusion) I employ the term 'disclosure' or 'publication'.

4. The jurisdiction—to employ a neutral term—of the European Court and its interpretation of the ECHR, have not been treated with universal acclaim in Britain—a disenchantment that, as will be evident from these pages, I share. This hostility has generated appeals for its replace-ment by an indigenous bill of rights. A 'Commission on a Bill of Rights' was established by the Government on 18 March 2011. Its terms of reference include to 'investigate the creation of a UK Bill of Rights that incorporates and builds on all our obligations under the European Con-vention on Human Rights, ensures that these rights continue to be enshrined in UK law, and protects and extend our liberties.' Its report was published on 18 December 2012. The majority of seven of the Commission's nine members concluded that, on balance, there was a strong argument in favour of a UK Bill of Rights on the basis that such a Bill would incorporate and

The English law, since the enactment of the Human Rights Act in 1998, has undergone tectonic shifts in its recognition of privacy or, to be precise, the protection of 'private life' under Article 8 of the European Convention on Human Rights (ECHR) which has been assimilated into domestic law by that historic statute. The new civil wrong: the 'misuse of personal information' now affords protection to an individual's 'private and family life, home and correspondence'. This is far from a full-blown right of privacy,[5] although, in the years since its inception, it has been all but treated as one.[6]

This is only part of the problem, for even the recognition of the 'right of personal privacy'[7] invites controversy and uncertainty. Why should this be so? For something approaching four decades I have argued that we ought to avoid the various conceptual and doctrinal ambiguities of 'privacy', by acknowledging that the protection of 'personal information' is at the heart of our anxieties about the increasing fragility of this important value. The law, I contended, ought to focus on the protection of 'personal information' which lies at the heart of our increasing apprehension about the vulnerability of sensitive or intimate facts about us. My definition of 'personal information' was an objective one: what is reasonable for an individual to regard as private and therefore to wish to control or limit its use.

Indeed, I went as far as to assert that this woolliness obstructed its effective legal recognition. Except as an abstract description of an underlying value, I contended in 1980, 'privacy' should not be deployed as a legal right

---

build on Britain's obligations under the ECHR, and that it would provide no less protection than is contained in the current Human Rights Act, and the devolution settlements. The two dissenting members were not persuaded that the majority had identified any shortcomings in the Human Rights Act or its application by the courts.

5. The right enshrined in Art 8 is not a 'right to privacy', but a right to *respect* for privacy. See *M v Secretary of State for Work and Pensions* [2006] 2 AC 91, [83] per Lord Walker; *R (Gillan) v Commissioner of Police for the Metropolis* [2006] 2 AC 307, [28] per Lord Bingham.

6. It is not easy to see how the House of Lords in *Campbell v MGN Ltd* [2004] 2 AC 457 made the interpretive leap from Art 8's protection of 'private life' to its recognition of the right to 'privacy'—even if confined to the misuse of private information. Why, if privacy was the right protected by Art 8—and the speeches are replete with broad declarations of its importance and value—did this exclude 'intrusion' such as electronic surveillance (which, in any event, sits more comfortably within the purport of that Article?) Was the court perhaps hidebound by its (correct) decision in *Wainwright v Home Office* [2003] 3 WLR 1137 that 'there is no general tort of invasion of privacy'?, [43], but (in my view, mistaken) conclusion in that case that strip-searches were, in theory, an example of what I here call 'intrusion'? I expand on this criticism in Chapter 8. See too my discussion in Chapter 6 of the role of intrusion in determining whether Art 8 is 'engaged'.

7. '[W]e have reached a point at which it can be said with confidence that the law recognises and will appropriately protect a right of personal privacy', *Douglas v Hello! Ltd* [2000] 1 QB 967, [110] per Sedley LJ.

or cause of action. Over twenty years later an echo of this view was heard in the House of Lords:[8]

> There seems to me a great difference between identifying privacy as a value which underlies the existence of a rule of law (and may point the direction in which the law should develop) and privacy as a principle of law in itself. The English common law is familiar with the notion of underlying values—principles only in the broadest sense—which direct its development. A famous example is…freedom of speech [as an]…underlying value…But no one has suggested that freedom of speech is in itself a legal principle which is capable of sufficient definition to enable one to deduce specific rules to be applied in concrete cases. That is not the way the common law works.[9]

My own disquiet sprang not merely from terminological or linguistic imprecision, but also from the promiscuous application of 'privacy', especially in the United States, to a varied assortment of issues that ranged from abortion, contraception, and sexual preference to noise and pornography. The birth of the new cause of action, fashioned though it was from the less than precise phraseology of Article 8 of the ECHR, was therefore, for me, something of a vindication of my protracted campaign. But my satisfaction that, in their wisdom, the judges identified the quintessence of privacy was tempered by a number of misgivings about the application of what has been styled the 'new approach'.

The recognition of this 'right of privacy' (chronicled especially in Chapter 4) is thus a mixed blessing. It is, on the one hand, heartening that the law has, at last, affirmed the existence of an independent right that was hitherto tethered to the uncertain regimen of confidentiality. Its provenance, on the other hand, is disconcerting. The concept of 'private life' is unhappily as vague as the 'right to be let alone' that bedevils this matter.[10] And the European Court of Human Rights is content that it should be so. Hence, to

---

8. *Wainwright v Home Office* [2003] UKHL 53, [31] per Lord Hoffmann.
9. *Au contraire*, would be Warren and Brandeis's response. Their case for the legal recognition of the right of privacy was the precise opposite. They reasoned that the common law had developed from the protection of the physical person and corporeal property to the protection of the individual's '[t]houghts, emotions and sensations', SD Warren and LD Brandeis, 'The Right to Privacy' (1890) 4 Harvard Law Review 193, 195. An individual's right to determine the extent to which these were communicated to others was already legally protected, but only in respect of authors of literary and artistic compositions and letters who could forbid their unauthorized publication. And though English cases recognizing this right were based on protection of property, in reality they were an acknowledgement of privacy, of 'inviolate personality' (205). The soundness and impact of their legendary essay are explored in Chapters 3, 4, and 8.
10. And whose deficiences I have sought to expose. See R Wacks, 'The Poverty of "Privacy"' (1980) 96 Law Quarterly Review 73, and Chapter 3.

take only one instance, it decided that Article 8 protects the right to sleep.[11] Should this, admittedly important, interest be regarded as a human right? The very concept of 'private life' invites obscurity and abstraction. This is evident in an early decision of the Court that declared:

> [T]he right to respect for private life does not end (at the right to privacy, i.e., the right to live, as far as one wishes, protected from publicity). It comprises also, to a certain degree, the right to establish and to develop relationships with other human beings, especially in the emotional field for the development and fulfilment of one's own personality.[12]

This is an unambiguous confirmation of the immense scope of Article 8. And herein lies the problem. 'We cannot', it has been rightly observed, 'inflate the concept of human rights so much that it covers the whole realm of justice. Human rights would lose their distinctive moral force.'[13] There is, as yet, little evidence of the English courts reading Article 8 in so expansive a manner. But that might simply be a consequence of the actions that have so far reached them. The reality, however, is that, if presented with such an application, the judges have little choice but to look to the jurisprudence of the European Court, for Articles 8 and 10 are 'the very content of the domestic tort that the English court has to enforce.'[14] This is not to deny the importance of rights or even their formulation in broad terms which facilitate their recognition by the common law; however, as one American commentator has acknowledged, 'a natural "right" to privacy is simply inconceivable as a legal right—sanctioned perhaps by society but clearly not enforceable by government...Privacy itself is beyond the scope of law.'[15]

Unlike manna, the new cause of action did not fall from heaven. For centuries, Equity has included the protection of personal information

---

11. See, eg, the decision in *Hatton v United Kingdom* App 36022/97 (2002) 34 EHRR 37 which accepted the proposition that sleep disturbance, distress, and illness caused by night flights at Heathrow Airport could constitute a violation of the claimants' right to private life under Art 8 of the ECHR. See Chapter 8.
12. *X v Iceland* App 6825/74 (1976) 5 DR 86, 87.
13. G Letsas, *A Theory of Interpretation of the European Convention on Human Rights* (Oxford: Oxford University Press, 2007), 25. Indeed, the relentless practice of human rights inflation has devalued the currency. In the words of James Griffin, 'The term "human right" is nearly criterionless. There are unusually few criteria for determining when the term is used correctly and when incorrectly—not just among politicians, but among philosophers, political theorists, and jurisprudents as well. The language of human rights has, in this way, become debased', J Griffin, *On Human Rights* (Oxford: Oxford University Press, 2008), 14–15.
14. *McKennitt v Ash* [2008] 1 QB 73, [11] per Buxton LJ.
15. RF Hixson, *Privacy in a Public Society: Human Rights in Conflict* (New York/Oxford: Oxford University Press, 1987), 98.

within the remedy for breach of confidence, and, it is out of this cocoon that the new cause of action was born. This development from chrysalis to creature—and how it has taken flight—are described in Chapters 3 and 4. Suffice it to say at this juncture that the major impediment to that ancient remedy providing greater protection in the archetypal privacy case was the requirement that the defendant owe the claimant a duty of confidence.[16] Once liberated from this restraint, the law of confidence might have been considered equipped to proffer the required protection for privacy, but it was instead held that 'the essence of the tort is better encapsulated now as misuse of personal information.'[17]

Personal information

My argument has been misunderstood. Critics have suggested that I overlook an important characteristic of private data: that on its own, an item of information may be perfectly innocuous, but when combined with another piece of equally inoffensive data, the information is transformed into something that is genuinely private. The example frequently cited is of Ms Brown's address which is publicly available and, on its own, hardly constitutes 'private' information. Connect this with, say, her occupation, and the combination converts the data into vulnerable details that Ms Brown has a legitimate interest in concealing.

My analysis would indeed be deficient if it failed to account for this obvious factor. The objective model of personal information that I postulate recognizes the need to consider the complete context in which the data occur. In evaluating whether the information in question satisfies the threshold requirement of 'personal', the facts that are the subject of the individual's complaint will plainly need to be examined 'in the round'. It is hardly reasonable for victims to conceive of publicly accessible data (telephone numbers, addresses, number plates, etc) as information whose disclosure or circulation they wish to control or curtail. In general, it is only when these data are rendered sensitive, for example by their linkage to other data, that a justifiable complaint could be said to materialize.

---

16. As long ago as 1972, the Younger Committee concluded that the action offered 'the most effective protection of privacy in the whole of our existing law, civil and criminal', *Report of the Committee on Privacy* (Cmnd 5012, 1972) (Chairman: Kenneth Younger), para 87.
17. *Campbell v MGN Ltd* [2004] 2 AC 457, [14] per Lord Nicholls.

Reasonableness does not wholly exclude the operation of individual idiosyncrasy where its effect would be relevant to the circumstances of the case. Nor would an objective test deny the significance of such factors in determining whether it is reasonable for an individual to consider information as personal. The British, for example, are notoriously coy about revealing their salaries; Scandinavians far less so. Cultural factors will inevitably influence the judgment of whether it is reasonable to regard information as personal. And this is no less true within a specific society. In any event, no item of information is—in and of itself—personal. An anonymous medical file, bank statement, or lurid disclosure of a sexual affair is innocuous until linked to an individual. Only when the identity of the subject of the information is revealed does it become personal. And this is no less true once this threshold is crossed; what is now personal information is worthy of protection only when it satisfies an objective test. But this does not occur in a conceptual or social vacuum; it must be evaluated by reference to the specific conditions.

I shall need to show the benefits of adopting this analysis, especially when personal information is misused or sought to be misused by the media. This I hope to do in Chapters 3 and 4. Nevertheless I remain (stubbornly) convinced that, at least in the United States, the promiscuous extension of the concept to 'decisional' matters (abortion, contraception, sexual preference), and its—comprehensible—conflation with freedom and autonomy, is a conceptual mistake. Its impact, however, may be diminishing: in the routine dystopian prognoses of privacy's decline, rarely is mention made of these and other 'decisional' matters (noise, pollution, and the like) that often infiltrate into the province of privacy. Why do privacy advocates rarely agonize about these questions, important though they are, when they warn of the countless dangers posed by our information society? Does this constitute a white flag: an implicit recognition that the proper meaning of privacy corresponds with our intuitive understanding and use of the notion of privacy as primarily an interest in protecting personal information? When we bewail its demise, do we not mourn the loss of control over intimate facts about ourselves? And is the essence of that control not the explicit exercise of autonomy in respect of our most sensitive details, whether they be pried upon or gratuitously published?

I could, of course, be wrong. Why should disparate privacy rights be unable to coexist as different, but related, dimensions of the same fundamental idea? Why not allow the 'informational privacy' under discussion here to live in peace with 'decisional privacy'? Most scholars in this enormous, ever-expanding field would express little or no resistance to this proposition. Why do I? My resistance to the equation of 'privacy' and personal autonomy springs not from a denial of the importance of rights or even their formulation in broad terms which facilitate their legal recognition. It rests instead on the belief that by addressing the problem as the protection of personal information, the pervasive difficulties that are generally forced into the straitjacket of privacy might more readily be resolved.

The concept of privacy has become too vague and unwieldy to perform constructive analytical work.[18] This uncertainty has, as I have already suggested, undermined the importance of this value and thwarted its effective protection. It has grown into as nebulous a notion as 'freedom' (with which it is not infrequently equated) or 'autonomy' (with which it is often confused).[19] Moreover, it seems to me to arrest the development of an acceptable theory of privacy. The more capacious the concept, the less likely is its susceptibility to lucid conceptual expression. Some might reply that the early, magnanimous 'right to be let alone' could comfortably accommodate all manner of privacy-invading conduct. But it is only by the most tortuous reasoning that the misuse of personal data (data mining, data scraping, profiling, etc), let alone—in this Facebook age—the manifold forms of online exploitation and abuse (including the scourges of deep packet inspection, data aggregation, flash cookies, and sites such as spokeo.com) could be satisfactorily captured within even so munificent a slogan. I continue this assault in the pages that follow.

But quite apart from its utility or application as a *legal* concept, the coherence of the very idea of 'privacy' is suspect. This is evident in two respects. First, it is sometimes argued that by protecting the values underpinning 'privacy' (property rights, human dignity, preventing or compensating the infliction of emotional distress, etc), moral and legal discourse concerning 'privacy' may be dispensed with. This essentially reductionist argument obviously has its major purchase in relation to the need for the *legal* protection of 'privacy'. If, however, it can be demonstrated that the concept is largely parasitic, that its protection may be secured by safeguarding other (primary)

---

18. An early expression of these difficulties is F Davis, 'What Do We Mean by "Right to Privacy"?' (1959) 4 South Dakota Law Review 1.
19. For an attempt to derive the right to privacy from the 'moral principle...of respect for individual liberty,' see RB Hallborg, 'Principles of Liberty and the Right to Privacy' (1986) 5 Law and Philosophy 175.

interests, its conceptual distinctiveness is thrown into considerable doubt.[20] Secondly, even among those who deny the parasitical character of 'privacy', there is little agreement concerning its principal defining features.

Again, these concerns are especially important in the context of arguments about the *legal* protection of 'privacy'. But it is clear that unless a concept is sufficiently distinctive to facilitate coherent analytical identification and description, the prospects for its satisfactory legal recognition and application are bound to be poor. Such problems are not, of course, peculiar to the notion of 'privacy'. 'Freedom', 'security', 'liberty', and other values are, to a greater or lesser extent, vulnerable to similar criticism. But unless it is to be argued that subscribing to generalized values exhibits our commitment to them, it seems perverse not to attempt to refine the nature and scope of the problem, especially if this might actually engender more effective protection. This analytical extravagance is not confined to academic commentary. It is evident also in a number of judicial decisions. We should, I think, prefer the circumspection of Gleeson CJ when in *Lenah* he declared, 'the lack of precision of the concept of privacy is a reason for caution in declaring a new tort of the kind for which the respondent contends.'[21]

Without undermining the significance of 'privacy' as a value, a less problematic and more direct method of attempting to resolve the difficulties associated with its protection is to isolate the essential issues that give rise to such claims. Indeed, in view of the confusion that generally afflicts discussions of the concept, there is an overwhelming case for seeking to liberate the subject from the presumptive force of its value-laden starting point concerning the desirability of 'privacy'. If it is replied that it is possible to arrive at a *neutral* definition of 'privacy', it must be said that such attempts inevitably strip the concept of much of its intuitive meaning and explanatory

---

20. The elaborate endeavour by Daniel Solove to formulate his 'taxonomy of privacy' is afflicted with this elemental deficiency. Solove proposes abandoning the search for a common denominator or essence of privacy. Instead, he suggests that privacy can usefully be conceptualized in terms of Wittgenstein's notion of 'family resemblances': though certain concepts might not share one common characteristic, they might form a 'network of similarities overlapping and criss-crossing'. Solove therefore proposes that instead of seeking an overarching concept of 'privacy', we ought to focus on specific forms of interferences or disruptions. But, on what basis, then, do certain practices constitute *privacy*-invading conduct if there is no shared concept of 'privacy'? The core idea of 'family resemblance' seems to invite the very vagueness that Solove is at pains to avoid. His meticulous analysis produces, I think, an admirable theory of *infringement* of privacy, rather than of privacy itself—perhaps confirming my own view that the concept is intractably incoherent. See DJ Solove, *Understanding Privacy* (Cambridge, MA: Harvard University Press, 2008).

21. *Australian Broadcasting Corporation v Lenah Game Meats Pty Ltd* [2001] HCA 63, para 41.

power. Thus, to conceive of 'privacy' as 'limited accessibility' avoids loading the concept with a positive value, but it also results in *any* loss of solitude by or information about an individual having to be counted as a loss of 'privacy'.[22]

A loss of privacy, as distinct from an infringement of the right of privacy, occurs, in this account, where others obtain information about an individual, pay attention, or gain access to him or her. The claimed virtues of this approach are, first, that it is neutral, facilitating an objective identification of a loss of privacy. Secondly, it demonstrates the coherence of privacy as a value. Thirdly, it suggests the utility of the concept in legal contexts (for it identifies those occasions calling for legal protection). And, fourthly, it includes 'typical' invasions of privacy and excludes those issues mentioned earlier which, though often thought to be privacy questions, are best regarded as moral or legal issues in their own right (noise, odours, prohibition of abortion, contraception, homosexuality, and so on).

Yet even this analysis presents certain difficulties. In particular, in attempting to define privacy in such a way as to avoid pre-empting questions as to its desirability, the analysis is driven to rejecting definitions which limit themselves to the *quality* of the information divulged. It therefore dismisses the view that, to constitute part of privacy, the information concerned must be *private* in the sense of being intimate or related to the individual's identity. If a loss of privacy occurs whenever *any* information about an individual becomes known (the secrecy component), the concept loses its intuitive meaning. But it seems to me to be a distortion to describe *every* instance of the dissemination of information about an individual as a loss of privacy, yet the requirement of a value-free definition of privacy dictates that to confine the ambit of privacy-invading conduct to the transfer or communication of private information is to invoke a value judgment in respect of the desirability of privacy. To the extent, however, that privacy is a function of information or knowledge about the individual, this seems to be inevitable. In other words, in so far as the question of information about an individual is concerned, a limiting or controlling factor is required; I think that the most acceptable limiting factor is that the information be 'personal'.

22. R Gavison, 'Privacy and the Limits of Law' (1980) 89 Yale Law Journal 412. Her concept of 'limited accessibility' comprises a cluster of three related but independent components: *secrecy*—information known about an individual; *anonymity*—attention paid to an individual; and *solitude*—physical access to an individual.

To claim that whenever an individual is the subject of attention or when access to him or her is gained, he or she necessarily loses privacy is again to divest our concern for privacy of much of its intuitive meaning. Having attention focused upon you or being subjected to uninvited intrusions upon your solitude are objectionable in their own right, but our concern for the individual's privacy in these circumstances is strongest when he or she is engaged in activities which we would normally consider private. The Peeping Tom is more likely to affront our conception of what is 'private' than someone who follows an individual in public.

There are, moreover, a number of associated problems that might be obviated by adopting the alternative approach proposed here. In particular, three specific analytical difficulties might be briefly mentioned. First, arguments about the meaning of 'privacy' frequently proceed from fundamentally different premises. Thus, for instance, where 'privacy' is described as a 'right',[23] issue is not seriously joined with those who conceive it to be a 'condition'.[24] The former is usually a normative statement about the need for privacy (however defined); the latter merely makes a descriptive statement about 'privacy'.

Secondly, claims about the desirability of 'privacy' confuse its instrumental and inherent value; 'privacy' is regarded by some as an end in itself,[25] while others view it as instrumental in the securing of other social ends such as creativity,[26] love,[27] or emotional release.[28] Thirdly, there is, among discussions of 'privacy', confusion between descriptive accounts especially of the law on the one hand, and normative accounts on the other. A considerable effort has been made in an ultimately futile attempt to reconcile these two fundamentally antagonistic perspectives.

23. The *Report of the Committee on Privacy* (n 16), confused 'rights' and 'liberties': N MacCormick, 'A Note upon Privacy' (1973) 89 Law Quarterly Review 23 and 'Privacy: A Problem of Definition' (1974) 1 Journal of Legal Studies 75. Cf N Marsh, 'Hohfeld and Privacy' (1973) 89 Law Quarterly Review 183.
24. L Lusky, 'Invasion of Privacy: A Clarification of Concepts' (1972) 72 Columbia Law Review, 693, 709; MA Weinstein, 'The Uses of Privacy in the Good Life' in JR Pennock and JW Chapman (eds), *Nomos* XIII (New York: Atherton, 1971), 27.
25. EL Beardsley, 'Privacy: Autonomy and Selective Disclosure' in JR Pennock and JW Chapman (eds), *Nomos* XIII (New York: Atherton, 1971; SI Benn, 'Privacy, Freedom and Respect for Persons' in *Nomos* XIII, 1.
26. Weinstein (n 24).
27. C Fried, *An Anatomy of Values: Problems of Personal and Social Choice* (Cambridge, MA: Harvard University Press).
28. AF Westin, *Privacy and Freedom* (New York: Atheneum, 1967), 33.

There is little doubt that originally the 'archetypal' complaints in the 'privacy' field related to the 'public disclosure of private facts' and the 'intrusion upon an individual's seclusion, solitude or private affairs'. And the problems generated by the collection and use of computerized personal data have become a central feature of the analysis of contemporary threats to privacy.[29] It is clear that, at bottom, these three questions share a concern to limit the extent to which 'private facts' about the individual are respectively published, intruded upon, or misused. My own view is therefore that a more rational, direct, and effective method of seeking to address the central questions of 'privacy' is to avoid the conceptual labyrinth that has so far impaired their satisfactory resolution. This is not to suggest that certain conditions (eg, being alone) or certain activities (eg, the hacking of mobile telephone voicemail) ought not to be characterized as 'privacy' or 'invasions of privacy' respectively. My entreaty that, except to describe the underlying value, the term 'privacy' ought to be resisted, has gone unheeded. It is now perhaps too late.

In locating the problems of privacy at the level of personal information, two obvious questions arise. First, what is to be understood by 'personal' and, secondly, under what circumstances is a matter to be regarded as 'personal'? Is something 'personal' by virtue simply of the claim by an individual that it is so, or are certain matters *intrinsically* personal? The assertion, in other words, that something is 'personal' may be norm-dependent or norm-invoking. To claim that my political views are personal must depend on certain norms which prohibit or curtail enquiries into, or unauthorized reports of, such views. It may, however, suffice for me to invoke the norm that I am entitled to keep my views to myself.

These norms are clearly culture-relative as well as dynamic. Anthropological evidence suggests that primitive societies have differential 'privacy' attitudes. And it can hardly be doubted that in modern societies, conceptions of what is 'private' will differ and change. There is certainly less diffidence

---

29. See, eg, DH Flaherty, 'On the Utility of Constitutional Rights to Privacy and Data Protection' (1991) 41 Case Western Reserve Law Review 831; S Simitis, 'Reviewing Privacy in an Information Society' (1987) 135 University of Pennsylvania Law Review 707: DJ Solove, *The Digital Person: Technology and Privacy in the Information Age* (New York: New York University Press, 2004); JB Rule, *Privacy in Peril* (New York: Oxford University Press, 2007); JB Rule and G Greenleaf (eds), *Global Privacy Protection: The First Generation* (Cheltenham: Edward Elgar, 2008); L Bygrave, *Data Protection Law: Approaching its Rationale, Logic and Limits* (The Hague: Kluwer Law International, 2002); P Schwartz and J Reidenberg, *Data Protection Law: A Study of United States Data Protection* (Dayton, OH: Michie, 1996).

in most modern communities with regard to several aspects of private life than characterized societies of even fifty years ago. Is there not a class of information that may plausibly be described as 'personal'? Normally it is objected that 'privateness' is not an attribute of the information itself; that the *same* information may be regarded as very private in one context and not so private or not private at all in another.

Naturally, Jane may be more inclined to divulge intimate facts to her psychiatrist or to a close friend than to her employer or spouse. And her objection to the disclosure of the information by a newspaper might be expected to be even stronger. But the information remains 'personal' in all three contexts. What changes is the extent to which she is prepared to permit the information to become known or to be used. It is counter-intuitive to describe the information in the first context (the psychiatrist) as 'not private at all' or even 'not so private'. We should surely want to say that the psychiatrist is listening to *personal* facts being discussed. Were the conversation to be surreptitiously recorded or the psychiatrist called upon to testify in court as to his or her patient's homosexuality or infidelity we should want to say that *personal information* was being recorded or disclosed. The context has manifestly changed, but it affects the degree to which it would be reasonable to expect an individual to object to the information being used or spread abroad, not the *quality* of the information itself.

Any definition of 'personal information' must therefore include both elements. It should refer both to the *quality* of the information and to the *reasonable expectations of the individual concerning its use*. The one is, in large part, a function of the other. In other words, the concept of 'personal information' postulated here functions both descriptively as well as normatively. Since 'personal' relates to social norms, to so describe something implies that it satisfies certain of the conditions specified in the norms, without which the normative implications would have no validity. Thus, if a letter is marked 'personal' or if its contents clearly indicate that it is personal, the implication is that it satisfies one or more of the conditions necessary for its being conceived as 'personal'; this is a descriptive account.

'Personal information' may therefore be defined to include *those facts, communications, or opinions which relate to an individual and which it would be reasonable to expect him or her to regard as intimate or sensitive and therefore to want to withhold, or at least to restrict their collection, use, or publication.* 'Facts' are not, of course, confined to textual data, but encompass a wide range of data including images, DNA, and other genetic and biometric data such as fingerprints, face and iris recognition, and the ever-increasing types of information about us that technology is able to uncover and exploit.

It might immediately be objected that, by resting the notion of 'personal information' on an *objective* determination of an individual's expectations, the definition is actually an exclusively normative one and therefore pre-empts enquiries concerning the desirability or otherwise of protecting 'personal information'. But any attempt to classify information as 'personal', 'sensitive', or 'intimate' is based on the assumption that such information warrants special treatment. To the extent that it is necessary to define the information by reference to some objective criterion (since a subjective test would clearly be unacceptable), it is inevitable that the classification depends on what may legitimately be claimed to be 'personal'. Only information which it is reasonable to wish to withhold is likely, under any test, to be the focus of our concern. An individual who regards information concerning say, his car, as personal and therefore seeks to withhold details of the size of its engine will find it difficult to convince anyone that his vehicle's registration document constitutes a disclosure of 'personal information'. An objective test of what is 'personal' will operate to exclude such species of information.

But this becomes more difficult where the individual's claim relates to information which affects his or her 'private life'. It would not be unreasonable, for instance, for an individual to wish to prevent the disclosure of facts concerning his trial and conviction for theft. Applying the proposed definition of 'personal information' as a first-order test of whether such information is 'personal' may suggest that the claim is a legitimate one. But such a claim is likely to be defeated on the ground that the administration of justice is an open and public process. The passage of time may, however, alter the nature of such events and what was once a *public* matter may, several years later, be reasonably considered as private.

Similarly, the publication of what was once 'public' information garnered from old newspapers may several years later be considered an offensive disclosure of personal information. It does not therefore follow that the objective test pre-empts the 'balancing' of the individual's right or claim to withhold 'personal information' on the one hand, and the competing interests of the community in, say, freedom of expression on the other. By voluntarily disclosing or acceding to the use or dissemination of personal information, the individual does not relinquish his claim that he retains certain control over it. He may, for instance, allow the information to be used for one purpose (eg, medical diagnosis), but object when it is used for another (eg, employment).

In the case of opinions about an individual expressed by a third party, the existence of which the individual is *aware* (eg, references sought by him for a job application), it would be reasonable to expect him to permit access to such material only by those who are directly concerned in the decision whether or not to employ him. Where he does *not* know that assessments have been made about him (where, for example, he is described as a 'bad risk' on the computerized files of a credit reference agency) or that his communications have been intercepted or recorded, he may reasonably be expected to object to the use or disclosure (and in the case of surreptitious surveillance, to the actual acquisition) of the information, particularly if it is (actually or potentially) misleading or inaccurate *were he aware* of its existence. There is naturally a whole range of 'items' of 'personal information' the use or disclosure of which one might expect individuals to wish to resist. A complete catalogue of such information would be impossible (and probably pointless).

Yet, while much of our contemporary disquiet about privacy tends to spring from the malevolent capacity of technology, a yearning for a private realm long precedes the Brave New World of bits and bytes, of electronic surveillance, and CCTV. Indeed, anthropologists have demonstrated that there is a near-universal desire for individual and group privacy in primitive societies, and that this is reflected in appropriate social norms. The manner in which information is collected, stored, exchanged, and used has altered forever—and with it, the character of the threats to individual privacy. But while the electronic revolution touches almost every part of our lives, it is not, of course, technology itself that is the villain, but the uses to which it is put.

At the core of our concern to protect privacy lies a conception of the individual's relationship with society. Once we acknowledge a separation between the public and the private domain, we presume both the existence of a community in which such a division makes sense, but also an institutional structure that facilitates an organic representation of this sort. In other words, to postulate the 'private' presupposes the 'public'. Participation in the public—in society—has undergone steady and profound erosion over the last century or so. Our post-modern psychological preoccupation with 'being in touch' with our feelings has, Richard Sennett vividly demonstrates, devastated the prospect of a genuine political community:

I think the defeat that intimate contact deals to sociability is...the result of a
long historical process, one in which the very terms of human nature have
been transformed, into that individual, unstable, and self-absorbed phenomenon we call 'personality.' That history is of the erosion of the delicate balance which maintained society in the first flush of its secular and capitalist
existence. It was a balance between public and private life, a balance between
an impersonal realm in which men could invest one kind of passion and a
personal realm in which they could invest another...As both secularity and
capitalism arrived at new forms in the (nineteenth) century, [the] idea of a
transcendent nature gradually lost its meaning. Men came to believe that they
were the authors of their own characters, that every event in their lives must
have a meaning in terms of defining themselves...Gradually this mysterious,
dangerous force which was the self came to define social relations. It became
a social principle. At that point, the public realm of impersonal meaning and
impersonal action began to wither.[30]

Paradoxically, excessive intimacy has destroyed it: 'The closer people come,
the less social, the more painful, the more fratricidal their relations.'[31]

The concern to protect 'privacy' in its broadest, and least lucid, sense
is founded upon a conception of the individual and his or her relationship with society. The idea of private and public spheres of activity assumes a community in which such a classification is possible, though
this positive conception of 'privacy' is a modern one which grew out of
a twin movement in political and legal thought. The emergence of the
nation-state and theories of sovereignty in the sixteenth and seventeenth
centuries produced the idea of a distinctly public realm.[32] On the other
hand, a delineation of a private sphere free from the encroachment of the
state emerged as a response to the claims of monarchs (and subsequently of
parliaments) to untrammelled power to make law.[33] Thus, the development
of the modern state, the regulation of social and economic behaviour, the

30. R Sennett, *The Fall of Public Man* (Harmondsworth: Penguin, 1974), 338.
31. Sennett (n 30), 338.
32. See AH Saxonhouse, 'Classical Greek Conceptions of Public and Private' in SI Benn and GF
    Gaus (eds), *Public and Private in Social Life* (London: Croom Helm and St Martin's Press, 1983),
    380; D Hanson, *From Kingdom to Commonwealth: The Development of Civic Consciousness in Eng-
    lish Political Thought* (Cambridge, MA: Harvard University Press, 1970), 1–19, quoted by MJ
    Horwitz, 'The History of the Public/Private Distinction' (1982) 130 University of Pennsylva-
    nia Law Review 1423; H Arendt, *The Human Condition* (Chicago, IL: University of Chicago
    Press, 1958), 38ff; T Nagel, 'Concealment and Exposure' (1998) 27 Philosophy and Public Af-
    fairs 3. Cf MC Nussbaum, *Hiding from Humanity: Disgust, Shame, and the Law* (Princeton, NJ:
    Princeton University Press, 2004), ch 6, IV.
33. J Appleby, *Economic Thought and Ideology in Seventeenth Century England* (Princeton, NJ: Princ-
    eton University Press, 1978), 62–3, quoted by Horwitz (n 32).

perception of a 'private' zone, and so on, are natural prerequisites to this form of demarcation.[34]

But while there is ample historical evidence for this phenomenon, it is best captured by sociological models in which it is shown to be expressive of the values of certain forms of society. In other words, there is an apparent relationship between the existence of a public/private dichotomy and other fundamental features of a society. Such models powerfully express the social values that capture this transformation. A particularly useful typology is the distinctive representation of societies as exhibiting the characteristics either of *Gemeinschaft* or *Gesellschaft*. The former, broadly speaking, is a community of internalized norms and traditions regulated according to status but mediated by love, duty, and a shared understanding and purpose. The latter, on the other hand, is a society in which self-interested individuals compete for personal material advantage in a so-called free market.[35]

The division between a public and private sphere is a central tenet of liberalism. Indeed, 'liberalism may be said largely to have been an argument about where the boundaries of [the] private sphere lie, according to what principles they are to be drawn, whence interference derives and how it is to be checked'.[36] The extent to which the law might legitimately intrude upon the 'private' is a recurring theme, especially in nineteenth-century liberal doctrine: 'One of the central goals of nineteenth century legal thought was to create a clear separation between constitutional, criminal and regulatory law—public law—and the law of private transactions—torts, contracts, property and commercial law.'[37] The question of the limits of the criminal law in enforcing 'private morality' also continues to vex legal and moral philosophers.[38]

The Greeks regarded a life spent in the privacy of 'one's own' (*idion*), as, by definition, 'idiotic'. And the Romans perceived privacy as merely a

---

34. See RH Mnookin, 'The Public/Private Dichotomy: Political Disagreement and Academic Reputation' (1982) 130 University of Pennsylvania Law Review 1429.
35. F Tonnies, *Gemeinschaft und Gesellschaft* [1887] (trans CP Loomis), *Community and Association* (East Lansing, MI: Michigan State University Press, 1955).
36. S Lukes, *Individualism* (Oxford: Basil Blackwell, 1973), 62. See too E Kamenka, 'Public/Private in Marxist Theory and Marxist Practice' in Benn and Gaus (n 32), 267, 273–4.
37. Horwitz (n 32), 1424.
38. This is, of course, illustrated by that old chestnut, the Hart/Devlin debate concerning, in particular, the issue of homosexual acts between consenting adults. The liberal position is, of course, exemplified by the Wolfenden Report (*Report of the Committee on Homosexual Offences and Prostitution*, Cmnd 247, 1957), which based itself on JS Mill's 'harm principle' expressed in *On Liberty* (1859). See too the *Report of the Committee on Obscenity and Film Censorship* (Cmnd 7772, 1979) (Chairman: Bernard Williams).

temporary refuge from the life of the *res publica*. Indeed, only in the late Roman Empire can one discern the initial stages of the recognition of privacy as a zone of intimacy. Hannah Arendt captures this transformation:

> In ancient feeling the private trait of privacy, indicated in the word itself, was all-important; it meant literally a state of being deprived of something, and even of the highest and most human of man's capacities. A man who lived only a private life, who like the slave was not permitted to enter the public realm, or like the barbarian had chosen not to establish such a realm, was not fully human.[39]

Our contemporary separation between public and private zones occurred as a result of a twin movement in political and legal thought. The emergence of the nation-state and theories of sovereignty in the sixteenth and seventeenth centuries generated the concept of a distinctly public realm. Conversely, the identification of a private domain free from the encroachment of the state emerged as a response to the claims of monarchs, and, in due course, parliaments, to an untrammelled power to make law. In other words, the appearance of the modern state, the regulation of social and economic activities, and the recognition of a private realm, are natural prerequisites to this partition.

The segregation of public and private spheres is, of course, also a central tenet of liberalism. Indeed, 'liberalism may be said largely to have been an argument about where the boundaries of [the] private sphere lie, according to what principles they are to be drawn, whence interference derives and how it is to be checked.'[40] The extent to which the law might legitimately intrude upon the 'private' is a recurring theme especially in nineteenth-century liberal doctrine: 'One of the central goals of nineteenth-century legal thought was to create a clear separation between constitutional, criminal, and regulatory law public law and the law of private transactions torts, contracts, property, and commercial law.'[41] And the question of the limits of the criminal law in enforcing 'private morality' continues to perplex legal and moral philosophers.

More than 150 years since its publication, John Stuart Mill's 'harm principle' expounded in *On Liberty*, still provides a litmus test for most libertarian accounts of the limits of interference in the private lives of individuals. For

---

39. Arendt (n 32), 38.
40. Lukes (n 36), 62.
41. Horwitz (n 32), 1424.

Mill, 'the sole end for which mankind are warranted, individually or collectively in interfering with the liberty of action of any of their number, is self-protection. That the only purpose for which power can be rightfully exercised over any member of a civilized community, against his will, is to prevent harm to others. His own good, either physical or moral, is not a sufficient warrant.'[42]

What is 'privacy'?

These accounts frequently assume a meaning of the concept of privacy. This is, however, a vexed, contentious matter. It is, moreover, one that has engaged scholars from a host of disciplines. Thousands of pages have been devoted to the quest for definition, or at least for clarity. Each author trawls vainly through the multitude of preceding efforts to describe this elusive notion.[43] Every new generation of privacy scholars feels bound to navigate anew these murky waters, relentlessly citing every prior definition in an exasperating pursuit of a breakthrough. None materializes. Nor can it.

This far I have employed the term 'privacy' promiscuously to describe a variety of conditions or interests—from seeking refuge from others to the intimacy of close relations. But the notion is anything but coherent. While there is general consensus that our privacy is violated by onslaughts on the private domain—in the shape of surveillance, the interception of our communications, and the activities of the paparazzi, the waters grow ever muddier when a multitude of additional grievances are crowded under the privacy umbrella.

The mammoth literature on the subject has, sadly, failed to produce a lucid or consistent meaning of a value that has become a forum for contesting, amongst other things, the rights of women (especially in respect of abortion), the use of contraceptives, the freedom of homosexuals and lesbians, the right to read or see obscene or pornographic material, and some of the problems of confidentiality generated by AIDS. An important consequence of this Procrustean use of privacy in support of so many disparate, sometimes competing, political ideals has been inevitable analytical disarray.

---

42. JS Mill, *On Liberty* (London: Longman, Roberts & Green, 1869), 9.
43. I suppose I too must enter a guilty plea to this charge.

For instance, one particularly ubiquitous and influential conception—
especially in the legal literature—conceives of 'privacy' as a claim: the 'claim
of individuals, groups, or institutions to determine for themselves when,
how, and to what extent information about them is communicated to others'.[44] To regard 'privacy' as a claim (or, a fortiori, a right) not only presumes
the value of 'privacy', but fails to define its content,[45] and is well described
as a kind of 'logical synecdoche'[46] for it is defining the part by the whole.
It would, moreover, include the use or disclosure of *any* information about
an individual. A similar criticism may be levelled at those conceptions of
'privacy' as an 'area of life' or a psychological state.

Another popular definition views 'privacy' in terms of the extent to
which an individual has *control* over information about himself or herself.[47]
For control over information to be coextensive with 'privacy', an individual
would have to be said to have lost 'privacy' if he or she is prevented from
exercising this control, even if he or she is unable to disclose personal information. This suggests a pre-emptive view of 'privacy'[48] by which its value
is assumed. Similarly, if I knowingly and voluntarily disclose personal information, I do not thereby lose 'privacy' because I am exercising (rather
than relinquishing) control. But this sense of control does not adequately
describe 'privacy', for although I may have control over whether to disclose the information, it may be obtained by other means. And if control is
meant in a stronger sense (namely that to disclose information, even voluntarily, constitutes a loss of control because I am no longer able to curtail
the dissemination of the information by others), it describes the *potential*
rather than the *actual* loss of 'privacy'. Hence, I may not attract any interest
from others and therefore I will be accorded 'privacy' whether I want it or
not. There is a distinction between my controlling the flow of information about myself and my being known about in fact. In order to establish

44. A Westin, *Privacy and Freedom* (London: Bodley Head, 1967), 7.
45. See N MacCormick, 'Privacy: A Problem of Definition' (1974) 1 British Journal of Law &
    Society 75.
46. T Gerety, 'Redefining Privacy' (1977) Harvard Civil Rights–Civil Liberties Law Review 233.
47. See, eg, Charles Fried, 'Privacy' (1968) 77 Yale Law Journal 482; R Parker, 'A Definition of Pri-
    vacy' (1974) 27 Rutgers Law Review 275, 280–1; A Miller, *The Assault on Privacy* (Ann Arbor,
    MI: University of Michigan Press, 1971), 25; EL Beardsley, 'Privacy: Autonomy and Selective
    Disclosure' in JR Pennock and JW Chapman (eds), *Nomos* XIII (New York: Atherton, 1971),
    56, 70; E Shils, 'Privacy: Its Constitution and Vicissitudes' (1966) 31 Law & Contemporary
    Problems 281; Hyman Gross, 'The Concept of Privacy' (1967) 42 New York University Law
    Review 475.
48. Ruth Gavison, 'Privacy and the Limits of Law' (1980) 89 Yale Law Journal 421.

whether such control actually protects my 'privacy', according to this argument, it is also necessary to know, for instance, whether the recipient of the information is bound by restrictive norms.

The purpose of privacy

A life without privacy is inconceivable. But what ends does privacy actually serve? In addition to its significance in liberal democratic theory, privacy stakes out a 'space' for creativity, psychological well-being, our ability to love, forge social relationships, promote trust, intimacy, and friendship.

In his classic work, Alan Westin identifies four functions of privacy that combine the concept's individual and social dimensions. First, it engenders personal autonomy; the democratic principle of individuality is associated with the need for such autonomy—the desire to avoid manipulation or domination by others. Secondly, it provides the opportunity for emotional release. Amongst the numerous situations that privacy affords us to shake off the unwanted gape, is the removal of one's social masks:

> On any given day a man may move through the roles of stern father, loving husband, car-pool comedian, skilled lathe operator, union steward, water-cooler flirt, and American Legion committee chairman—all psychologically different roles that he adopts as he moves from scene to scene on the individual stage…Privacy…gives individuals, from factory workers to Presidents, a chance to lay their masks aside for rest. To be always 'on' would destroy the human organism.[49]

Thirdly, it allows us to engage in self-evaluation: the ability to formulate and test creative and moral activities and ideas. And, fourthly, privacy offers us the environment in which we can share confidences and intimacies, and engage in limited and protected communication.

Privacy and personal information

The focus of this book is on the law, and though the drawing of the public/private boundary is logically anterior to any conception of the role of law, it is also *constituted* by the law. This circularity is compounded by the fact that

49. Westin (n 28), 34–5.

non-legal regulation of what is apparently 'private' may exercise significant controls over such behaviour. Moreover, it would be misleading to assume that, even in liberal thought, there is a consistent or definitive boundary between what is 'private' and what is 'public'. A vast literature devoted to the resolution of these difficulties inevitably raises complex methodological and epistemological questions which frequently obscure rather than illuminate.

Without suggesting that sociological and philosophical enquiries of this kind be neglected, I have long argued that a more constructive means of resolving some of the problems encountered in regulating the collection, storage, and use of private facts about an individual might be found by seeking to identify what *specific interests* of the individual we think the law ought to protect. At the core of the preoccupation with the 'right to privacy' is protection against the misuse of personal, sensitive information. This, at last, appears to be the English law, though it stands in need of greater judicial analysis and elucidation. I suggest a direction this might take in subsequent chapters.

Privacy and the state

In view of decisions such as *Griswold*, *Roe*, *Hardwick*, and *Casey*, it is not surprising that 'privacy' discourse has expanded well beyond Warren and Brandeis's limited concern to establish a legal means of containing unwanted publicity.[50] Though aspects of their original formulation of 'inviolate personality' have had a powerful influence on the concept of 'personhood'[51] as an essential philosophical basis of 'privacy', even this idea has been deployed in an expansive attempt to locate the right to privacy within a theory of democracy. Thus, two recent essays proceed from explicitly political

---

50. *Griswold v Connecticut*, 381 US 479 (1965); *Roe v Wade*, 410 US 113 (1973); *Bowers v Hardwick*, 478 US 186 (1986); *Planned Parenthood v Casey*, 505 US 833 (1992). These judgments of the US Supreme Court concerned, respectively, the use of contraception, abortion, sodomy, and, again, abortion.

51. See J Reiman, 'Privacy, Intimacy, and Personhood' (1976) 6 Philosophy and Public Affairs 26; DAJ Richards, 'Sexual Autonomy and the Constitutional Right to Privacy: A Case Study in Human Rights and the Unwritten Constitution' (1979) 30 Hastings Law Journal 965; JB Craven, 'Personhood: The Right to Be Let Alone' (1976) Duke Law Journal 699; SJ Schnably, 'Beyond *Griswold*: Foucauldian and Republican Approaches to Privacy' (1991) 23 Connecticut Law Review 861–2; J Rubenfeld, 'The Right of Privacy' (1989) 102 Harvard Law Review 737, 739.

perspectives of state power. After rejecting both a republican account[52] and an anti-totalitarian analysis of privacy,[53] Schnably[54] argues that

> [P]rivacy theory needs to make a decisive break from the idea of cordoning individuals from state power. That ideal is a chimera. Rather...a theory of privacy needs to ask how the power of the state *should* be deployed both to foster individual responsibility and freedom in decision-making and to make the politics that directs the deployment of state power more democratic.[55] ...Properly understood, the right to privacy addresses the problem of unequal power and the way it distorts individuals' attempts to come to grips with moral issues.[56]

A similar political strategy informs Thomas's analysis of the US Supreme Court's decision that the Constitution did not confer 'a fundamental right to engage in homosexual sodomy'.[57]

He postulates a different approach that is based on the 'individual right of corporeal integrity' from which he derives 'a right to be free from homophobic violence'.[58] Contending that 'the argument from privacy is predominantly an axiological case against the legal regulation of private, consensual sexual conduct',[59] Thomas claims:[60]

> The corporeal paradigm...differs from the privacy framework in that its case against homosexual sodomy laws relies first and primarily on concepts about power and the state taken from political theory....[S]odomy statutes necessarily presuppose a political conception regarding the relationship between the arm of the state and the body of the individual....[T]he corporeal model permits us to apprehend the unique way in which homosexual sodomy law has historically promoted and reflected illegitimate power relationships among the citizens who make up the body politic.

Since its seminal decision in *Griswold*, the expression by the US Supreme Court of 'unenumerated rights'[61] such as 'privacy' has inevitably led not

---

52. F Michelman, 'Law's Republic' (1988) 97 Yale Law Journal 1493.
53. Rubenfeld (n 51).
54. Schnably (n 51).
55. Schnably (n 51), 875.
56. Schnably (n 51), 933.
57. *Bowers v Hardwick*, 478 US 186 (1986). K Thomas, 'Beyond the Privacy Principle' (1992) 92 Columbia Law Review 1431.
58. Thomas (n 57), 1512.
59. Thomas (n 57), 1513.
60. Thomas (n 57).
61. 'We deal with a right of privacy older than the Bill of Rights—older than our political parties, older than our school system' (at 486, per Douglas J). See R Dworkin, 'Unenumerated Rights: Whether and How *Roe* should be Overruled' (1992) 59 University of Chicago Law Review 381.

only to its colonization of liberties,[62] but has resulted in confusion between the political and social foundations of 'privacy' on the one hand, and its explication as an individual right on the other.[63] It is difficult not to support the libertarian and feminist assault on the state's intrusion into private and even public lives,[64] but the concept of privacy is ill-suited to this task.[65] Arguments about the nature and limits of state power are fundamental to any serious consideration of constitutional freedom. But they are far from conclusive; nor may they be substituted for the difficult and careful analysis that is required when attempting to delineate the precise nature of the right that it is sought to protect.

Privacy as deception

In seeking to withhold or limit the circulation of 'personal information', some would claim that the individual is engaged in a form of deception, especially where the information depicts him or her in an unfavourable light. This is the burden of Posner's application of his 'economic analysis of law' to the subject of personal information.[66] In his view, 'To the extent that people conceal personal information in order to mislead, the economic case for according legal protection to such information is no better than that for permitting fraud in the sale of goods'.[67]

But even if one were to accept the 'economic' perspective, it does not follow that one would accept the assessment of the economic 'value' of

62. See Wacks (n 10), 79–80.
63. See Robert C Post, 'The Social Foundations of Privacy: Community and Self in the Common Law Tort' (1989) 77 California Law Review 957.
64. '[I]t is wrong to think of abortion as an essentially private matter', Schnably (n 51), 944.
65. Thus, while attacking the involvement of the state in homophobic violence, Thomas concedes that 'the use of the term "privacy" to describe [membership of gay and lesbian rights organizations and patronage of gay and lesbian coffeehouses, etc] introduces an avoidable analytical ambiguity, and ultimately confuses as much as it clarifies'; see Thomas (n 57), 1500 n 243. Indeed, Thomas argues that the rights of homosexuals be grounded, not in the right to privacy, but in the Eighth Amendment's prohibition against 'cruel and unusual' punishments (1435).
66. Though he employs (with little clarity) the term 'privacy', Judge Posner (rightly) concentrates his attention on the question of personal information. See RA Posner, 'The Right of Privacy' (1978) Georgia Law Review 393 and 'An Economic Theory of Privacy' in Schoeman (ed), Philosophical Dimensions of Privacy (Cambridge: Cambridge University Press, 1984); RA Epstein, 'A Taste for Privacy? Evolution and the Emergence of a Naturalistic Ethic' (1980) 9 Journal of Legal Studies 665. Cf CE Baker, 'Posner's Privacy Mystery and the Failure of the Economic Analysis of Law' (1978) 12 Georgia Law Review, 475; EJ Bloustein, 'Privacy is Dear at Any Price: A Response to Professor Posner's Economic Theory' (1978) 12 Georgia Law Review 429.
67. Posner, 'The Right of Privacy' (n 66), 401.

withholding personal information; individuals may be willing to trade off their interest in restricting the circulation of such information against their 'societal' interest in its free flow. In other words, Posner has not shown, and may be unable to show, that his calculation of 'competing' interests is necessarily the correct, or even the most likely, one. This analysis cannot be pursued here, but it is worth noting that Posner's claim that his economic theory 'explains' the operation of law produces a certain dissonance if one compares the protection of privacy in the United States with that prevailing in the United Kingdom.

Posner argues also that transaction-cost considerations may militate against the legal protection of personal information. Where the information is discrediting and accurate, there is a social incentive to make it generally available: accurate information facilitates reliance on the individual to whom the information relates. It is therefore socially efficient to allow a society a right of access to such information rather than to permit the individual to conceal it. In the case of non-discrediting or false information, the value to the individual of concealment exceeds the value of access to it by the community. Information which is false does not advance rational decision-making and is therefore of little use.

The limits of privacy

Privacy is not an unqualified good. A number of its shortcomings may be briefly identified. First, privacy is sometimes perceived as a rather quaint, prudish Victorian value; it has, in the words of one writer, 'an air of injured gentility'. Secondly, and more seriously, the shroud of privacy may conceal domestic oppression, especially of women by men. Feminists claim that a significant cause of women's subjugation is their relegation to the private realm of the home and family. Moreover, while the state is disposed to control the public sphere, there is a reluctance to encroach into the private realm—frequently the site of the exploitation of and violence against women:

> [W]hen the law of privacy restricts intrusions into intimacy, it bars change in control over that...It is probably not coincidence that the very things feminism regards as central to the subjection of women—the very place, the body; the very relations, heterosexual; the very activities, intercourse and reproduction; and the very feelings, intimate—form the core of what is covered by

privacy doctrine. From this perspective, the legal concept of privacy can and has shielded the place of battery, marital rape, and women's exploited labor.[68]

Thirdly, the sanctuary of privacy may emasculate the detection and apprehension of criminals and terrorists. Threats to security presently, of course, occupy centre stage. Some fear that an excessively zealous defence of privacy may hinder law enforcement authorities in the execution of their responsibilities. Fourthly, it may hamper the free flow of information, impeding transparency and candour. Fifthly, privacy may obstruct business efficiency and increase costs. An undue preoccupation with privacy can undermine the collection of crucial personal information, and slow down the making of commercial decisions thereby reducing productivity. Sixthly, as Richard Posner contends, withholding unflattering personal information is to deceive. Seventhly, certain communitarian critics regard privacy as an unduly individualistic right that should not be permitted to trump other rights or community values.[69]

Reviews, reports, and re-examinations

The common law's inadequacies, especially those relating to protection against unwanted publicity, have long been acknowledged. For more than half a century, there have been a variety of attempts to reform the law. In 1961 Lord Mancroft presented a Right of Privacy Bill in the House of Lords. Its purpose was to protect a person from unjustifiable publication relating to his private affairs. It was withdrawn after a Second Reading. In 1969 Brian Walden MP's Privacy Bill was withdrawn after its Second Reading when the Government undertook to pursue a comprehensive examination of the subject.[70]

68. C MacKinnon, *Feminism Unmodified: Discourses on Life and Law* (Cambridge, MA: Harvard University Press, 1987), 101. The notion of 'privacy' described in these critical appraisals presupposes a sweeping conception which I seek in these pages to contest. Another important positive consequence of my theory of privacy as the protection of personal information may be to remove the shroud with which the comprehensive right to a 'private life' envelops the domestic sphere, and which, as MacKinnon puts it, 'keeps the private beyond public redress and depoliticizes women's subjection within it.' (102).
69. See A Etzioni, *The Limits of Privacy* (New York: Basic Books, 1999).
70. The Bill was identical to that drafted by the British section of the International Commission of Jurists (JUSTICE) in 1970.

The following year the Committee on Privacy of the British section of JUSTICE published *Privacy and the Law*.[71] It recommended that legislation should be passed to create a general right of privacy applicable to all situations. In 1972 the National Council for Civil Liberties submitted a draft Right of Privacy Bill to the Younger Committee which concluded that, on balance, a general law of privacy was not required.[72] It proposed, however, that surveillance by means of a technical device should be actionable in tort, and that it ought to be tortious to disclose or use information which the discloser knows or ought to know was obtained by unlawful means.[73]

John Browne MP introduced a Protection of Privacy Bill in 1989 which provided for remedies for the unauthorized public use or public disclosure of private information. Although it passed the Committee stage, it was withdrawn at Report stage when the Government announced that it was appointing a committee, to be chaired by David Calcutt QC, to consider what measures were needed to give further protection to individual privacy from the activities of the press. In 1990 the Calcutt Committee published its report concluding that while 'there is now a problem about privacy'[74] there was no overwhelming case in support of a statutory tort of infringement of privacy.[75]

One could have been forgiven for experiencing *déjà vu* when, in his 1993 *Review of Press Self-Regulation*, Sir David Calcutt QC concluded that press self-regulation under the Press Complaints Commission (PCC) had been ineffective.[76] He recommended that the Government give further consideration to the introduction of a new tort of infringement of privacy. The National Heritage Committee of the House of Commons published a report on *Privacy and Media Intrusion* in the same year.[77] It expressed dissatisfaction with the manner in which the PCC had dealt with complaints, and recommended a Protection of Privacy Bill with both civil and criminal provisions. The first part of the Bill listed various civil offences leading to a tort of infringement of privacy.

71. JUSTICE, *Privacy and the Law* (London, Stevens & Sons, 1970).
72. *Report of the Committee on Privacy* (n 16).
73. [563]–[565]; [629]–[633].
74. [13.10].
75. *Report of the Committee on Privacy and Related Matters* (Cm 1102, 1990).
76. *Review of Press Self-Regulation* (Cm 2135, 1993) (Chairman: Sir David Calcutt, QC).
77. National Heritage Committee, *Privacy and Media Intrusion* (HC 294-I, 1993).

Also in 1995 the Lord Chancellor's Department and the Scottish Office issued a consultation paper on *Infringement of Privacy*.[78] It considered the question whether there was a need for a general tort of infringement of privacy. This was a busy year for privacy; the Government's response to the National Heritage Committee Report and the 1993 Consultation Paper was contained in a paper entitled *Privacy and Media Intrusion* published also in 1995.[79] It concluded that statutory intervention in this area would be a significant development of the law, and the Government was not convinced that a case for legislation had been made out.

In 1998 the Government introduced the Human Rights Act incorporating the European Convention on Human Rights into UK law. In its 2003 report on *Privacy and Media Intrusion*, the House of Commons Culture, Media and Sport Committee 'firmly recommended' that legislation was required to clarify the protection that individuals could expect from unwarranted intrusion into their private lives.[80] The Government's negative response was that specific privacy legislation was 'not only unnecessary but undesirable' because:[81]

(a) various aspects of privacy are already protected by legislation (eg, the Data Protection Act);

(b) the 1998 Human Rights Act protected the right to respect for private life;

(c) the weighing of competing rights in individual cases is the quintessential task of the courts, not of Government, or Parliament;

(d) seeking a remedy in the courts could lead to a further loss of privacy for those not normally in the public eye;

(e) the focus should be on ensuring that the press are meeting their responsibilities under the industry's Code of Practice.

---

78. Lord Chancellor's Department and the Scottish Office, *Infringement of Privacy—Consultation Paper* (1993).
79. Department of National Heritage, *Privacy and Media Intrusion: The Government's Response* (Cm 2918, 1995).
80. House of Commons Culture, Media and Sport Committee, *Privacy and Media Intrusion*, Fifth Report of Session 2002–03, vol 1 (HC 458-I, 2003).
81. Department for Culture, Media and Sport, *Privacy and Media Intrusion—The Government's Response to the Fifth Report of the Culture, Media and Sport Select Committee on 'Privacy and Media Intrusion' (HC 458–1) Session 2002–2003* (Cm 5985, 2003), [2.3]–[2.6].

In 2007 the Culture, Media and Sport Select Committee, in its *Self-Regulation of the Press*,[82] rejected the idea of statutory regulation of the press, declaring that it was 'almost impossible' to draft a law that adequately defined a right to privacy. Its 2010 report on privacy and libel did not directly address the question of whether a privacy statute was required, but expressed a preference for self-regulation of the press, proposing that the PCC should have the power to impose fines for serious breaches of its code.[83] In 2012 the Parliamentary Joint Committee on Privacy and Injunctions supported the status quo:

> We conclude that a privacy statute would not clarify the law. The concepts of privacy and the public interest are not set in stone, and evolve over time. We conclude that the current approach, where judges balance the evidence and make a judgment on a case-by-case basis, provides the best mechanism for balancing article 8 and article 10 rights.[84]

Media apprehension

The endeavours to control—or at least to contain—the worst excesses of the tabloids, thus span more than four decades. There have been numerous false dawns. Stars linger in the sky, while an eager band of terrestrial stars— pop stars, sports stars, stars of screen, radio, television, and the catwalk—accepts defeat; their dejection is matched only by the misery of their lawyers. Despite this celestial image—the private lives of 'ordinary' individuals are also vulnerable to unwanted publicity and warrant legal protection.

I shall not recount that forty-year saga here;[85] save to note that each attempt has been repulsed by the introduction of a variety of modifications to fortify

---

82. House of Commons Culture, Media and Sport Committee, *Self-Regulation of the Press*, Seventh Report of Session 2006–07 (HC 375, 2007).

83. House of Commons Culture, Media and Sport Committee, *Press Standards, Privacy and Libel*, Second Report of Session 2009–10 (HC 362, 2010). The committee's recommendations in respect of 'super injunctions' are discussed in Chapter 7.

84. Joint Committee on Privacy and Injunctions, *Privacy and Injunctions*, Session 2010–12, HL Paper 273 (HC 1443, 27 March 2012), Executive Summary. This conclusion is explicitly endorsed by the Leveson Inquiry Report: Part J, ch 3, para 4.3. See Chapter 8.

85. See R Wacks, *Privacy and Press Freedom* (London: Blackstone Press, 1995), ch 1, and perhaps the references in n 1. Dissatisfaction with judicial inertia periodically reaches a crescendo; see, eg, the debate that followed the denial of a remedy to the plaintiff television actor in *Kaye v Robertson* [1991] FSR 62 whose photograph was taken while he was convalescing in a private room of a hospital from which the press were explicitly barred. See BS Markesinis, 'Our Patchy Law of Privacy—Time to Do Something About It' (1990) 53 Modern Law Review 802; P Prescott,

the regulatory regime of what is now the PCC.[86] Most recently, provoked
by public revulsion at the hacking of the voicemail of the mobile telephone
of a murdered teenager, the Government appointed Lord Justice Leveson
to conduct an inquiry into the culture, practices, and ethics of the press,
including its relations with the public, with the police, with politicians, and,
as to the police and politicians, the conduct of each. The comprehensive,
not to say exhaustive, report of the findings and recommendations of the
inquiry runs to some 2,000 pages.[87] In so far as they touch on protecting
privacy against infringement by the media, the proposals are considered in
the relevant sections of this book. In respect of the conduct of the media,

> the clearest message which comes out of the entirety of this lengthy part of the
> Report addressing the culture, practices and ethics of the press overall is that,
> time and time again, there have been serious and uncorrected failures within
> parts of the national press that may have stretched from the criminal to the
> indefensibly unethical, from passing off fiction as fact to paying lip service to
> accuracy. In doing so, far from holding power to account, in these regards the
> press is exercising unaccountable power which nobody holds to account. In
> my view, the maintenance of the status quo is simply not an option; the need
> for change in internal but most importantly in external regulation has been
> powerfully identified.[88]

Identifying several serious weaknesses in the existing system of self-regulation
by the PCC,[89] Lord Justice Leveson declared:

> With some measure of regret, therefore, I am driven to conclude that the
> Government should be ready to consider the need for a statutory backstop
> regulator being established, to ensure, at the least, that the press are subject to
> regulation that would require the fullest compliance with the criminal and civil
> law, if not also to ensure consequences equivalent to those that would flow
> from an independent self-regulatory system. Independence of the regulatory
> body is absolutely critical.[90] I recommend that an independent self-regulatory
> body should be governed by an independent Board. In order to ensure the
> independence of the body it is essential to ensure that the Chair and members

'Kaye v Robertson—A Reply' (1991) 54 Modern Law Review 451; BS Markesinis, 'The Calcutt
Report Must Not Be Forgotten' (1992) 55 Modern Law Review 118, D Feldman, *Civil Liberties and Human Rights in England and Wales*, 2nd edn (Oxford: Oxford University Press, 2002),
Part III; G Phillipson, 'Transforming Breach of Confidence? Towards a Common Law Right
of Privacy under the Human Rights Act' (2003) 66 Modern Law Review 726.

86. See Chapters 2, 6, and 7.
87. *An Inquiry into the Culture, Practices and Ethics of the Press* (HC 780, 2012).
88. *An Inquiry into the Culture, Practices and Ethics of the Press* (n 87), para 4.7, p 739.
89. See Chapter 7.
90. *An Inquiry into the Culture, Practices and Ethics of the Press* (n 87), para 3.34, p 1758.

of the Board are appointed in a genuinely open, transparent and independent way, without any influence from industry or Government.[91]

Astonishingly, although the catalyst for the inquiry was the brazen invasion of countless individuals' privacy, instead of questioning the extent to which the proposals in the Report provide adequate protection for individual privacy, the hullabaloo centred on the recommendation that, to achieve public confidence in the suggested media regulator, its independence be secured by an independent body.[92] The PCC's dismal record of self-regulation (which one witness to the inquiry dubbed 'self-interested regulation') inspires little confidence that—even in its beefed up, independent incarnation—the new body would offer an effective or appropriate means by which to enunciate what are, after all, fundamental constitutional principles. Charting the boundaries of freedom of expression is an onerous challenge best left to judges. A statute—along the lines proposed in the Appendix—would create a framework within which the legitimate rights of victims of media infractions, on the one hand, and freedom of expression, on the other, could be judiciously weighed. It would offer clear guidance to the courts in regard to key concepts such as 'personal information' and 'public interest'. Moreover, judicial interpretation of the legislation would generate a body of binding precedent on the manner in which the inevitable balancing exercise is to be conducted.

Regrettably, the Leveson Inquiry Report did not consider the question of a statutory privacy tort, though its terms of reference would appear to include it.[93] The Report concluded:

> It might have been possible to review the law of privacy and there have been suggestions that a statutory enunciation of such a tort could be of value. Again, how it might be formulated and its possible extent has not been the subject of detailed evidence. In any event, the way in which the common law has addressed these issues has allowed flexibility of approach and a sensible enunciation of the relevant factors to be taken into account when balancing the competing issues in fact sensitive cases.[94]

91. *An Inquiry into the Culture, Practices and Ethics of the Press* (n 87), para 4.5, p 1759.
92. Part K, ch 7, para 6.4. The Report proposes Ofcom as the ideal agency to assume responsibility for recognition and certification of the regulator, Part K, ch 7, para 6.23.
93. '1. To inquire into the culture, practices, and ethics of the press, including…2. To make recommendations…(b) for how future concerns about press behaviour, media policy, regulation and cross-media ownership should be dealt with by all the relevant authorities, *including Parliament, Government*, the prosecuting authorities and the police…' Emphasis added.
94. Part J, ch 3, para 4.2.

It would be surprising were the vigorous media in Britain untroubled by the efforts to circumscribe their freedom to publish personal information. Is it a lost cause? 'Some degree of abuse', James Madison recognized, 'is inseparable from the proper use of every thing; and in no instance is this more true than in that of the press...[I]t is better to leave a few of its noxious branches to their luxuriant growth, than, by pruning them away, to injure the vigor of those yielding the proper fruits.'[95]

But what are the 'proper fruits'? And who is to decide? In general, those who oppose legal, or even stringent regulatory, checks on the unwanted public disclosure of private facts tend to depict concern for the victim as quaint, even prudish. This is contrasted with the aggressively robust pursuit of the truth by the press. In many cases, of course, newspapers, like all commercial institutions, are moved by the interests of their shareholders who may evince less interest in what appears in the paper than what appears in its balance sheet. Moreover, since the press, in its code of conduct, has itself recognized the individual's right to a private life,[96] it is hardly in a position to characterize such apprehensions as pious or censorious.

Privacy advocates may well include enemies of free speech, but that is no more a legitimate argument against them than the argument that advocates of free speech may include avaricious newspaper proprietors. Much is likely to transpire between my typing these words and their appearance on this page, yet the likelihood of MPs (some of whom must dream of little else) passing legislation on this volatile subject remains negligible. How many politicians, whose careers often hang by a slender thread, wish to invite the animosity of the tabloids by championing curbs on their power to report personal information of those in the public eye?

The media and its influential lobby have over the years deployed a number of arguments to stave off legislation. It is instructive to examine some of them and, to this end, I consider the views of two leading journalists on what they perceive to be an objectionable encroachment on editorial freedom. The first was written some seventeen years before the Leveson Inquiry, the second was penned in the midst of the proceedings in 2012. Though published almost two decades apart, they postulate remarkably similar views and are representative of the standpoint of the British press in

95. J Madison, *Report on the Virginia Resolutions, House of Representatives*: 20 January 1800, p 571, in *Letters and Other Writings of James Madison* (1865), vol 4 (Cornell University Library, 2009), 544.
96. PCC, *Editors' Code of Practice*, clause 3.

general, though, since both authors are prominent members of the 'quality' press, they might justly be described as less partial in this regard. Both articles appeared in the same periodical.

The first article, written by a distinguished former editor of *The Times*, and member of the Calcutt Committee,[97] is typical of the media standpoint. Simon Jenkins states:

> My objection is not to the gun but to its aim, the archaic obsession of the tabloids with sex. All but two of the 17 scalps that Fleet Street claims to have cut from the heads of senior Tories of late are for sexual 'misbehaviour'. The misbehaviour is usually of a sort that none of the journalists would recognise as such in themselves or their colleagues. No politician is hounded from office for incompetence or wasting public money. It simply does not happen. The thinnest of justifications for sexual intrusion is that the victims are 'hypocrites', that those who preach family values and back-to basics lay themselves open to intrusion, even if they are doing nothing that impinges on their public duties. That is garbage.[98]

The truth is, as Jenkins points out, that while most tabloids preach family values, they show little concern or respect for the families of their victims. Nor does the cry of 'investigative journalism' wash:

> The revelation of the contents of private phone calls or of the personal misfortunes of relatives of relatives of the royal family are ethically indefensible. They are rarely 'investigative' and merely involve paying money to a snooping intermediary. They are also breaches of the code drawn up by all newspapers back in 1990.[99]

Yet despite this scathing indictment of press conduct, he rejects a 'privacy law': 'I cannot imagine anything more ludicrous or cumbersome or ineffective. I appreciate the tabloids and the irresponsibility and tastelessness they bring to Britain's otherwise dour public life.'

The logic of this line of reasoning is hard to discern. The charges against the tabloids include humbug (for its disingenuous use of 'public interest'), hypocrisy (for exposing intimate information about all except journalists), duplicity

---

97. *Review of Press Self-Regulation* (n 76).
98. Simon Jenkins, *The Spectator*, 15 April 1995.
99. Jenkins (n 98). The code has in this respect changed little over the years, and defines 'public interest' to include detecting or exposing crime or serious impropriety, protecting public health and safety, and preventing the public from being misled. 'The public interest does not include whatever the public is interested in, and it was crucial to maintain the distinction—especially for those in public life. This is a distinction which will cause considerable problems for many tabloid editors in future', R Snoddy, *The Good, the Bad and the Unacceptable* (London: Faber, 1992), 112. Prescient words.

and chicanery (for tricking victims or others into disclosing sensitive facts), dishonesty (for defending virtually any disclosure of private lives as being connected to public office), and insensitivity (for intruding upon private grief). His denunciation nevertheless fails to disclose a case for legislative protection which is summarily dismissed as 'ludicrous', 'cumbersome', and 'ineffective'. The charges are then dropped for the evidence reveals no case to answer!

It hardly requires stating that these three colourful epithets might themselves apply to the media's own attempts at self-regulation. More importantly, however, any serious argument against the statutory protection of privacy surely rests on none of these grounds, but on its potential chilling effect. While the evidence from other jurisdictions gives little cause for pessimism, it would be rash to predict the fall-out of legislation to protect publications that are not in the public interest (with legislative pointers as to its meaning). The burden of proof nonetheless falls on those who, like me, contend that such legislation would not threaten media freedom and the good government it frequently engenders.

The proposition by a respected journalist that to value privacy is somehow wimpish ('irresponsibility' becomes a virtue) or puritan ('tastelessness' is laudable) is curious enough. But his rationale for free speech in this context is even more grotesque: to enliven Britain's allegedly dull public life. This end could, of course, be achieved by any number of artless endeavours. Are those who suffer genuine emotional distress or embarrassment at the hands of the media to be informed that they ought not to complain for their humiliation has invigorated our political life?

A similar position is adopted by Toby Young whose defence of tabloid journalism is also based on its role in entertaining readers:

> This is the real threat posed by the Leveson inquiry—not that Lord Justice Leveson will recommend full-blown statutory regulation, though he has declared that simply 'tinkering around the edges' of existing regulation won't be nearly enough. But that the red-tops will feel obliged to behave more like the broadsheets, thereby losing much of their mass-market appeal. No more celebrity tittle-tattle, no more kiss-and-tells. The *News of the World* has already gone to the wall. How long will the rest of them survive in a post-Leveson world? Most of the red-tops are on their knees as it is and if they find themselves having to abide by an FT-style 'code of ethics', they won't last 12 months.

This is a perfectly legitimate argument for, as Young points out, along with this aspect of their journalism ('irreverent, funny, rambunctious, saucy, anti-Establishment'), the tabloids publish also a good deal of serious news and analysis, brilliantly condensed into readable, clear little paragraphs without all the self-important throat-clearing broadsheets enjoy. If they go to the wall, their readers are unlikely to get that information from anywhere else…[A] cleaned-up tabloid press is unlikely to last very long in the current economic climate.

But while this may be true, does it constitute a persuasive, or even a plausible, case for intrusive, sensationalist journalistic practices? It rests on two questionable assumptions. First, that the tabloids will be driven out of business and, secondly, that, as a consequence, their readers will be deprived of access to news.[100]

Neither cuts much ice. What evidence is there that stripped of their kiss-and-tell stories, the red-tops would expire? And even if this were the case, should their survival be made to depend on offensive newsgathering methods and unsolicited disclosures of private information? Moreover, in a world of online news and satellite television, the prospects of a news famine—for even the most diehard tabloid enthusiast—seem exceedingly remote.

Indeed, Young concedes this point, though in support of an additional dubious claim; he writes:

Another thing to bear in mind is that paparazzi photographs and celebrity tittle-tattle are hardly likely to disappear, however successful Leveson's efforts. If the red-tops become too fearful of public censure to carry salacious stories, their readers will turn to the internet instead. The difference is that sites like TMZ don't include any serious content alongside the pictures of Paris Hilton and Lindsay Lohan flashing their knickers.

This is to patronize the tabloid reader. What impediment is there to his or her clicking on any of a huge number of online newspapers, blogs, or other websites that provide 'serious content'? And, echoing Jenkins, he concludes with a flourish:

---

100. This is not a wholly tendentious claim. Lord Woolf CJ was to similar effect in *A v B plc* [2003] QB 195 where he declared (at [11] xii): 'The courts must not ignore the fact that if newspapers do not publish information which the public are interested in, then there will be fewer newspapers published, which will not be in the public interest.' The Court of Appeal has since distanced itself from this view, pronouncing Lord Woolf's view irreconcilable with the decision of the European Court of Human Rights in *von Hannover v Germany* (2005) 40 EHRR 1, which cautioned against equating what is interesting to the public (and hence in the commercial interests of the press to publish) with what may be in the public interest to know: *McKennitt v Ash* [2008] QB 73, [62] per Buxton LJ. See Chapter 5.

How much more satisfying it would be to see the red-tops engaging in a last hurrah, using every weapon in their arsenal to ridicule Lord Justice Leveson and his army of pompous lawyers. Yes, it might have been tantamount to signing their own death warrants, but if you're going to die anyway, why not go out in a blaze of glory? It would have been the tabloid version of Rorke's Drift. And perhaps it would have brought the public to their senses, and encouraged them to rally behind tabloids and remember our national sense of fun.

We all love fun, but at whose expense is it being enjoyed? It may sound sanctimonious, even priggish, but as I argue in Chapter 5, the true motives for the intrusion and publication are material elements in the contest between privacy and public disclosure. It is not unreasonable to enquire whether the media are acting out of a genuine desire to serve the public interest, or whether publication of the story is in pursuit of profit, prurience, or even rancour. This question will strike some as unfashionably high-minded in our brash new world. But, while the literature on privacy is dominated by a focus upon the interests of the victim and the violation of his or her dignity, personhood, and so on, the unconscionability of the defendant's acts is no less significant a consideration—especially where refuge is sought in an appeal to the public interest. In other words, if it can be demonstrated that the media's appeal to its freedom of expression is spurious, and merely conceals other less laudable motives, the scales must perforce be tipped in favour of the claimant.

Privacy advocates may well include enemies of free speech, but that is no more a legitimate argument against them than the argument that champions of free speech include avaricious newspaper proprietors. The power of the press lobby can, however, never be underestimated. How many politicians wish to invite the animosity of the tabloids by supporting curbs on reporting of what has been called 'bonk journalism'? The media, while quick to condemn the exposure of private lives in the name of the public interest, inevitably close ranks against the prospect of legislation. While most tabloids preach family values, they often show lamentably little concern or respect for the families of their victims.

2

Freedom to express what?

Little controversy surrounds the argument that, in a liberal democracy, freedom of expression is a paramount right. It is difficult to see how a democracy could exist without it. In the words of Lord Nicholls:

> The high importance of freedom to impart and receive information and ideas has been stated so often and so eloquently that the point calls for no elaboration in this case. At a pragmatic level, freedom to disseminate and receive information on political matters is essential to the system of parliamentary democracy cherished in this country. This freedom enables those who elect representatives to Parliament to make an informed choice, regarding individuals as well as policies, and those elected to make informed decisions... Likewise, there is no need to elaborate on the importance of the role discharged by the media in the expression and communication of information and comment on political matters. Without freedom of expression by the media, freedom of expression would be a hollow concept.[1]

But what exactly does this right entail? What, in other words, should one be free to express?[2] Incitement to commit crime? Hate speech? Intimate facts about another?

In any free society, the debate about what rights and freedoms warrant safeguarding (and the nature, scope, and manner of their protection) gives rise to a predictable contest between those of a utilitarian disposition, on

---

1. *Reynolds v Times Newspapers Ltd* (2001) 1 AC 127, [200]. The Strasbourg Court was to similar effect in *Castells v Spain* (1992) 14 EHHR 445, [43], see n 27.
2. When confronting the legitimate limits of this freedom, it is best to avoid Justice Homes's celebrated—but unhelpful—aphorism about shouting fire in a crowded theatre. His actual dictum was: 'The most stringent protection of free speech would not protect a man in falsely shouting fire in a theatre and causing a panic.' But is this 'expression' or even 'speech'? *Schenck v United States*, 249 US 47 (1919). Moreover, if we take this maxim seriously, the false cry of alarm is malicious: a far cry from the exercise of freedom—even under the First Amendment. The wide currency accorded this exemplar in accounts of media freedom has long been a mystery to me.

the one hand, and those who advocate the recognition of individual rights, on the other. The former espouse the view that, broadly speaking, justice is to be measured by reference to the consequences of an act or rule. The latter look to the protection of the rights of the individual as a more effective means of securing liberty.[3] Those who justify free speech by consequentialist arguments normally draw on the arguments of Milton and Mill (from truth or democracy), while those who employ rights-based justifications conceive of speech as an integral part of an individual's right to self-fulfilment.[4] Sometimes, however, these positions tend to be amalgamated, and even confused. So, for example, Thomas Emerson discerns four primary justifications which include both sorts of claim: individual self-fulfilment, attainment of the truth, securing the participation by members of society in social, including political, decision-making, and providing the means of maintaining the balance between stability and change in society.[5]

There is much to commend Spinoza's claim that individuals should be free and unimpeded in their beliefs, both by right and in fact. He refers to the impossibility for the mind to be completely under another's control— 'for no one is able to transfer to another his natural right or faculty to reason freely and to form his own judgment on any matters whatsoever, nor can he be compelled to do so.'[6] Hence, any attempt by the government to seek to control citizens' beliefs and opinions is bound to fail, and will ultimately weaken its own authority. When it comes to an individual expressing his or her opinions Spinoza warns that any attempt to limit this freedom is bound to fail. Suppressing speech or writing offends the natural right of citizens to express their views. In any event, they will speak their minds—even in the face of restraints, though government interference with their freedom

---

3. Some of these points are made in R Wacks, *Privacy and Press Freedom* (London: Blackstone Press, 1995), ch 3. See too R Wacks, *Privacy: A Very Short Introduction* (Oxford: Oxford University Press, 2010), ch 4.
4. See, in particular, F Schauer, *Free Speech: A Philosophical Enquiry* (Cambridge: Cambridge University Press, 1982) and 'Reflections on the Value of Truth' (1991) 41 Case Western Reserve Law Review 699. See too E Barendt, *Freedom of Speech*, 2nd edn (Oxford: Clarendon Press, 2006); T Gibbons, *Regulating the Media* (London: Sweet & Maxwell, 1991).
5. T Emerson, 'The Right of Privacy and Freedom of the Press' (1979) 14 Harvard Civil Rights–Civil Liberties Law Review 329, 331. See too J Raz, 'Free Expression and Personal Identification' (1991) 2 Oxford Journal of Legal Studies 303; T Emerson, 'Towards a General Theory of the First Amendment' (1963) 72 Yale Law Journal 877; R Dworkin, 'Censorship and a Free Press' in Part 6 of *A Matter of Principle* (Cambridge, Mass: Harvard University Press, 1985), 335–87; R Gavison, 'Too Early for a Requiem: Warren and Brandeis were Right on Privacy vs Free Speech' (1992) 43 South Carolina Law Review 437.
6. B Spinoza, *Tractatus Theologico-Politicus*, XVIII, 225.20/276 (1677, trans RHM Elwes, 1883).

may drive them to do so in secret. Such compulsion can only endanger the power of the state.

Some contend that the harm principle does not go far enough. Joel Feinberg has famously argued that we may require a—less restrictive—'offence principle' that provides a yardstick by which to fix the limits of, inter alia, free speech. 'Harm' in many instances, he suggests, sets the bar too high; we should be able to prohibit certain forms of expression when they seriously offend others. As he puts it, 'It is always a good reason in support of a proposed criminal prohibition that it would probably be an effective way of preventing serious offense (as opposed to injury or harm) to persons other than the actor, and that it is probably a necessary means to that end…The principle asserts, in effect, that the prevention of offensive conduct *is* properly the state's business.'[7] Its application will inevitably prove difficult given the prejudices and excessive sensitivity of some.

In regard to offensive speech, rather than conduct, Feinberg proposes a number of criteria that ought to be considered in determining whether proscription is justified. They include the extent, duration, and social value of the speech, the ease with which it might have been avoided, the speaker's motives, the number of individuals who are offended, the intensity of the offence, and the general interests of the community at large.

In other words, even if such speech causes no harm, as understood by Mill, or offence, it should be limited or restricted since it is incompatible with democracy itself. The argument from democracy claims that political speech not only legitimates the government, but creates an environment in which individuals may pursue their aspirations. Should hate speech curb this important feature of a free society, we may justify prohibiting such speech, on the ground of protecting free speech itself.

Article 10 of the European Convention on Human Rights (ECHR) includes within its conception of 'the right to freedom of expression' the freedom to hold opinions, and to receive and impart information and ideas without interference by public authority and regardless of frontiers. It does, however, explicitly permit states to require the licensing of broadcasting, television, or cinema enterprises. It provides also that these freedoms may be subject to such formalities, conditions, restrictions, or penalties as are

---

7. J Feinberg, *Offense to Others: The Moral Limits of the Criminal Law* (Oxford: Oxford University Press, 1985), 1. See too his *Harm to Others: The Moral Limits of the Criminal Law* (Oxford: Oxford University Press, 1985); S Fish, *There's No Such Thing as Free Speech…and it's a good thing too* (New York: Oxford University Press, 1994).

prescribed by law and are necessary in a democratic society, in the interests of national security, territorial integrity or public safety, for the prevention of disorder or crime, for the protection of health or morals, for the protection of the reputation or rights of others, for preventing the disclosure of information received in confidence, or for maintaining the authority and impartiality of the judiciary.

In the United States the issue of freedom of expression is, of course, fiercely debated against the background of the First Amendment's injunction that 'Congress shall make no law...abridging the freedom of speech, or of the press'.[8] And in Britain, there are signs that, under the unfolding sway of the Human Rights Act 1998, the courts may embrace a more expansive understanding of this liberty.[9]

Individual or community?

Does free speech serve the welfare of the individual or of the community? The individualist, rights-based justification argues for the interests in autonomy, dignity, self-fulfilment, and other values that the exercise of free speech safeguards or advances. The communitarian justification is consequentialist or utilitarian and draws on democratic theory or the promotion of 'truth' to support free speech as facilitating or encouraging the unfettered exchange of ideas, the dissemination of information, and associated means of enlarging participation in self-government.

Thus Spinoza advances also a utilitarian case for free speech: it promotes the discovery of truth, economic progress, and the development of creativity. An open marketplace of ideas is required if science, philosophy, and other disciplines are not to be compromised: 'This freedom is of the first importance in fostering the sciences and the arts, for it is only those whose judgment is free and unbiased who can attain success in these fields.'[10] He

---

8. It is generally treated as if it were not the First Amendment, but the First Commandment! For an absorbing account of the history of the First Amendment, see A Lewis, *Freedom for the Thought That We Hate: A Biography of the First Amendment* (New York: Basic Books, 2010).

9. Article 10 of the ECHR, unlike the First Amendment, bristles with exceptions to the right. See the chapters following for several examples of the new order and the application of, in particular, Arts 8, 10, and 12. For a detailed analysis of the Human Rights Act as it affects the media, see H Fenwick and G Phillipson, *Media Freedom under the Human Rights Act* (Oxford: Oxford University Press, 2007).

10. B Spinoza, *Tractatus Theologico-Politicus* [Gebhardt ed, 1925] (trans S Shirley) (Leiden: Brill, 1991), 295.

does not advocate absolute freedom of expression. Sedition or speech that promotes revolution, disobedience to law, or harm to others may legitimately be restricted. Those who seek to change or repeal laws must do so peacefully and through rational argument. Should their argument fail to persuade the sovereign to amend or revoke the law, they ought to accept that judgment. Drawing a line between words and action, Spinoza contends that the government is justified in criminalizing certain types of action. But he explicitly excludes ideas, even the expression of ideas, as falling within the category of 'action'. Under the social contract, man relinquished the right to act as he thought fit, but not his right to reason and judge.

Freedom of expression may also be characterized as a right or interest of both the individual *and* the community as a whole. Among liberal theorists, it is generally regarded as an individual right. So, for example, for Dworkin[11] it is a fundamental right related to the basic concept of human dignity and the background right to be treated with equal respect and concern. This is the right, in other words, to be heard or read. This right 'trumps' the interest in suppressing speech where it might be considered necessary to protect the community.[12]

Speaker or audience?

Theories of free speech that seek to protect the audience are generally arguments of policy (based on the importance of that freedom to the community). Theories that advance the interests of the speaker are generally arguments of principle which give primacy to the individual over the community.[13] Dworkin submits that free speech is likely to receive stronger protection when it is regarded as safeguarding, as a matter of principle,

---

11. See generally R Dworkin, *Taking Rights Seriously*, 2nd edn (Cambridge, Mass: Harvard University Press, 1977).
12. This formulation does run into certain difficulties, for 'it does not appear to provide any clear basis for distinguishing a free speech principle from general libertarian claims concerning, say, the choice of a dress or sexual life-style which might be favoured by individuals. Moreover, unlimited speech may well be contrary to a respect for human dignity. The restrictions imposed by libel and obscenity laws can easily be justified by reference to this value', Barendt (n 4), 16. Moreover, the extent to which we are 'fulfilled' by exercising (or at least by non-restriction of) our right to free speech is moot. How, eg, am I 'fulfilled' by publishing pornography?
13. R Dworkin, 'Is the Press Losing the First Amendment?' in R Dworkin, *A Matter of Principle* (Cambridge, Mass: Harvard University Press, 1985), 386.

the rights of the *speaker*. But the matter is not so straightforward. At first blush, it would seem to provide a coherent basis for claiming that publications which harm other individuals cannot seriously be said to advance the speaker's or publisher's self-fulfilment. But who is to say whether or not certain forms of speech are instrumental in achieving this object?[14] Also, the argument 'suffers from a failure to distinguish intellectual self-fulfilment from other wants and needs, and thus fails to support a distinct principle of free speech'.[15] The argument does not, moreover, work especially well in defence of *press* freedom which appears to rest almost entirely on the interests of the community, rather than the individual journalist, editor, or publisher.

What of the *motive* of the speaker? It would not be unduly disingenuous to suggest that profit may be of interest to newspaper editors and proprietors. And, as Professor Barendt observes, a 'rigorous examination of motives to exclude speech made for profit would leave little immune from regulation'.[16] Nor does the audience necessarily care; a good read is a good read whether its author is moved by greed or edification.

The argument from truth

The essence of John Stuart Mill's celebrated argument from truth is that any suppression of speech is an 'assumption of infallibility' and that only by the unrestricted circulation of ideas can the 'truth' be discovered.[17] But this theory, taken to its logical conclusion, would prevent any inroads being made into the exercise of the right to speak (at least truthfully). But Mill's assumption that there exists some objective truth 'out there'—and his confidence

---

14. A more sophisticated version of the theory is suggested by Thomas Scanlon who argues that government ought never to endanger the autonomy of individuals rationally to determine the validity of other arguments, not on the basis of the argument from truth, but because of the rights of the individual as *listener*. See T Scanlon, 'A Theory of Freedom of Expression' (1972) 1 Philosophy and Public Affairs 204 and 'Freedom of Expression and Categories of Expression' (1979) 40 University of Pittsburgh Law Review 519. But, as Dworkin asks, how does this protect the rights of the *speaker*?
15. Schauer, *Free Speech* (n 4), 56.
16. Barendt (n 4), 24.
17. Thomas Scanlon argues that the argument from truth is a 'natural' (or non-instrumental) argument; see T Scanlon, 'A Theory of Freedom of Expression' (n 14); J Milton, *Areopagitica and Of Education* (ed KM Lea) (Oxford: Clarendon Press, 1973); DA Richards, 'Free Speech as Toleration' in WJ Waluchow (ed), *Free Speech: Essays in Law and Philosophy* (Oxford: Clarendon Press, 1994).

in the prevalence of reason are both rather questionable. The assumption asserts that freedom of expression is a social good because it is the best process by which to advance knowledge and discover truth, starting from the premise that the soundest and most rational judgment is arrived at by considering all facts and arguments for and against. This free marketplace of ideas, Emerson argues, should exist irrespective of how pernicious or false the new opinion appears to be 'because there is no way of suppressing the false without suppressing the true'.[18]

Frederick Schauer expresses doubts that truth is indeed ultimate and non-instrumental; does it not secure a 'deeper good' such as happiness or dignity?[19] If truth is instrumental, then whether more truth causes a consequential strengthening of this deeper good is a question of fact and not an inevitable logical certainty from definition. For Schauer the argument from truth is an 'argument from knowledge';[20] an argument that the value in question is having people *believe* that things are in fact true. He formulates the argument in this way to concentrate not on the abstract truth of a proposition but how its propagation 'is directed towards human action'.[21] One may fail to possess knowledge, or what Schauer calls 'justified true belief', in three ways: 'one's belief can be unjustified, one's belief can be false, and one can have no belief at all'.[22] 'Is it necessarily or generally the case', he asks, 'that knowledge is better than ignorance?'[23] In many instances, new knowledge does not replace existing beliefs about a particular subject but adds to what was previously 'epistemological empty space'.[24] Thus, a gain in knowledge is simply an addition rather than substitution of the true for the false. In such cases, the concept of a marketplace of ideas begins to collapse and one is left with the value of truth actually being contingent upon a theory which links truth to the aim to which it is instrumental. Schauer concludes that *this* theory depends upon a balancing exercise between members of a class or sub-class; many increases in someone's knowledge are at the expense

18. Emerson, 'The Right of Privacy and Freedom of the Press' (1979) 14 Harvard Civil Rights–Civil Liberties Law Review 329, 882.
19. Schauer, *Free Speech* (n 4), p 699.
20. Schauer, *Free Speech* (n 4), p 707.
21. Schauer, *Free Speech* (n 4), p 708.
22. Schauer, *Free Speech* (n 4).
23. Schauer, *Free Speech* (n 4). Ruth Gavison, addressing the argument from truth, claims that 'this particular rationale cannot support the many privacy-invading statements that do not concern ideas or attempt to explain the truth. To recall, the interest that is protected is an interest in not being discussed at all, not an interest in being known in an accurate way', 463.
24. Schauer, *Free Speech* (n 4), p 709.

of someone else's well-being or dignity. He concedes that if we view society as a whole,

> ...more knowledge, as a class, will benefit the well-being or happiness or util-ity or dignity of the recipients of that knowledge, as a class, more than it will detract from the well-being or happiness or utility or dignity of the subjects of that knowledge, as a class.[25]

But if the class is subdivided, it becomes possible to identify sub-classes within which this tendency is reversed. Therefore, proceeding upon the assumption that knowledge is power, if, by law, we curtail the dissemina-tion by A of information about B, then B is empowered at the expense of A who is relatively disempowered. The power struggle is therefore between possessors of information and the class of potential users of that informa-tion. Schauer's approach liberates us from the straitjacket of the inviolabil-ity of free speech. Nevertheless support for a 'categories approach' may be drawn from Schauer's acceptance that certain increases in knowledge have no value at all.[26]

Self-government

The argument that freedom of expression provides the tools for successful self-governance is an extension of the argument from truth.[27] As Alexander Meiklejohn puts it:

> The principle of the freedom of speech springs from the necessities of the pro-gram of self-government. It is not a Law of Nature or Reason in the abstract.

25. Schauer, *Free Speech* (n 4), p 711.
26. Schauer, *Free Speech* (n 4). The argument from truth, as Professor Barendt, observes, has greater pertinence in respect of assertions of opinion than propositions of fact, op.cit., 191.
27. In *Castells* v *Spain* 14 EHRR 445, the European Court of Human Rights noted, in relation to Art. 10, 'the freedom of expression enshrined in [Art. 10], constitutes one of the essential foundations of a democratic society and one of the basic conditions for its progress... it is ap-plicable not only to "information" or "ideas" that are favourably received or regarded as inof-fensive, but also to those that offend, shock or disturb. Such are the demands of that pluralism, tolerance and broadmindedness without which there is no "democratic society"' [42]. This standpoint appears to have dictated the outcome of the important (and controversial) decision of that court in *von Hannover v Germany* Application 59320/00 (2005) EHRR 1 which held that legal protection of private life is warranted only where publication of private information contributes 'to a debate of general interest.' [76]. I discuss this case in subsequent chapters. In *R v Secretary of State for the Home Department, ex parte Simms* [2000] 2 AC 115, 125–6, Lord Steyn stated, 'In a democracy it is the primary right: without it an effective rule of law is not possible. Nevertheless, freedom of expression is not an absolute right. Sometimes it must yield to other

It is a deduction from the basic American agreement that public issues shall be decided by universal suffrage.[28]

In certain specific instances such information may be relevant to self-government. Where, for instance, the people acting through their democratically elected government consider a certain 'action' to be sufficiently antisocial to constitute a criminal offence, then it is in the interest of self-governance that offenders are apprehended and punished. Similarly, where an individual holds a public office, and thereby actually acts on behalf of the people, representing and implementing their political beliefs, any activity of that person which pertains directly to his or her fitness to perform that function is a legitimate interest of the community.

Media freedom

Arguments from democracy are in full flower here. For Milton and Blackstone, it was the prior restraint of the press that represented the most sinister threat to freedom of speech. Blackstone declares:

> The liberty of the press is indeed essential to the nature of a free state; but this consists in laying no *previous* restraints upon publications and not in freedom from censure for criminal matter when published. Every free man has an undoubted right to lay what sentiments he pleases before the public: to forbid this, is to destroy the freedom of the press: but if he publishes what is improper, mischievous, or illegal, he must take the consequence of his own temerity.[29]

Nor is the scope of press freedom restricted to prohibitions against 'prior restraint'.[30] Both the conception of the media and the boundaries of their freedom are, however, considerably wider today. Thus, the term 'media' normally extends beyond newspapers and periodicals, and includes television,

---

cogent social interests...[I]t promotes the self fulfilment of individuals in society...Freedom of speech is the lifeblood of democracy. The free flow of information and ideas informs political debate. It is a safety valve: people are more ready to accept decisions that go against them if they can in principle seek to influence them. It acts as a brake on the abuse of power by public officials. It facilitates the exposure of errors in the governance and administration of justice of the country.'

28. A Meiklejohn, *Political Freedom: The Constitutional Powers of the People* (Oxford: Oxford University Press, 1965), p27.

29. *Blackstone's Commentaries*, 17th edn (1830), Book IV, 151 (as quoted by Lord Denning MR in his dissenting judgment in *Schering Chemicals Ltd v Falkman Ltd* [1981] 2 WLR 848, 860).

30. See the discussion of media pre-notification in Chapter 7.

radio, and the Internet.[31] We are all publishers now. The Internet has created hitherto unthinkable opportunities for freedom of expression. Bloggers proliferate at an astonishing rate. Social networking is the new form of
community; Facebook has a billion users.

There is nothing new about the law's struggle to keep abreast with technology. In this case, however, the contest may not be worth the candle.
Attempts to control the Internet, its operation, or content, have been notoriously unsuccessful. Its anarchy and resistance to regulation is, in the minds
of many, its strength and attraction. Inevitably, the advances in electronic
media will continue to test the appropriateness of existing standards. Can
the same regulation that is applied, for example, to broadcasting be applied to computer networks? The print media appear to enjoy a preferred
position, grounded in their historical supremacy and ubiquity, notwithstanding the fact that the electronic word is the dominant means of communication in advanced societies. As the differences between the media
dissolve, there is clearly a need to establish a regime that recognizes the
rights of both the users and operators of the new technology. It can no
longer matter whether the information you receive appears in the pages of
your newspaper or online.

Yet, though the form in which a message is transmitted may cease to be
a significant factor, users of the Internet experience communication in a
fundamentally different way from other electronic media. Thus, in the case
of television and radio, the number of speakers is limited by the available
spectrum, the ability to speak is limited by the high cost of speaking, and
listeners are, at least in general, merely passive recipients of the communications. With the Internet, on the other hand, the number of speakers is infi-
nite, and interactivity is standard. And, unlike television and radio, a speaker
online can reach the entire world, yet at the same time is able to direct his or
her speech to individuals who share an interest in a particular subject.

Does this digital world require a modified, or even a new, approach in
the pursuit of an elusive equilibrium between privacy and free speech?
Lord Justice Leveson remarked upon the suggestion that 'the burgeoning of
the internet is likely to render irrelevant much of the work of the Inquiry
even assuming that it has not already done so. If, for example, celebrity X's

---

31. There is a rapidly expanding literature on the impact of the Internet on numerous elements
of freedom of expression, including the use of social network sites such as Facebook and Twitter. See, for example, L Bollinger, *Uninhibited, Robust, and Wide-Open: A Free Press for a New
Century* (New York: Oxford University Press, 2010). See Chapter 6.

privacy is violated online, then the metaphorical cat is well out of the bag, and there is no reason why open season should not exist in the printed media.' He (rightly) found this argument flawed on two grounds. First, because 'the internet does not claim to operate by any particular ethical standards, still less high ones. Some have called it a "wild west" but I would prefer to use the term "ethical vacuum".'[32] Newspapers, on the other hand, claim to adhere to an ethical code of conduct:

> [T]he premise on which newspapers operate remains constant: that the Code will be adhered to, that within the bounds of natural human error printed facts whether in newsprint or online will be accurate, and that individual rights will be respected. In contrast, the internet does not function on this basis at all. People will not assume that what they read on the internet is trustworthy or that it carries any particular assurance or accuracy; it need be no more than one person's view. There is none of the notional imprimatur or kitemark which comes from being the publisher of a respected broadsheet or, in its different style, an equally respected mass circulation tabloid.[33]

Secondly, there is a qualitative difference between photographs online and those published on the front page of a newspaper such as *The Sun*:

> The fact of publication in a mass circulation newspaper multiplies and magnifies the intrusion, not simply because more people will be viewing the images, but also because more people will be talking about them. Thus, the fact of publication inflates the apparent newsworthiness of the photographs by placing them more firmly within the public domain and at the top of the news agenda.[34]

In many ways the Internet constitutes Emerson's quintessential 'free marketplace of ideas': it provides an authentic rough-and-tumble environment of critical scepticism with the freedom to express the uncomfortable, the unpalatable, and the unconventional. The marketplace should exist, Emerson

---

32. *An Inquiry into the Culture, Practices and Ethics of the Press*, HC 780 (2012), Part F, Chapter 7, para 3.1.
33. *An Inquiry into the Culture, Practices and Ethics of the Press*, HC 780 (2012), Part F, Chapter 7, para 3.3.
34. *An Inquiry into the Culture, Practices and Ethics of the Press*, HC 780 (2012), Part F, Chapter 7, para 3.4. He adds: 'Ultimately, this is most decidedly not a debate about free speech. A newspaper's right to publish what it chooses within the general law (whether or not it complies with the Editors' Code) is not in question, although within a more robust regulatory framework the consequences of a breach of the Code, publication having occurred, might well be such as to have a deterrent effect. To turn this into a debate about free speech both misses the point and is in danger of creating the sort of moral relativism which has already been remarked on. This is, or at least should be, a debate about freedom with responsibility, and about an ethical press not doing something which it is technically quite able to do but decides not to do.' *An Inquiry into the Culture, Practices and Ethics of the Press*, HC 780 (2012), Part F, Chapter 7, para 3.5. But it *is* a debate about free speech. Nor does the question of moral relativism seem to arise here.

argued, irrespective of how pernicious or false the new opinion appears to be because there is no way of suppressing the false without suppressing the true. Such a model may nevertheless preserve the rights of those harmed by the exercise of this liberty, including their right to privacy. The protection of anonymous speech is likely to attract greater attention as a vital element both of free speech and privacy in cyberspace. If treated as analogous to public space, it may be that if you object to what you see or hear online, you may simply have to look away, as pedestrians do when offended by a billboard.[35]

Yet, these extraordinary developments notwithstanding, the central question is inescapable: how is privacy to be reconciled with freedom of expression? Our electronic age has still to address Warren and Brandeis's entreaty (discussed in Chapter 3) that the law ought to thwart the distress caused by the gratuitous publication of private information.

The political justification for freedom of the press is an application of the argument from truth. Mill's second hypothesis, it will be recalled, is the 'assumption of infallibility' that specifies the conditions under which we are able to have confidence believing that what we think is true, actually is true. The safest way to achieve this, the argument runs, is to allow freedom to debate ideas, to subject them to contradiction and refutation. Interference with this freedom diminishes our ability to arrive at rational beliefs. These are powerful principles, even if they occasionally appear to be based on an idealized model of the political process in which individuals actively participate in government.

On the other hand, a free press clearly has the potential to engender such interest and to facilitate its exercise. As Gibbons puts it:

> As a principle based upon democratic theory, freedom of speech derives its force much more from a sceptical tendency which stresses the fallibility of those in power, and displays a healthy attitude of incredulity towards the claims of authority. The need is for political choices to be justified and for mistakes, with their potential for serious and wide-reaching consequences, to be avoided. In this task, the media have come to play a significant part, both in providing a forum for political debate and in helping to mould opinion.[36]

---

35. American law conceives this to be an aspect of privacy since *Stanley v Georgia* 394 US 557 (1969). The idea is that what I read in the privacy of my home should not be subject to regulation. With mobile devices and increasingly ubiquitous wi-fi, the analogy loses much of its purchase.
36. Gibbons, *Regulating the Media*, p 16. The Leveson Inquiry Report expressed the view that a 'free press performs its communication role in a democracy in a myriad ways, day in and day

The attraction of the arguments from truth and from democracy is that they establish independent grounds for freedom of speech in a way that arguments based on the interests of the speaker do not.[37] But the media publish a good deal that, even by the most magnanimous exercise of the imagination, is not remotely connected to these noble pursuits. Does this suggest that the media are entitled to no special treatment? Arguments to support special treatment for the press tend to fall on stony judicial ground in most common law jurisdictions.

A stronger case can be made where the media offend decorum rather than the law. This (thinner) argument may then be made to turn on the importance to the political process of the publication of a *particular* report. This strategy collapses into an undifferentiated argument for freedom of expression, whether exercised in the press or the pub. There may be much to commend such a position, for it avoids the difficulties in defining what is to be understood by the 'media' or 'press'. Indeed, as Schauer argues:

> We may wish to say that some forms of communication represent a constraint on governmental power even greater than that established by a general Free Speech Principle, but this powerful constraint would properly be keyed to political content, and not to the presence or absence of a printing press or transmitter.[38]

The First Amendment

US courts and commentators have developed several theories of free speech, both rights-based and consequentialist[39] that seek to account for

out. It is by no means only through political journalism and holding authority to account that the press proves its value in this way (although those are very important aspects in their own right). All forms of journalistic content potentially perform this vital role. Debate and comment, information and speculation, news and opinion, education and entertainment, all play their part. It is exactly this multifunctional and multifaceted package of content, produced with such verve and to deadline week in, week out, which makes the press such a marvel, such a matter of pride.' Part B, Chapter 4, para 3.2.

37. Gibbons, *Regulating the Media*, pp 16–17.
38. Schauer, *Free Speech* (n 4), p 109.
39. See F Schauer, 'The Role of the People in First Amendment Theory' (1986) 74 *California Law Review* 761, 769–78. Professor Schauer finds rights-based and especially deontological theories (i.e., those that suggest free speech is good *in itself* because, for example, it encourages self-fulfilment) to be unsound. But he is also critical of consequentialist theories (such as Meiklejohn's) which are premised on popular participation. He concludes that 'it is time to face up to the paternalism of the First Amendment', and 'the fact that a system of government has essentially been forced on us, and there is little we can do about it', 788.

the exercise of free speech in all its protean forms. In particular, there is a tendency to adopt a purposive construction of the First Amendment; to ask, in other words, what forms of speech or publication warrant protection by virtue of their contribution to the operation of political democracy. This is evident in the decisions which distinguish, with variable consequences, between 'public figures' and ordinary individuals. The US Supreme Court in the seminal libel case of *New York Times v Sullivan* expressed its philosophy in unequivocal terms:

> [W]e consider this case against the background of a profound national commitment to the principle that debate on public issues should be uninhibited, robust and wide open, and that it may well include vehement, caustic, and sometimes unpleasantly sharp attacks on government and public officials.[40]

The principal purpose of the First Amendment is, in this approach, the protection of the right of all citizens to understand political issues in order that they might participate effectively in the operation of democratic government.[41] This formula allows considerable scope for actions by private individuals who have been subjected to gratuitous publicity. In practice, however, it is frequently those who are in the public eye that—for this very reason—attract the attention of the tabloids. The difficult question which the theory is then required to answer is the extent to which such public figures are entitled to protection of aspects of their personal lives.[42] And this, in turn, involves a delicate investigation of what features of a public figure's life may legitimately be exposed—in the furtherance of political debate. His sex life? Her health? Their finances?

Although this theory seeks to distinguish between voluntary and involuntary public figures, its application, except as a general rationale for the existence of the freedom of speech itself, provides uncertain guidance as to the respective rights and obligations in cases involving unwanted publicity. In the absence of an attempt to define the kinds of information in respect of which all individuals might prima facie expect to receive protection (even if such protection is subsequently to be outweighed by considerations of the

---

40. *New York Times v Sullivan,* 376 US 254 (1964), 270 *per* Brennan J. See too *Whitney v California,* 274 US 357 (1927), 375–8 *per* Brandeis J.
41. See A Lewis, *Freedom for the Thought That We Hate: A Biography of the First Amendment* (New York: Basic Books, 2010).
42. Recent developments of the English law are outlined in Chapter 5. For a valuable, comprehensive account of freedom of expression in the English law and under the European Convention, see R Clayton and H Tomlinson, *Privacy and Freedom of Expression,* 2nd edn (Oxford: Oxford University Press, 2010), Chapter 15.

public interest) one of the central purposes of recognizing an individual's interest in restricting information—the trust, candour, and confidence it fosters—is diminished.

Speech and action

The First Amendment explicitly protects 'speech' (though this has been given a fairly generous interpretation by the US Supreme Court). Emerson argues that while expression is good in itself and should not be restricted, actions may be susceptible to control for the mutual good. One ground for this dichotomy is that expression is normally less harmful than action. He argues that expression 'generally has less immediate consequences, is less irremediable in its impact'.[43] But far from providing the main justification for the primacy of free speech, Stanley Fish argues that this duality suggests that such freedom should never be championed in the abstract but only as a result of a weighing of the consequences of the protection of that particular speech.[44] Fish's reasoning is based on the assertion that 'speech always seems to be crossing the line into action'.[45] In reality, then, the 'zone of constitutionally protected speech'—speech which has no provocative effect to anyone, which is mere abstract expression—is empty:

> [W]hen a court invalidates legislation because it infringes on protected speech, it is not because the speech in question is without consequences but because the consequences have been discounted in relation to a good that is judged to outweigh them.[46]

Hence, speech is never protected per se, but compared 'in relation to a value—the health of the republic [or] the vigour of the economy'.[47]

The contentious subject of how privacy might be reconciled with freedom of expression is the subject of Chapter 5.

---

43. Emerson (n 5), 881. See generally DA Farber, *The First Amendment*, 3rd edn (New York: Foundation Press, 2010).
44. Fish (n 7), 106.
45. Fish (n 7), 105.
46. Fish (n 7), 106.
47. Fish (n 7), 106.

3
The genesis

Queen Victoria and Prince Albert were not amused. Accomplished etch-ers, they wanted copies made for their private use, and sent a number of plates to the Palace printer, one Strange. Several of the impressions managed to fall into the hands of a third party, Judge, who evidently obtained them through a 'mole' employed by Strange. In turn, Strange acquired them from Judge in the honest belief that they were to be publicly exhibited with the consent of the couple. A catalogue was prepared, and they set about arrang-ing the exhibition. When he discovered that no Royal Assent had been con-ferred, Strange withdrew his participation from the exhibition, but decided to proceed with the printing of the catalogue. His plan was to offer it for sale along with autographs of the regal artists. The Prince obtained an injunction to prevent the exhibition and the intended circulation of the catalogue, the court openly acknowledging that 'the importance which has been attached to this case arises entirely from the exalted station of the Plaintiff...'[1]

Though the judgments in the case turn largely on the fact that the plates were the property of the Prince, the court explicitly recognized that this af-forded a wider basis upon which the law 'shelters the privacy and seclusion of thoughts and sentiments committed to writing, and desired by the author to remain not generally known.'[2]

Prophets of privacy

This decision was a significant factor in the legendary article that in 1890 was to give birth to the legal recognition of privacy in the United States.

1. (1849) 2 De Gex & Sm 652, 64 ER 293; (on appeal) (1849) 1 Mac & G 25, 41 ER 1171, 1177.
2. (1849) 2 De Gex & Sm 652, 64 ER 293; (on appeal) (1849) 1 Mac & G 25, 41 ER 1171, 1177.

Written by Samuel D Warren and Louis D Brandeis, their commentary was published in the influential *Harvard Law Review*.[3] A few years before, the invention of the inexpensive and portable 'snap camera' by Eastman Kodak had changed the world. Individuals could be snapped at home, at work, or at play. The beginning of the end of privacy was nigh.

The two lawyers, Warren, a Boston attorney and socialite, and Brandeis, who would be appointed to the Supreme Court in 1916, angered by the earliest paparazzi and so-called 'yellow journalism' wrote what is often characterized as the most influential law review article ever published.[4] It is usually claimed that the catalyst for their annoyance was that the press had snooped on Warren's daughter's wedding. But this seems unlikely since, in 1890, she was six years old! The more plausible source of their fury was a series of articles in a Boston high-society gossip magazine, describing Warren's glamorous dinner parties.

Their celebrated essay condemned the press for their effrontery, and contended that the onslaught by the journalists constituted an invasion of their privacy which right, they argued, was immanent in the common law. Drawing upon decisions of the English courts relating to, in particular, breach of confidence, property, copyright, and defamation, they contended that these cases were merely instances and applications of a general right to privacy, of the 'right to be let alone'.[5] The common law, they claimed, albeit under different forms, protected an individual whose privacy was invaded by the likes of a snooping journalist. In so doing, the law acknowledged the importance of the spiritual and intellectual needs of man. They declared:

> The intensity and complexity of life, attendant upon advancing civilization, have rendered necessary some retreat from the world, and man, under the refining influence of culture, has become more sensitive to publicity so that solitude and privacy have become more essential to the individual; but modern enterprise and invention have, through invasion upon his privacy, subjected

3. SD Warren and LD Brandeis, 'The Right to Privacy' (1890) 4 Harvard Law Review 193; WL Prosser, 'Privacy' (1960) 48 California Law Review 383, describes Warren and Brandeis's article as 'the outstanding example of the influence of legal periodicals upon American law'. See too WF Pratt, 'The Warren and Brandeis Argument for a Right to Privacy' (1975) Public Law 161; H Kalven, 'Privacy in Tort Law: Were Warren and Brandeis Wrong?' (1966) 31 Law and Contemporary Problems 326; DL Zimmerman, 'Requiem for a Heavyweight: A Farewell to Warren and Brandeis's Privacy Tort' (1983) 68 Cornell Law Review 297.
4. The essay 'enjoys the unique distinction of having theoretically outlined a new field of jurisprudence', D Larremore, 'The Law of Privacy' (1912) 12 Columbia Law Review 693.
5. It is a mystery to me why the authors felt the need to refer to this nebulous right in order to buttress their argument. I consider this anomaly in Chapter 7.

him to mental pain and distress, far greater than could be inflicted by mere bodily injury.[6]

The common law, they reasoned, has developed from the protection of the physical person and corporeal property to the protection of the individual's '[t]houghts, emotions and sensations'.[7] But as a result of threats to privacy from recent inventions and business methods and from the press, the common law needed to go further. An individual's right to determine the extent to which his thoughts, emotions, and sensations were communicated to others was already legally protected but only in respect of authors of literary and artistic compositions and letters who could forbid their unauthorized publication. And though English cases recognizing this right were based on protection of property, in reality they were an acknowledgement of privacy, of 'inviolate personality'.[8]

In 1902 their line of reasoning was put to the test. The plaintiff complained that her image had been used without her consent to advertise the defendant's merchandise. She was portrayed on bags of flour with the dismal pun, 'Flour of the family'. The majority of the New York Court of Appeals rejected Warren and Brandeis's thesis, holding that the privacy argument had 'not as yet an abiding place in our jurisprudence, and ... cannot now be incorporated without doing violence to settled principles of law ...'[9] The minority, however, warmed to the idea, Gray J declaring that the plaintiff had a right to be protected against the use of her image for the defendant's commercial advantage: 'Any other principle of decision ... is as repugnant to equity as it is shocking to reason.'[10]

The court's decision provoked general disapproval[11] that led to the enactment by the State of New York of a statute rendering unlawful the unauthorized use of an individual's name or image for advertising or trade purposes.[12] But three years later in a case involving similar facts, the Supreme Court of Georgia adopted the reasoning of Gray J. The Warren and

6. Warren and Brandeis (n 3), 196.
7. Warren and Brandeis (n 3), 195.
8. Warren and Brandeis (n 3), 205.
9. *Roberson v Rochester Folding Box Co*, 171 NY 538, 64 NE 442, 447 (1902).
10. *Roberson v Rochester Folding Box Co*, 171 NY 538, 64 NE 442, 450 (1902).
11. A criticism of the judgment by the *New York Times* seems to have been the cause of one of the majority judges taking the unusual step of defending the decision: O'Brien, 'The Right of Privacy' (1902) 2 Columbia Law Review 437.
12. NY Sess Laws (1903), ch 132, paras 1–2, subsequently amended in 1921, NY Civil Rights Law, paras 50–1.

Brandeis argument, fifteen years after its publication, had triumphed. Since that momentous judgment, most US states have incorporated the 'right to privacy' into their law. Yet, despite the authors' heavy reliance on the judgments of English courts, it has taken more than a century for the right of privacy to be recognized in England, albeit in a rather different form.

Over the years the US common law maintained its steady expansion of the notion of privacy. In 1960 Dean Prosser, a leading tort expert, expounded the view that the law now recognized not one tort, 'but a complex of four different interests... tied together by the common name, but otherwise [with] nothing in common.'[13] He delineated their nature as follows:

1. Intrusion upon the plaintiff's seclusion or solitude or into his private affairs

The wrongful act consists in the intentional interference with the plaintiff's solitude or seclusion. It includes the physical intrusion into the plaintiff's premises and eavesdropping (including electronic and photographic surveillance, 'bugging' and telephone-tapping). Three requirements must be satisfied:[14] (a) there must be actual prying (disturbing noises or bad manners will not suffice); (b) the intrusion must offend a reasonable man; and (c) it must be an intrusion into something private.

2. Public disclosure of embarrassing private facts about the plaintiff

Three elements of the tort are indicated by Prosser: (a) there must be publicity (to disclose the facts to a small group of people would not suffice); (b) the facts disclosed must be private facts (publicity given to matters of public record is not tortious); and (c) the facts disclosed must be offensive to a reasonable man of ordinary sensibilities.

13. *Prosser and Keeton on Torts*, 5th edn (St Paul, MN: West Publishing, 1984), 855.
14. Prosser (n 13), 856–7; *Restatement (Second) of the Law of Torts* (Philadelphia, PA: American Law Institute, 1977), para 652D.

3. Publicity which places the plaintiff in a false light in the public eye

According to Prosser,[15] this tort normally arises in circumstances in which some opinion or utterance (eg, spurious books or views) is publicly attributed to the plaintiff, or where his picture is used to illustrate a book or article with which he has no reasonable connection. The overlap with the tort of defamation is at once apparent and, though the false light 'need not necessarily be a defamatory one',[16] it is submitted that an action for defamation will invariably lie in such cases. The publicity must be 'highly offensive to a reasonable person'.[17]

4. Appropriation, for the defendant's advantage, of the plaintiff's name or likeness

Under the common law tort, the advantage derived by the defendant need not be a financial one;[18] it has, for instance, been held to arise where the plaintiff was named as father in a birth certificate. The statutory tort (which exists in several states) normally requires the unauthorized use of the plaintiff's identity for commercial (usually advertising) purposes; the New York statute,[19] upon which most of the current legislation is modelled, confines itself to advertising or 'purposes of trade'.[20] The recognition of this tort establishes what has been called a 'right of publicity'[21] under which an individual is able to decide how he or she wishes to exploit his or her name or image commercially. It is difficult to see how the protection of this essentially proprietary interest is connected with the protection of even a general 'right to privacy'.[22] It is only the torts of 'intrusion' and 'public disclosure' that 'require the invasion of something secret, secluded or private pertaining

---

15. Prosser (n 13), 863–4; *Restatement* (n 14), para 652E.
16. Prosser (n 13), 863–4; *Restatement* (n 14), para 652E. For my argument that 'false light' claims can invariably be accommodated by defamation, see Chapter 5.
17. *Restatement* (n 14), para 652E, comment b.
18. Prosser (n 13), 853; *Restatement* (n 14), para 652C, comment b.
19. New York Civil Rights Law 1921, Titles 50–1.
20. This has been widely defined; see eg *Spahn v Julian Messner, Inc*, 23 App Div 2d 216, 260 NYS 2d 451 (1964).
21. MB Nimmer, 'The Right of Publicity' (1954) 19 Law and Contemporary Problems 19, 203; Kalven (n 3), 331.
22. See RC Post, 'Rereading Warren and Brandeis: Privacy, Property, and Appropriation' (1991) 41 Case Western Reserve Law Review 647.

to the plaintiff'.[23] It might therefore be argued that the torts of 'appropriation' and 'false light' are not properly conceived of as aspects of 'privacy'.[24]

This fourfold segregation of the right to privacy is regarded by some as
misconceived because it undermines the Warren and Brandeis axiom of
'inviolate personality' and neglected its moral basis as an aspect of human
dignity.[25] The classification has nevertheless assumed a prominent place in
US tort law, although, as predicted by one legal scholar, Harry Kalven, it has
to a large extent ossified the conception into four types:

> [G]iven the legal mind's weakness for neat labels and categories and given
> the deserved Prosser prestige, it is a safe prediction that the fourfold view will
> come to dominate whatever thinking is done about the right of privacy in
> the future.[26]

The vicissitudes of these four torts have been charted in an enormous spate
of academic and popular literature. Nor has this development been restricted
to the United States. Virtually every advanced legal system has, to a greater
or lesser extent, sought to recognize various aspects of privacy, not always
with clarity or consistency.[27]

A constitutional right

These four torts remained for some time the principal tools by which US
law protected privacy in different forms. And they marked, more or less, the
confines of the constitutional protection of privacy as well. The principal
concern of Warren and Brandeis was, of course, what we would now call
media intrusion. Several years after the publication of their seminal essay,
however, Justice Brandeis (as he now was) delivered a powerful dissent in

23. WL Prosser, *Law of Torts*, 4th edn (St Paul, MN: West Publishing, 1971), 814.
24. 'Its splendid pedigree notwithstanding, false light has proved in practice to illuminate nothing. From the viewpoint of coherent first amendment theory, it has served to deepen the darkness', DL Zimmerman, 'False Light Invasion of Privacy: The Light that Failed' (1989) 64 New York University Law Review 364, 453.
25. EJ Bloustein, 'Privacy as an Aspect of Human Dignity: An Answer to Dean Prosser' (1964) 39 New York University Law Review 962.
26. Kalven (n 3).
27. They include Austria, Canada, China, Denmark, Estonia, France, Germany, Hong Kong, Hungary, India, Ireland, Italy, Lithuania, the Netherlands, New Zealand, Norway, the Philippines, Russia, South Africa, South Korea, Spain, Taiwan, Thailand, and the majority of Latin American countries.

the case of *Olmstead v United States* in 1928.[28] He declared that the Constitution conferred 'as against the Government, the right to be let alone', adding, 'To protect that right, every unjustifiable intrusion by the Government upon the privacy of the individual, whatever the means employed, must be deemed a violation of the Fourth Amendment.'[29] That view was adopted by the US Supreme Court in *Katz v United States*.[30] Since then privacy as the right to be let alone has been invoked by the Court in this context.

But the most significant—and controversial—development came in 1965 with the Supreme Court's decision in *Griswold v Connecticut*.[31] It declared unconstitutional a Connecticut statute prohibiting the use of contraceptives—because it violated the right of marital privacy, a right 'older than the Bill of Rights'.[32] The word 'privacy' appears nowhere in the Constitution, yet in a series of cases the Supreme Court has—via the Bill of Rights (particularly the First, Third, Fourth, Fifth, and Ninth Amendments) recognized, amongst other privacy rights, that of 'associational privacy',[33] 'political privacy',[34] and 'privacy of counsel'.[35] It has also set the limits of protection against eavesdropping and unlawful searches.[36]

By far the most divisive 'privacy' decision that the Court has decided is the case of *Roe v Wade* in 1973.[37] It held by a majority that the abortion law of Texas was unconstitutional as a violation of the right to privacy. Under that law abortion was criminalized, except when performed to save the pregnant woman's life. The Court held that states may prohibit abortion to protect the life of the foetus only in the third trimester. The judgment, which has been described as 'undoubtedly the best-known case the United States Supreme Court has ever decided',[38] is simultaneously embraced by feminists, and deplored by many Christians. It is the slender thread by which the right of American women to a lawful abortion hangs. There appears to

---

28. 277 US 438 (1928).
29. 277 US 438 (1928) at 473.
30. 398 US 347 (1967). This is a classic case of 'intrusion'. See my argument that it be analytically segregated from 'disclosure' in Chapters 5 and 8. I return to this seminal decision in Chapter 4.
31. 381 US 479 (1965).
32. 381 US 479 (1965) at 486.
33. *NAACP v Alabama*, 357 US 442 (1958).
34. *Sweezy v New Hampshire*, 364 US 234 (1957).
35. *Massiah v US*, 377 US 201 (1964).
36. *Olmstead v US*, 277 US 438 (1928); *Goldman v US*, 316 US 129 (1942).
37. 410 US 113 (1973). See too *Planned Parenthood v Casey*, 505 US 833 (1992).
38. R Dworkin, *Life's Dominion: An Argument about Abortion and Euthanasia* (London: HarperCollins, 1993), 4.

be no middle ground. The jurist Ronald Dworkin bluntly describes the fervour of the contest:

> The war between anti-abortion groups and their opponents is America's new version of the terrible seventeenth-century European civil wars of religion. Opposing armies march down streets or pack themselves into protests at abortion clinics, courthouses, and the White House, screaming at and spitting on and loathing one another. Abortion is tearing America apart.[39]

Another privacy judgment of the Court that generated a hullabaloo was *Bowers v Hardwick* in 1986 in which a bare majority held that the privacy protections of the due process clause did not extend to homosexual acts between consenting adults in private: 'No connection between family, marriage, or procreation on the one hand and homosexual conduct on the other has been demonstrated.'[40] This decision was explicitly overruled in *Lawrence v Texas* in which, by 6–3, the Supreme Court decided that it had construed the liberty interest too narrowly. The majority held that substantive due process under the Fourteenth Amendment entailed the freedom to engage in intimate consensual sexual conduct.[41] Its effect is to nullify all legislation throughout the United States that purports to criminalize sodomy between consenting same-sex adults in private.

The US experience is both influential and instructive. Other common law jurisdictions continue to wrestle with the intractable problems of definition, scope, and reconciling privacy with other rights, especially freedom of expression. It is fair to say, as a generalization, that the approach of the common law is largely interest-based, while the continental tradition of civil law jurisdictions tends to be rights-based. In other words, while the English law, for example, adopts a pragmatic case-by-case approach to the protection of privacy, French law conceives privacy as a fundamental human right. This disparity has nevertheless been attenuated by the impact of the European Convention on Human Rights (ECHR) and other declarations and directives emanating from Brussels. The intensity of this side-wind is most conspicuously evident in the adoption by the United Kingdom of its Human Rights Act of 1998, as will become clear later.

39. Dworkin (n 38), 103.
40. 478 US 186, 284 (1986).
41. 539 US 558 (2003).

Common law caution

It is not only the English law that still grapples with the problem of privacy. Australia, New Zealand, Ireland, Canada, Hong Kong, and other common law jurisdictions languish, to a greater or lesser extent, in a quagmire of ambiguity and indecision.

The English law

Despite several commissions, committees, and attempts at legislation, the law, though recently vivified by the Human Rights Act 1998, remains uncertain. In 1972 the Younger Committee rejected the idea of a general right of privacy created by statute. It concluded that it would burden the court 'with controversial questions of a social and political character'.[42] Judges would be likely to encounter problems balancing privacy with competing interests such as freedom of expression. Indeed. The committee recommended the creation of a new crime and tort of unlawful surveillance, a new tort of disclosure or other use of information unlawfully acquired, and the consideration of the law on breach of confidence (which protects confidential information entrusted by one party to another) as a possible means by which privacy could be safeguarded. Similar reports have been produced in other common law jurisdictions.[43]

In recent years a flurry of celebrity litigation has presented the courts with an opportunity to examine whether, in the absence of explicit common law privacy protection, the remedy of breach of confidence might provide a makeshift solution. Lord Hoffmann declared in the House of Lords that the

> ...coming into force of the Human Rights Act 1998 weakens the argument for saying that a general tort of invasion of privacy is needed to fill gaps in

---

42. *Report of the Committee on Privacy* (Cmnd 5012, 1972) (Chairman: Kenneth Younger), para 653.
43. See eg Australian Law Reform Commission, *For Your Information: Australian Privacy Law and Practice* (Report 108, 2012); New Zealand Law Commission, *Review of the Law of Privacy* (4 stages: 2006–11); Law Reform Commission of Hong Kong, *Privacy and Media Intrusion* (2004), *Civil Liability for Invasion of Privacy* (2004), *Privacy: The Regulation of Covert Surveillance* (2006); New South Wales Law Commission, *Invasion of Privacy* (Law Com No 120, 2009); Victorian Law Reform Commission, *Final Report into Surveillance in Public Places* (2010).

the existing remedies. Sections 6 and 7 of the Act are in themselves substantial gap fillers; if it is indeed the case that a person's rights under article 8 [of the ECHR] have been infringed by a public authority, he will have a statutory remedy.[44]

The impact of this Act (which incorporates into English law Art 8 of the ECHR) cannot be overstated. It provides for the protection of the right to respect for family life, home, and correspondence. The consequences of its enactment are, of course, a major concern of this book.

As in Britain, deliberations about the need for legal protection have pre-occupied law reform commissions at both state and federal level in Australia. Nor have the courts been idle. In a significant decision in 2001, a majority of the High Court of Australia leaned, albeit tentatively, towards the recognition of a privacy tort. In *Australian Broadcasting Corporation v Lenah Game Meats Pty Ltd*[45] the court, acknowledging the inadequacy of Australian law, expressed its support for the judicial development in common law jurisdictions of a common law action for invasion of privacy. In specifying what might constitute an unwarranted invasion of privacy, the court stated:

> Certain kinds of information about a person, such as information relating to health, personal relationships, or finances, may be easy to identify as private; as may certain kinds of activity, which a reasonable person, applying contemporary standards of morals and behaviour, would understand to be meant to be unobserved. The requirement that disclosure or observation of information or conduct would be highly offensive to a reasonable person of ordinary sensibilities is in many circumstances a useful practical test of what is private.[46]

The decision, though inconclusive on the central issue, does suggest that the High Court, if, when presented with a more deserving plaintiff (this one was an abattoir whose cruel practices the Australian Broadcasting Corporation wished to expose), the recognition of a privacy tort may not be entirely improbable. This dictum—and the court's significant attempt to identify 'private facts'—is considered in greater detail later.[47]

In 2004 the New Zealand Court of Appeal took a significant step towards recognizing a common law tort of privacy. In the case of *Hosking v*

---

44. *Wainwright v Home Office* [2003] UKHL 53, [34].
45. [2001] HCA 63.
46. [2001] HCA 63 [42].
47. Commonwealth, state, and territory legislation either do not apply to, or explicitly exempt, the media. Legislative provisions prohibit stalking and surveillance that could have an impact on the media, eg the Victorian Surveillance Devices Act 1999.

Runting[48] the defendants took pictures of the plaintiffs' 18-month-old twin daughters in the street, being pushed in their stroller by their mother. The father is a well-known television personality. The couple sought an injunction to prevent publication. The trial court held that New Zealand law did not recognize a cause of action in privacy based on the public disclosure of photographs taken in a public place. But, though the Court of Appeal dismissed the plaintiffs' appeal, it decided (3–2) that a case had been made out for a remedy for 'breach of privacy by giving publicity to private and personal information'.[49] This view was based principally upon its interpretation of the English courts' analysis of the remedy for breach of confidence, as well as the fact that it was consistent with New Zealand's obligations under the International Covenant on Civil and Political Rights and the United Nations Convention on the Rights of the Child. The court also considered that its judgment facilitated the reconciliation of competing values, and enabled New Zealand to draw upon the extensive experience in the United States. In their majority judgments, Gault P and Blanchard J specified two essential requirements for a claim to succeed. First, the plaintiff must have a reasonable expectation of privacy and, secondly, there must be publicity given to private facts that would be considered highly offensive to an objective reasonable person.

The New Zealand Privacy Act of 1993 provides that any person may complain to the Privacy Commissioner alleging that any action is or appears to be 'an interference with the privacy of an individual'.[50] If the Privacy Commissioner finds that the complaint has substance, he or she may refer it to the Proceedings Commissioner appointed under the Human Rights Act 1993, who may in turn bring proceedings in the Complaints Review Tribunal. The Tribunal may make an order prohibiting a repetition of the action complained of or requiring the interference to be rectified. It has the power to award damages. The Bill of Rights Act has no explicit privacy provision.

---

48. [2005] I NZLR I (NZCA). See too *Rogers v Television New Zealand* [2008] 2 NZLR 277, NZSC. See the surprising decision of the High Court in *C v Holland* [2012] NZHC 2155, which decided that invasion of privacy by surreptitious videoing—without publicity or the prospect of publicity—was an actionable tort. Whata J held that the similarity to the tort of public disclosure formulated in *Hosking v Runting* was 'sufficiently proximate to enable an intrusion tort to be seen as a logical extension or adjunct to it', [86]. See Chapter 8.
49. [148].
50. Section 66. Note that the Act (which is, in large part, a data protection statute), specifically excludes application to 'any news medium…engaged in news activities'. Section 2(1).

While Ireland does not explicitly recognize a general right to privacy at common law, the courts have fashioned a constitutional right to privacy out of Article 40.3.1 of the Constitution under which the state guarantees to respect, defend, and vindicate the personal rights of the citizen. So, for example, in 1974 the majority of the Supreme Court held that privacy was included among these rights.[51] Succeeding judgments have indicated that the Article extends to some invasions of privacy by interception of communications and surveillance.[52] The European Convention on Human Rights Act 2003 gives legal effect to Article 8. The Irish Press Council and Ombudsman system includes the explicit protection of privacy.[53]

While neither the Canadian Constitution nor its Charter of Rights and Freedoms include an explicit reference to privacy, the courts have filled the gap by construing the right to be secure against unreasonable search or seizure (Section 8 of the Charter) to embody an individual's right to a reasonable expectation of privacy. There is no common law right of privacy along US lines,[54] but the lower courts have shown a willingness to stretch existing causes of action, such as trespass or nuisance, to protect the privacy of the victim. The common law deficiency has been resolved in four Canadian provinces by the enactment of a statutory tort of invasion of privacy. In British Columbia, Manitoba, Newfoundland, and Saskatchewan the tort of 'violation of privacy' is actionable without proof of damage. The precise formulation of the tort differs in each province. Federal and provincial legislation protects the collection and use of personal data in a commercial context.[55] The federal statutes are the Privacy Act, and the Personal Information Protection and Electronic Documents Act.

Quebec, as a civil law jurisdiction, has developed its remedy through the interpretation of general provisions of civil liability in the former Civil Code. The present protection, however, is explicitly incorporated in the new Civil Code. It provides that every person has a right to the respect of

51. *McGee v Attorney General* [1984] IR 36. See too *Herrity v Associated Newspapers* [2008] IEHC 249.
52. *Kennedy v Ireland* [1987] IR 587. But see *Atherton v DPP* [2005] IEHC 429.
53. As an independent body with statutory underpinning, it was cited as a possible model for Britain in the Leveson Inquiry Report, Part K, ch 5. The Report contains a valuable survey of press regulation in China, France, Germany, the Netherlands, Scandinavia, and the United States. See Part K, ch 2.
54. The matter is not without uncertainty, though the better view is that no explicit judicial recognition has occurred, despite suggestions to the contrary: see eg *Somwar v McDonald's Restaurants of Canada Ltd* (2006) 263 DLR (4th) 752. But see too *Hung v Gardiner* [2002] BCSC 1234, [2003] BCCA 257, (2003) 227 DLR (4th) 282.
55. The federal statutes are the Privacy Act, and the Personal Information Protection and Electronic Documents Act.

his or her reputation and privacy, and that no one may invade the privacy of another person except with the consent of the person or his or her heirs or unless it is authorized by law. The forms of privacy-invading conduct specified cover a fairly wide range of conduct. In addition, Section 5 of the Quebec Charter of Human Rights and Freedoms declares that every person has a right to respect for his or her private life. This provision is directly enforceable between citizens. The 1994 Uniform Privacy Act clarifies and augments the existing provincial statutes.

Scots law, like the law of South Africa, with its Roman roots, is able to recognize privacy under the *actio iniuriarum* which protects an individual's *dignitas*.[56] It has, however, long recognized the action for breach of confidence and, since the enactment of the Human Rights Act 1998, has implemented the protection afforded by Article 8 of the ECHR.[57] The South African law of delict which requires that, to establish liability, the plaintiff must prove that the act in question was both wrongful and intentional, recognizes invasions that take the form of both intrusion and disclosure. In respect of the disclosure by the media of personal information, the courts allow the defence of public interest in the publication.[58]

Section 14 of the post-apartheid South African Constitution which enshrines 'the right of privacy' has been interpreted by the Constitutional Court to apply in a wide range of activities that extend well beyond the conception of privacy advanced in these pages.[59]

The European approach

The continental attitude to privacy is based on the concept of the 'right of personality'.[60] In Germany this right is guaranteed by the Basic Law. Article 1 of the Constitution imposes on all state authorities a duty to respect and

56. See *Robertson v Keith*, 1936 SC 29. *Duchess of Argyll v Duke of Argyll*, 1962 SC (HL) 88; discussed later, began life, of course, in Scotland: [1967] Ch 302. Cf *Nicol v Caledonian Newspapers Ltd*, 2003 SLT 109.
57. See *Martin v McGuiness*, 2003 SLT 1424; *X v BBC*, 2005 SLT 796. Cf *Response Handling Ltd v BBC*, 2008 SLT 51.
58. *Financial Mail v Sage Holdings* [1993] 2 SA 451 (A); *MEC for Health, Mpumalanga v M-Net* [2002] 6 SA 714 (T).
59. Eg the possession of obscene and pornographic material: *De Reuck v DPP (WLD)* [2004] 1 SA 406, CC; search and seizure: *Investigating Directorate: Serious Economic Offences v Hyundai Motor Distributors (Pty) Ltd* [2001] 1 SA 545, CC; and prostitution: *S v Jordan* [2002] 6 SA 642, CC.
60. Excellent accounts of the legal protection of privacy in Europe, and in various common and civil jurisdictions, are provided in *Tugendhat and Christie on the Law of Privacy and the Media*,

protect 'the dignity of man'. Article 2(1) provides that 'Everyone shall have the right to the free development of his personality in so far as he does not violate the rights of others or offend against the constitutional order or the moral code.' These two articles combine to establish a general right to one's own personality; and the right to respect for one's private sphere of life is an emanation of this personality right.

In addition, the courts protect privacy as part of the right of personality under the Civil Code. They also employ the law of delict to provide a remedy against conduct injurious to human dignity such as the unauthorized publication of the intimate details of a person's private life; the right not to publish medical reports without the patient's consent; the right not to have one's conversation recorded without one's knowledge and consent; the right not to have one's private correspondence opened—whether or not it is actually read; the right not to be photographed without consent; the right to a fair description of one's life; and the right not to have personal information misused by the press.

The German courts recognize three spheres of personality: the 'intimate', the 'private', and the 'individual' spheres. The 'intimate sphere' covers one's thoughts and feelings and their expression, medical information, and sexual behaviour. Given its particularly private nature, this species of information enjoys absolute protection. The 'private sphere' includes information which, while neither intimate nor secret (eg facts about one's family and home life) is nevertheless private and therefore attracts qualified protection; disclosure might be justified in the public interest. The 'individual sphere' relates to an individual's public, economic, and professional life, one's social and occupational relations. It attracts the lowest degree of protection.[61]

Privacy is zealously protected in France.[62] Though it is not explicitly mentioned in the French Constitution, the Constitutional Council in 1995 extended the concept of 'individual freedom' in Article 66 to the right to privacy. Privacy was thus elevated to a constitutional right. In addition,

2nd edn (M Warby, N Moreham, and I Christie eds) (Oxford: Oxford University Press, 2011), ch 3 and R Clayton and H Tomlinson, *The Law of Human Rights*, 2nd edn (Oxford: Oxford University Press, 2009), Appendices 2 to 6.

61. The landmark decision in *von Hannover v Germany* App 59320/00 (2005) 40 EHRR 1, discussed in Chapters 4 and 5, was critical of German law's inadequate protection of public figures.
62. As one 'witness' to the United Kingdom Joint Parliamentary Committee on Privacy and Injunctions put it, 'we have a tradition in this country where [Dominique] Strauss-Kahn would not have got away for so many years with portraying himself in a way that he clearly is not.'

Article 9 of the French Civil Code provides that 'Everyone has the right to respect for his private life…' This has been interpreted by the courts to include a person's identity (name, date of birth, religion, address, etc) and information about a person's health, matrimonial situation, family, sexual relationships, sexual orientation, and his or her way of life in general. It is also a criminal offence to encroach intentionally upon a private place by taking a photograph or by making a recording. Damages may be awarded for violations.[63]

The Italian Constitution protects the right to privacy as a constituent of an individual's personality. Thus, an invasion of privacy may give rise to a claim under the Civil Code, which provides that a person who intentionally or negligently commits an act that causes unreasonable harm to another is liable to compensate the latter. The Civil Code declares also that the publication of a person's image may be restrained if it causes prejudice to his or her dignity or reputation.

Article 10 of the Dutch Constitution guarantees the right to privacy, but it is a right subject to qualification; though the Supreme Court has held that the right to freedom of speech does not excuse an infringement of privacy, it will consider all circumstances in a privacy action, and a journalist may demonstrate that the publication in question was reasonable. Article 1401 of the Civil Code imposes a general liability for causing wrongful harm to others; it has been interpreted to include harm caused by publishing injurious private information without justification. The criminal law punishes trespassing into a person's home, eavesdropping on private conversations, and the unauthorized taking of photographs of individuals on any private property, and to publish the photographs so acquired.

The international dimension

A fairly generous right to privacy is an acknowledged human right, and is recognized in most international instruments. So, for example, Article 12 of the United Nations Declaration of Human Rights and Article 17 of the International Covenant on Civil and Political Rights both provide,

63. A distinction is drawn between photographing public figures exercising their official functions, on the one hand, and their unauthorized use for commercial purposes, on the other. See *Sarkozy and Bruni Tedeschi v Ryanair TGI Paris*, 5 February 2008, JCP 2008, Act 117. See E Steiner, 'The New President, His Wife and the Media: Pushing Away the Limits of Privacy Law's Protection in France' (2009) 13 Electronic Journal of Comparative Law.

1. No one shall be subjected to arbitrary or unlawful interference with his privacy, family, home or correspondence, nor to unlawful attacks on his honour and reputation.

2. Everyone has the right to the protection of the law against such interference or attacks.

Article 8 of the ECHR declares,

1. Everyone has the right to respect for his private and family life, his home and his correspondence.

2. There shall be no interference by a public authority with the exercise of this right except such as is in accordance with the law and is necessary in a democratic society in the interests of national security, public safety or the economic well-being of the country, for the prevention of disorder or crime, for the protection of health or morals, or for the protection of the rights and freedoms of others.

The European Court of Human Rights in Strasbourg has long been energetically adjudicating complaints from individuals seeking redress for alleged infractions of Article 8. Their grievances have exposed deficiencies in the domestic law of several European jurisdictions. For example, in *Gaskin v United Kingdom*[64] the Court held that the right to respect for private and family life imposed a duty to provide an individual with personal information about himself held by a public authority. In *Leander v Sweden*[65] the Court had ruled that such access could be legitimately denied to an applicant where the information related to national security, for example for the purpose of vetting an individual for a sensitive position, provided there is a satisfactory process by which the decision not to provide the information may be reviewed.

The English experience: breach of confidence

Four decades ago the Younger Committee concluded that the equitable remedy for breach of confidence offered 'the most effective protection of privacy in the whole of our existing law, civil and criminal'.[66] It requested

---

64. (1989) 12 EHHR 36.
65. (1987) 9 EHHR 36.
66. *Report of the Committee on Privacy* (n 42), para 87.

the Law Commissions to clarify the law in legislative form which they did.[67] But Parliament has failed to act. Perhaps they were right. Few tears would be shed by Professor Jones who regarded the report in the following light:[68]

> At the end of the day the large question remains: is it desirable *at this time* to enact legislation on the lines suggested by the Law Commission, legislation which will, in some ways, petrify the development of this branch of the law. Certainly there are few signs in the last few years that the common law has failed to deal adequately with the problems which it has been required to solve. This area of the law is not crying out for reform. It is still in an embryonic state; and there may well be questions lurking unseen in the shadows.

This, of course, begs the question what are 'the problems which it has been required to solve?' In the years since these words were written, the ability of the remedy of breach of confidence to solve the problem of the protection of personal information might justly be questioned. In this regard, I have attempted to show that, though 'privacy' and 'confidence' often overlap, the action for breach of confidence provided an unsuitable means by which to safeguard privacy.[69] Recent developments appear to have supported this view.

Indeed, while many of the requirements of the traditional cause of action have been all but demolished by the English courts, thanks to the super-model, Naomi Campbell, the 'new approach' announced by the House of Lords, 'takes a different view of the underlying value which the law protects…' This 'underlying value', at least in respect of personal information, is no longer the protection of a *relationship* of confidence, but 'the right to control the dissemination of information about one's private life and the right to the esteem and respect of other people.'[70]

---

67. Law Commission, *Breach of Confidence* (Law Com No 110, Cmnd 8388, 1981); Scottish Law Commission, *Breach of Confidence* (Scot Law Com No 90, Cmnd 9385, 1984).
68. G Jones, 'The Law Commission's Report on Breach of Confidence' [1982] Cambridge Law Journal 40, 47.
69. My whingeing on this subject began many moons ago, see R Wacks, 'Breach of Confidence and the Protection of Privacy' (1977) 127 New Law Journal 328.
70. *Campbell v MGN Ltd* [2004] 1 AC 457 (HL), [51] per Lord Hoffmann. The reference to 'esteem and respect' seems inappropriate; they are more properly the province of defamation than privacy. See Chapter 5.

It appears that, in respect of personal information (and perhaps even beyond),[71] the 'old fashioned'[72] remedy has been consigned to history. While few may mourn its apparent demise, it must be true that cases will arise straddling the frontier between personal and commercial information, or combining both species of information (as occurred in *Douglas v Hello! Ltd*).[73] It therefore remains important to evaluate, if only briefly, the jurisdictional foundation of the action in order to establish what is left of the remains.

It is arguable that the remedy may now fairly be described as *sui generis*.[74] Moreover, since the judicial unshackling of the action's 'relational' chains, the action—facilitated of course by the authority of the Human Rights Act— affords protection against the misuse of personal information. Whether this is an agreeable outcome is another matter. I reserve my reservations for the final chapter of this book.

What follows is neither a comprehensive nor exhaustive account of the law of confidence, but an outline of its principal features in so far as they pertain to the protection of personal information.[75] The action is overwhelmingly deployed in commercial or industrial disputes, but the subject of personal privacy has always fallen within its ambit, albeit in a secondary role. My purpose is to re-examine the question whether, even if the protection of privacy and the protection of confidence are, as I believe, based on 'two alternative theories'[76] (the former being 'primarily designed to protect

71. The full impact of these post-Human Rights Act decisions on the future of the action for breach of confidence will take time to unfold. For some reflections on how far these ripples may extend, including the waves they may cause in other common law jurisdictions, see M Richardson, M Bryan, M Vranken, and K Barnett, *Breach of Confidence: Social Origins and Modern Developments* (Cheltenham: Edward Elgar, 2012), ch 8. The metamorphosis of the protection of privacy under the wing of breach of confidence to the new cause of action for the misuse of personal information is described in greater detail in Chapter 4.
72. *Mosley v News Group Newspapers Ltd* [2008] EMLR 20, [7] per Eady J.
73. In *Douglas v Hello! Ltd (No 1)* [2001] QB 967 the claim was for the invasion of privacy occasioned by the publication of the claimants' wedding photographs. In *Douglas v Hello! Ltd (No 6)* [2008] 1 AC 1, the magazine that had purchased the rights to publish the photographs successfully claimed damages.
74. Gurry would seem to be correct in claiming that 'the action for breach of confidence is *sui generis* in nature and that it is difficult to confine the action exclusively within one conventional jurisdictional category. Instead, courts have invoked different jurisdictions—primarily contract and equity and to a lesser extent property and tort—on a pragmatic basis', T Aplin, L Bently, P Johnson, and S Malynicz, *Gurry on Breach of Confidence: The Protection of Confidential Information*, 2nd edn (Oxford: Oxford University Press, 2012), 99. This pragmatism is evident in numerous cases in both England and other common law jurisdictions. See eg *Lac Minerals Ltd v International Corona Resources Ltd* [1989] 2 SCR 574 (SC) and *Cadbury Schweppes Inc v FBI Foods Ltd* [1999] 1 SCR 142 (SCC) and *Hunt v A* [2008] 1 NZLR 368. (NZCA). Similar instances of this pragmatic approach may be found in other decisions cited by Gurry, para 4.11.
75. The most authoritative source is Gurry (n 74).
76. *Copley v Northwestern Mutual Life Insurance Co*, 295 F Supp 93, 95 (1968).

feelings and sensibilities'),⁷⁷ the action has nevertheless provided the courts with the means by which to protect an individual against unwanted publicity being given to his or her private life. I return to the subject in Chapter 4 where some of the cases touched on in the following sections (in order to provide a general picture of the principal features of the remedy) are discussed in greater detail.

The elements of the action

It is little more than a truism that the leading cases failed to establish with adequate clarity the circumstances in which (either direct or indirect) recipients of confidential information may be restrained from using or disclosing it.⁷⁸ This may, in part, be a consequence of the actions frequently arising in the form of applications for interlocutory injunctions which call for speedy adjudication. More modern decisions recognize a wider equitable principle of good faith or conscience on which to base the jurisdiction,⁷⁹ but its precise scope is not always easy to delineate.⁸⁰

In order to found a cause of action, three general requirements must be satisfied:

(a) The information itself must 'have the necessary quality of confidence about it'.⁸¹ (This requirement is normally satisfied by demonstrating that the information is 'not...public property and public knowledge'.)⁸²

(b) The information must have been imparted in circumstances imposing an obligation of confidence. Such an obligation will normally arise when

77. *Copley v Northwestern Mutual Life Insurance Co*, 295 F Supp 93, 95 (1968).
78. In particular, *Prince Albert v Strange* (1849) 1 H & Tw 1, 1 Mac & G 25; *Morison v Moat* (1851) 9 Hare 241.
79 *Seager v Copydex (No 1)* [1967] 2 All ER 415, 417 per Lord Denning MR; *Fraser v Evans* [1969] 1 All ER 8, 11 per Lord Denning MR.
80. 'The jurisdictional basis of the action...has been a source of lingering uncertainty and controversy. Contract, equity, and property have at times each provided the basis on which the courts have granted relief and, in some cases, a mixture of these bases has been relied on. The situation has been regarded as unsatisfactory and as evidence of conceptual confusion on the part of the courts', Gurry (n 74), 97 (footnotes omitted).
81. *Saltman Engineering Co Ltd v Campbell Engineering Co Ltd* (1948) 65 RPC 203, [1963] 3 All ER 413, 415 per Lord Greene MR.
82. *Saltman Engineering Co Ltd v Campbell Engineering Co Ltd* (1948) 65 RPC 203, [1963] 3 All ER 413, 415 per Lord Greene MR.

information is imparted—either explicitly or implicitly—for a limited purpose, and extends to any third parties to whom the information is disclosed, in breach of confidence, by the original confidant.[83]

(c) There must have been an unauthorized use of the information by the party who was under an obligation of confidence.

Each of these requirements will be briefly examined with particular reference to the protection of personal information.

The information

Although, as already mentioned, the vast majority of decisions involve cases concerning trade secrets (including business[84] and technical secrets[85]), government secrets[86] and artistic and literary confidences,[87] as well as personal information, have all been the subject of litigation.[88] The main concern here is, of course, the last.[89]

---

83. *Lord Ashburton v Pape* [1913] 2 Ch 469.
84. Eg *Thomas Marshall (Exporters) Ltd v Guinle* [1978] 3 WLR 116, 136 where Megarry V-C considered the sort of information 'capable of being confidential'. Sir Nicolas Browne-Wilkinson V-C opined that, 'Neither in principle nor on authority [is] there any reason why information relating to sexual matters should not be the subject of an enforceable duty of confidentiality': *Stephens v Avery* [1988] 2 WLR 1280.
85. Eg *Ackroyds (London) Ltd v Islington Plastics Ltd* [1962] RPC 97 (invention of tool to manufacture plastic 'swizzle sticks'); *Vestergaard Frandsen A/S v Bestnet Europe Ltd* [2009] EWHC 657 (Ch), [2009] EWHC 1456 (Ch) (a database of ingredients and proportions to manufacture insecticidal fabrics).
86. *Attorney-General v Guardian Newspapers Ltd (No 2)* [1988] 2 WLR 805 (Scott J); (Court of Appeal) [1988] 2 WLR 805; *Attorney-General v Guardian Newspapers Ltd* [1987] 1 WLR 1248; *Attorney-General v Jonathan Cape Ltd* [1976] 1 QB 752; *Commonwealth of Australia v John Fairfax & Sons Ltd* (1981) 55 ALJR 45; *Attorney General v Blake* [2001] 1 AC 268 (HL).
87. Eg *Fraser v Thames Television Ltd* [1983] 2 WLR 917 (idea for a television series); *Burrows v Smith and Crush Digital Media Ltd* [2010] EWHC 22 (idea for a computer video game).
88. *Saltman Engineering Co Ltd v Campbell Engineering Co Ltd* (1948) 65 RPC 203, 215, [1963] 3 All ER 413, 415: the information must have 'the necessary quality of confidence about it, namely, it must not be something which is public property and public knowledge', per Lord Greene MR.
89. While in *Mosley v News Group Newspapers Ltd* [2008] EWHC 687 (QB) an injunction was declined, in *Barclays Bank plc v Guardian News and Media Ltd* [2009] EWHC 591 (QB) the court held that posting confidential information online will not necessarily obliterate its confidentiality. The matter turns on the scope of the dissemination: 'general availability of material upon the internet would mean that it would be likely to lose its confidential character. However, equally, there is guidance and observations that very limited dissemination and only partial dissemination, perhaps in some remote or expert site that is not generally available to the public without a great deal of effort, may not result in such a loss of confidentiality', [22] per Blake J. The confidential information had appeared on the newspaper's website overnight (for about five hours); the injunction was therefore continued. See too *Attorney General v Greater*

So, for example, in *Duchess of Argyll v Duke of Argyll*[90] the Duchess successfully sought an injunction to prohibit the Duke and a newspaper from
publishing confidences she had reposed in her husband in the course of
their marriage. Ungoed-Thomas J, relying largely on *Prince Albert v Strange*,
held that such communications between spouses were protected against
breach of confidence—notwithstanding the Duchess's subsequent adultery
and divorce from the Duke. He declared, 'there could hardly be anything
more intimate or confidential than is involved in [the relationship of mar-
riage], or than in the mutual trust and confidence which are shared between
husband and wife.'[91]

Similarly, in *Stephens v Avery*,[92] the information concerned the plaintiff's
lesbian affair with a Mrs Telling. On application to strike out the plaintiff's
pleadings as disclosing no cause of action at interlocutory stage, Sir Nicolas
Browne-Wilkinson V-C stated, first, that grossly immoral conduct will not
be protected[93] but that because of the inability in modern times to determine the mores of a nation, 'only in a case where there is still a generally
accepted moral code can the court refuse to enforce rights in such a way
as to offend that generally accepted code.'[94] The Vice-Chancellor also recognized the test propounded by Megarry J in *Coco*.[95] He doubted 'whether
equity would intervene unless the circumstances are of sufficient gravity;
equity ought not to be invoked merely to protect trivial tittle-tattle, however confidential.'[96] On the facts, the disclosure of intimate details regarding
someone's sexual life was held by the Vice-Chancellor not to be trivial: 'I
have the greatest doubt whether wholesale revelation of the sexual conduct of an individual can properly be described as "trivial" tittle-tattle.'[97] He
added, 'I can see no reason why information relating to that most private

---

Manchester Newspapers Ltd [2001] EWHC QB 451; *Aegis Defence Services Ltd v Stoner* [2006]
EWHC 1515 (Ch). See Chapter 5.

90. [1967] Ch 302.
91. [1967] Ch 302 at 619.
92. [1988] 2 All ER 477, [1988] 2 WLR 1280. See too *Barrymore v News Group Newspapers Ltd*
    [1997] FSR 600. See W Wilson, 'Privacy, Confidence and Press Freedom: A Study in Judicial
    Activism' (1990) 53 Modern Law Review 43.
93. Following *Glyn v Western Feature Film Co* [1916] 1 Ch 261.
94. [1988] 2 All ER 477, 481.
95. *Coco v AN Clark (Engineers) Ltd* [1969] RPC 41.
96. *Coco v AN Clark (Engineers) Ltd* [1969] RPC 41 at 48.
97. *Stephens v Avery* [1988] 2 WLR 1280, 1285.

sector of everybody's life, namely sexual conduct, cannot be the subject matter of a legally enforceable duty of confidentiality.'[98]

In the infamous decision of *Woodward v Hutchins*,[99] the exploits of pop-stars, and in particular the 'outrageous' behaviour of one of them aboard an aircraft, was the subject of the action. There were no submissions in respect of the quality of the information revealed per se and Lord Denning MR proceeded on the basis that it was prima facie susceptible to the protection of a duty of confidentiality. In *Lennon v News Group Newspapers Ltd*[100] the former wife of John Lennon sold the 'story' of her marriage to the ex-Beatle to the *News of the World* which commenced a serialization of it. The articles disclosed intimate details of the relationship between the plaintiff and his ex-wife. The Court of Appeal denied an injunction on the ground that 'the relationship of these parties has ceased to be their own private affair …'

Similarly, in *Khashoggi v Smith*[101] the former housekeeper of the plaintiff, an affluent socialite who had attracted considerable publicity, disclosed intimate facts to the *Daily Mirror* concerning the plaintiff. But as there was an investigation proceeding into the alleged commission of an offence by the plaintiff, the Court of Appeal, on an interlocutory motion, refused to enjoin publication on the principal ground that there could be no confidence where it was sought to exploit information for investigation into the commission of alleged offences.

Many disclosures assume the form of a photograph taken or used without the subject's consent. It is a problem that, though its contemporary form assumes rather different proportions, begins in the early days of photography. So in *Pollard v Photographic Co*,[102] Mrs Pollard had her picture taken at the defendant's shop. An employee of the defendant used it in the shop window in the form of a Christmas card. There was some evidence that the employee may have been selling the cards for commercial gain (rather than using the card to advertise the services of the photographic company). North J held that a breach of confidence had occurred, declaring that 'where a person obtains information in the course of a confidential

---

98. *Stephens v Avery* [1988] 2 WLR 1280 at 1286.
99. [1977] 1 WLR 760. See R Wacks, 'Pop Goes Privacy' (1978) 31 Modern Law Review 67.
100. [1978] FSR 573.
101. (1980) 130 NLJ 168.
102. (1889) 40 Ch 345.

employment, the law does not permit him to make any improper use of the information so obtained.'[103] And he further emphasized that,

> The customer who sits for the negative…puts the power of reproducing the object in the hands of the photographer: and in my opinion, the photographer who uses the negative to produce other copies for his own use, without authority, is abusing the power of confidentiality placed in his hands namely for the purpose of supplying the customer.[104]

This dictum supports the view that the law protects also a person's likeness,[105] but such a conclusion cannot be reached without an analysis of the following, second limb of the *Saltman* test.

The obligation of confidence

The recipient of information generally incurs an obligation of confidence by virtue of the relationship in the course of which the information is imparted. Such an obligation may arise, with or without a contract, in a variety of circumstances, ranging from marriage[106] to cabinet meetings.[107]

Even before the *Campbell* correction, the absence of an explicit undertaking by the recipient of information to maintain its confidentiality did not negate the imposition of an obligation of confidence where the circumstances are such as to indicate that he or she knew or ought to have known that the information is to be treated as confidential.[108] Moreover, where a third party receives confidential information and, at the time she receives it is unaware that she has acquired it as a result of a breach of confidence, she

---

103. (1889) 40 Ch 345 at 349.
104. (1889) 40 Ch 345 at 349. The court also held that it was an implied term of the contract that prints developed from the negative of photographs taken at the defendant's shop were not to be used for an unauthorized purpose. By extension a hotel guest who has been surreptitiously photographed in his or her room by hotel staff could claim an implied term of the contract that the room is surveillance-free.
105. See *Li Yau-wai v Genesis Films Ltd* [1987] HKLR 711.
106. *Duchess of Argyll v Duke of Argyll* [1967] Ch 302.
107. *Attorney-General v Jonathan Cape Ltd* [1976] QB 752.
108. The objectivity of the test was—presciently—proposed, *obiter*, by Megarry J in *Coco v AN Clark (Engineers) Ltd* [1969] RPC 41, 48: 'It may be that the hard-worked creature, the reasonable man, may be pressed into service once more; for I do not see why he should not labour in equity as well as at law. It seems to me that if the circumstances are such that any reasonable man standing in the shoes of the recipient of the information would have realised that upon reasonable grounds the information was being given to him in confidence, then this should suffice to impose upon him the equitable obligation of confidence.'

will, on being given notice of the breach, be prima facie subject to a duty of confidence. This is clear from the judgment of Sir Robert Megarry V-C in *Malone v Commissioner of Police for the Metropolis (No 2)*.[109]

> If A makes a confidential communication to B, then A may not only restrain B from divulging or using the confidence, but may also restrain C from divulging or using it if C has acquired it from B, even if he acquired it without notice of any impropriety…In such cases it seems plain that, however innocent the acquisition of the knowledge, what will be restrained is the use or disclosure of it after notice of the impropriety.

The key question—at least before the advent of the Human Rights Act in respect of personal information—has long been whether an obligation of confidence arises in the *absence* of some pre-existing confidential relationship in which the claimant imparts confidential information to another. This would constitute a serious limitation on the action's viability as a tool by which to protect privacy. I therefore consider it in the section entitled 'Reappraising orthodoxy'.

Unauthorized use

For the claimant in a breach of confidence action to establish that the defendant has actually used or disclosed the confidential information, he or she must prove that the information was 'directly or indirectly obtained from a plaintiff, without the consent, express or implied, of the plaintiff'.[110] The claimant does not have to show that the defendant has acted dishonestly or even consciously in using the information. Thus, in *Seager v Copydex Ltd*[111] the defendant was held liable for 'unconscious plagiarism'[112] in using the plaintiff's idea for a carpet grip; the two parties had discussed—apparently in rather general terms—the plaintiff's idea, but their negotiations broke down and the Court of Appeal found that the defendant honestly believed the idea to be his own.[113]

---

109. [1979] 2 All ER 620, 634.
110. *Saltman Engineering Co Ltd v Campbell Engineering Co Ltd* (1948) 65 RPC 203, 213 per Lord Greene MR.
111. [1967] RPC 349.
112. [1967] RPC 349 at 374.
113. See, too, *Terrapin Ltd v Builders Supply Co (Hayes) Ltd* [1967] RPC 375; (on appeal) [1960] RPC 128.

Whether a claimant need establish that he or she has suffered (or will suffer) detriment as a result of the breach of confidence is a matter of some uncertainty. While Megarry J (as he then was) in *Coco v AN Clark (Engineers) Ltd*[114] suggested that this might be a requirement of the action, the better view would seem to be that this factor ought to be conceived as relevant only to the determination of the appropriate remedy. In the context of the misuse of personal information it would not, of course, always be easy to see how, other than the injured feelings, embarrassment, or distress suffered by the claimant, he or she could realistically be said to have suffered any detriment, at least in the strict sense of material disadvantage.[115]

In principle, it ought not to matter whether the personal information disclosed was true or false or whether it lowered or enhanced the plaintiff's reputation (a view accepted by Knight Bruce V-C in *Prince Albert v Strange*[116] and by Megarry J in *Coco*[117]). There is no denying the fact that 'some people want privacy largely so that they can turn it to their own financial advantage'[118] and the detriment in such cases would not be different from the normal commercial confidence case. There is also much in Professor Cornish's view[119] that:

> It is tempting to say that liability ought to follow simply upon the breaking of the confidence without looking also for detriment. But one should remember that a very wide range of subject-matter is involved, and also that there is always some public interest in the freedom to use information. Restriction of that freedom accordingly requires sufficient reason.

The limits of the action

A number of obstacles have always beset the path of the law of confidence as a protector of personal information. First is the apparent requirement, just mentioned, of a relationship of confidence between the person who

---

114. [1969] RPC 41, 48; see, too, *Dunford & Eliot Ltd v Johnson & Firth Brown Ltd* [1978] FSR 143, 148 per Lord Denning MR.
115. In *Attorney-General v Guardian Newspapers Ltd (No 2)* [1988] 3 WLR 776, 782, Lord Keith stated, *obiter*, 'I would think it a sufficient detriment to the confider that information given in confidence is to be disclosed to persons whom he would prefer not to know of it, even though the disclosure would not be harmful to him in any positive way.' Lord Goff (at 806) preferred to keep the question open. See, too, *X v Y* [1988] 2 All ER 648, 657. *Li Yau-wai v Genesis Films Ltd* [1987] HKLR 711; M Pendleton, (1987) 17 Hong Kong Law Journal 362.
116. (1849) 2 De Gex & Sm 652, 697.
117. [1969] RPC 41, 48; see, too, Scott J in *Cork v McVicar* [1984] The Times, 1 November.
118 W Cornish, D Llewelyn, and T Aplin, *Intellectual Property: Patents, Copyright, Trade Marks and Allied Rights*, 7th edn (London: Sweet & Maxwell, 2010), 357.
119. Cornish et al (n 118), ibid.

confides the information and the person to whom it is confided. Such a relationship will not necessarily (or even normally) be present where the claimant's grievance is that personal facts have been published without his or her consent (eg, by a newspaper which has obtained the information without any breach of confidence). But it no longer appears to be a prerequisite of the action, at least in cases involving personal information.[120] I examine this question later.

Secondly, the possible requirement that in order to succeed the claimant must show detriment may mean, in a privacy case, that the only detriment suffered would be mental distress. This may suffice for the claimant to be awarded an injunction, but may deprive him or her of an award of damages. Thirdly, the claimant must establish that the information was inaccessible to the public, not in the 'public domain'; a requirement which may produce artificial results in the context of privacy claims, especially in the case of publication on the Internet.[121]

Fourthly, the action is available only to the person to whom the obligation of confidence is owed, and it is only the person who has actual, imputed, or constructive knowledge that he or she is acting in breach of confidence who may be sued. Under a strict interpretation of this requirement, the action was of limited utility to the claimant who is subjected to unwanted press publicity, but *Campbell* has lifted this barrier.

Fifthly, the application of the defence of 'clean hands' to a privacy action results in the court refusing relief where, on a 'balance of perfidy',[122] the claimant has himself disclosed information which is of a greater order

---

120. The 'new approach' enunciated in *Campbell v MGN* [2004] 2 AC 457 (HL), [51], all but annihilates this requirement.

121. Thus, in *Mosley v News Group Newspapers Ltd* [2008] EWHC 687 (QB), when faced with the extensive availability of the offending video online, Eady J warned that a court 'should guard against slipping into playing the role of King Canute. Even though an order may be desirable for the protection of privacy, and may be made in accordance with the principles currently being applied by the courts, there may come a point where it would simply serve no useful purpose and would merely be characterised, in the traditional terminology, as a *brutum fulmen*. It is inappropriate for the Court to make vain gestures', [34]. As Gurry points out, 'the principal questions in cases involving misuse of private information relate to notions of intrusiveness, harassment, and control of one's image…so that it often makes little sense to make a distinction between whether the information is in the public domain or not', Gurry (n 74), 659. For examples of the limitations of 'public domain' in the context of 'privacy' claims, see *Douglas v Hello! Ltd (No 3)* [2006] QB 125; *HRH Prince of Wales v Associated Newspapers Ltd* [2008] Ch 57; *Green Corns v Claverly* [2005] EWHC 958 (QB); *Murray v Express Newspapers plc* [2009] Ch 481.

122. *Duchess of Argyll v Duke of Argyll* [1967] Ch 302, 331 per Ungoed-Thomas J. This rarely arises in privacy claims, though, as I argue in Chapter 4, there are circumstances in which the

of impropriety or where he has himself exhibited little concern for the maintenance of the confidential relationship.

Sixthly, the occasional application of the rule accepted in libel cases that an interlocutory injunction will not be granted against a defendant who intends to justify or plead fair comment,[123] is inappropriate in cases involving breach of confidence, especially where personal information is concerned, for not only is the disclosure of a secret irrevocable, but, since compensation is unlikely to be awarded for mental distress (the claimant's usual injury in such cases), to leave the claimant to her remedy in damages is effectively to deprive her of effective relief. An injunction (including the so-called 'super injunction' and anonymous injunction) is plainly the most fitting remedy where the threat of publication is known to the claimant. Whether prior notification of an intention to publish ought to be required by the law, as well as the issue of injunctive relief are considered in Chapter 7.

It is not unreasonable to conclude that, in general terms, until recently the action for breach of confidence was inadequate to deal with the archetypal privacy complaint because the action is largely concerned with: (a) disclosure or use rather than publicity; (b) the source rather than the nature of the information; and (c) the preservation of confidence rather than the possible harm to the claimant caused by its breach.

These deficiencies are most effectively demonstrated by contrasting the action with the US tort of 'public disclosure of private facts' or what is called in the *Restatement (Second) of the Law of Torts*[124] 'publicity given to

conscience of the *defendant* might be called into question! The limitations of the principle are, as emerges from the judgment in *Attorney General v Heinemann Publishers Australia* [1989] 2 FSR 349, at 506, fairly strict. In *Gray v Thames Trains* [2009] UKHL 33, [30], Lord Hoffmann suggested that the maxim *ex turpi causa non oritur actio* 'expresses not so much a principle as a policy'. I presume the learned judge was not employing these terms (as he has done elsewhere) in the Dworkinian sense, for surely this is a textbook example of what Dworkin calls 'a standard that is to be observed, not because it will advance or secure an economic, political, or social situation, but because it is a requirement of justice or fairness or some other dimension of morality', R Dworkin, *Taking Rights Seriously* (London: Duckworth, 1978), 22.

123. *Bonnard v Perryman* [1891] 2 Ch 289. The courts are far more amenable when it comes to awarding injunctions in a breach of confidence action: *Cream Holdings v Banerjee* [2005] 1 AC 253.

124. *Restatement (Second) of the Law of Torts* para 652D. See Dean Prosser's account earlier.

private life'.[125] As already mentioned, the *Restatement*[126] defines the tort as follows:

> One who gives publicity to a matter concerning the private life of another is subject to liability to the other for invasion of his privacy, if the matter publicized is of a kind that (a) would be highly offensive to a reasonable person, and (b) is not of legitimate concern to the public.

The tort has the following three elements:

(a) there must be *publicity*: for example, to inform his employer or a small group that the claimant is a homosexual, would not suffice;

(b) the information disclosed must be *private* facts: publicity given to matters of public record will not be actionable;

(c) the facts disclosed must be *offensive* to a reasonable person of ordinary sensibilities.

The US tort therefore differs in a number of respects from the 'traditional' remedy for breach of confidence. In Table 1, I identify the essential differences. The fundamental distinction lies, of course, in the fact that while the tort of unwanted publicity is based on the protection against the disclosure of certain information which is categorized as 'private', the action for breach of confidence rests on the more limited protection against disclosure of certain information which is categorized as 'confidential' and is subject to an obligation of confidence owed normally to the person who has confided it.

The US tort therefore protects the plaintiff against wide publicity being given to certain classes of information. The purpose of the law of confidence, on the other hand, though it requires the information to be confidential, is essentially to maintain the fidelity or trust that the plaintiff has reposed in the person to whom he or she has confided (or, at any rate, who ought to recognize that he or she is violating such trust). The policy of the law is principally to promote the honesty which is important to commercial

---

125. But note that the US tort has generated less litigation than might have been anticipated, and in formulating certain, sometimes fundamental, elements there is a degree of imprecision and even speculation. Reports of the death of the tort may, however, be exaggerated. Compare DL Zimmerman, 'Requiem for a Heavyweight: A Farewell to Warren and Brandeis's Privacy Tort' (1983) 68 Cornell Law Review 291 and R Gavison, 'Too Early for a Requiem: Warren and Brandeis Were Right on Privacy vs Free Speech' (1992) 48 South Carolina Law Review 437. Furthermore, some of the drawbacks of the tort may be explained in part by the existence of a remedy for breach of confidence.

126. See n 14.

Table 1. PUBLIC DISCLOSURE AND BREACH OF CONFIDENCE COMPARED

Public disclosure	Breach of confidence
Publicity given to 'private facts'	Use or disclosure of confidential information
Wide publicity generally required	Not required
Not required	Information must be imparted in circumstances imposing a duty of confidence
Facts disclosed must be 'highly offensive'	Not required, but 'trivial tittle-tattle' not protected
Disclosures in the public interest not actionable	Similar limitation obtains
Public figures may forfeit some protection	Similar limitation obtains
Anyone who is subject to unauthorized publicity may sue	Only the person to whom the duty of confidence is owed may sue
Anyone who publishes private facts without authority may be sued	Only the person who is subject to a duty of confidence may be sued

transactions. It is not therefore illogical that the action for breach of confidence should concentrate on the *source* rather than, as in the privacy tort, the *content* of the information.

Moreover, there is no requirement in the law of confidence that the disclosure be 'highly offensive' (or indeed offensive at all) since its principal object is not to prevent harm to the plaintiff, but to ensure that information communicated in confidence (actually or constructively) will, in general, be protected. Under the US tort, I do not have a cause of action where the published information about me is, by reference to an objective standard, innocuous—even if its disclosure causes me embarrassment or distress. Where, however, I impart the *same* facts in the course of a confidential relationship, it is arguable that, because, in the absence of an expectation of confidentiality, I might not have revealed them, I should be able to prevent their disclosure by the action for breach of confidence.

Hence in privacy cases the action for breach of confidence always had the potential to protect a wider range of subject matter relating to the claimant, subject, of course, to the existence of a relationship of confidence or, at any rate, circumstances in which the defendant knew or ought to have known that he or she was acting in breach of confidence. This is consistent with the law's objective in protecting the interest in the maintenance of confidential relationships. And even if the revelations made in breach of confidence were innocuous it would not be unreasonable for the confider to fear that possible future disclosures may be less trivial.

Similarly, whereas the privacy tort requires wide publicity,[127] in the case of breach of confidence the claimant will have a legitimate objection if disclosure is made in breach of confidence to a single individual.

Reappraising orthodoxy

Prior relationship

The Law Commission concluded that 'an obligation of confidence will arise when the circumstances of the relationship [between confider and confidant] import it.'[128] And this principle figured in the Commission's draft bill.[129] An obligation of confidence was only to be imposed if the confidant had agreed to treat the information as confidential in the form of an express undertaking or in circumstances where, by conduct in relation to the confider, or by virtue of the relationship between them, such an undertaking on the part of the confidant could be inferred.[130] However, the Commission could not state any clear overarching principle to guide the courts.[131] At the time of formulating its recommendations, however, there were no authorities in which a prior relationship between the confider and confidant was absent.

Since then, though, a number of decisions have illuminated the grounds upon which the action is based. But straws were already in the wind. For example, Laws J in *Hellewell v Chief Constable of Derbyshire*[132] stated,

> If someone with a telephoto lens were to take from a distance and with no authority a picture of another engaged in some private act, his subsequent disclosure of the photograph would, in my judgment, as surely amount to a breach of confidence as if he had found or stolen a letter or diary in which the act was recounted and proceeded to publish it. In such a case, the law would

127. *Peterson v Idaho First National Bank*, 367 P2d 284 (1967). Cf *Beaumont v Brown*, 257 NW 522 (1977).
128. *Breach of Confidence* (n 67), para 4.2.
129. *Breach of Confidence* (n 67), Appendix A.
130. *Breach of Confidence* (n 67), section 3(1)(a) and (b).
131. The Law Commission was content to restate its comments in its Working Paper No 58 that: 'No one can say with any assurance how a particular issue will be decided in the future' (*Breach of Confidence* (Working Paper No 58, Cmnd 5012, 1972)), para 5.2.
132. [1995] 1 WLR 804, 807.

protect what might reasonably be called a right of privacy, although the name accorded to the cause of action would be breach of confidence.

Claimants now have the model Naomi Campbell to thank for the recognition that the action is not predicated upon a prior relationship between the parties but is based upon the straightforward protection of the right to a private life. Such a position was, I believe, already discernible from a careful reading of several decisions since the Law Commission's Report, in particular *Francome*,[133] *Stephens*,[134] *Spycatcher*,[135] and *Franklin*[136] (which was considered by the Law Commission).[137]

In *Franklin* the defendant occasionally lent a hand at the plaintiff's orchard, subsequently set up his own rival orchard, and then, surreptitiously, stole budwood cuttings from the plaintiff's premises. The cuttings provided the defendant with information regarding a new strain of nectarines that the plaintiff had cross-bred. Dunn J did not consider the obligation of confidence to be predicated upon a relationship between the parties during the course of which the information was divulged from confider to confidant. He found himself 'quite unable to accept that a thief who steals a trade secret, with the intention of using it in commercial competition with its owner, to the detriment of the latter and so uses it, is less unconscionable than a traitorous servant.'[138] Though I earlier characterized this decision as one which would be best understood as being based on the infringement of the plaintiff's property in his budwood,[139] this now seems a rather restrictive interpretation. There is, I think, justification for reading the judgment as the

133. *Francome v Mirror Group Newspapers Ltd* [1984] 1 WLR 892.
134. *Stephens v Avery* [1988] 2 WLR 1280.
135. *Attorney-General v Guardian Newspapers (No 1)* [1987] 1 WLR 1248 and *Attorney-General v Guardian Newspapers (No 2)* [1988] 3 All ER 545.
136. *Franklin v Giddins* [1978] 1 Qd R 72 and see case note by WJ Braithwaite, 'The Secret of Life: A Fruity Trade Secret' (1979) 95 Law Quarterly Review 323.
137. The Law Commission stressed that its terms of reference 'are not directed to the protection of privacy as such', para 2.1. However, it was explicitly asked to consider whether the law in this area protected information 'unlawfully obtained', ibid. It was in response to this question that it concluded, 'it is very doubtful to what extent, if at all, information becomes impressed with an obligation of confidence by reason solely of the reprehensible means by which it has been acquired', para 4.10. Implicit in this statement is the further conclusion that *Franklin* could not be taken as authority, in England at least, that the law was moving to receipt-based conscionability principles.
138. [1978] 1 Qd R 72, 80.
139. R Wacks, *Personal Information: Privacy and the Law* (Oxford: Clarendon Press, 1989), 255–6.

beginning of the demise of the need for a relationship for the imposition of an obligation of confidence.[140]

The limitations of the decision must, however, be acknowledged. The information was of a wholly commercial nature and, more importantly, the cutting—the carrier of the information—was obtained unlawfully from the plaintiff's orchard. This point is considered later,[141] suffice it to observe here that the result could well have been very different if the defendant had stumbled upon the cutting lying on a road near the plaintiff's property.[142]

In *Stephens*, though on the facts there clearly was a strong prior relationship between the plaintiff and Mrs Telling, the Vice-Chancellor, in response to counsel for the defendant's submission that there must be such a relationship for the duty of confidence to be imposed, stated that 'the basis of the intervention...is that it is unconscionable for a person who has received information on the basis that it is confidential subsequently to reveal that information.'[143] These sentiments were explicitly restated by Lord Goff:

> [A] duty of confidence arises when confidential information comes to the knowledge of the person (the confidant) in circumstances where he has notice, or is held to have agreed, that the information is confidential, with the effect that it would be just in all the circumstances that he should be precluded from disclosing the information to others.[144]

Kaye v Robertson,[145] which became something of a *cause célèbre*, involved the use of a photograph of the plaintiff, a television actor, taken by newspaper reporters while he was convalescing in a private room of a hospital from which they were expressly barred. Breach of confidence was not pleaded (presumably because counsel recognized the same limitations of the action

---

140. As suggested by Braithwaite (n 136). He considers it authority for the proposition that an individual who surreptitiously obtains confidential information (as distinct from learning through a confidential disclosure) will be subject to an obligation of confidence.

141. See the text at n 184.

142. The Law Commission specifically reviewed *Franklin* under the heading 'Can information initially become impressed with an obligation of confidence by only of the reprehensible means by which it has been acquired?', Part IV, Section C. As remarked earlier, this unwillingness to discuss the case in relation to the wider issue may be a result of the terms of reference of the Commission's considerations (n 67).

143. [1988] 2 All ER 477, 482.

144. *Spycatcher (No 2)* [1988] 3 All ER 545, 658.

145. [1991] FSR 62. See BS Markesinis, 'Our Patchy Law of Privacy—Time to Do Something about It' (1990) 53 Modern Law Review 802; P Prescott, '*Kaye v Robertson*—A Reply' (1991) 54 Modern Law Review 450; BS Markesinis, 'The Calcutt Report Must Not be Forgotten' (1992) 55 Modern Law Review 118; and D Feldman, *Civil Liberties and Human Rights in England and Wales*, 2nd edn (Oxford: Oxford University Press, 2002), 387–8.

as I did)[146] but, apart from the question of a prior relationship between the parties, the case has much in common with *Pollard*.[147] Both concern the unauthorized use of the plaintiff's likeness, though in *Kaye* the plaintiff's objection is to the unauthorized publicity, while in *Pollard* it is against the defendant's commercial use.[148]

The absence of a relationship between the parties did not inhibit the a Hong Kong court from imposing liability for breach of confidence. In *Koo and Chiu v Lam*,[149] Hong Kong Court of Appeal held that a medical researcher was under a duty of confidence in respect of a questionnaire that had been prepared by a rival research team and which, by the appellant's admission, he had used formulating his own questionnaire. It is unfortunate that there is no clear evidence as to how the appellant obtained access to the respondents' questionnaire. Penlington JA, commenting upon the trial judge's finding that the appellant had obtained the information 'surreptitiously', remarked,

> [H]e did somehow come into possession of the document, and he must have known it was confidential because of the amount of work which had gone into its preparation. It had not been given to him by the persons whose information it was and again he must have realised he was not entitled to use it.[150]

This dictum takes the law considerably further than both *Franklin* and *Francome* for in those decisions the 'surreptitious taker' acted contrary to law (theft and an offence contrary to the British Wireless Telegraphy Act 1949, respectively). In *Koo*, Penlington JA emphasized that the finding of 'surreptitious obtaining' did not extend as far as theft which, he said, 'cannot be supported by the evidence'.[151] But if surreptitious taking extends to the mere fact that the appellant 'did somehow come into possession' of the questionnaire with the knowledge that it was confidential, the Hong Kong Court of Appeal appears (by accident or design) to have grasped the nettle and embraced the notion of receipt-based liability, albeit under cover of surreptitiousness rather than unconscionability.

---

146. Scott LJ, writing extra-judicially, after having noted that the breach of confidence action was not argued before the court in *Kaye*, could only ask 'Why not?' (*Confidentiality and the Law* (London: LLP, 1990)), xxiii.
147. (1888) 40 Ch 345.
148. See MP Thompson, 'Confidence in the Press' (1993) The Conveyancer 347; and *Li Yau-wai v Genesis Films Ltd* [1987] HKLR 711.
149. Civil Transcript No 116 (1992).
150. Civil Transcript No 116 (1992), 30.
151. Civil Transcript No 116 (1992), 29.

But one could not, on the basis of this judgment, have thrown caution to the wind. First, the actual finding, at first instance, that the information was imparted in circumstances imposing an obligation of confidence (the second *Saltman* limb) was not challenged upon appeal.[152] Secondly, the rival teams of researchers worked at the same university which implied a 'course of dealing' between the parties during which the appellant arguably became aware that the questionnaire was confidential. This could, to some extent, approximate to a relationship of confidence on orthodox principles. The case was clearly not one of a stranger stumbling across a diary in the street. Nevertheless, assuming it is correct, the decision is another demonstration of the utility of the breach of confidence action where the strict requirement of a prior relationship is relaxed. It does not, however, remove all the obstacles in the path of the protection of privacy, for the finding that the appellant knew that the information contained in the questionnaire was confidential was derived less from the nature of the information than from his personal experience, and the relationship, albeit limited, between the parties.

Kaye exemplified the difficulties associated with predicating the action for breach of confidence upon a relationship between the parties. The archetypal invasion of privacy complaint is not, of course, based on a direct relationship between the victim and the wrongdoer; indeed, this is the primary objection to the US tort of breach of confidence which centres upon the fiduciary nature of certain relationships and prohibits the disclosure of information imparted within them.[153] Thus, it has been argued that this tort is capable (at least in the context of the relationship between employer and employee) of assuming the—frayed—mantle of Warren and Brandeis's public disclosure tort as a means of protecting privacy. This interpretation of the tort[154] suggests that it affords protection to any unauthorized disclosure within a non-public relationship 'that goes beyond mere friendship, family, or confessor-confidant',[155] such relationship which must be 'customarily understood to carry an obligation of confidence'.[156]

---

152. One is bound to ask why not? The decision of the trial judge represented a significant divergence from present authority.
153. See SL Fast, 'Breach of Employee Confidentiality: Moving Toward a Common-Law Tort Remedy' (1993) 142 University of Pennsylvania Law Review 431.
154. Relying upon *Vassiliades v Garfinckel's*, 492 A2d 580 (DC 1985).
155. Fast (n 153), 452.
156. Fast (n 153), 452.

An approach of this kind (apart from inviting the problems under discussion) is plainly too narrow. How would it assist the victim against the disloyal friend in *Stephens*? Or the claimant against the newspaper reporters in *Kaye*?

Constructive knowledge

If the principle of unconscionability is indeed at the heart of the action, the insistence on the need for a prior relationship between confider and confidant may be explained as the threshold of circumstantial evidence that the claimant must satisfy in order to show that the recipient's conscience has been pricked by the confidential nature of the information. The question therefore becomes one of the standard of proof: under what circumstances will *constructive* knowledge be attributed to a confidant—that he or she has received information he or she is expected to keep secret when such knowledge cannot be said to exist in fact?

In *Coco* Megarry J said,

> It seems to me that if the circumstances are such that any reasonable man standing in the shoes of the recipient of the information would have realised that upon reasonable grounds the information was being given to him in confidence, then this should suffice to impose upon him the equitable obligation of confidence.[157]

This dictum pertains both to the confidant and to third party recipients. In the case of the latter, however, the court has never required any kind of relationship directly between confider and third party, nor between confidant and third party, though as conceded earlier, there has in fact been a relationship between confider and confidant in all but two of the cases.[158]

In another Hong Kong decision, *Li Yau-wai v Genesis Films Ltd*,[159] the plaintiff, an insurance salesman, allowed his photograph to be taken by the defendant film company upon the understanding it would facilitate his being considered for casting in a future film. Instead, the defendant used the photograph as a prop in a 'ribald comedy', causing the plaintiff considerable embarrassment. The court held that, in addition to liability in defamation,

---

157. [1969] RPC 41, 48.
158. Namely, *Franklin* and *Francome*.
159. [1987] HKLR 711; and see note by M Pendleton (1987) 17 Hong Kong Law Journal 362.

the defendant owed the plaintiff an obligation of confidence in respect of the photograph and, accordingly, the unauthorized use constituted breach of that obligation. Rhind J applied the reasoning of North J in *Pollard* to find that the photograph had the necessary quality of confidence about it, adding that 'where a person makes himself accessible to be photographed by another in circumstances where one would expect confidentiality to be respected, a duty of confidence on the part of the person taking the photograph will arise.'[160]

The court applied Megarry J's objective test to determine the second limb of the traditional test of actionability: was the information imparted in circumstances importing an obligation of confidence? It was satisfied that 'any officious bystander would emphatically pronounce that when Genesis took Mr Li's photograph, it knew that it was for use only for casting purposes.'[161] The application of the standard of the reasonable person to impose upon the defendant an obligation of confidence represents a significant development, especially because the actual intentions of the parties had to be drawn by inference rather than by reference to a specific remark or their relationship. It demonstrates the potential of the unconscionability test in protecting privacy.

In the case of a third party, his or her obligation to keep information secret is parasitic upon there being an obligation owed to the confider by a confidant.[162] A fortiori, a relationship between the confider and confidant is required, without which third party obligations cannot arise. Third party obligation may have assisted in paving the way towards the 'new approach' and its elimination of the strict requirement of a relationship between confider and recipient. The law attaches such a duty in respect of the confidences of a person whom the third party has not even met because a duty of confidence has arisen at the primary level between confidant and confider. Why then should that duty *at the primary level* require a prior relationship? Why, in other words, should the court be satisfied that the third party acted unconscionably according to a lower standard of proof than it applies to the confidant?

In 1995 I argued that since the principle of unconscionability admits of a lower standard of proof, this could be the basis for the protection against unauthorized publicity by the law of confidence. If, as is suggested earlier, the

---

160. [1987] HKLR 711, 719.
161. [1987] HKLR 711, 719.
162. See the exemplary analysis of this question in Gurry (n 74), 286–300.

principal rationale of the law *is* unconscionability, then there would seem to be no obvious obstacle in the way of attaching an obligation to a person by virtue merely of receipt of information whose *nature* is such that the person, on the principles of constructive knowledge, is taken to have realized that he or she may not divulge it to another. This is the mechanism by which personal information may be protected from transactions which take place outside a relationship between the person who is the subject of that information and the person who disseminates it.[163] And so it has come to pass. But what of the pre-Human Rights Act authority for this metamorphosis?

Reconsidering the cases

In *Stephens* the Vice-Chancellor noted that 'the relationship between the parties is not the determining factor. It is the acceptance of the information on the basis that it will be kept secret that affects the conscience of the recipient of the information.'[164] This remark, though plainly *obiter* (there was a close relationship between the plaintiff and Mrs Avery) explicitly recognizes that the requirement of a relationship is not a rule of law but merely a means of proving to an acceptably high standard that the information is received *on the basis that it will be kept secret*.

Was this a (belated) creative leap towards Younger? If, as I formerly argued, the action is generally concerned to protect the source rather than the nature of the information such decisions (or at least their reasoning)[165] may legitimately be so regarded. Thus, on the basis of *Stephens* and *Spycatcher (No 2)*, Wilson adopts this view because for him the basis of the jurisdiction for breach of confidence in cases of personal information is the protection of 'the integrity of certain types of relationships',[166] whereas in cases of commercial confidences it is the protection of 'the pre-existing rights of the plaintiff'.[167] He refers to Ungoed-Thomas J's view in *Argyll* that 'the

---

163. This must be read in the light of the fundamental principle that the only person who may call for the fulfilment of the obligation of confidence is the person to whom that obligation is owed: *Fraser v Evans* [1969] 1 QB 349. The Law Commission observed that a person who has only 'an *interest* in the secrecy of the information cannot, therefore, enforce any obligation owed in respect of that information', para 5.9. This question is discussed later.

164. [1988] 2 All ER 477, 482.

165. Though not in their result.

166. Wilson (n 92), 49.

167. Wilson (n 92), 49.

protection of confidential information between husband and wife is not designed to intrude into the marital domain, but to protect it, not to break their confidential relation, but to encourage it.'[168]

This was how I, too, understood the decisions.[169] But a more faithful reading might suggest that, though in both instances clear relationships between the parties existed,[170] the courts were chiefly concerned with unconscionable conduct. Thus, the question of a relationship becomes a sufficient but not a necessary condition of liability. It is, in other words, an important factor in determining whether the evidence supports the inference that the recipient of the information either knew or ought reasonably to have known that the information was subject to a duty of confidence. But it is not a requirement of the action.

In *Francome*[171] the nature of the information unlawfully intercepted was not considered by the court for it was an interlocutory application by the defendant newspaper to discharge an injunction restraining it from publishing until trial extracts from the recordings of the conversations between the plaintiff and his wife. It is clear, however, that the information was such that both sides were aware of its value: the plaintiff in destroying his reputation, the newspaper in profiting from a scoop concerning alleged illicit activities by one of Britain's leading jockeys. On a conventional analysis, it is plausible, if slightly artificial, to consider Mr Francome (the plaintiff) as the confider and his wife, the confidant. But here there is an important factor: the confidant has herself committed no breach of confidence.

How then could a third party (the tapper) be held liable? To what does the parasite of third party liability attach? The court directed itself to the *mens rea* of the tapper. Could it be said that his conscience was pricked? The answer, according to the Court of Appeal, was emphatically in the affirmative. The only basis upon which such a conclusion could have been reached was the tacit assumption that a person who unlawfully listens to another's telephone conversation acquires information that was intended to be received by no one other than the person on the end of the line. A tapper is, by definition, on notice, either explicitly (and it seems difficult to avoid the conclusion that he knew precisely the confidential nature of the

---

168. *Duchess of Argyll v Duke of Argyll* [1965] 1 All ER 611, 626.
169. Wacks (n 139), 87 and 97.
170. As Wilson (n 92) puts it, 'the obligation imposed was clearly indebted to a "special" relationship between the confider and confidant', 49.
171. [1984] WLR 892.

information) or implicitly (on the ground that he or she ought reasonably to know).

This decision is difficult to square with orthodoxy. Wilson asserts that 'in the absence of...a relationship the courts have nevertheless shown themselves ready to intervene to protect a confidence where it would advance or support a particular right of the plaintiff.'[172] Such rights, he continues, are 'socially based'.[173] But this begs the question: if Mr Francome's 'right' not to have his telephone tapped (and his conversation overheard) had not been recognized by the court, he would have had no legal right at all. And Wilson's reference to the dictum in *Argyll* must be read in the light of Lord Keith's observation in *Spycatcher (No 2)* that 'as a general rule it is in the public interest that confidences should be respected, and the encouragement of such respect may *in itself* constitute a sufficient ground for recognizing and enforcing the obligation of confidence.'[174]

Thus, while the scope of the action has manifestly enlarged, this has occurred on the basis of principles that have long supplied its equitable underpinning.[175] And these limitations that I earlier identified[176] led me to conclude, inter alia, that in the absence of a relationship of confidence between the person who confides the information and the confidant, no duty of confidence can be born. So, I suggested, a newspaper may publish with impunity personal information which it has obtained without a pre-existing relationship of confidence. Similarly, to use the well-worn example already

---

172. Wilson (n 92), 54.
173. Wilson (n 92), 52.
174. [1988] 3 All ER 545, 640.
175. See Jones (n 68). Even in 1970, Jones identified a general principle of unconscionability from cases such as *Seager v Copydex* [1967] 1 WLR 923. He argues: 'The plaintiff's right is based upon the broad equitable principle that the defendant shall not *knowingly* take advantage of the plaintiff's confidence', ibid, 492 (emphasis added). The new edition of Gurry adopts the following position, 'it was suggested in the first edition of this book that surreptitious acquisition could be accommodated within the action for breach of confidence "without doing violence to the way in which the action has developed" by characterizing the "spy" as having forced an unwanted communication on the confider...The spy..."should, therefore, be attributed with the obligation of confidence..." [I]t seems artificial to squeeze the surreptitious acquisition cases into a "relationship of confidence" type analysis, and the better view is that the courts' intervention in these instances serves the policy of protecting confidential or private information, rather than any relationship of confidence', 266.
176. See Wacks (n 139), 100–34. I there consider in detail what I call the structural, functional, doctrinal, and (with scant regard for elegance) the 'functional-structural' problems in applying the action to protect privacy. See too N Moreham, 'Breach of Confidence and Misuse of Private Information: How Do the Two Actions Work Together?' (2010) Media and Arts Law Review 265 and 'The Protection of Privacy in English Common Law: A Doctrinal and Theoretical Analysis' (2005) 121 Law Quarterly Review 628.

mentioned, I cannot be restrained from publishing the contents of a private diary which I happen to discover lying on a public highway. If this is indeed the law it would represent a formidable restriction upon the utility of the action, and an attractive argument in support of the enactment of specific privacy legislation. It does not follow, of course, that were the action capable of accommodating these kinds of activities, the case for explicit legislation would be defeated, though it would weaken it. What then is the status of the argument that a duty arises on discovery or receipt of obviously confidential information?

In *Spycatcher (No 2)* Lord Goff remarked that the duty of confidentiality, as currently defined, embraced the situation 'where an obviously confidential document is wafted by an electric fan out of a window into a crowded street or when an obviously confidential document, such as a private diary, is dropped in a public place, and is then picked up by a passer-by.'[177] He then, somewhat cryptically, continued:

> I have deliberately avoided the fundamental question whether, contract apart, the duty [of confidentiality] lies simply in the notion of an obligation of conscience arising from the circumstances in or through which the information was communicated or obtained.[178]

Although the latter comment (and the fact that there was in fact a relationship of confidence) suggests that these observations were *obiter*, the importance of the first dictum hardly requires pointing out. It plainly contemplates attaching a duty of confidence to a person who receives information that is *obviously confidential* by virtue only of the *nature of the information*. Hence, the reasonable person who stumbles across a private diary would clearly apprehend that the information unintentionally imparted to him or her should not be passed on to others.

Moreover, the court's willingness in *Francome* (at the interlocutory stage) to recognize a duty of confidence imposed by virtue of the receipt of confidential information *simpliciter* is significant. Indeed, *Francome* demonstrates that the traditional distinction between the obligation on a confidant within a relationship of confidence with the confider, and imposed on a third party whose conscience may be pricked simply by notice, is, at least on certain facts, difficult to sustain. It looks like a straightforward acceptance of a duty based on unconscionable behaviour per se. The decision does,

---

177. [1988] 3 All ER 545, 658–9.
178. [1988] 3 All ER 545, 659.

however, have its limits. First, it was an interlocutory hearing. And, secondly, the court appears to condemn the manner in which the information was obtained, rather than its nature. In respect of the first matter, the Master of the Rolls warned:

> It is of paramount importance that everyone should understand the exercise on which…we are engaged. There is to be a speedy trial at which the rights of the parties will be determined…It is not our function to decide questions of law or fact which will be in issue at the trial.[179]

Yet though the force of *Francome* may be reduced by its interlocutory setting, the court was nevertheless faced with clear authority that in the case of telephone-tapping, no cause of action would lie. And while one presumes that in awarding an injunction it was influenced by the fact that the plaintiff's remedy of damages if the article were published before trial was a fairly hollow one, the court explicitly addressed the conflicting authority on the point. It was obviously persuaded that there was a reasonable prospect of the plaintiff's substantive claim succeeding at trial.

It will be recalled that in *Malone*,[180] on the other hand, the Vice-Chancellor declined an injunction to protect an individual whose telephone had been tapped by the police who had acted according to law under directions from the Home Secretary. In his view, 'however secret and confidential the information, there can be no binding obligation of confidence if that information is blurted out in public or is communicated in other circumstances which negative any duty of holding it confidential.'[181] He added, 'it seems to me that a person who utters confidential information must accept the risk of any unknown overhearing that is inherent in the circumstances of communication.'[182]

This reasoning was, however, distinguished by the court in *Francome*. Fox LJ observed:

> The Vice-Chancellor was clearly dealing with a case of authorised tapping by the police…Illegal tapping by private persons is quite another matter, since it must be questionable whether the user of a telephone can be regarded as accepting the risk that in the same way as, for example, he accepts the risk

---

179. [1984] 1 WLR 892, 893.
180. See page 75 for a detailed discussion of the case, see Wacks (n 139), 276–85.
181. [1979] Ch 345, 375.
182. [1979] Ch 345, 376.

that his conversation may be overheard in consequence of the accidents and imperfections of the telephone system itself.[183]

Despite this backsliding, straws remained for the traditionalist to clutch at. It might, for example, have been contended that the true rationale of *Francome* and *Franklin* was that the court will not condone the improper or unlawful obtaining of information.[184] It is tempting to distinguish between such conduct and the innocent finding of a diary or, indeed, lawful telephone-tapping. How might *Franklin* have been decided if the defendant had innocently found the budwood cutting on a path? Thus, George Wei argues that the concept of 'illegality of means' provides the best explanation of these two decisions,[185] and he proposes a number of factors that the court ought to take into account including the legality of the means used to acquire the secret information, the standards and practices of the relevant industry, and the general circumstances of the case.[186] But, apart from those circumstances which have a bearing on the reasonable person's knowledge of the obligation of confidence, the means of taking should not be directly relevant when imposing a duty of confidence.[187]

In any event, the distinction drawn by Fox LJ in *Francome* rests on the *quality of the information*. The information in *Malone* was information in the public domain; the conversations in *Francome* were not. Moreover, in *Francome* there was no breach of duty apart from the eavesdropping by a 'third party'. On what other ground could the telephone conversations be protected than that the conscience of the recipient was pricked by the confidentiality of the information? If that is an acceptable category of *confidential information* it requires, of course, only a limited exercise of the legal imagination to extend protection to the victim of the zoom lens for, 'in principle, there cannot be any distinction between eavesdropping on telephone conversations and intruding on private occasions by the use of long-range cameras or binoculars.'[188]

---

183. [1984] 1 WLR 892, 900.
184. The Law Commission's view on this matter was almost entirely based on *Malone* and is therefore questionable in the light of *Francome*. See *Breach of Confidence* (n 67), paras 4.7–4.10.
185. G Wei, 'Surreptitious Takings of Confidential Information' (1992) 12 Oxford Journal of Legal Studies 302, 308.
186. Wei (n 185), 315.
187. See Wacks (n 139), 169–71.
188. P Milmo, 'Confidence and Privacy' (1993) New Law Journal 1647.

This at once raises the prospect of the vexatious litigant, for if the traditional test is to be supplanted by criteria defining when information is confidential, how is the law to regulate the circumstances in which the information is imparted? Ultimately this is a matter of policy. And the guardian of policy is whether that information is in the public domain, the question to which I now turn.

Public domain

That information is generally available or accessible is better regarded as a factor negating the obligation of confidence *ab initio*, than as a defence to an action for breach of confidence. In the commercial context, the classic formulation of the test is, as expounded in *Saltman*, that the information is public property and public knowledge. This has been refined by concepts like the springboard doctrine (see later). Hence, in a typical trade secrets case, *O Mustad v Dosen*,[189] the defendant, allegedly in breach of confidence, informed a rival company about details of the plaintiff's process for making fish hooks (the defendant having formerly worked for the plaintiff company). The details had to some extent been revealed by the plaintiff in their patent. In Lord Buckmaster's view,

> Of course, the important point about the patent is not whether it was valid or invalid, but what it was that it disclosed, because after the disclosure had been made by the plaintiff to the world, it was impossible for them to get an injunction restraining the defendant from disclosing what was common knowledge.[190]

In the case of personal information, this test sits a little less comfortably, though much of the confusion has arisen as a consequence of an incomplete analysis of the commercial doctrines or of the factual circumstances of the particular decisions in issue. The apparent difficulty of applying the test in a non-technical context emerges from *Spycatcher (No 1)*,[191] and in particular the comments of Sir John Donaldson MR in the Court of Appeal where he stated,

189. [1963] RPC 41.
190. [1963] RPC 41, 43.
191. [1987] 1 WLR 1248.

[I] accept that to the extent that these publications have been read the information to which they relate has become public knowledge, but not that it has
entered the public domain, so losing the seal of confidentiality because that
only occurs when information not only becomes a matter of public knowledge, but also public property.[192]

He added,

The only post-July 1986 publication which could render confidential information public property is that revealed in the Australian proceedings or in the
UK Parliament. On the hypothesis that the Government would otherwise
successfully establish its right to confidentiality at the trial, it will be able to
require the court to treat all other publications as tainted by the fact that Mr
Wright was their source and so incapable of becoming public property.[193]

July 1986 was the date when the Government first attempted to enjoin
publication in Britain of information concerning the revelations in *Spycatcher*. The Master of the Rolls's reasoning might therefore be formulated
as follows:

(a) Peter Wright may be subject to a duty of confidentiality (if such is
    proved in law);

(b) at the time the Government first attempted to restrain publication of
    the information it was not in the public domain;

(c) the only releases which might be held to have caused the information
    to enter the public domain are those which are the subject of the main
    action;

(d) if, therefore, a possible right of action was denied at the interlocutory
    stage owing to revelations made since the right was first attempted to
    be exercised, the court would allow the breach to defeat the action to
    prevent the breach.

Sir John was concerned to maintain the plaintiff's rights at the interlocutory stage. The critical element is that the revelations which the court
would not allow to be considered to be in the public domain were revelations made *after* the Government sought to exercise its rights. Until then the
public was unaware of the *Spycatcher* allegations apart from the reports of the
Australian litigation. As in *Francome*, any other reasoning would have left the
Government with a hollow right at trial, for the disclosure would have been

192. [1987] 1 WLR 1248, 1275.
193. [1987] 1 WLR 1248, 1275.

permitted, and the plaintiff's only remedy would be in damages. Indeed, at trial none of the judges who heard the substantive action had any doubt that the information was in the public domain. And in the second *Spycatcher* case Lord Goff remarked that 'on any sensible view the information contained in the book was, at the date of the trial, in the public domain.'[194]

More difficult is *Schering Chemicals Ltd v Falkman Ltd.*[195] In effect, the court imposed on the second defendant a blanket duty not to disclose matters which he had learned as an interviewer for the course which Schering had provided to counteract adverse publicity which had surrounded their pregnancy-testing drug. The court appeared to annihilate the public domain test to determine liability and instead treated it as one of the factors to be taken into account in the 'public interest' balancing exercise (see Chapter 5). The decision may be read as an application of the springboard doctrine; in other words, a case where a party who acquires confidential information may not take advantage of that information even if it subsequently enters the public domain.

The springboard doctrine

The scope of the principle is well expressed by Roxburgh J in *Terrapin Ltd v Builders Supply Co (Hayes) Ltd*[196] where the learned judge states that 'springboard it remains even when all the features have been published or can be ascertained by actual inspection by any member of the public.'[197] But the obvious problem with this expression of the doctrine is that it appears to nullify the public domain test—that is, that information obtained prima facie under an obligation of confidentiality can never be used, even if it is subsequently published. This places the recipient of the information in a worse position than anyone else. And it contradicts *Mustad* which specifically acknowledges the inability of the courts to enforce a duty of confidence in respect of information available to the public at large. Attempts to reconcile *Mustad* and *Terrapin* have not been especially successful (see later).

194. [1988] 3 All ER 545, 665.
195. [1981] 2 WLR 848.
196. [1967] RPC 375.
197. [1967] RPC 375, 391.

There is much to be said for Gurry's view that emphasis be placed on the 'inaccessibility of the information to the public':

> What the courts are protecting, therefore, is essentially an original process of mind which produces inaccessible information, and the protection operates against anyone, who, by taking unfair advantage of the information which has been disclosed to him, saves himself the time, trouble and expense of going through the same process.[198]

And it is worth recalling that Roxburgh J in *Terrapin* was considering the specific argument that, although the defendant had received information concerning the plaintiff's building units, publication by the plaintiff of brochures rendered the information in the public domain. Roxburgh J maintained:

> The brochures are certainly not equivalent to the publication of the plans, specifications, other technical information and know-how. The dismantling of a unit might enable a person to proceed without plans or specifications, or other technical information, but not, I think, without some of the know-how, and certainly not without taking the trouble to dismantle. I think it is broadly true to say that a member of the public to whom the confidential information had not been imparted would still have to prepare plans and specifications. He would probably have to construct a prototype, and he would certainly have to conduct tests. Therefore, the possessor of the confidential information still has a long start over any member of the public.[199]

This approach may be used to explain *Schering*. Support may be drawn from a remark by Shaw LJ:

> To extend the knowledge or to revive the recollection of matters which may be detrimental or prejudicial to the interests of some person or organisation is not to be condoned because the facts are already known to some and linger in the memories of others.[200]

In other words, although the information in *Schering* had, at some time, been accessible in the press and on television, the defendant, by virtue of his position 'inside the story', had a permanent advantage over all others since, even though the public could rekindle and augment their knowledge concerning the affair from existing media sources, the defendant was one

198. F Gurry, *Breach of Confidence* (Oxford: Clarendon Press, 1984), 646.
199. [1967] RPC 375, 391.
200. [1981] 2 WLR 848, 870.

step ahead in terms of the time, money, and effort required to perform the requisite investigation.[201]

The cases which have (ineffectively) sought to reconcile *Mustad* with *Terrapin*, do so on the basis of the author of the disclosure. In *Mustad* the confider itself released the information and this fact was used in *Cranleigh Precision Engineering Ltd v Bryant*[202] and in *Speed Seal Products Ltd v Paddington*,[203] concerning disclosure by a third party and the confidant respectively, to hold that in such cases the information would not be held to have entered the public domain. The underlying principle appears to be that no man may profit from his own wrong.

In *Spycatcher (No 2)* the House of Lords explored the reach of this principle.[204] For Lord Goff, *Cranleigh* involved merely an extension of the springboard doctrine and, accordingly, the reasoning in *Speed Seal* (the identity of the discloser) which was widely thought to be embodied in *Cranleigh*, 'cannot in my mind be supported'.[205] He was unequivocal:

> I have to say, however, that I know of no case in which the maxim [no man may profit from his own wrong] has been invoked in order to hold that a person is not released from [an] obligation by the destruction of the subject matter of that obligation.[206]

On the other hand, Lord Griffiths[207] explicitly maintained that the obligation of confidence owed by Peter Wright to the Crown could not be destroyed by a deliberate act of disclosure by Wright (and, hence, that *The Sunday Times*, as third parties with knowledge of Wright's obligation, should not be permitted to publish future serializations of *Spycatcher*),[208] Cripps calls this a 'major departure from orthodoxy'.[209]

---

201. The Law Commission described *Schering* as an 'unfortunate and paradoxical result', (*Breach of Confidence* (n 67), para 6.67). The effect of the decision taken to its logical conclusion is that information once acquired in confidence could not be used by the acquirer even though the information was, at the time of acquisition, in, or subsequently entered, the public domain (ibid.)
202. [1966] RPC 375.
203. [1986] 1 All ER 91.
204. See Y Cripps, 'Breaches of Copyright and Confidence: The *Spycatcher* Effect' [1989] Public Law 13.
205. [1988] 3 All ER 545, 662.
206. [1988] 3 All ER 545, 662.
207. Lord Jauncey concurred with Lord Griffiths's reasoning but stopped short of restraining *The Sunday Times* from future serialization. He considered that such an injunction would be illogical in the face of the various other newspapers which were capable of serializing *Spycatcher*, [1988] 3 All ER 545, 668.
208. [1988] 3 All ER 545, 652.
209. Cripps (n 204), 17.

Lord Goff's seems to be the better view and, although *obiter*, supports Gurry's approach as to the nature and scope of the springboard doctrine. It certainly provides a more logical foundation for the public domain test.[210] Lord Griffiths's approach may legitimately perhaps be confined to the secret-service context.[211]

Public domain and personal information

Does the test work when it is personal information that is disclosed? I expressed doubts in my earlier work.[212] And some of these misgivings persist, but, in practical terms, the concept of the public domain and the associated springboard doctrine has operated reasonably successfully in non-commercial contexts. Consider again the telephone-tapping cases of *Francome* and *Malone*. The former involved the interception of telephone conversations by a private individual, the latter by the police in the exercise of their statutory powers. In exercising their discretion as to what kind of disclosure constitutes a statement to the public (and thus one which is in the public domain and hence 'unprotectable'), the courts may be interpreted as concluding that while it is wholly unreasonable to regard the unlawful tapping of one's telephone conversation by a private individual as an everyday risk of using the telephone, it is not unreasonable to consider it so if the listener is an arm of the state acting in pursuance of its lawful authority. In other words, the question of public domain is pressed into service to decide whether the conduct in question occurs in circumstances in which it is reasonable to expect to be unobserved. Being naked in one's garden is different from parading nude on a public highway. The question in both situations is whether the risk of having personal information divulged to others is a natural, reasonable, and foreseeable consequence of that conduct. If it is, the

---

210. The Law Commission in its Report adopts a standpoint identical to that taken by Gurry in respect of the interpretation and scope of the springboard doctrine (*Breach of Confidence* (n 67), paras 4.24–4.31).

211. 'It would make a mockery of the duty of confidence owed by members of the security and intelligence services if they could discharge it by breaching it', [1988] 3 All ER 545, 651. The reasoning of Roxburgh J was explicitly accepted by Arnold J in *Vestergaard Frandsen A/S v Bestnet Europe Ltd* [2009] EWHC 657 (Ch), [2010] FSR 2, 29. See too *BBC v HarperCollins* [2010] EWHC 2424 (Ch), [2011] EMLR 6.

212. See eg Wacks (n 139), 59–68.

information is in the public domain and cannot be the subject of a duty of confidence.

Yet problems linger. Earlier I suggested that the principal complaint in breach of confidence cases is one of disclosure—even to a single individual—whereas with privacy the wrong involves publicity.[213] This distinction was adopted in the consultation paper published by the Lord Chancellor's Department.[214] Thus, as pointed out in both the paper and the Law Commission's Report (and mentioned earlier), once information has entered the public domain, it can no longer be protected from further disclosures to the public at large, even by someone formerly obliged to keep the information secret.[215] The Law Commission gives two examples to illustrate the difficulty. The first[216] concerns information imparted by a patient to his doctor in confidence and which is later revealed to a small local newspaper by the doctor. If the story, initially published to a limited audience in breach of confidence, is taken up by a national newspaper does the patient lose his or her right to restrain the national paper from re-publishing, to a far wider audience, information which is already in the public domain?[217]

The second example[218] relates to the assiduous researcher who combs through back copies of newspapers to compile a list of facts regarding a particular person, all of which individually, at some stage, were known to the public (and thus did enter the public domain), but as a collective article can be said not to be 'generally' known.[219] The researcher may be restrained by application of the springboard doctrine, as explained earlier. If the extraction of information, though accessible to the public, requires 'a significant expenditure of labour, skill or money'[220] then the information cannot be

---

213. Wacks (n 139), para 4.5. See R Wacks, 'The Poverty of "Privacy"' (1980) 96 Law Quarterly Review 73, 82.
214. *Infringement of Privacy* (Lord Chancellor's Department, Scottish Office, 1993).
215. Upon the formulation of the springboard doctrine advanced earlier. If *Schering* is strictly followed, the complainant would be saved from repeated disclosures by the confidant (see earlier).
216. *Breach of Confidence* (n 67), para 5.12.
217. The Law Commission remarks, 'The patient's real complaint is based, not on considerations of confidentiality, but on the ground that his medical history is a private matter that should be protected by a right of privacy', *Breach of Confidence* (n 67), para 5.12.
218. *Breach of Confidence* (n 67), para 6.68.
219. As in the infamous US decision, *Sidis v FR Publishing Co*, 113 F2d 806 (2d Cir 1940), in which a former child prodigy was denied a remedy to prevent his past from being dug up in an article compiled exclusively from information in the public domain. See Chapter 5.
220. Clause 2(2) of the draft bill.

said to be in the public domain, and the complainant may well be able to restrain its disclosure.[221] I grapple again with this difficulty in Chapter 4.

Conclusion

The action for breach of confidence manifestly provided—and continues to provide—considerable adventitious protection to personal information. It was, however, in 1990 too extravagant to assert that since *Stephens* 'discrete areas of law which enjoy no obvious thematic unity have been united and organised by a new moral principle—privacy.'[222] At best, these cases pointed to a growing recognition of the principle of unconscionability, in respect to the defendant's disregard for the claimant's privacy. It is only now that we are able to greet a new dawn of privacy protection. But, on a practical level, the action for breach of confidence still goes some way towards equipping the courts with a useful means by which to restrain several forms of conduct which are most likely to *cause* an invasion of privacy.[223] In short, 'the early emphasis in breach of confidence actions was to protect the secrecy of information confided by one person to another...the law seems to be moving beyond this, to afford protection to secret information *which may not have been confided to anyone*.'[224] And so, under the sway of Article 8 of the ECHR, it has done so.

Perhaps the Law Commission underestimated the ability of Equity to treat the right of confidence as one *in rem* where the recipient of information is held to owe an obligation by virtue of its nature. It is true that Equity acts *in personam*. But the nature of certain information puts a reasonable man or woman on notice that confidential or personal information would not have been revealed to him or her unless he or she undertook to keep it secret. The courts therefore needed to begin to identify types of information which carry with them (like a health warning) a clear obligation of

---

221. For criticism of the Law Commission's change of heart (from its original proposals in its Working Paper No 57, para 103), see Wacks (n 139), 63–8.
222. Wilson (n 92), 54.
223. It is therefore difficult to accept Lord Keith's dictum in *Spycatcher* that '[Since] breach of confidence involves no more than an invasion of privacy...The right to personal privacy is clearly one which the law should in this field seek to protect', [1988] 3 All ER 545, 639.
224. Thompson (n 148), 73.

confidence.[225] And so it has done, though, as I complain in Chapter 8, with less precision than might have been hoped.

225. Such an approach would also obviate another barrier to the use of the action in the protection of privacy: the requirement that the obligation of confidence is owed only to the confider (*Fraser v Evans* [1969] 1 All ER 415). It is sometimes suggested that the action would therefore be unable to provide a remedy to a father whose child's body is photographed after, say, a disaster at a football match, a harrowing example that materialized at Hillsborough. By protecting 'information pertaining to the health of one's family', a remedy might be available. This is the definition proposed in the Lord Chancellor's consultation paper: 'privacy shall be taken to include matters appertaining to [a person's] health, personal communications and family and personal relationships', *Infringement of Privacy* (n 214), para 5.22. Another route to protection in such cases is via the cause of action for the intentional infliction of emotional distress, see Chapter 6.

4

The new order

It fell to Sedley LJ to deliver the message. No longer would the old idol be worshipped; breach of confidence had given way to new commandments that promised better protection for all: 'we have reached a point at which it can be said with confidence that the law recognises and will appropriately protect a right of personal privacy.'[1]

This revelation was received with contentment by the House of Lords.[2] The exodus from the outmoded equitable remedy had begun. The new dispensation was welcomed by Lord Nicholls:

> This cause of action has now firmly shaken off the limiting constraint of the need for an initial confidential relationship. In doing so it has changed its nature. In this country this development was recognised clearly in the judgment of Lord Goff of Chieveley in *Attorney-General v Guardian Newspapers Ltd (No 2)* [1990] 1 AC 109, 281. Now the law imposes a 'duty of confidence' whenever a person receives information he knows or ought to know is fairly and reasonably to be regarded as confidential. Even this formulation is awkward. The continuing use of the phrase 'duty of confidence' and the description of the information as 'confidential' is not altogether comfortable. Information about an individual's private life would not, in ordinary usage, be called 'confidential'. The more natural description today is that such information is private. The essence of the tort is better encapsulated now as misuse of private information.[3]

1. *Douglas v Hello! Ltd* [2000] 1 QB 967, [110]. Lord Woolf MR in *A v B plc* [2002] EWCA Civ 337, [2003] QB 125, [9] pronounced—perhaps somewhat precipitately—that decisions prior to the Human Rights Act 1998 were 'largely of historic interest only'. See too Buxton LJ in *McKennitt v Ash* [2006] EWCA Civ 1714, [2007] EMLR 113.
2. *Campbell v MGN Ltd* [2004] 2 WLR 1232.
3. *Campbell v MGN Ltd* [2004] 2 WLR 1232 at [14]. In *McKennitt v Ash* [2008] QB 73, Buxton LJ went so far as to declare that since the enactment of the Human Rights Act 1998, the action for breach of confidence had developed beyond 'old-fashioned breach of confidence' which applied to 'conduct inconsistent with a pre-existing relationship' to embrace 'the purloining of private information' under the new tort of misuse of private information (at 80–1). Similar statements are expressed in *HRH Prince of Wales v Associated Newspapers* [2008] Ch 87, 124–5 per Lord Phillips, and *Murray v Express Newspapers plc and Another* [2009] Ch 481, 500 per Sir Anthony Clark MR.

The focus of the numerous actions generated since the Act opened the door more widely to victims of privacy-invading publications is the 'balancing' of Article 8 of the European Convention on Human Rights (ECHR) with Article 10's protection of the 'right to freedom of expression'.

The Articles

ARTICLE 8
Right to respect for private and family life

1. Everyone has the right to respect for his private and family life, his home and his correspondence.

2. There shall be no interference by a public authority with the exercise of this right except such as is in accordance with the law and is necessary in a democratic society in the interests of national security, public safety or the economic well-being of the country, for the prevention of disorder or crime, for the protection of health or morals, or for the protection of the rights and freedoms of others.

ARTICLE 10
Freedom of expression

1. Everyone has the right to freedom of expression. This right shall include freedom to hold opinions and to receive and impart information and ideas without interference by public authority and regardless of frontiers. This Article shall not prevent States from requiring the licensing of broadcasting, television or cinema enterprises.

2. The exercise of these freedoms, since it carries with it duties and responsibilities, may be subject to such formalities, conditions, restrictions or penalties as are prescribed by law and are necessary in a democratic society, in the interests of national security, territorial integrity or public safety, for the prevention of disorder or crime, for the protection of health or morals, for the protection of the reputation or rights of others, for preventing the disclosure of information received in confidence, or for maintaining the authority and impartiality of the judiciary.

How the judges have sought to reconcile these two rights is the subject of Chapter 5. Here I sketch the essentials of the modern, 'Europeanized' approach to the protection of personal information.

The Human Rights Act 1998 (which came into effect on 2 October 2000) incorporates into English law Article 8 of the ECHR which provides: 'Everyone has the right to respect for his private and family life, his home and his correspondence.' This measure, at least in the mind of one senior judge, gives 'the final impetus to the recognition of a right of privacy in English law'.[4] Though his sanguine view may not be shared by all members of the judiciary, the analysis of privacy exhibited in recent cases suggests that the effect of Article 8 is to offer fairly considerable potential for the horizontal application of the rights contained in Article 8.[5]

'The interplay between articles 8 and 10', Lord Steyn declared in *Re S (A Child)*[6]

> has been illuminated by the opinions in the House of Lords in *Campbell v MGN Ltd* [2004] 2 WLR 1232. For present purposes the decision of the House on the facts of *Campbell* and the differences between the majority and the minority are not material. What does, however, emerge clearly from the opinions are four propositions. First, neither article has *as such* precedence over the other. Secondly, where the values under the two articles are in conflict, an intense focus on the comparative importance of the specific rights being claimed in the individual case is necessary. Thirdly, the justifications for inter-fering with or restricting each right must be taken into account. Finally, the proportionality test must be applied to each. For convenience I will call this the ultimate balancing test.

The flurry of decisions by both the Court of Appeal and the Supreme Court, although they have won plaudits from privacy advocates, give rise to a number of fundamental questions about the conceptual basis of the action. Some will arise in the course of this and the following chapter, but, as already mentioned, I shall—in the interests of convenience and, I hope, clarity—attempt to explain my major concerns separately in Chapter 8.

In *Douglas v Hello! Ltd*[7] photographs of the wedding of Michael Doug-las and Catherine Zeta-Jones were surreptitiously taken, notwithstanding explicit notice having been given to all guests forbidding 'photography or video devices at the ceremony or reception'. The couple had entered into an exclusive publication contract with *OK!* magazine but its rival, *Hello!*,

---

4. *Douglas v Hello! Ltd* [2000] 1 QB 967, para 111 per Sedley LJ. Cf Lord Hoffmann in *Wainwright* [2003] 3 WLR 1137: 'the coming into force of the Human Rights Act 1998 weakens the argu-ment for saying that a general tort of invasion of privacy is needed to fill gaps in the existing remedies.' In this section I draw on parts of R Wacks, 'Why There Will Never Be An English Common Law Privacy Tort' in M Richardson and AT Kenyon, *New Directions in Privacy Law* (Cambridge: Cambridge University Press, 2006) which has, to some extent, been overtaken by recent decisions.

5. Whether such horizontality is a consequence of the Act is left uncertain by the House of Lords in *Campbell*.

6. [2004] UKHL 47, [2005] 1 AC 593, [17].

7. [2001] 2 WLR 992 (CA).

sought to publish these pictures. The Court of Appeal permitted it to do so, largely on the ground the wedding reception was not an essentially 'private' matter. Indeed, the court was of the view that it had become a commercial transaction. From the point of view of the action for breach of confidence, there was little to support the proposition that the information was indeed 'confidential'. The case, therefore, resembles in some respects what the US courts have called the 'appropriation of name and likeness'—though, oddly, none of the judges in the Court of Appeal mention this tort. The House of Lords' decision is obviously critical in its recognition of a new cause of action, but the seeds of this development were unmistakably planted in the Court of Appeal whose judgments, especially that of Sedley LJ, seem to be central.

Announcing the coming of the right to 'personal privacy', he explained that it rested on two factors. First, the growing recognition of a need for 'private space' and, secondly, in order to give effect to the right to 'respect for family life' provided for by Article 8 of the Human Rights Act. Neither of these grounds, it must be said, affords a precise or persuasive argument for 'the confidence' expressed by the learned judge in the recognition of this right. I return to this case later. Suffice it to say that his analysis of what he entitles the 'tort' of breach of confidence leaves several questions unanswered. Moreover, the nebulous equation of 'privacy' and 'the fundamental value of autonomy' merely compounds the woolly contours of a decision which, though it may be supportable in its outcome, provides an unsatisfactory analysis of the action for breach of confidence and, in particular, its application to the protection of personal information.

The court appears sensibly to have drawn a distinction between what US law calls a 'right to publicity', on the one hand, and a right to privacy, on the other. The former has provided celebrities with the means to assert that by publishing private information about them, the defendant has deprived them of their 'right' to exploit their celebrity status for profit. Restraints on the exercise of freedom of expression would, the court held, be ordered only where 'privacy' properly so called has been invaded by unwanted publicity. In view of the alacrity with which the Court of Appeal, and particularly Sedley LJ, proclaimed a new dawn of privacy, it is necessary to quote their judgments at some length. Heralding the new order, Sedley LJ declared,

> The courts have done what they can, using such legal tools as were to hand, to stop the more outrageous invasions of individuals' privacy; but they have

felt unable to articulate their measures as a discrete principle of law....The reasons are twofold. First, equity and the common law are today in a position to respond to an increasingly invasive social environment by affirming that everybody has a right to some private space. Secondly, and in any event, the Human Rights Act 1998 requires the courts of this country to give appropriate effect to the right to respect for private and family life set out in Article 8 of the European Convention on Human Rights and Fundamental Freedoms. The difficulty with the first proposition resides in the common law's perennial need (for the best of reasons, that of legal certainty) to appear not to be doing anything for the first time. The difficulty with the second lies in the word 'appropriate'. But the two sources of law now run in a single channel because, by virtue of section 2 and section 6 of the Act, the courts of this country must not only take into account jurisprudence of both the Commission and the European Court of Human Rights which points to a positive institutional obligation to respect privacy; they must themselves act compatibly with that and the other Convention rights. This, for reasons I now turn to, arguably gives the final impetus to the recognition of a right of privacy in English law.[8]

He concluded that 'at lowest':

Mr Tugendhat has a powerfully arguable case to advance at trial that his two first-named clients have a right of privacy which English law will today recognise and, where appropriate, protect. To say this is in my belief to say little, save by way of a label, that our courts have not said already over the years. It is to say, among other things, that the right, grounded as it is in the equitable doctrine of breach of confidence, is not unqualified...What a concept of privacy does, however, is accord recognition to the fact that the law has to protect not only those people whose trust has been abused but those who simply find themselves subjected to an unwanted intrusion into their personal lives. The law no longer needs to construct an artificial relationship of confidentiality between intruder and victim: it can recognise privacy itself as a legal principle drawn from the fundamental value of personal autonomy.[9]

Sedley LJ then turned to section 6 of the Human Rights Act that provides that the court as a public authority cannot act in a manner incompatible with a Convention right:

If it is not—for example if the step from confidentiality to privacy is not simply a modern restatement of the scope of a known protection but a legal innovation— then I would accept his submission...that this is precisely the kind of incremental change for which the Act is designed: one which without undermining

8. [2001] 2 WLR 992 (CA) at [110]–[111].
9. [2001] 2 WLR 992 (CA) at [125]–[126].

the measure of certainty which is necessary to all law gives substance and effect to section 6.[10]

He added that, 'Such a process would be consonant with the jurisprudence of the European Court of Human Rights, which section 2 of the Act requires us to take into account and which has pinpointed Article 8 as a locus of the doctrine of positive obligation.'[11]

In the course of his judgment Keene LJ noted that, although the particulars of claim were put in terms of breach of confidence, it was said in argument for the claimants that the case has more to do with privacy than with confidentiality:

> [I]t is clear that there is no watertight division between the two concepts. *Argyll v Argyll*[12] was a classic case where the concept of confidentiality was applied so as, in effect, to protect the privacy of communications between a husband and wife. Moreover, breach of confidence is a developing area of the law, the boundaries of which are not immutable, but may change to reflect changes in society, technology and business practice.

Regarding the application of section 6(1), it:

> ...arguably includes their activity in interpreting and developing the common law, even where no public authority is a party to the litigation. Whether this extends to creating a new cause of action between private persons and bodies is more controversial, since to do so would appear to circumvent the restrictions on proceedings contained in section 7(1) of the Act and on remedies in section 8(1). But it is unnecessary to determine that issue in these proceedings, where reliance is placed on breach of confidence, an established cause of action, the scope of which may now need to be approached in the light of the obligation on this court arising under section 6(1) of the Act.[13]

Citing *Guardian Newspapers (No 2)* as authority that a pre-existing confidential relationship between the parties is not required for a breach of confidence suit, Keene LJ elaborated:

> The nature of the subject matter or the circumstances of the defendant's activities may suffice in some instances to give rise to liability for breach of confidence. That approach must now be informed by the jurisprudence of the Convention in respect of Article 8. Whether the resulting liability is described

10. [2001] 2 WLR 992 (CA) at [129].
11. [2001] 2 WLR 992 (CA) at [130].
12. [1990] 1 AC 109.
13. [1990] 1 AC 109 at [166].

as being for breach of confidence or for breach of a right to privacy may be little more than deciding what label is to be attached to the cause of action, but there would seem to be merit in recognising that the original concept of breach of confidence has in this particular category of cases now developed into something different from the commercial and employment relationships with which confidentiality is mainly concerned.[14]

There is much to digest in the rich diet of these sweeping, positive[15] dicta, but I shall resist the tempting feast here,[16] and simply reiterate that as discussed in Chapter 3, the equitable remedy for breach of confidence has long been recognized as a means by which personal privacy may be, and has been, protected. Indeed, as shown there, there is a tendency in some of the breach of confidence litigation to treat confidence as synonymous with or, at least, a surrogate of privacy. Nor is this development confined to English decisions. Notwithstanding the existence of the tort of wrongful publication of private information in New Zealand, its High Court recently found that the equitable remedy for breach of confidence (as developed by the English judges) afforded an adequate cause of action for the claimant, a celebrity who had been subjected to intrusive photography by the media.[17]

The class of confidential information, and therefore the reach of the action, appear to be expanding to reflect the range of activities undertaken by the rich and famous, though not always with obvious consistency. Consequently, the majority of the House of Lords held that the details of Naomi Campbell's attendance at Narcotics Anonymous (NA) were private information which imported a duty of confidence. This was based largely on the view that a breach of confidence had occurred which could not be justified in the public interest.

---

14. [1990] 1 AC 109 at [166].
15. Lord Hoffmann, in both *Campbell* and *Wainwright*, declined Sedley LJ's invitation to the privacy party. In *Wainwright* he declared: 'the coming into force of the Human Rights Act 1998 weakens the argument for saying that a general tort of invasion of privacy is needed to fill gaps in the existing remedies. Sections 6 and 7 of the Act are in themselves substantial gap fillers; if it is indeed the case that a person's rights under article 8 have been infringed by a public authority, he will have a statutory remedy. The creation of a general tort will, as Buxton LJ pointed out in the Court of Appeal, at [2002] QB 1334, 1360 [92], pre-empt the controversial question of the extent, if any, to which the Convention requires the state to provide remedies for invasions of privacy by persons who are not public authorities', [2003] 3 WLR 1137.
16. See Chapters 5 and 6 for a closer analysis of the decision.
17. *Hosking and Hosking v Simon Runting* [2004] NZCA 34.

On the other hand, details of the sexual infidelities of a well-known footballer[18] and the activities of a famous TV presenter in a brothel[19] either fell short of the required 'confidential' nature of the information, or their disclosure was found to be in the public interest. Thus in *Theakston v MGN Ltd*[20] the court declared:

> I do not consider it likely that the nature or detail of the sexual activities engaged in within the brothel are confidential. They are activities with a number of prostitutes in return for promises of payment in a brothel accessible to anyone with the money and the inclination. There is nothing about the activity, the participants or the location beyond the mere fact that the activities were of a sexual nature to warrant the imposition of confidentiality.

This clearly demonstrates the limits of breach of confidence for, while sex is, of course, a central aspect of privacy, the remedy may not extend to transitory or commercial sexual relationships. Thus, despite the court's dissolution of the requirement of a pre-existing relationship of confidence, adulterous relationships lie 'at the outer limits of relationships which require the protection of the law'.[21] Details of sex between a prostitute and her client were not, in the absence of an agreement to maintain confidentiality, protected—notwithstanding the client's wish that they should be.[22]

In *Naomi Campbell v MGN Ltd*[23] the House of Lords held that the supermodel was entitled to damages for the publication by the *Daily Mirror* of articles and photographs concerning the fact that she was receiving treatment by NA for her drug addiction. Campbell had publicly denied that she was addicted to drugs, and the Court of Appeal had held that by mendaciously asserting to the media that she did not take drugs, she had rendered it legitimate for the media to put the record straight. Phillips LJ stated:

> We do not consider that a reasonable person of ordinary sensibilities, on reading that Miss Campbell was a drug addict, would find it highly offensive, or

18. *A v B plc* [2002] EWCA Civ 337. See also n 15. *Hosking and Hosking v Simon Runting* [2004] NZCA 34.
19. *Theakston v MGN Ltd* [2002] EWHC 137 (QB).
20. [2002] EWHC 137 (QB).
21. *A v B plc* [2002] EWCA Civ 337, [2002] 2 All ER 545, [11(xi)], [43(iii)], [47].
22. *Theakston v MGN Ltd* [2002] EWHC 137 (QB), [57]–[64], [72]–[76]; endorsed by the Court of Appeal in *A v B plc* [2002] EWCA Civ 337, [2002] 2 All ER 545. See G Phillipson, 'Transforming Breach of Confidence? Towards a Common Law Right of Privacy under the Human Rights Act' (2003) 66 Modern Law Review 726, 744–8, 757–8.
23. [2004] 2 WLR 1232.

even offensive that the *Mirror* also disclosed that she was attending meetings of Narcotics Anonymous. The reader might have found it offensive that what were obviously covert photographs had been taken of her, but that, of itself, is not relied upon as ground for legal complaint.

[I]t is not obvious to us that the peripheral disclosure of Miss Campbell's attendance at Narcotics Anonymous was, in its context, of sufficient significance to shock the conscience and justify the intervention of the court. On the contrary, we have concluded that it was not.[24]

Since the disclosure of this confidential information was in the public interest, the court took the view that a journalist must be given 'reasonable latitude as to the manner in which that information is conveyed to the public'.[25] If not, his or her Article 10 right to freedom of expression would be unnecessarily inhibited.

The Court of Appeal expressed also certain fairly expansive opinions upon the relationship between privacy and breach of confidence, and between the latter and the Data Protection Act 1998. In respect of the first, it stated that the development of the law of confidence since the Human Rights Act came into force has seen information described as 'confidential' not only where it has been confided by one person to another, but where it relates to an aspect of an individual's private life which he or she does not choose to make public. It considered that the unjustifiable publication of such information would better be described as 'breach of privacy' rather than 'breach of confidence'.[26]

The House of Lords demonstrated a similar alacrity to dissolve the distinction between confidence and privacy. Thus, in the now widely mentioned statement quoted earlier, Lord Nicholls seemed to administer the *coup de grace* to the action for breach of confidence as a means of protecting privacy. It is not entirely surprising that, since the adoption of the Human Rights Act in 1998, there is a tendency for the courts to administer the withering away of the distinction between 'privacy' and 'confidence'.[27] But

24. *Campbell v MGN Ltd* [2002] EWCA Civ 1373, [54].
25. [2003] QB 633, 662, [64].
26. In the words of Phillips LJ: 'The development of the law of confidentiality since the Human Rights Act came into force has seen information described as "confidential" not where it has been confided by one person to another, but where it relates to an aspect of an individual's private life which he does not choose to make public. We consider that the unjustifiable publication of such information would better be described as breach of privacy rather than breach of confidence', *Campbell v MGN Ltd* [2002] EWCA Civ 1373, [70].
27. See *McKennitt v Ash* [2006] EWCA Civ 1714, [2008] QB 73, and *Lord Browne of Madingley v Associated Newspaper Ltd* [2007] EWCA Civ 295, [2008] QB 103. An encouraging exception is *Associated Newspapers Ltd v HRH Prince of Wales* [2006] EWCA Civ 1776. See Chapter 8.

this may reflect less the development of the law than the spate of recent cases involving unwanted publicity. While it may seem unduly doctrinaire to insist upon a clearer analytical differentiation between the two causes of action (thus, eg, the equitable remedy differs from any putative 'privacy tort' in respect, for instance, of both who may sue and who may be sued), the court also neglected the question whether, first, given the equitable nature of the remedy for breach of confidence, Miss Campbell ought perhaps to have come to Equity with clean hands, or, on the other hand, what effect the defence that 'there is no confidence in iniquity' might have had. The court's reasoning is not accompanied by a comprehensive discussion of the leading cases on breach of confidential personal information steeped in the notion of conscience that have afforded the very means by which the remedy has been widened—especially in respect of third party rights, and the development of an objective standard of liability.[28]

As to the—waning—action for breach of confidence as a guardian of privacy, therefore, the courts now seem content to satisfy themselves that the essentials of Article 8 are met by the law of confidence, but this is unlikely to foreclose wider consideration of the concept of privacy (and its relation to other apparently competing rights) in the future. In any event, it is not unreasonable to find in several of these recent judgments a willingness to allow Article 8 to thwart the conception of a full-blown privacy tort. Occasionally one can almost hear the clang of the sword being returned to its scabbard. This resistance is most keenly evident when Article 10 of the Human Rights Act (protecting freedom of expression) is invoked. This matter is further pursued in Chapter 5.

The triumph of privacy in *Campbell* was moderated by the House of Lords' unanimous acknowledgement that in respect of Articles 8 and 10, there was no question of either right being accorded supremacy.[29] Each was to be balanced against the other at this second stage of the enquiry, and among the considerations that entered into this process were, on the one hand, the duty of the media 'to impart information and ideas of public interest which the public has a right to receive' and the need for the court

---

28. On the extent to which the traditional breach of confidence action can, and should, survive in cases involving personal information, see NA Moreham, 'Breach of Confidence and Misuse of Private Information: How Do the Two Actions Work Together?' (2010) 15 Media and Arts Law Review 265. I return to this subject in Chapter 8.

29. *Campbell v MGN Ltd* [2002] EWCA Civ 1373, at [12] per Lord Nicholls, [55] per Lord Hoffmann, [113] per Lord Hope, [138] per Baroness Hale, [167] per Lord Carswell.

'to leave it to journalists to decide what material needs to be reproduced to ensure credibility'[30] and, on the other, the potential of the unauthorized disclosure or publication of the information 'to cause harm to the claimant'.[31]

Lord Hope added that in implementing this balancing exercise, 'the right of the public to receive information about the details of [Campbell's] treatment was of a much lower order than the undoubted right to know that she was misleading the public when she said that she did not take drugs... [T]he more intimate the aspects of private life which are being interfered with, the more serious must be the reasons for doing so before the interference can be legitimate.'[32] The key factor was that the disclosure of the details of the model's treatment at NA, especially the publication of the photographs had the potential to cause harm to her (eg, by obstructing her efforts to conquer her addiction, by causing her substantial distress). The risk of harm was the principal factor that determined the majority view that her Article 8 right to a private life had been violated by the newspaper.[33]

Lords Hoffmann and Nicholls were unconvinced by this argument, and held that Article 10 trumped the applicant's privacy claim, Lord Hoffmann pointing to the 'practical exigencies of journalism' which required that editorial decisions 'be made quickly and with less information than is available to a court which afterwards reviews the matter at leisure.'[34]

Early cases under the new regime reveal reluctance by judges to distinguish the various categories of speech, as well as the circumstances and manner in which the new right is exercised. The consequences of their treatment of speech in a monolithic, undifferentiated manner inevitably generated an unacceptable conflation between gossip and politically relevant publications.[35] In attempting to 'balance' the claimant's claim to freedom from public disclosure, on the one hand, against the defendant's claim to exercise freedom of expression, on the other, a number of factors ought to be taken into account, including: (a) the defendant's motives and beliefs; (b) the timing of the disclosure; (c) the recipient of the disclosure; and (d) the burden and standard of proof. Moreover, the volatile concept of

---

30. *Campbell v MGN Ltd* [2002] EWCA Civ 1373, at [116] per Lord Hope.
31. *Campbell v MGN Ltd* [2002] EWCA Civ 1373, at [118] per Lord Hope.
32. *Campbell v MGN Ltd* [2002] EWCA Civ 1373, at [117].
33. *Campbell v MGN Ltd* [2002] EWCA Civ 1373, at [119] per Lord Hope, [157] per Baroness Hale, [169] per Lord Carswell.
34. *Campbell v MGN Ltd* [2002] EWCA Civ 1373, at [62].
35. This is evident in, eg, *Theakston v MGN* [2002] EMLR 22, and *A v B plc* [2002] EWCA 337, [2002] 3 WLR 542.

'public interest' should itself be subjected to a careful scrutiny. The courts must—perforce—consider some of the following:

(a) To whom was the information given?
(b) Is the claimant a 'public figure'?
(c) Was the claimant in a public place?
(d) Is the information in the public domain?
(e) How was the information acquired?
(f) What was the defendant's motive?
(g) Was it essential for the claimant's identity to be revealed?
(h) How serious was the invasion of the claimant's privacy?[36]

In a number of the earlier decisions the importance of these considerations often appeared to be lost on the judges whose equation of privacy and confidentiality, and their proclivity to privilege free speech generally, eclipsed the need for the careful investigation of such questions.[37] Happily, there is now evidence of a greater degree of careful scrutiny of the elements of the new cause of action, and explicit recognition of the rationale for freedom of expression where it serves the public interest.[38] Thus, in mediating between Articles 8 and 10 (and taking into account, by necessity, the Strasbourg jurisprudence), the judges have developed a two-stage test which asks:

1. Is Article 8 engaged by virtue of the information in question relating to the claimant's 'private and family life, his home and his correspondence'?

2. If so, is the defendant's conduct such that, upon analysis of the proportionality of the interference with competing rights under Articles 8 and 10, the protection of the rights of others is necessary for freedom of expression to yield?[39]

---

36. R Wacks, *The Protection of Privacy* (London: Sweet & Maxwell, 1980), 98–106, R Wacks, *Privacy and Press Freedom* (London: Blackstone Press, 1995), 105–12. See the Appendix where these elements are included in a draft bill that I have the audacity to propose.
37. See *A v B plc* [2002] EWCA 337, [2002] 3 WLR 542.
38. This is the subject of Chapter 5.
39. *Campbell v MGN Ltd* [2004] 2 AC 457, [19]–[21] per Lord Nicholls, [92] per Lord Hope, [134], [137], [140] per Baroness Hale, [166]–[167] per Lord Carswell.

A 'reasonable expectation of privacy'

In answering the first question, the court will enquire whether the victim had 'a reasonable expectation of privacy'.[40] Although this standard is appropriate in cases of *intrusion*, it is less apposite in regard to the separate question of the *publication* of private facts. Where one is subjected to surveillance, for example, the question is properly addressed to whether, in all the circumstances, one had a reasonable expectation of privacy. When pursued by paparazzi using zoom lenses, or when spied upon with hidden electronic devices, when one's telephone is intercepted, one's room or office is bugged, or one's computer is hacked into, the first question that must arise under Article 8 is whether there was a reasonable expectation of privacy.

What does this mean? It surely provides an objective measure by which to decide whether, in all the circumstances, the claimant is entitled to assume that his or her privacy is secure. It therefore examines the *circumstances* rather than merely the *information* that may warrant protection. Thus, to take a recent notorious example, was the Duchess of Cambridge, sunbathing nude beside the swimming pool on private premises, reasonably entitled to expect that her privacy was secure? But of what exactly must she have a reasonable expectation? That she would not be seen? By whom? That she would not be photographed? That, if photographed, the images would not be published?

The last question moves the enquiry out of the zone of physical privacy (the overriding concern in cases of intrusion) into that of the misuse of the personal information thereby garnered. And, here, I suggest, the 'reasonable expectation' test on its own is inadequate. Why? Because it raises different issues that relate to the *use* to which the victim is willing to consent. It is, in other words, a matter of *control* over the dissemination of one's private information. Failing to differentiate the two forms of invasion of privacy,

---

40. In *Murray v Express Newspapers* [2008] EWCA Civ 446, [87] the Court of Appeal declared that 'the question whether there is a reasonable expectation of privacy is a broad one, which takes account of all the circumstances of the case. They include the attributes of the Claimant, the nature of the activity in which the Claimant was engaged, the place at which it was happening, the nature and purpose of the intrusion, the absence of consent and whether it was known or could be inferred, the effect on the Claimant and the circumstances in which and the purposes for which the information came into the hands of the publisher.' See too *Goodwin v News Group Newspapers* [2011] EWHC 1437 (QB), [87]; *Trimingham v Associated Newspapers Ltd* [2012] EWHC 1296 (QB).

the enquiry not only neglects the separate interests of the claimants that are generated by each activity, but it also renders more complex the balancing exercise with Article 10 that arises in cases of disclosure.[41]

The distinction is between the victim's *expectation* in the case of *intrusion*, and his or her *wishes* in respect of *disclosure*.[42] The two are often intimately linked, but not ineluctably so. It is entirely possible for a celebrity to object to her photograph being taken surreptitiously, but happy to allow its publication. Even if her disapproval extends to both, however, the wrongfulness of the intrusion rightly turns on her reasonable expectation of privacy, while the unlawfulness of the subsequent publication should be adjudged by reference to her right to control the use or misuse of her image.[43]

Segregating the two activities, it should be added, may also have constitutional implications. For example, in the United States employees and ex-employees of a Senator surreptitiously removed papers from his files, copied them, and handed the duplicates to two newspaper columnists. The journalists, with full knowledge of the circumstances of its acquisition, included the information in their column. The court held, dealing separately with disclosure and intrusion, that, in respect of the former, the First Amendment protected the revelation of such information and, as to

41. See Chapter 8.
42. The centrality of the victim's wishes features in two recent attempts to conceptualize 'privacy'. Moreham includes the element of 'desire' when defining privacy as 'the state of "desired inaccess" or as "freedom from unwanted access". In other words, a person will be in a state of privacy if he or she is only seen, heard, touched or found out about if, and to the extent that, he or she wants to be seen, heard, touched or found out about. Something is therefore "private" if a person has a desire for privacy in relation to it: a place, event or activity will be "private" if a person wishes to be free from outside access when attending or undertaking it and information will be "private" if the person to whom it relates does not want people to know about it', NA Moreham, 'Privacy in the Common Law: A Doctrinal and Theoretical Analysis' (2005) 121 Law Quarterly Review 628, 636. And Solove is to similar effect when he argues that privacy 'involves more than avoiding disclosure; it also involves the individual's ability to ensure that personal information is used for the purposes she desires', D Solove, 'Conceptualizing Privacy' (2002) 90 California Law Review 1087, 1108. See too D Solove, 'A Taxonomy of Privacy' (2006) 154 University of Pennsylvania Law Review 477.
43. There are a handful of decisions in which a severance is espoused. In *Wood v Commissioner of Police for the Metropolis* Laws LJ distinguished between 'the fact or threat of publication in the media, and ...the snapping of the shutter', [2010] EMLR 1 (CA), [33]. A dichotomy of this kind was adopted also in *Theakston v MGN* [2002] EMLR 22, where the court drew a distinction between the intrusion into the claimant's sexual activities (which it did not protect), on the one hand, and the publication of photographs of him in a brothel (which it did), on the other. Moreover, as pointed out earlier, in the leading authority, to which the courts routinely defer, *von Hannover* [2004] EMLR 379 (ECtHR), the European Court applied the 'reasonable expectation of privacy' test to the intrusive activities of the media, not to the publication of

the latter, the columnists could not be liable for the intrusion merely upon proof of their knowledge of its occurrence.[44]

First Amendment protection extends only to disclosure. In regard to the protection afforded to the media by the newsworthiness defence to otherwise actionable disclosures of private facts, it has been asserted that, 'The values of the First Amendment would be seriously subverted if such protection were withdrawn on the ground of knowledge on the part of the media that the truth had come to light through legally reprehensible means employed by others.'[45]

The concept of 'reasonable expectation of privacy' is at the heart of the US tort of intrusion. The US Supreme Court has held that a person has a reasonable expectation of privacy if (a) he, by his conduct, has exhibited an actual (or subjective) expectation of privacy, that is, he has shown that he seeks to preserve something as private, and (b) his subjective expectation of privacy is one that society is prepared to recognize as reasonable, that is, the expectation, viewed objectively, is justifiable under the circumstances.[46] Moreover, the judicial origin of the test involved the interception of telephone calls: from the Supreme Court's decision in *Katz v United States*[47] which, interpreting the Fourth Amendment's protection against 'unreasonable searches and seizures',[48] held that in order to warrant protection, the plaintiff must have had a 'reasonable expectation of privacy'.[49]

the material so obtained. And it followed its earlier decision in *Halford v United Kingdom* (1997) EHRR 523.

44. *Pearson v Dodd*, 410 F2d 701 (DC Cir 1969), *cert denied*, 395 US 947 (1969).

45. A Hill, 'Defamation and Privacy under the First Amendment' (1976) Columbia Law Review 1205, 1279–80.

46. *Smith v Maryland*, 442 US 735 (1979). In US tort law, factors determining the reasonableness of an expectation of privacy include: (a) whether the area is generally accessible to the public; (b) whether the individual has a property interest in the area; (c) whether the individual has taken normal precautions to maintain his or her privacy; (d) how the area is used; and (e) the general understanding of society that certain areas deserve the most scrupulous protection from intrusion. See *Rakas v Illinois*, 439 US 128, 152–3 (1978); *Oliver v United States*, 466 US 170, 178–83 (1984).

47. 389 US 347 (1967).

48. The Fourth Amendment provides: 'The right of the people to be secure in their persons, houses, papers, and effects, against unreasonable searches and seizures, shall not be violated, and no Warrants shall issue, but upon probable cause, supported by Oath or affirmation, and particularly describing the place to be searched, and the persons or things to be seized.' In *United States v Jones*, 132 S Ct 945 (2012) the Supreme Court held that installing a GPS tracking device on a person's car and the use of that device to monitor the vehicle's movements on public streets, constitutes a search or seizure within the meaning of the Fourth Amendment and therefore required a search warrant.

49. The Supreme Court famously stated, that the Fourth Amendment 'protects people, not places'. What an individual knowingly exposes to the public, even in his or her home or office, is not

I believe that a more constructive approach would be one that attempts to identify what *specific interests* of the individual the law ought to protect. At the core of the preoccupation with the right to privacy is the individual's interest in protection against the misuse of personal, sensitive information. Although Article 8 employs the phrase 'private life' the judges have, willy-nilly, engineered the concept to protect 'private facts' against unauthorized disclosure. I hope I do not over-complicate the matter, since an intuitive understanding of private facts (sex, health, and finance tend to dominate) will normally suffice. But if the starting point of any enquiry were whether the facts sought to be protected were indeed private or, as I prefer to call them, personal, it might assist in identifying the genuinely intimate or sensitive facts that are worthy of legal protection.[50] And this would assist in providing more robust protection to freedom of speech, a matter I consider in Chapter 5. In other words, by concentrating on identifying the *categories* of private information, rather than the *circumstances* that may give rise to a reasonable expectation of privacy, the law would broadcast a clearer message—to both the media and the public—as to where the law draws the line between privacy and freedom of expression.

I stress that such an approach is not a panacea; it would not automatically obviate the evaluation that is inevitably required when deciding whether to proscribe or permit publication of personal information. But it does promise a greater measure of certainty in interpreting the amorphous terms, particularly of Article 8. In any event, as the law now stands, the approach turns on a number of factual circumstances, including some of the criteria I have mentioned earlier. In deciding this matter, the courts have formulated the following five-stage enquiry:[51]

1. Is Article 8 engaged? If not, that is the end of the matter.

2. If Article 8 is engaged, is Article 10 also engaged?

protected by the Fourth Amendment. But what he or she seeks to preserve as private, even in an area accessible to the public, may be constitutionally protected.

50. I have argued elsewhere that any definition of 'personal information' must include *both* the quality of the information and the reasonable expectation of the individual concerning its use. The one is, in large part, a function of the other. In other words, the concept of 'personal information' postulated here functions both descriptively and normatively.

51. For an invaluable, detailed analysis of how the courts have wrestled with these criteria, see *Tugendhat and Christie on the Law of Privacy and the Media,* 2nd edn (M Warby, N Moreham, and I Christie eds) (Oxford: Oxford University Press, 2011), especially ch 5. An admirable survey of the law and practice up to mid-2006 may be found in H Fenwick and G Phillipson, *Media Freedom under the Human Rights Act* (Oxford: Oxford University Press, 2006), Part IV.

3. If so, then the court will seek to 'balance' the competing rights, applying an 'intense focus' upon the facts to decide which Article should yield.

4. Other rights (ECHR and non-ECHR) may need to be taken into account, and, in respect of the former, the same balancing approach should be adopted as is the case in respect of Article 10.

5. The 'balancing' process should avoid mere generalities.

The old order changeth...

Yielding place to...what? In steering the law away from the protection previously afforded to personal information by the equitable remedy for breach of confidence, the House of Lords has promulgated a new cause of action styled the misuse of personal—or sometimes private—information. At first blush, the new dispensation appears to be an acceptable consequence of the transition from confidence to privacy. But, as I have suggested earlier, when the complaint relates to publication, to allow the category of 'private facts' to turn exclusively on the claimant's 'reasonable expectation of privacy' may result in uncertainty. This is not to suggest that by adopting my (or indeed anyone's) objective definition of 'personal information' the conceptual thicket is instantly cleared. But, as a guide to claimants, the media, and the courts, a clearer notion of what constitutes the category or type of information that warrants protection seems fundamental.

Why does the current test not satisfy this requirement? While it rests on an objective standard by which to determine whether, in all the circumstances, the claimant is entitled to assume that his or her privacy is secure, it directs the enquiry to the *circumstances*, while neglecting the *information* that may warrant protection. Thus, while a consideration of this kind is perfectly appropriate when deliberating whether an *intrusion* is justified (spying, telephone-tapping, hacking, bugging, etc, see Chapter 6), it does not, I believe, satisfactorily address the separate question of *disclosure* of private facts.[52] And if it is replied that the courts are in this respect merely

---

52. The Press Complaints Commission's *Editors' Code of Practice* appears to recognize this distinction when in Art 3 it states, '(iii) It is unacceptable to photograph individuals in private places without their consent', adding 'Note: Private places are public or private property where there is a reasonable expectation of privacy.' The PCC is considered in Chapters 5 and 6.

following Strasbourg jurisprudence, and, in particular, the seminal case of *von Hannover*,[53] the European Court there applied the test to the intrusive activities of the media, not to *publication* of the material so obtained. In other words, the Princess's complaint that Article 8 had been breached related to harassment by the media. Indeed, in utilizing this test, the Court explicitly refers to its decision in *Halford v United Kingdom*[54] which involved the interception of telephone calls. The Court there stated that the applicant would 'have had a reasonable expectation of privacy for such calls'.[55]

Intrusion and disclosure are, as I have said, often inextricably connected. The media generally intrudes in order to publish the fruits of its invasion. The Peeping Tom's intrusion, however, normally ends there. Thus, it seems to me that infractions of Article 8 ought to distinguish between straightforward spying (in which the 'reasonable expectation' test is properly applied), on the one hand, and public disclosures of personal information (whether or not obtained by intrusive conduct), on the other.

Indeed, this dichotomy has been accepted in a number of decisions of the English courts. In *Theakston*,[56] as mentioned earlier, the court distinguished between the confidentiality of the claimant's sexual activities and his visiting a brothel (which it held were not confidential) and the publication of photographs of him in the brothel (which were). Though the judge treated the matter as one of breach of confidence, the distinction he draws between the intrusion that occurred in the brothel and the photographs that the newspaper sought to publish is a legitimate one:

> I considered that even though the fact that the Claimant went on to the brothel and the details as to what he did there were not to be restrained from publication, the publication of photographs taken there without his consent could still constitute an intrusion into his private and personal life and would do so in a peculiarly humiliating and damaging way. It did not seem to me remotely inherent in going to a brothel that what was done inside would be photographed, let alone that any photographs would be published.[57]

---

53. *Von Hannover v Germany* [2004] EMLR 379 (ECtHR). I discuss this decision in Chapters 6 and 7. Note that the Court employs the phrase '*legitimate* expectation of privacy'. This does not seem, on balance, significantly to affect the 'reasonableness' or objective nature of the test.
54. (1997) EHRR 523.
55. (1997) EHRR 523 at [45].
56. *Theakston v MGN* [2002] EMLR 22.
57. *Theakston v MGN* [2002] EMLR 22, [78].

While one may contest the court's conclusion (that the fact that the claimant visited a brothel was not confidential), it is submitted that the distinction between 'intrusion' and 'disclosure' was properly drawn,[58] as it was by Laws LJ in *Wood v Commissioner of Police for the Metropolis*.[59]

On the other hand, the Court of Appeal in *Murray*[60] explained how the 'reasonable expectation' test is to be applied:

> This is an objective test but is a broad one and essentially a question of fact. The court must take account of all the circumstances of the case. They include the attributes of the claimant, the nature of the activity in which the claimant was engaged, the place at which it was happening, the nature and purpose of the intrusion, the absence of consent and whether it was known or could be inferred, the effect on the claimant and the circumstances in which and the purposes for which *the information came into the hands of the publisher*.

As the italicized sentence shows, the court exhibits no hesitation in applying the test to *publication* of personal information obtained by intrusion. The judges ought to resist the tendency—evident in this dictum—to conflate the *intrusion* practised by the prying journalist or photographer with the *publication* of the information thereby acquired. The intruder is not always the discloser.

And here lies another difficulty that I have with the 'new approach'. The House of Lords christened the new cause of action '*misuse* of personal information'. It protects 'the right to control the *dissemination* of information about one's private life ...'[61] There is plainly no 'misuse' when the claimant is spied upon. Although no general cause of action for intrusion has been recognized by the courts, there are numerous dicta that appear to acknowledge that, in theory, the clandestine recording of private matters 'engages

---

58. As Gurry (rightly) does: 'It is submitted that the decision ...[is] wrong according to a test of "private information". The information ...related to the claimant's sexual life, for which there surely has to be a "reasonable expectation of privacy"...Further, the fact that the other party to the relationship [probably a prostitute] wished to disclose the information should not have been relevant to whether the information was "private".' Of course, while agreeing with this criticism, I would prefer to adjudge the quality of the information by reference to a different test. In this case, the outcome will have been the same, but that will not always be the case—or else I have proposed a distinction without a difference!

59. [2010] EMLR 1 (CA): 'ordinarily the taking of photographs in a public street involves no element of interference with anyone's private life and therefore will not engage Article 8(1), although the later publication of such photographs may be a different matter', [31].

60. *Murray v Express Newspapers plc* [2009] 1 Ch 481 (CA), [27] (emphasis added).

61. *Campbell*, [51] per Lord Hoffmann.

Article 8',[62] that the mere taking of a photograph of a child[63] or an adult in a public place[64] might fall within the category of 'misuse'. Why this wrongful act has evaded inclusion within the liberal terms of Article 8 (where it could be congenially accommodated) is a mystery I attempt to solve in Chapter 8.

How might my approach operate in cases involving the misuse of private information? Instead of equating (or, at least, failing to separate) the determination of what constitutes 'private facts' with the claimant's 'reasonable expectation of privacy', the first stage of the enquiry would consist in establishing whether 'private facts' are in issue at all. Thus, rather than seeking to discover what the victim's reasonable expectations were (an apposite question in cases of intrusion) the court would ask whether the complaint refers to facts, communications, or opinions about the claimant which it would be reasonable to expect him or her to regard as intimate or sensitive and therefore to want to withhold, or at least to restrict their collection, use, or circulation.

'Private facts'

The practical consequences of this uncertainty are evident in the House of Lords' failure in *Naomi Campbell v MGN Ltd*[65] to define with adequate precision the central concept of 'private facts'. The court, by 3–2, found in favour of the supermodel who sought damages for the publication by the *Daily Mirror* of articles and photographs concerning the fact that she was receiving treatment by NA for her drug addiction. The model had publicly denied that she was addicted to drugs, and the Court of Appeal had held that by mendaciously asserting to the media that she did not take drugs,

---

62. *Mosley v News Group Newspapers Ltd* [2009] EMLR 20, [104].
63. *Murray v Express Newspapers plc* [2008] EWCA Civ 446, [2008] 3 WLR 1360. An appeal against Patten J's decision was allowed by the Court of Appeal. With respect, this aspect of the judge's reasoning—that, following *von Hannover* 'there remains an innocuous conduct in a public place which does not raise a reasonable expectation of privacy', [68]—seems correct, notwithstanding the majority's judgment in *Campbell* that the supermodel would have had no complaint had she been photographed merely walking on a public street rather than emerging from a meeting of NA. The latter conclusion was based on the *publication* of the pictures, whereas I understand Patten J's analysis in the sentence quoted relates to the issue of *intrusion*. See further later.
64. *Wood v Commissioner of Police of the Metropolis* [2010] EMLR 1 (CA).
65. [2004] 2 WLR 1232. I return to this question in Chapter 8.

she had rendered it legitimate for the media to put the record straight. The House of Lords nevertheless held that she was entitled to compensation. The judgments reveal several perspectives of the emerging tort, particularly in the developing environment of Article 8 of the Human Rights Act. The majority regarded the disclosure of Campbell's attendance at an NA meeting, along with the publication of the images of her leaving the meeting, as intimate medical information that warranted protection, notwithstanding Article 10's protection of speech provision. The view of the minority, on the other hand, was that this information did not amount to sensitive health data, and, in any event, as Lord Hoffmann puts it,

> The practical exigencies of journalism demand that some latitude must be given. Editorial decisions have to be made quickly and with less information than is available to a court which afterwards reviews the matter at leisure.[66]

The court recognizes that the claim is based solely on the *publication* of the images, not the intrusive photography by which they were obtained. Thus, Lord Nicholls declares:

> In the case of individuals this tort, however labelled, affords respect for one aspect of an individual's privacy. That is the value underlying this cause of action. An individual's privacy can be invaded in ways not involving publication of information. Strip-searches are an example. The extent to which the common law as developed thus far in this country protects other forms of invasion of privacy is not a matter arising in the present case. It does not arise because, although pleaded more widely, Miss Campbell's common law claim was throughout presented in court exclusively on the basis of breach of confidence, that is, the wrongful *publication* by the 'Mirror' of private *information*.[67]

There is, as I have pointed out, no clear consensus among the judges in *Campbell* on the critical question of what constitutes 'private facts' or what the court prefers to call 'private information'. Lord Nicholls expresses a strong preference for a test based on whether in regard to the disclosed facts 'the person in question had a reasonable expectation of privacy'.[68] He explicitly rejects Gleeson CJ's formulation in *Australian Broadcasting Corporation v Lenah Game Meats Pty Ltd* that asks whether the disclosure 'would be highly offensive to a reasonable person'.[69] The learned judge conceded:

---

66. [2004] 2 WLR 1232 para 62.
67. [2004] 2 WLR 1232 para 15.
68. [2004] 2 WLR 1232 para 21.
69. (2001) 185 ALR 1, 13, para 42.

There is no bright line which can be drawn between what is private and what is not. Use of the term 'public' is often a convenient method of contrast, but there is a large area in between what is necessarily public and what is necessarily private. An activity is not private simply because it is not done in public. It does not suffice to make an act private that, because it occurs on private property, it has such measure of protection from the public gaze as the characteristics of the property, the nature of the activity, the locality, and the disposition of the property owner combine to afford. Certain kinds of information about a person, such as information relating to health, personal relationships, or finances, may be easy to identify as private; as may certain kinds of activity, which a reasonable person, applying contemporary standards of morals and behaviour, would understand to be meant to be unobserved. The requirement that disclosure or observation of information or conduct would be highly offensive to a reasonable person of ordinary sensibilities is in many circumstances a useful practical test of what is private.[70]

But this test, according to Lord Nicholls, is stricter than his proposed 'reasonable expectation' test. Moreover, the 'highly offensive' test goes 'more properly to issues of proportionality; for instance, the degree of intrusion into private life, and the extent to which publication was a matter of proper public concern. This could be a recipe for confusion.'[71]

Lord Hope, in formulating his test of what constitutes 'private information', expresses support for the so-called Gleeson test, and held that the Court of Appeal was in error

...when they were asking themselves whether the disclosure would have offended the reasonable man of ordinary susceptibilities. The mind that they examined was the mind of the reader: para 54. This is wrong. It greatly reduces the level of protection that is afforded to the right of privacy. The mind that has to be examined is that, not of the reader in general, but of the person who is affected by the publicity. *The question is what a reasonable person of ordinary sensibilities would feel if she was placed in the same position as the claimant and faced with the same publicity.*[72]

Baroness Hale also gives short shrift to the Gleeson test, declaring:

An objective reasonable expectation test is much simpler and clearer than the test sometimes quoted from the judgment of Gleeson CJ in the High Court of Australia in *Australian Broadcasting Corporation v Lenah Game Meats Pty Ltd.*[73]

---

70. [2004] 2 WLR 1232 para 42.
71. [2004] 2 WLR 1232 at [22].
72. [2004] 2 WLR 1232 para 99 (emphasis added).
73. [2004] 2 WLR 1232 para 135.

Like Lord Hope, she acknowledges the importance of judging the privateness of the disclosed information from the point of view of 'the sensibilities of a reasonable person placed in the situation of the subject of the disclosure rather than to its recipient.'[74] The learned judge adds:

> It should be emphasised that the 'reasonable expectation of privacy' is a threshold test which brings the balancing exercise into play. It is not the end of the story. Once the information is identified as 'private' in this way, the court must balance the claimant's interest in keeping the information private against the countervailing interest of the recipient in publishing it. Very often, it can be expected that the countervailing rights of the recipient will prevail.[75]

As mentioned in Chapter 1, my suggested definition of 'personal information' includes those facts, communications, or opinions which relate to the individual and which it would be reasonable to expect him or her to regard as intimate or sensitive and therefore to want to withhold, or at least to restrict their collection, use, or publication. Since 'personal' relates to social norms, to so describe something implies that it satisfies certain of the conditions specified in the norms, without which the normative implications would have no validity. Thus, if a letter is marked 'personal', or if its contents clearly indicate that it is personal, the implication is that it satisfies one or more of the conditions necessary for its being conceived as 'personal'; this is a descriptive account.

To the extent that it is necessary to define the information by reference to some objective criterion (since a subjective test would clearly be unacceptable), it is inevitable that the classification depends on what may legitimately be claimed to be 'personal'. Only information which it is reasonable to wish to withhold is likely, under any test, to be the focus of our concern. An individual who regards information concerning say, his car, as personal and therefore seeks to withhold details of the size of its engine will find it difficult to convince anyone that his vehicle's registration document constitutes a disclosure of 'personal information'. An objective test of what is 'personal' will operate to exclude such species of information.

The question of the offensiveness of the publication relates to the *publicity* given to the personal information.[76] But there are other considerations,

---

74. [2004] 2 WLR 1232 para 136.
75. [2004] 2 WLR 1232 para 137.
76. The New Zealand Court of Appeal in *Hosking v Runting* [2004] NZCA 34 appears to have adopted this approach.

including, of course, the 'profile' of the new cause of action for misuse of personal information. I examine these in the next chapter.

Public places

The extent to which there is a reasonable expectation of privacy in a public place is a recurring theme in many judgments, and is revisited in Chapter 5. The following two decisions of the European Court are instructive, not only in respect of this question but also because they address the (neglected) relationship between intrusion and disclosure that I mentioned earlier. The first is relevant also to media regulation discussed in the next chapter.

One evening while walking down Brentwood High Street, Peck attempted to slash his wrists with a kitchen knife.[77] He was unaware that he had been captured on CCTV by a camera installed by Brentwood Borough Council. The CCTV footage did not show him actually cutting his wrists. The operator was alerted only to the image of an individual in possession of a knife. The police were notified and arrived at the scene, where they seized the knife, provided Peck with medical assistance, and transported him to a police station, where he was detained under the Mental Health Act 1983. After being examined and treated by a doctor, he was released without charge and taken home by police officers. A few months later the council published two photographs obtained from the CCTV footage to accompany an article headed 'Defused—the partnership between CCTV and the police prevents a potentially dangerous situation.' Peck's face was not masked. The article revealed the circumstances as described earlier. A few days afterward, the *Brentwood Weekly News* used a photograph of the incident on its front page to illustrate an article on the use and benefits of CCTV. Peck's face was not concealed. Subsequently, another local newspaper published two similar articles along with a picture of Peck taken from the CCTV footage, and referred to the applicant having been intercepted with a knife, and that a potentially dangerous situation had been resolved. It added that Peck had been released without charge. Several readers recognized Peck from the picture.

---

77. *Peck v United Kingdom* App 44647/98 (2003) EHRR 41.

Extracts from the CCTV footage were included in a local television programme with an average audience of 350,000. This time Peck's identity had been masked at the council's oral request. A month or two later Peck discovered from a neighbour that he had been filmed on CCTV, and that footage had been released. He took no action as he was still suffering from severe depression. The CCTV footage was also supplied to the producers of *Crime Beat*, a BBC series on national television with an average of 9.2 million viewers. The council imposed several conditions, including that no one should be identifiable in the footage. Nevertheless, trailers for an episode of the programme showed Peck's unmasked face. When friends informed him that they had seen him in the trailers, Peck complained to the council. It contacted the producers who confirmed that his image had been covered in the main programme. But when the programme was aired, despite the pixilation, he was recognized by friends and family.

His complaints to the Broadcasting Standards Commission and the Independent Television Commission (both now replaced by Ofcom) alleging, among other things, an unwarranted infringement of his privacy, were successful. His objection about the published articles to the Press Complaints Commission was, however, unproductive. Peck then sought leave from the High Court to apply for judicial review concerning the council's disclosure of the CCTV material. His application and a further request for leave to appeal to the Court of Appeal were both rejected. He therefore pursued his grievance in the European Court which decided that the disclosure of the CCTV footage by the council was a disproportionate interference with his private life, contrary to Article 8. The expression 'private life' in the Article was, it held, to be interpreted generously to include the right to identity and personal development. Merely because the footage was taken on a public street did not render it a public occasion since Peck was not attending a public event, nor was he a public figure, and it was late at night. Moreover, the disclosure of the footage to the media resulted in its being seen by a significantly larger audience than Peck could reasonably have foreseen. It was the extent of disclosure by the media that breached his Article 8 rights. The Court concluded that the council could have obtained Mr Peck's consent prior to disclosure and it should have hidden his face. The case is important authority for the proposition that merely because an individual is in a public place does not render his or her conduct public, except in so far as passers-by witness it. It was the extent of the *further disclosure* by various forms of media that breached Peck's Article 8 rights.

In *Perry v United Kingdom*[78] the applicant complained that he had been covertly filmed by CCTV while in custody. The Government argued that the filming was not conducted in a private place with any intrusion into the 'inner circle' of his private life. The custody suite of the police station, it contended, was a communal administrative area through which all suspects had to pass and where the conspicuously placed camera operated as a matter of security routine. The images also related to public, not private, matters. Perry, it claimed, must have realized that he was being filmed; he could have no reasonable expectation of privacy. Acknowledging that the normal use of security cameras in the public street, shopping centres, or police stations serve a legitimate and foreseeable purpose, did not raise issues under Article 8(1), the European Court nevertheless found against the Government. Its reasoning was that whether or not Perry had been aware of the CCTV, there was no indication that he had any expectation that he was being filmed for use in a video identification procedure and, potentially, as evidence prejudicial to his defence at trial. This, it held, went beyond the normal or expected use of that sort of camera. The footage had been obtained involuntarily or in circumstances where it could be reasonably anticipated that it would be recorded and used for identification purposes. It therefore concluded that both the recording and use of the footage constituted an interference with his right to respect for private life.[79]

The fact, therefore, that the claimant happens to be in a public place when the infringement occurs, does not in itself exclude the operation of Article 8. The key question is whether, at the time of the infringement, the extent of subsequent publicity exceeded what was reasonably foreseeable. In Professor Phillipson's words:

> Where there is no expectation either of being photographed or overheard, as where surreptitious photographs are taken of a person relaxing by a hotel pool, on a beach, or in a restaurant, or where there is no expectation that any images recorded will be afforded mass publicity—as in *Peck* itself—the fact that the location was a public or semi-public one will not prevent there being an invasion of private life.[80]

With this—prophetic—observation, the Duchess of Cambridge would doubtless concur.[81]

---

78. App 63737/00 (2004) 39 EHRR 3.
79. App 63737/00 (2004) 39 EHRR 3 at [40]–[43], [48].
80. Phillipson (n 22), 739.
81. See Chapter 5.

5

Striking a balance

It is little more than a cliché that the limits to the right of privacy are drawn by the right to publish information that is in the public interest. Far less certainty, however, attends the question of what constitutes the 'public interest' and the circumstances under which private facts may be disclosed in its name. In this chapter, I examine how the courts have addressed this complex, malleable term both in cases of breach of confidence, and under the 'new approach' that has seen a fairly sophisticated doctrinal analysis of the concept.

The fundamental question that arises under both the action for breach of confidence and the new tort of misuse of private information is the same: when may personal facts be published on the ground that it is in the public interest so to do? The answer in both cases must of course be sought against the background of the value of free speech: any restriction of the free circulation of ideas and information requires powerful justification, as discussed in Chapter 2.

Until the passage of the Human Rights Act in 1998, and, in particular, the decision of the House of Lords in *Campbell v MGN Ltd*,[1] breach of confidence remained the principal means by which to provide protection against the gratuitous publication of personal information. Although this cause of action has all but been superseded by the tort of misuse of private information, it remains an important remedy, and I shall here outline the essentials of this jurisprudence and how it has influenced current developments.[2]

---

1. [2004] 2 AC 457.
2. See generally T Aplin, L Bently, P Johnson, and S Malynicz, *Gurry on Breach of Confidence: The Protection of Confidential Information*, 2nd edn (Oxford: Oxford University Press, 2012); M Richardson, M Bryan, M Vranken, and K Barnett, *Breach of Confidence: Social Origins and Modern Developments* (Cheltenham/Northampton, MA: Edward Elgar, 2012).

I shall then consider how courts now address these problems, identifying some of the more thorny problems that the new law has generated.

US law tends to apply a test of 'newsworthiness' which in many cases generates a similar set of questions, though it seems unnecessarily to complicate the matter. Still, it is worth asking whether there is anything the English law can learn from the US approach. I consider the position later.

A number of other legal environments exist where attempts are made to balance free speech and privacy. They too tend to concentrate on whether the publication is in the 'public interest' and how that concept is to be understood. Victims of unwanted publicity may in some cases—instead of, or as a complement to, a legal remedy—turn to the various media regulatory bodies whose codes of practice attempt to define the concept of 'public interest'. The structure and operation of these institutions are returned to in Chapter 7; here I focus on the approaches of their codes.

The Data Protection Act 1998 has certain relevance here, as does the law of defamation, which continues to provide a means by which claimants may seek relief for unwanted publicity. Their significance in relation to reconciling privacy and freedom of expression is also briefly considered.

Breach of confidence

It is trite law that the action for breach of confidence is circumscribed by a public interest test.[3] Less clear is the strict nature of the test: whether its absence constitutes a substantive requirement of the action, or whether it operates as a defence to what would otherwise be a protected confidence. This analysis turns in large part upon the conceptual basis of the action

---

3. See Y Cripps, 'The Public Interest Defence to the Action for Breach of Confidence and The Law Commission's Proposals on Disclosure in the Public Interest' (1984) 4 Oxford Journal of Legal Studies 361; and Law Commission, *Breach of Confidence* (Law Com No 110, Cmnd 8388, 1981), paras 4.36–4.53. It is worth bearing in mind Eady J's prudent admonition in respect of the public interest and personal information: 'it would hardly be appropriate to clutter up the courts with cases of spanking between consenting adults taking place in private property without disturbing the neighbours. That would plainly not be in the public interest. It would not be logical...to pray in aid the public interest when trying to justify hidden cameras and worldwide coverage. It is worth remembering that even those who have committed serious crimes do not thereby become outlaws as far as their own rights including rights of personal privacy are concerned', *Mosley v News Group Newspapers* [2008] EWHC 1777, [117].

itself. If the action is grounded in equitable considerations, the nature of the public interest test falls to be treated in like manner.[4]

The essence of any equitable action is that the court may *recognize* the claimant's equitable right, yet refuse to grant a remedy to protect it. Unlike the common law position, protection does not follow recognition *as of right*; equitable remedies are discretionary. Accordingly, if the obligation of confidence never came into existence 'the court would be deprived of the opportunity to exercise the discretionary features of their equitable jurisdiction.'[5] Moreover, if the obligation were struck down *ab initio* by the public interest element of the information in question, a court of equity could not assess the appropriateness of damages in lieu of the granting of an injunction preventing disclosure.[6]

For these reasons, it is submitted that the public interest qualification acts as a *defence* in that it operates to bar the enforcement of the right rather than to deny its existence.[7] The Law Commission, however, with specific reference to the judgment of Lord Widgery CJ in *Attorney-General v Jonathan Cape Ltd*,[8] felt itself unable to draw such a conclusion. In that case the Lord Chief Justice considered that it was for the claimant to show: '(a) that...publication would be a breach of confidence; (b) that the public interest requires that the publication be restrained, and (c) that there are no other facets of the public interest contradictory of and more compelling

---

4. Cripps (n 3) outlines five separate conceptual bases: equity, contract, property, tort, and 'an action *sui generis*', 362–7. Gurry is to similar effect, see Chapter 4.

5. Cripps (n 3), 363.

6. See s 50 of the Senior Courts Act 1981 for the modern-day embodiment of Lord Cairns' Act. In *Church of Scientology of California v Kaufman* [1973] RPC 627, 658, Goff J did not feel that the successful invocation of the public interest defence could deprive the plaintiff of its remedy in damages. This, it is contended, is strong evidence for the rejection of the test as a substantive requirement. 'He simply refused to grant an injunction to enforce the obligation', Y Cripps, *The Legal Implications of Disclosure in the Public Interest* (Oxford: ESC Publishing, 1986), 31.

7. The acceptance of this view leads to a further difficulty recognized by the Commission in respect of the observations of the courts in this area: '(1) whether they relate to the proper scope of the public interest in being informed of the subject matter of an action for breach of confidence, which, to determine whether the defendant is liable for the breach, has to be weighed by the court against the public interest in the preservation of the obligation; or (2) whether they refer to the extent to which the public interest in being so informed should be taken into account by a court in determining whether or not to grant an interlocutory injunction; or (3) whether they are concerned with the extent to which such public interest is a factor to be considered by the court in determining whether or not to grant a final injunction, irrespective of any claim which the plaintiff may make for damages', *Breach of Confidence* (n 3), para 4.49.

8. [1976] QB 752.

than that relied upon.'[9] It cited this dictum as authority for the view that the disclosure of the information *not* being in the public interest is a 'positive requirement of the action'[10] and, hence, on the basis of the jurisprudence in this area, it concluded that whether the test constituted a defence was a 'further uncertainty'.[11]

It is arguable, however, that Widgery CJ's remarks pertain more to the burden of proof of the public interest test than to its legal rationale. It is, admittedly, unusual to cast the legal burden of disproving a defence in civil matters upon the claimant;[12] this may well be due to the importance of free speech which would otherwise be subjugated in a successful action for breach of confidence. As the Commission put it,

> [T]he law on breach of confidence…is a not insubstantial check on freedom of speech. If Lord Widgery's test is applicable to the action…in all circumstances this check may be more acceptable in that it only operates if the plaintiff can show that it is justified on a balance of the public interests involved.[13]

I return to this question later.

9. [1976] QB 752, 770.
10. *Breach of Confidence* (n 3), para 4.42.
11. *Breach of Confidence* (n 3), para 4.53. See MW Bryan, 'The Law Commission Report on Breach of Confidence: Not in the Public Interest?' (1982) Public Law 188. The Commission recommend that 'the courts should have a broad power to decide in an action for breach of confidence whether in the particular case the public interest in protecting the confidentiality of the information outweighs the public interest in its disclosure or use', para 6.77. As to the substantive requirements of the issue, the plaintiff must satisfy the court that the public interest relied upon by the defendant is 'outweighed by the public interest involved in upholding the confidentiality of the information', cl 11(1)(b). In its Fourth Report, *Privacy and Media Intrusion* (HC 294-I, 1993), para 55, the National Heritage Committee recommended a defence of public interest which, as defined, would include any act done for the purpose of preventing, detecting, or exposing the commission of any crime; or, informing the public about matters directly affecting the discharge of any public functions of the individual concerned; or, preventing the public from being harmfully misled by some public statement or action of the individual concerned; or, for the protection of health or safety; or, under any lawful authority. This mirrors quite closely the test propounded by the Calcutt Committee except that the Committee eschews the emphasis on the 'public interest' and, instead, justifies specific revelations which: expose crime or seriously antisocial conduct; or, protect the health or safety of the public; or, concern the behaviour of an individual in his or her private life which so adversely affect his or her public duties or is so hypocritical, that the public is likely to be seriously misled: *The Report of the Committee on Privacy and Related Matters* (Cmnd 1102, 1990), paras 3.19–3.27, 12.20–12.23.
12. This, of course, is the requirement in criminal evidence.
13. *Breach of Confidence* (n 3), para 4.44.

What is in the public interest?

In *Gartside v Outram*[14] Wood V-C declared,

> [T]here is no confidence as to the disclosure of an iniquity. You cannot make me the confidant of a crime or a fraud, and be entitled to close up my lips upon any secret which you have the audacity to disclose to me relating to any fraudulent intention on your part: such a confidence cannot exist.[15]

The court therefore declined to impeach the actions of a former clerk to the plaintiff who informed certain individuals that they had been defrauded by his ex-employer. On the other hand, in *Weld-Blundell v Stephens*[16] the defendant's partner in a firm of chartered accountants negligently published libellous statements, made by the plaintiff, to those who had been defamed. The plaintiff successfully recovered damages, Warrington LJ commenting that he could see 'no reason founded on public policy or any other ground why an agent should be at liberty to disclose evidence of a private wrong committed by his principal.'[17] The Court of Appeal saw *Gartside* as an example of the Court of Chancery declining to exercise its equitable discretion and leaving the plaintiff to his remedy at law because he came to court with 'unclean hands'.[18]

It is possible to reconcile *Gartside* and *Weld-Blundell* on their facts, a position reinforced by Viscount Finlay's remarks on the latter in the House of Lords when he acknowledged that 'there may, of course, be cases in which some higher duty is involved. Danger to the State, or public duty may supersede the duty of the agent to the principal.'[19] In *Initial Services v Putterill*[20] Lord Denning MR dismissed the suggestion that the public interest defence was confined to cases where the party seeking enforcement of the obligation of confidence had been 'guilty of an actual or contemplated crime or fraud':[21]

---

14. (1856) 26 LJ Ch 113.
15. (1856) 26 LJ Ch 113, 114.
16. [1919] 1 KB 520.
17. [1919] 1 KB 520, 535.
18. Cripps considers this to be inconsistent with Wood V-C's proprietary analysis in *Gartside*: 'The real ground of the jurisdiction, as it is properly put, is founded first upon property', (1856) 26 LJ Ch 113, 116. See Cripps (n 6), 31.
19. [1920] AC 956, 965–6.
20. [1968] 1 QB 396.
21. A suggestion of Bankes LJ in *Weld-Blundell* [1919] 1 KB 520, 527.

[I] do not think that it is so limited. It extends to any misconduct of such
a nature that it ought in the public interest to be disclosed to others...The
exception should extend to crimes, frauds and misdeeds, both those actually
committed as well as those in contemplation, provided always—and this is
essential—that the disclosure is justified in the public interest.[22]

But he qualified this principle by imposing a requirement that, even where
the information in question does relate to matters in which there is a legitimate public interest:

The disclosure must...be to one who has a proper interest to receive the information. There may be cases where the misdeed is of such a character that
the public interest may demand, or at least excuse, publication on a broader
field, even to the press.[23]

This point receives further elaboration later. Suffice it to say that it may be a
potent counter-argument against those who regard the action for breach of
confidence when applied to personal information as an unjustifiable restriction on free speech. As *Francome*[24] demonstrates, the competing public interest of having confidences preserved may be upheld notwithstanding that
the court orders the information to be disclosed to interested parties.[25]

In *Woodward*, an archetypal privacy case, the plaintiffs, three pop-stars,
were denied the injunction they sought to restrain their press agent revealing information relating to the various 'outrages' committed by them. Lord
Denning MR stated:

If a group of this kind seek publicity which is to their advantage, it seems to
me that they cannot complain if [their servant or agent] afterwards discloses
the truth about them. If the image which they fostered was not a true image, it
is in the public interest that it should be corrected. In these cases of confidential information it is a question of balancing the public interest in maintaining
the confidence against the public interest in knowing the truth.[26]

---

22. [1968] 1 QB 396, 405.
23. [1968] 1 QB 396, 405.
24. [1984] 1 WLR 892.
25. Sir John Donaldson MR commented: 'Assuming that the tapes reveal evidence of the com-
    mission of a criminal offence or a breach of the rules of racing—and I stress that this is an
    assumption—it may well be in the public interest that the tapes...be made available to the
    police or the Jockey Club', [1984] 1 WLR 892, 899.
26. [1977] 1 WLR 760, 762–3. Lord Denning's approach seems no longer to be good law. See eg
    McKennitt v Ash [2007] 3 WLR 194; *Campbell v Frisbee* [2002] EWCA Civ 1374, [203] EMLR
    3. For criticism of this and other aspects of the judgment, see R Wacks, 'Pop Goes Privacy'
    (1978) 31 Modern Law Review 67.

In *Fraser v Evans*, however, Lord Denning modified this balancing test, with specific reference to the public interest.[27] The court held that the obligation of confidence may be enforced only by the person to whom it is owed. Nevertheless, the Court of Appeal was willing to consider the question of the public interest defence and to introduce a test of considerably wider ambit and flexibility than had hitherto been propounded. The Master of the Rolls remarked,

> [T]he Court will in a proper case restrain the publication of confidential information. The jurisdiction is based not so much on property or on contract as on the duty to be of good faith. No person is permitted to divulge to the world information which he has received in confidence, unless he has *just cause* for doing so.[28]

The 'just cause or excuse' phraseology may have increased the range of factors to be taken into account when assessing whether to enjoin publication.[29] But Lord Denning MR cast doubt on the universal applicability of his new formulation in *Hubbard v Vosper*,[30] by reverting to the public interest expression of the test. This ambiguity, it is submitted, is more a question of form than substance. In *Church of Scientology v Kaufman* Goff J adopted the 'just cause or reasonable excuse for breaking confidence'[31] test but reasoned that it comprised both a 'narrow basis'[32]—the public interest test in *Hubbard* and *Putterill*—and a 'wider basis'[33]—*Fraser v Evans*. This bifurcation was adopted by Megarry V-C in *Malone*,[34] but one must be wary of drawing any general conclusions from his application of the test.

The significance of the motives and beliefs of the 'public informer' is discussed later. In *Malone* it was necessary for the Vice-Chancellor to excuse the actions of the police in tapping the plaintiff's telephone, even though they were, to some extent, on 'fishing expeditions' which *might* satisfy their suspicions of iniquity. Hence, Sir Robert eschewed the 'narrow basis' and adopted the 'wider' one because 'that is not confined to misconduct or misdeeds. There may be cases where there is no misconduct or misdeed but yet

27. [1969] 1 QB 349.
28. [1969] 1 QB 349, 362 (emphasis added).
29. Cripps (n 6), 39.
30. [1972] 2 QB 84.
31. [1973] RPC 627, 648.
32. [1973] RPC 627, 648.
33. [1973] RPC 627, 648.
34. [1979] 2 WLR 700, 729.

there is a just cause or excuse for breaking confidence.'[35] In other words, if Megarry V-C had accepted only the narrow basis, it would not have justified the police's measures if the information subsequently revealed did not disclose misconduct on the part of Malone.

In *British Steel Corporation v Granada TV Ltd*[36] Granada Television broadcast a programme seeking to show that the huge losses being incurred by British Steel at the time were due to mismanagement and poor quality control. This information, which Granada knew to be confidential, had been passed to them by an unknown person. It is important to note that the only contended issue was an order granted to British Steel that Granada disclose its source. In spite of this, the House of Lords took it upon themselves to consider the public interest test, and the majority view was the traditional one. As Lord Wilberforce stressed,

> There is an important exception to the limitations which may exist upon the right of the media to reveal information otherwise restricted. That is based on what is commonly known as the 'iniquity rule.' It extends in fact beyond 'iniquity' to misconduct generally…It must be emphasised that we are not in this field in the present case. The most that it is said the papers reveal is mis-management and government intervention.[37]

Uncertainties surrounding the nature and scope of the public interest test have, to a large extent, been clarified by the *Lion Laboratories* case.[38] This concerned Intoximeters manufactured by the plaintiff to be used to breath-test drivers suspected of being over the prescribed alcohol limit.[39] Two ex-employees of the plaintiff had disclosed internal memoranda to a newspaper relating to their concern about the accuracy of the device in calibration tests. At first instance, Leonard J granted the plaintiff an interlocutory injunction. The Court of Appeal, without hesitation, discharged the injunction on the ground that the information contained in the memoranda concerned matters in the public interest. In the course of his

---

35. [1979] 2 WLR 700, 716.
36. [1980] 3 WLR 774.
37. [1980] 3 WLR 774, 821–2. However, Lord Salmon (dissenting) foreshadowed the approach in *Lion Laboratories* case when he declared, 'No doubt crime, fraud and misconduct should be laid bare in the public interest; and these, of course, did not occur in BSC. There was however much else, even more important in all the circumstances, which called aloud to be revealed in the public interest', 843. Among the factors which Lord Salmon identified was the fact that BSC was a nationalized undertaking and thus any losses would affect the public purse, 837.
38. *Lion Laboratories Ltd v Evans* [1984] 3 WLR 539.
39. See Y Cripps, 'Alcohol Measuring Devices and Breaches of Copyright and Confidence' (1985) Cambridge Law Journal 35.

judgment, Stephenson LJ highlighted four points. First, he emphasized that the courts were concerned only with what was *in* the public interest not what was *of* interest to the public.[40] Secondly, he recognized that the media have their own private interest in increasing circulation.[41] Thirdly, he said that the public interest is not always best served by disclosure to the press. Fourthly, and most significantly, the court rejected counsel's submission that the public interest test was confined to cases of iniquity. Stephenson LJ expressed the view that iniquity was 'merely an instance of just cause or excuse for breaking confidence'[42] and accordingly there was no need to show misconduct on the part of the plaintiff. He believed that the just cause or excuse in the instant case was 'the public interest [in admittedly confidential information]'.[43]

The decision represents 'a deeper inroad into actions for breach of confidence...than any other case on the public interest defence',[44] but an important feature of this case is that the alleged inaccuracy of the Intoximeter could have had an effect on 'the life, and even the liberty, of an unascertainable number of Her Majesty's subjects.'[45]

Factual influences on the public interest test

The defendant's motives and beliefs

The tabloids depend heavily upon members of the public 'selling' them information concerning either themselves or, more pertinently in the present context, others. Accordingly, the motive of the informant may be a crucial factor in the application of the public interest test. In *Putterill* Lord Denning

---

40. [1984] 3 WLR 539, 546 (quoting Lord Wilberforce in *British Steel* [1980] 3 WLR 780, 1168: 'there is a wide difference between what is interesting to the public and what is in the public interest').
41. In respect of the publication of personal information, this might be described as an injudicious understatement.
42. [1984] 3 WLR 539, 547.
43. [1984] 3 WLR 539, 547.
44. Cripps (n 39), 39.
45. [1984] 3 WLR 539, 554 per Stephenson LJ. In *Spycatcher (No 2)* Lord Goff explicitly embraced the *Lion Laboratories* approach. He said that, although the 'defence of iniquity' was originally 'narrowly stated, on the basis that a man cannot be made the confidant of a crime or a fraud...It is now clear that the principle extends to matters of which disclosure is required in the public interest', [1988] 3 All ER 545, 659.

MR qualified his general public interest test[46] with reference to informants disclosing information 'out of malice or spite or...for reward'.[47] He thought such to be 'a different matter. It is a great evil when people purvey scandalous information for reward.'[48]

The only decision which gives any weight to this proposition is *Schering*. The case presents several difficulties in its treatment of the public domain issue, but paramount to the Court of Appeal was the public interest defence and, in particular, the majority view that the informant Elstein had acted with improper motives. Shaw LJ warned that 'the Law of England is indeed, as Blackstone declared, a law of liberty, but the freedoms it recognises do not include a licence for the mercenary betrayal of business confidences.'[49] Nevertheless Lord Denning MR, who in *Putterill* supported the importance of motive, thought it 'quite unfair to accuse [Elstein], on the present evidence, of a flagrant breach of duty, or of being a traitorous adviser seeking to make money out of his misconduct.'[50] It is arguable that this is his conclusion *on the facts* and not on legal principle,[51] but in the light of his comments in *Woodward*, it is hard to escape the conclusion that he did dismiss motive as a matter of law. Indeed, 'it is difficult to imagine a clearer case of a person purveying scandalous information for reward.'[52] Yet the Master of the Rolls discerned a public interest in there being truth in publicity.[53]

Additional difficulties arise from *Malone*, primarily because the factual context concerned the exercise of the police of their executive powers. Cripps warns that Megarry V-C's views are to be treated 'with caution'[54] because he was 'careful to limit his comments to the particular facts of the case and hence to the special considerations involved in telephone tapping at the behest of the police.'[55] The Vice-Chancellor took as his starting point the observation that 'the detection and prosecution of criminals, and the discovery of projected crimes, are important weapons in protecting the

46. As discussed above in the text after n 21.
47. [1968] 1 QB 396, 406.
48. [1968] 1 QB 396, 406.
49. [1981] 2 WLR 848, 869. Templeman LJ was equally explicit on the matter: 'It is important in the present case that, if the injunction is withheld, the court will enable a trusted adviser to make money out of his dealing in confidential information', 881.
50. [1981] 2 WLR 848, 859.
51. 'Lord Denning...openly disregarded the fact that the defendant had been paid for his disclosures', Cripps (n 3), 374.
52. Cripps (n 3), 374.
53. [1977] 1 WLR 760, 763–4.
54. Cripps (n 3), 378.
55. Cripps (n 3), 378.

public.'[56] He then went on to limit the implication of this statement (that all confidences could be disclosed if they furthered the aim of 'crime prevention') in two ways. First, the information could not be used for any purpose other than the prevention and detection of crime and, secondly, that the informant must have had reasonable grounds for believing that the disclosure of the information would facilitate such a purpose.[57] As to the latter, it is obviously for the court and not for the informant to decide what matters are in the public interest to be disclosed in breach of confidence. As to the first limitation, it is most doubtful whether the court would censure the disclosure of information revealing criminal behaviour on account of the professedly opportunistic attitude of the informant.

The correct approach in this case, it is submitted, is to disregard the motive of the informant. The public interest test should focus on the value of the information to the public. If the community has a legitimate interest in preserving confidences (against which must be balanced the interest in free speech) taking account of the motive of the informant, this effectively introduces a further value of preventing the transfer of information for money. If the recipient is willing to pay, it is difficult to see what comprises this third value. Moreover, this 'value' cannot be a factor in assessing the other two. The interest in protecting confidences springs from commercial and social considerations. Access to information rests on the (often competing) needs of a free society. Upon what basis are the motives of the informant to be evaluated?[58]

Following *Lion Laboratories*, it is, in any event, unlikely that defendant's motives will be taken into account. In his definition of the public interest balancing test, Stephenson LJ said,

> There is confidential information which the public may have a right to receive and others, in particular the press...may have a right and even a duty to publish, even if the information has been unlawfully obtained in flagrant breach of confidence and *irrespective of the motive of the informer*.[59]

---

56. [1979] 2 WLR 700, 730.
57. [1979] 2 WLR 700, 730.
58. 'If there is a public interest in the receipt of certain information then that public interest ought not to be said to be diminished, extinguished or, indeed, affected by a defendant's ulterior motives for publication', Cripps (n 3), 377. She rightly acknowledges that this argument may have less force in relation to the 'just cause or excuse' formulation of the defence (ibid).
59. [1984] 3 WLR 539, 546. Stephenson LJ (at 548) drew upon the formulation of the balancing test of Lord Fraser in *British Steel* which he considered 'so apt that I follow the judge in quoting it': 'The answer to the question therefore seems to me to involve weighing up the public

A rather different application of the defendant's motives arises where the media claim to be acting in the public interest, but this is merely charade; their real motives are otherwise. This raises a (neglected) moral question that I discuss later.

The timing of the disclosure

In *Initial Services* Lord Denning MR observed,

> In [*Weld-Blundell*], Bankes LJ rather suggested that the exception is limited to the proposed or contemplated commission of a crime or a civil wrong. But I should have thought that was too limited. The exception should extend to crimes, frauds and misdeeds, *both those actually committed as well as those in contemplation*, provided always—that the disclosure is justified in the public interest.[60]

The timing of the disclosure is not, as a general rule, relevant, but there are certain exceptions. In *Schering* Shaw LJ remarked that the public no longer had an interest in the drug Primodos and its side effects because the drug had been taken off the market by Schering Chemicals Ltd. He believed that 'neither the public nor any individual stands in need of protection from its use at this stage in the history.'[61] Similarly, the timing of the disclosures played a crucial role in *Jonathan Cape* where the Attorney-General sought, unsuccessfully, to restrain the publication of the first volume of the diaries of the late Richard Crossman. The diaries disclosed Cabinet discussions and other governmental confidences, but Lord Widgery CJ held that the public interest defence must be subject to a limit of time. The events described in the diaries were a decade old, and the Lord Chief Justice found it hard to believe that 'the publication of anything in volume one would inhibit free discussion in the Cabinet of today, even though the individuals involved are

---

interest for and against publication...The informer's motives are, in my opinion, irrelevant', [1981] AC 1096, 1202.

60. [1968] 1 QB 396, 405 (emphasis added). Note that the *Initial Services v Putterill* formulation has now been superseded in so far as the scope of the public interest test is concerned. See *Lion Laboratories* discussed at n 37, and *Hellewell v Chief Constable of Derbyshire* [1995] 1 WLR 804; *Woolgar v Chief Constable of Sussex Police* [2000] 1 WLR 25; *The General Dental Council v Ruth Savery & others* [2011] EWHC 3011 (Admin).

61. [1981] 2 WLR 848, 869.

the same, and the national problems have a distressing similarity with those of a decade ago.'[62]

The recipient of the disclosure

The court is reluctant to allow the public interest defence to become a 'mole's charter'.[63] One of the methods used to circumscribe the scope of the defence is that disclosure, though in the public interest, ought to be sanctioned only when it is made to an appropriate body (and this will normally not include the media). Reference has been made to Lord Denning's comments in *Initial Services*[64] and their approval by Stephenson LJ in *Lion Laboratories*.[65] In that decision Griffiths LJ was at pains to explain why this was an appropriate occasion for disclosure to the press and not to the Home Office:

> The public stance of the Home Office is that there is no risk of a false conviction as a result of using the machine. The Home Office is an interested and committed party. Of course I do not suggest that the Home Office would deliberately shut their eyes to evidence that the machine, or the manufacturers, might not be as reliable as they thought; but civil servants are human, and beauty lies in the eye of the beholder. I think in all the circumstances that the Daily Express is not to be criticised for thinking that the impact of the revelations in their newspaper would be more likely to galvanise the authorities into action than a discreet behind-doors approach.[66]

In *Francome* the Court of Appeal, though declining to lift an injunction prohibiting the defendants from publishing allegations of breaches of the rules of horse-racing by the plaintiff, supported such disclosure being made to the police or the Jockey Club. As Stephenson LJ put it,

---

62. [1976] QB 752, 771. It was mentioned earlier that the Law Commission thought that Lord Widgery's test served to 'make more acceptable' the fact that the action for breach of confidence was a 'not insubstantial check on freedom of speech' (see text at n 13). The Commission went on to comment that the time factor, in the personal information sphere: 'would enable a court to hold that the balance of interest lay in favour of protecting the confidence; the claim of the individual to have this information kept secret may well with the passage of the years become stronger, while a claim on behalf of the public to have access to it may in time tend to be less compelling', *Breach of Confidence* (n 3), para 4.44.
63. *Lion Laboratories* [1984] 3 WLR 539, 562 per Griffiths LJ.
64. See text at n 22.
65. See text after n 40.
66. [1984] 3 WLR 539, 561.

In the instant case, pending a trial, it is impossible to see what public interest would be served by publishing the contents of the tapes which would not equally be served by giving them to the police or the Jockey-Club. Any wider publication could only serve the interests of the *Daily Mirror*.[67]

The burden and standard of proof

The comments of Lord Widgery CJ in *Jonathan Cape* and their interpretation by the Law Commission have been considered earlier.[68] The ambiguities which it identified concern the question upon whom the burden of proof of the public interest defence rests, and not whether the defence is a defence at all, but a mandatory requirement of the action for breach of confidence. *Lion Laboratories* has gone a long way towards resolving this problem, at the interlocutory stage at least. The court laid to rest the suggestion that the standard of proof for actions for breach of confidence was the same as that for libel actions—that is, if the public interest defence was raised then no interlocutory injunction should be granted, the plaintiff being left to his damages at trial.[69]

Stephenson LJ, agreeing with the remarks of Sir David Cairns in *Khashoggi*, said that 'to be allowed to publish confidential information, the defendants must do more than raise a plea of public interest; they must show *a legitimate ground for supposing it is in the public interest for it to be disclosed*.'[70] This was translated into a 'serious test of public interest which may succeed at the trial'.[71]

In respect of the burden of proving the defence at trial, the authorities point to a distinction between private and public actions for breach of confidence. *Jonathan Cape* concerned an action between the state and an individual and this may explain why Lord Widgery placed the burden of proof upon the plaintiff, whereas in decisions such as *Fraser*, the public interest

---

67. [1984] 1 WLR 892, 898.
68. See text after n 6. The final conclusion of the Law Commission was that it was: 'a further uncertainty in the light of *Cape's* case...whether, as Lord Widgery there held, it is for the plaintiff to satisfy the court that the balance of the public interest lies in favour of protecting confidence or whether, as previously widely accepted, it is for the defendant to raise the issue of public interest as a defence', para 4.53.
69. See the comments of Lord Denning MR in *Hubbard* [1972] 2 QB 84, 96; and in *Fraser* [1969] 1 QB 349, 360–1; and of Roskill LJ in *Khashoggi v Smith* (1980) 124 SJ 149 (CA).
70. [1984] 3 WLR 539, 548 (words of Sir David Cairns emphasized).
71. [1984] 3 WLR 539, 548 per Stephenson LJ.

defence failed because the *defendant* has not been able to make out a ground for publication. As Lord Goff pointed out in *Spycatcher (No 2)*:

> In cases concerned with government secrets,[72] it is incumbent on the Crown, in order to restrain disclosure of government secrets, not only to show that the information is confidential, but also to show that it is in the public interest that it should not be published. The reason for this additional requirement in cases concerned with government secrets appears to be that, although in the case of private citizens there is a public interest that confidential information should as such be protected, in the case of government secrets the mere fact of confidentiality does not alone support such a conclusion, because in a free society there is a continuing public interest that the workings of government should be open to scrutiny and criticism. From this it follows that, in such cases, there must be demonstrated some other public interest which requires that publication should be restrained.[73]

In cases involving personal information, it would appear that the burden of proof rests upon the defendant to show why the protection of confidence should be overridden in favour of the public interest in receiving the information. But even this may be subject to exceptions as is illustrated by comparing *Williams v Williams*[74] with the *Distillers* case.[75] In the former, Lord Eldon LC referring to the attempt by the plaintiff to prevent the disclosure of an unpatented eye medicine was not of the opinion 'that the Court ought to struggle to protect this sort of secrets in medicine'.[76] In the *Distillers* case, the information in question concerned the harmful side effects of the notorious drug Thalidomide on unborn children. At first instance, Talbot J phrased the defence in such a way as to leave no doubt that he thought it was for the defendant to prove that there is 'a competing public interest which overrides the plaintiff's private rights and the public interest arising out of discovery.'[77]

72. The learned judge referred to Lord Widgery CJ in the *Jonathan Cape* case [1975] 3 All ER 484, 495, and to Mason CJ in *Commonwealth of Australia v John Fairfax & Sons Ltd* (1980) 32 ALR 485, 492–3.

73. [1988] 3 All ER 545, 660. For a more contemporary instance—minus considerations of iniquity—of a court finding that there existed a public interest in passengers learning of deficiencies in the London Underground, see *London Regional Transport v Mayor of London* [2001] EWCA Civ 1491, [2003] EMLR 4.

74. (1817) 3 Mer 157, 36 ER 61.

75. *Distillers Co (Biochemicals) Ltd v Times Newspapers Ltd* [1975] 1 QB 613.

76. (1817) 3 Mer 157, 36 ER 61, 62.

77. [1975] 1 QB 613, 623. The reference to discovery indicates what may well have dominated the minds of the judges who dealt with the case up to the House of Lords. The information which *The Times* sought to publish had been passed to them as a result of a discovery order by the court in the action between Distillers and the users of Thalidomide. One of the competing

Distillers represents the better approach. The burden of proof should always rest upon the defendant in 'private' confidence actions. If there are very strong public interest considerations going against the plaintiff (eg the interest society has in the free circulation of information likely to lead to advances in medicine), apart from the omnipresent interest in free speech, then this should result in the evidential threshold being lowered, making it easier for the defendant to prove his or her defence. In stricter terms of evidence, the plaintiff should adduce a greater weight of evidence in rebuttal. In its draft bill, however, the Law Commission proposes the *Jonathan Cape* test for the tort of breach of confidence:

> Having regard to the importance in our view of the free circulation of information, we think it in principle right that the plaintiff should be required to establish that the balance of the public interest lies in his particular case in protecting the confidentiality of the relevant information.[78]

This conclusion resulted in clause 11 of the bill. Subclauses (1)(a) and (2) control the evidential burden of the defendant, whilst subclause (1)(b) imposes the legal burden on the plaintiff. Clause 11(2) provides,

> For the purposes of subsection (1) a defendant raises the issue of public interest in relation to a disclosure or use of information if he satisfies the court that, in view of the content of the information, there was, or (in the case of an apprehended disclosure or use) will be, at the time of the disclosure or use a public interest involved in the information being so disclosed or used.

This is an unattractive solution, for the reasons suggested later. Suffice it to say here that these proposals accord value to certain forms of free speech which have no intrinsic worth.[79]

In Chapter 4 I sketched the background to recent developments which, under the sway of the Human Rights Act 1998, has seen the courts all but supplant the action for breach of confidence with a new tort of 'misuse of private information'. Indeed, Lord Woolf MR consigned the pre-1998 case law to history.[80]

---

public interests was therefore the administration of justice—a consideration likely perhaps to be magnified in gravity by the administrators of that justice.

78. *Breach of Confidence* (n 3), para 6.82.
79. This question is considered in Chapter 2.
80. *A v B plc* [2002] EWCA Civ 337, [2003] QB 125, [9]: such cases were 'largely of historic interest only'. This dictum, I would respectfully submit, may overstate the position.

Breach of confidence and privacy

One of the law's great ironies is that, although rooted in the English law of confidence, the US privacy torts have failed to germinate in England. Ever wary of the 'grand style' of judicial interpretation, founded on sweeping principles,[81] the English courts tend to maintain a hard-headed hostility towards legal rights that are allegedly immanent in the law. Under the so-called 'new approach' there are signs of a more expansive attitude to the protection of rights, in general, and to the subject of privacy, in particular. The perceived shackles of the equitable remedy for breach of confidence were, as explained in Chapter 4, broken in *Campbell*, though the new jurisprudence does not entirely discard the tests developed by the courts over the centuries. Despite eliminating the need for a relationship of confidence between the parties, and the application of the Human Rights Act 1998,[82] some of these 'ancient' criteria are—inexorably—revivified when the complaint is one of misuse of personal information. They are considered later.

As mentioned also in Chapter 4, the 'ultimate balancing test' as proposed by Lord Steyn in *Re S (A Child)*[83] constitutes a recognition of the tension between Article 10 and Article 8 of the European Convention on Human Rights (ECHR) that is always likely to be difficult to address and, in some cases, the outcome will inevitably prove controversial. The court pointed out:

Where both Article 10 and Article 8 are engaged,

(a) neither Article *as such* has precedence over the other;

(b) where the values protected by the two Articles are in conflict, it is necessary to conduct a careful scrutiny of their comparative importance in the particular case;

---

81. The (doubtless) few uninitiated may find the following helpful: ch 6, 'Legal Realism' in R Wacks, *Understanding Jurisprudence: An Introduction to Legal Theory*, 3rd edn (Oxford: Oxford University Press, 2012).

82. In *Campbell* Lord Hoffmann appeared to sound the death knell for the requirement of a 're-lationship of confidence' between claimant and defendant when he stated, 'As Sedley LJ observed in a perceptive passage in his judgment in *Douglas v Hello! Ltd* [2001] QB 967, 1001, the new approach takes a different view of the underlying value which the law protects. Instead of the cause of action being based upon the duty of good faith applicable to confidential personal information and trade secrets alike, it focuses upon the protection of human autonomy and dignity—the right to control the dissemination of information about one's private life and the right to the esteem and respect of other people', [2004] 2 AC 457, [51].

83. [2004] UKHL 47, [2005] 1 AC 593.

(c) the necessity for limiting each right is assessed objectively in accordance with the principle of proportionality.[84]

Although the conflict is an unavoidable consequence of the factual circumstances of each case, the outcome may be disappointingly unpredictable. This much is acknowledged by the judges themselves.[85] It would be unfair therefore to condemn the courts for what may occasionally strike the observer as the uncertain state of the law. They are also bound to consider the judgments that issue from Strasbourg which are not always models of sagacity.

So, for instance, consider—again—the following three celebrated cases in both jurisdictions. Each found in favour of the victim, yet the circumstances were sufficiently diverse that one might reasonably have expected different results. In the first, supermodel Naomi Campbell was photographed leaving a meeting of Narcotics Anonymous (NA). The British tabloid newspaper, the *Daily Mirror*, published the pictures together with articles claiming that she was receiving treatment for her drug addiction. She had denied publicly that she was an addict, and sued the newspaper for damages. The trial court and the Court of Appeal found against her. They held that by mendaciously asserting to the media she did not take drugs, she had rendered it legitimate for the media to put the record straight. But her appeal to the House of Lords succeeded and she was awarded compensation for a violation of her privacy.[86]

84. *Re S (A Child) (Identification: Restrictions on Publication)* [2005] 1 AC 593 (HL). It is interesting to note that prior to the Human Rights Act, Lord Hoffmann robustly announced: 'It cannot be too strongly emphasised that outside the established exceptions, or any new ones which Parliament may enact in accordance with its obligations under the [ECHR], there is no question of balancing freedom of speech against other interests. It is a trump card which always wins', *R v Central Television Plc* [1994] 3 WLR 20, 30. He did, however, acknowledge that 'a right of privacy may be a legitimate exception to freedom of speech'. But see his more tempered remarks in Lord Hoffmann, 'Human Rights and the House of Lords' (1999) 62 Modern Law Review 159, 165. Similarly, Lord Denning MR in *Schering* went on to accept that there are 'exceptional cases, where the intended publication is plainly unlawful and would inflict grave injury on innocent people or seriously impede the course of justice', *Schering Chemicals Ltd v Falkman Ltd* [1981] 2 WLR 848, 861. In similar vein, Templeman LJ remarked that 'Blackstone was concerned to prevent government interference with the press. The times of Blackstone are not relevant to the times of Mr Murdoch', ibid, 861.
85. Thus Lord Carswell remarked, 'Weighing and balancing these factors is a process which may well lead different people to different conclusions, as one may readily see from consideration of the judgments of the courts below and the opinions given by the several members of the Appellate Committee of your Lordships' House', *Campbell v MGN Ltd* [2004] UKHL 22, [168]. The House in that appeal was divided 3–2.
86. *Campbell v MGN Ltd* [2004] UKHL 22.

In the second case, photographs of the wedding of Michael Douglas and Catherine Zeta-Jones were surreptitiously taken, notwithstanding explicit notice having been given to all guests forbidding 'photography or video devices at the ceremony or reception'. The couple had entered into an exclusive publication contract with *OK!* magazine but its rival, *Hello!*, sought to publish these pictures. The stars reached for their lawyers, and won.[87]

The European Court of Human Rights has, on a number of occasions, revealed the inadequacy of European domestic legal protection of privacy. In the third example, Princess Caroline of Monaco complained that paparazzi employed by several German magazines had photographed her while she was engaged in a variety of quotidian activities, including eating in a restaurant courtyard, horse riding, canoeing, playing with her children, shopping, skiing, kissing a boyfriend, playing tennis, sitting on a beach, and so on. A German court found in her favour in respect of the photographs which, though in a public place, were taken when she had 'sought seclusion'.

But, while accepting that some of the pictures were sufficiently intimate to warrant protection (eg those of her with her children or in the company of a boyfriend sitting at a secluded section of a restaurant courtyard), the court dismissed her complaint in regard to the rest. She turned to the European Court which acknowledged that Article 8 applied, but sought to balance the protection of the Princess's private life against that of freedom of expression as guaranteed by Article 10 of the ECHR. Taking and publishing photographs, it decided, was a subject in which the protection of an individual's rights and reputation assumed especial significance since it did not concern the dissemination of 'ideas', but of images containing personal or even intimate 'information' about that individual. Moreover, pictures published in the tabloid press were frequently snapped in an atmosphere of harassment that generated in the paparazzi's quarry a strong sense of intrusion or even of persecution.[88]

The critical factor in balancing the protection of private life against freedom of expression, the Court held, was the contribution that the published photographs and articles made to a debate of general interest. The pictures of the Princess were, it found, of a purely private nature, taken without her knowledge or consent and, in some instances, in secret. They made no

87. *Douglas v Hello! Ltd* [2001] QB 967.
88. *Von Hannover v Germany* [2004] EMLR 379 (ECtHR).

contribution to a debate of public interest given that she was not engaged in an official function and the photographs and articles related exclusively to details of her private life. Furthermore, while the public might have a right to information, including, in special circumstances, about the private life of public figures, they did not have such a right in this instance. It had no legitimate interest in knowing Princess Caroline's whereabouts or how she behaved in her private life—even in places that could not always be described as secluded. In the same way as there was a commercial interest for the magazines to publish the photographs and articles, those interests had, in the Court's view, to yield to the applicant's right to the effective protection of her private life.

Celebrities—stars of screen, radio, television, pop music, sport, and the catwalk—are regarded as fair game by the paparazzi.[89] Members of the British Royal family, most conspicuously, and tragically, the Princess of Wales, have long been preyed upon by the media. More recently, photographs of the Duchess of Cambridge, taken surreptitiously while she was sunbathing at a private villa in Provence, were published online and in countries other than the United Kingdom.

It is persistently claimed that public figures forfeit their right to privacy. This contention is generally based on the following reasoning. Either it is asserted that celebrities relish publicity when it is favourable, but resent it when it is hostile. They cannot, it is argued, have it both ways. Secondly, the opinion is heard that the media have the right to 'put the record straight'. So, in the case of Naomi Campbell, since she lied about her drug addiction, there is, the Court of Appeal held, a public interest in the press revealing the truth. The first assertion, advanced not surprisingly by the media, is a specious application of the idiom: 'Live by the sword, die by the sword.' It would sound the death knell for the protection of most public figures' private lives. The fact that a celebrity courts publicity—an inescapable feature

---

89. A 'public figure', according to Prosser, is a 'person who, by his accomplishments, fame, or mode of living, or by adopting a profession or calling which gives the public a legitimate interest in his doings, his affairs, and his character, has become a "public personage"', WL Prosser, 'Privacy' (1960) 48 California Law Review 383, 410. German law adopts a sophisticated distinction between 'public persons' who are known as 'persons of contemporary history', and 'private persons'. 'Public persons' are divided into two further sub-categories: an 'absolute public person' such as a head of state and a famous celebrity, and a 'relative public person' who is catapulted into the public eye by, eg, a criminal trial. See BS Markesinis and N Nolte, 'Some Comparative Reflections on the Right of Privacy of Public Figures in Public Places' in P Birks (ed), *Privacy and Loyalty* (Oxford: Oxford University Press, 1997).

of fame—cannot be allowed to annihilate his or her right to shield intimate features of their lives from public view.[90]

Nor is the second argument wholly persuasive. Suppose that a celebrity were HIV-positive or suffering from cancer. Can it really be the case that a legitimate desire on his part to deny that he is a sufferer of one of these diseases may be annihilated by the media's right to 'put the record straight'? If so, the protection of privacy becomes a fragile reed. Truth or falsity should not block the expectation of those who dwell in the glare of public attention.

It is easy to make this criticism; more difficult is to suggest practical solutions. The courts are often faced with complex, always contested, factual, philosophical, and legal issues that do not admit of simple resolution. I do not underestimate the challenges generated by the judicial undertaking involved in striking a balance between the competing rights of victim and media. Since the enactment of the Human Rights Act 1998, they have devised a number of tests in pursuit of this invariably contentious equilibrium. They include the following, each of which I shall briefly examine.

(a) What is 'private'?

Article 8, it will be recalled, refers to 'respect for private and family life...' It does not specify *where* one's life is lived. In other words, at first blush it would seem that in weighing this article against the free speech provisions of Article 10, 'private' would embrace only what occurs in private as opposed to those that take place in public. This is not what the courts have held. Nor is it clear whether the information sought to be protected need be secret or confidential in the sense that it is not a matter of public knowledge. The general conclusion is far from satisfactory, as Gurry points out, a matter may be private

> ...in the sense of being related to one's *private* life, whether known or not by others and whether taking place in public or private. [This] view...has

90. The Leveson Inquiry found 'ample evidence that parts of the press have taken the view that actors, footballers, writers, pop stars—anyone in whom the public might take an interest—are fair game, public property with little, if any, entitlement to any sort of private life or respect for dignity, whether or not there is a true public interest in knowing how they spend their lives. Their families, including their children, are pursued and important personal moments are destroyed. Where there is a genuine public interest in what they are doing, that is one thing; too often, there is not', *An Inquiry into the Culture, Practices and Ethics of the Press* (HC 780, 2012), Executive Summary, para 33.

predominated, largely because of the Strasbourg jurisprudence relating to Article 8 ECHR which itself, after all, refers to 'respect for private and family life…' without imposing any further requirements as to the where such a life is lived or whether such information is secret or not.[91]

Hence, in the case of Naomi Campbell, mentioned earlier, the newspaper had, along with a photograph of her leaving a meeting of NA in a public place with other drug addicts, published the fact that she was an addict for which she had attended NA for some time. Is this truly 'private' information? The House of Lords held that it was. And, in the case of Princess Caroline, the European Court, as we saw earlier, was even more generous in treating her 'interaction' with the world as 'private'. Such expansiveness flows ineluctably, I would contend, from the very phraseology of Article 8 which extends the zone of 'privateness' well beyond the protection of personal information as I should prefer the concept to be understood.[92] I return to this question later.

There are, fortunately, limits to this liberality. Elton John, it was held, had no reasonable expectation of privacy when he was photographed outside his home sporting a tracksuit and baseball cap.[93] But how, one may ask, is this judgment to be reconciled with the case of Princess Caroline going about her business in public?[94] Is there not a line to be drawn in respect of what constitutes 'private' or 'personal'? In Chapter 1, I attempted to demonstrate the perils of privacy inflation. Unless these expressions are confined to what is properly private, the law's protection loses its essential purpose. Part of the difficulty arises, of course, from the wording of Article 8 itself. Its

---

91. Gurry (n 2), 701.
92. It is conceded, of course, that there is no 'bright line' as Gleeson CJ called it in *Australian Broadcasting Corporation v Lenah Game Meats Pty Ltd* (2001) 185 ALR 1, by which to distinguish activities that occur in public, but nevertheless warrant protection. Disclosures relating to children have provided an opportunity for courts to draw clearer borders to the plaintiff's reasonable expectation of privacy. See eg *Murray v Express Newspapers* [2007] EWHC 1908 (photograph of the child of JK Rowling in his pram) in which the Court of Appeal found that a reasonable expectation of privacy arose notwithstanding that the picture was taken in a public place. See too *ETK v News Group Newspapers* [2011] EWCA Civ 439, [2011] 1 WLR 1827.
93. *John v Express Newspapers* [2006] EWHC 1611 (QB), [2006] 2 AC 457. In *Campbell* Baroness Hale drew a distinction between genuinely personal information relating to the supermodel, on the one hand, and 'when she pops out to the shops for a bottle of milk', [2004] UKHL 22, [2004] 2 AC 457. In the case of Elton John, Eady J held that the question of public interest was not engaged; Art 10 prevailed in the absence of the pop-star's Art 8 rights.
94. 'Was Elton John not in his zone of interaction outside his London home in just the same way that Princess Caroline had been?', Gurry (n 2), 703.

formulation of 'respect for private and family life...home and correspondence' opens the door to a wide assortment of activities and information that
do not always chime with an intuitive understanding of privacy. Commenting on the categories of information that, until 2009, had been regarded by
the courts as 'private', Eady J stated that it had

> ...been of a strictly *personal* nature concerning, for example, sexual relation-
> ships, mental or physical health, financial affairs, or the claimant's family or do-
> mestic arrangements. I am not aware of a case in which...there is a significant
> public element in the information sought to be restricted.[95]

That may be so, but even by eliminating 'a significant public element', the
net remains too widely cast.

(b) Are the media entitled to 'put the record straight'?

Superstars and supermodels attract little sympathy when they complain of
media intrusion. They cannot, it is generally maintained, have it both ways.
They bask in the glory of favourable publicity; they cannot therefore legitimately whinge when a disclosure reveals them in a less than satisfactory
light. But this simple judgment neglects the principal purpose of the legal
protection of personal information against its gratuitous disclosure. A law
that purports to defend the individual against unwanted publicity fails in
that objective when it is founded on this popular, but misconceived, notion.
There is, a fortiori, even less sympathy for public figures that lie. Indeed,
Miss Campbell conceded at trial that because she had lied about her drug
addiction, the media had a right to put the record straight. There is a public
interest in the media revealing the truth. She was

> ...a well-known figure who courts rather than shuns publicity, described as a
> role model for other young women, who had consistently lied about her drug
> addiction and compared herself favourably with others in the fashion business
> who were regular users of drugs. By these actions she had forfeited the protec-
> tion to which she would otherwise have been entitled and made the informa-
> tion about her addiction and treatment a matter of legitimate public comment
> on which the press were entitled to put the record straight.[96]

---

95. *Author of a Blog v Times Newspapers* [2009] EWHC 1358 (QB). The court declined to prevent
the disclosure of the identity of an anonymous blogger as it did not constitute private information.
96. *Campbell v MGN Ltd* [2004] UKHL 22.

One might have hoped that this question had been laid to rest following the criticism of the judgments in *Woodward v Hutchins*.[97] Yet this argument reared its head again in *Campbell* where both the Court of Appeal and the House of Lords accepted that the media had the right to 'put the record straight'. Since Miss Campbell lied about her drug addiction, there was, the courts both held, a public interest in the press revealing the truth. As stated earlier, it is difficult to accept this view.

It is arguable that under Lord Steyn's 'new approach' with its 'intense focus' on the relative importance of competing rights, 'putting the record straight' has lost a good deal of its power.[98] It is likely to work against a claimant only where he or she has exhibited a degree of hypocrisy or mendacity that the media has exposed.

(c) Is it relevant that the claimant is a 'role model'?

The putative public interest that arises under this head is closely related to (b). The claim that the claimant is a role model, especially to the young, is premised on the same consideration that animates the right of the media to put the record straight.[99] It is therefore subject to similar objection. Why should an individual, whether or not he or she happens to be a celebrity, forfeit Article 8 protection on the ground that those who regard such persons—frequently sportsmen—are 'let down' by their behaviour. Is it really 'self-evident', as Lord Woolf put it, that a famous footballer's activities off the field have 'a modicum of public interest...[because they] are role

---

97. [1977] 1 WLR 760. Not only by this author: Wacks (n 26), but, later, by others, see R Toulson and C Phipps, *Confidentiality*, 2nd edn (London: Sweet & Maxwell, 2006), paras 6.09 and 6.24, and *Tugendhat and Christie on the Law of Privacy and the Media*, 2nd edn (M Warby, N Moreham, and I Christie eds) (Oxford: Oxford University Press, 2011), paras 12.28 and 12.30. Bridge LJ (at 765) added, 'those who seek and welcome publicity of every kind bearing upon their private lives so long as it shows them in a favourable light are in no position to complain of an invasion of their privacy by publicity which shows them in an unfavourable light.' Similar sentiments were expressed by Roskill LJ in *Khashoggi v Smith* (1980) 130 NLJ 168. Such a position all but extinguishes the privacy rights of celebrities, and must be rejected.

98. Thus in *McKennitt v Ash* [2005] EWCA Civ 1714, [2008] QB 73, Eady J proposed that the limitation might apply where the plaintiff had exhibited 'a very high degree of misbehaviour', though the Court of Appeal regarded this test as too stringent: [2008] QB 73, [69].

99. All three elements—courting publicity, setting the record straight, and being a role model—merged in *Theakston v MGN* [2002] EWHC 137 (QB). The newspaper disclosed that the claimant (a children's TV presenter) had visited a brothel. The court held that there was a public interest in the publication of this fact, particularly in respect of the last factor, since children looked up to him as a person of probity.

models for young people and undesirable behaviour on their part can set an unfortunate example'?[100]

The former captain of the England football team failed to prevent the publication of details of his adulterous affair on the ground that, since in a press interview and his autobiography, he had asserted that he had abandoned his womanizing, there was a public interest in revealing that this was a false image. Yet, unlike Naomi Campbell, there was no evidence of mendacity by Ferdinand. What was the 'false image' that he had projected? It would seem that it was his assertion that he was a reformed man. But that 'image', the court appeared to accept, was falsified by contact—through text messaging—with a woman that he had known since his teenage years. A disquieting aspect of the judgment is the assumption that merely because the holder of the position of England captain is perceived by some as being a role model, such an individual's right to privacy is diminished. It is hard to see how the public interest is served by a disclosure of this kind.

More difficult, but no less troubling, is the decision with (yet another) football connection. A former manager of the England team sought to prevent publication by a newspaper of his adulterous affair. The woman involved had apparently disclosed the details to the newspaper (though it is not clear whether she sold the story to the paper). The Court of Appeal declined to award an injunction to the claimant. Lindblom J acknowledged that McClaren was a public figure, but was willing to disregard the fact that the journalist had acted furtively:

> Even if one allows for the degree of difference there must be between the position of a former manager and that of a serving captain of England's football team, he is clearly still a prominent public figure who has held positions of responsibility in the national game. Whether or not the defendant's story was a set-up—involving, as it did, a photograph taken surreptitiously by a journalist who seems to have been told where the claimant and SA would be—I saw as no more than peripheral to the balancing exercise I had to carry out.[101]

What seems to have counted against the claimant was the fact that some six years before he had conducted another extramarital relationship with his secretary. Details were published in *The Sun* when he was being considered for the position of England football manager. However, he did not

---

100. *A v B plc* [2002] EWCA Civ 337, [2003] QB 195. See too *Hutcheson (formerly known as KGM) v News Group Newspapers Ltd* [2012] EMLR 2.
101. *Steve McClaren v News Group Newspapers Ltd* [2012] EWHC 2466 (QB).

on that occasion attempt to prevent publication by seeking an injunction. More significantly, he sold this story through his publicity agent for £12,500.[102]

Should the claimant's readiness to publicize his previous infidelity (albeit self-seeking) constitute a bar to relief? I submit not. Nor is it clear why the court regarded the surreptitious manner in which the facts were garnered, or perhaps even the element of entrapment, as extraneous to the decision.

The Court of Appeal in *Campbell* retreated from the 'role model' argument, at least in its strong form as adopted in *Theakston* and *A v B plc*. Delivering the judgment of the court, Lord Phillips MR declared that 'the fact that an individual has achieved prominence on the public stage does not mean his private life can be laid bare by the media. We do not see why it should necessarily be in the public interest that an individual who has been adopted as a role model, without seeking this distinction, should be demonstrated to have feet of clay.'[103]

In *von Hannover v Germany*[104] the European Court recognized a 'fundamental distinction' 'between reporting facts—even controversial ones—capable of contributing to a debate in a democratic society relating to politicians in the exercise of their functions, for example, and reporting details of the private life of an individual.'[105] It added that 'the decisive factor in balancing the protection of private life against freedom of expression should lie in the contribution that the published photos and articles make to a debate of general interest.'[106] It rejected the argument that because she

---

102. *Steve McClaren v News Group Newspapers Ltd* [2012] EWHC 2466 (QB).
103. [2002] EWCA Civ 1373, [2003] QB 633, [41]. The House of Lords did not directly address this question.
104. App 59320/00 (2005) 40 EHRR 1.
105. App 59320/00 (2005) 40 EHRR 1 at [63].
106. App 59320/00 (2005) 40 EHRR 1 at [76]. The Court drew a 'fundamental distinction' between reporting facts that may contribute to 'a debate in a democratic society' relating to politicians in the exercise of their 'public functions', on the one hand, and reporting details of the private life of one who exercises no 'official function', [63]. In the former case, it opined, the media exercises its essential 'watchdog' role. In the latter case, it does not. Thus, the Court concluded, since the pictures and article in question pertained to Princess Caroline's private life, they did not fall within the sphere of public debate, and hence cannot 'be deemed to contribute to any debate of general interest to society', [65]. They are therefore not protected by Art 10. This reasoning is perplexing—both for its adoption of the a priori assumption that public figures *ipso facto* forfeit Art 8 protection, and because it confines the notion of 'public figure' to those who perform official functions. In *Edward Rocknroll v News Group Newspapers Ltd* [2013] EWHC 24 (Ch), the husband of the newly married actress Kate Winslet was held not to be a public figure. He was granted an injunction against *The Sun* which sought to publish photographs taken in 2010 at a private fancy dress party at which the claimant,

was a 'figure of contemporary society *par excellence*' there was a legitimate public interest in her comings and goings.[107]

The extent to which a role model surrendered her privacy arose in *McKennitt v Ash*[108] where the former friend of the Canadian folk singer published a book, *Travels with Loreena McKennitt*. The singer sought to restrain further publication of the work. Eady J granted an injunction despite the defendant's reliance on *A v B plc* that the claimant was a role model.[109] The Court of Appeal upheld the decision, Buxton LJ holding that the court was not bound by *A v B plc*. In the course of his judgment he expressed reservations about the 'role model' argument as stated by Lord Woolf in *A v B plc*:

> First, as to the position of Ms McKennitt, she clearly does not fall within the first category mentioned by Lord Woolf, and 'hold a position where higher standards of conduct can be rightly expected by the public': that is no doubt the preserve of headmasters and clergymen, who according to taste may be joined by politicians, senior civil servants, surgeons and journalists. Second, although on one view Ms McKennitt comes within Lord Woolf's second class, of involuntary role models, I respectfully share the doubts of Lord Phillips...as to the validity of that concept; and it would in any event seem difficult to include in the class a person such as Ms McKennitt, who has made such efforts not to hold herself out as someone whose life is an open book. Third, it is clear that Lord Woolf thought that role models were at risk, or most at risk, of having to put up with the reporting of *disreputable* conduct: such as was the conduct of claimant before him. Ms McKennitt does not fall into that category...[110]

The claimant not only belonged to none of these groups, but she had always striven to protect her privacy.

In *Mosley v News Group Newspapers*[111] the claimant, President of Federation Internationale de l'Automobile (FIA), had engaged in sado-masochistic

---

Edward Rocknroll, by his own admission, indulged in 'rather silly, schoolboy-like behaviour', [6]. Briggs J concluded that 'nothing in the conduct of the claimant which the Photographs portray gives rise to any matter of genuine public debate, however widely drawn is the circle within which such matters may genuinely arise', [33].

107. The question of whether she was a role model did not arise. It is at least arguable that, no less than celebrity footballers, the Princess might be a role model to her subjects or others. This argument seems not to have been advanced by the media. A helpful, comprehensive analysis of this—and other—aspects of the decision is provided by H Fenwick and G Phillipson, *Media Freedom under the Human Rights Act* (Oxford: Oxford University Press, 2006), 671 ff.

108. [2006] EWCA Civ 1714, [2008] QB 73.

109. [2003] QB 195 (CA).

110. [2007] 3 WLR 194, [65].

111. [2008] EWHC 1777 (QB).

activities which were surreptitiously filmed by one of the participants. She also gave an interview to the *News of the World* which was published under the heading 'F1 Boss has Sick Nazi Orgy with 5 Hookers'. An edited version of the video was uploaded to the tabloid's website. Between 30 and 31 March 2008 it had been viewed over 1.4 million times, while the online version of the article had been visited some 400,000 times. On 31 March the newspaper removed the edited video footage voluntarily from its website, and undertook not to show the images again without 24 hours' notice. A second article was published on 6 April 2008. On 9 April Eady J declined an application for an interim injunction to prevent further publication since the material was already in the public domain.

Mosley's action was based, in part, on breach of confidence arising out of a pre-existing relationship.[112] In respect of Article 8, Eady J accepted that in the case of photography, the mere fact of clandestine recording may be regarded as an intrusion, and an improper violation of Article 8. And he treated the subsequent publication of the material as a separate issue. The newspaper pleaded public interest in disclosure, and that Article 10 ought to prevail. The public interest as originally framed concerned the allegation that the S&M session involved Nazi or concentration camp role-play. This was subsequently widened to include the assertion that the acts involved illegality: assault occasioning actual bodily harm and brothel-keeping. The public interest, it was argued, related to Mosley being a role model as President of the FIA. On the evidence, Eady J found that the S&M session did not involve a Nazi theme. He accepted that the claimant's Article 8 rights had been engaged. As to the defendant's rights under Article 10, it was argued that Mosley's behaviour exhibited depravity and adultery; there was therefore a clear public interest in its disclosure. Eady J gave this moralistic contention short shrift:

> The modern approach to personal privacy and to sexual preferences and practices is different from that of past generations. First there is a greater willingness…to accord respect to an individual's right to conduct his or her personal life without state interference or condemnation. It has to be recognized that sexual conduct is a significant aspect of human life in respect of which people should be free to choose…It is important in this new rights-based jurisprudence to ensure that where breaches occur remedies are not refused because

112. See Chapter 4.

an individual journalist or judge finds the conduct distasteful or contrary to moral or religious teaching...'[113]

The *ratio* would seem to be that there is no 'open season' in respect of the privacy even of 'voluntary' role models. The test by which the public interest is to be judged is whether, as held in *von Hannover*, the disclosure makes a genuine contribution to the debate on matters of general interest and not 'vapid tittle-tattle'.[114]

The law is unambiguous: the media has a right—and often a duty—to report on matters that relate to or affect the ability, or indeed the suitability, of those public figures. So, whereas Princess Caroline succeeded in the case mentioned earlier, in 2012 the Court held that images of her and her husband on a skiing holiday in 2002, published beside an article regarding the health of her father, Prince Rainier III of Monaco, did not violate her privacy. The health of the reigning prince was, it declared, a subject of general interest and the media were entitled to report on 'the manner in which his children reconciled their obligations of family solidarity with the legitimate needs of their private life, among which was the desire to go on holiday'.[115]

---

113. [2008] EWHC 1777 (QB), [125]. He added, 'judges need to be wary about giving the impression that they are ventilating while affording or denying legal redress because of some personal moral or social views and especially at a time when society is less homogenous than in the past...a judge like anyone else is obviously entitled to hold personal moral views about the issues of the day but it is important not to let them intrude when interpreting and applying the law...', quoting *CC v AB* [2007] EMLR 11, [25].

114. Baroness Hale's felicitous phrase in *Jameel v Wall Street Journal* [2006] UKHL 44, [2007] 1 AC 359, [147] in which the House of Lords reiterated the 'general obligation of the press, media and other publishers to communicate important information upon matters of general public interest and the general right of the public to receive such information' established in *Reynolds v Times Newspapers Ltd* [2001] 2 AC 127, the so-called '*Reynolds* defence'. See too *Flood v Times Newspapers Ltd* [2012] UKSC 11 in which the Supreme Court unanimously supported a robust public interest defence. Lord Phillips stressed 'a need for care when applying to the law of defamation decisions on the tension between article 8 and article 10 in other contexts. The fact remains, however, that the creation of *Reynolds* privilege reflected a recognition on the part of the House of Lords that the existing law of defamation did not cater adequately for the importance of the article 10 right of freedom of expression', [46].

115. *Von Hannover v Germany (No 2)* [2012] ECHR 228. See too *Standard Verlags v Austria* App 21277/05 (2008) 47 EHRR 58 in which the European Court upheld the *von Hannover* distinction between 'information concerning the health of a politician...and idle gossip about the state of his or marriage or alleged extra-marital relationships.' 'Kiss and tell' stories are rarely likely to satisfy this test.

It does not follow, however, that a claimant's apparently inconsequential or trivial personal information will fail to be protected under Article 8, or indeed that its disclosure may not be in the public interest.[116]

(d) How far is the judgment of the media relevant?

It is unquestionably the case that many decisions of editors and journalists are made under pressure. As Lord Hoffmann declared in *Campbell*,

> The practical exigencies of journalism demand that some latitude must be given. Editorial decisions have to be made quickly and with less information than is available to a court which afterwards reviews the matter at leisure. And if any margin is to be allowed, it seems to me strange to hold the *Mirror* liable in damages for a decision which three experienced judges in the Court of Appeal have held to be perfectly justified.[117]

This does not, however, mean that the subjective judgment of the media, however sincerely held, is determinative of whether publication is in the public interest.[118] In *Reynolds*, Lord Nicholls suggested that, in the context of defamation,

> ...matters to be taken into account include the following. The comments are illustrative only.
>
> 1. The seriousness of the allegation. The more serious the charge, the more the public is misinformed and the individual harmed, if the allegation is not true.
>
> 2. The nature of the information, and the extent to which the subject-matter is a matter of public concern.
>
> 3. The source of the information. Some informants have no direct knowledge of the events. Some have their own axes to grind, or are being paid for their stories.
>
> 4. The steps taken to verify the information.
>
> 5. The status of the information. The allegation may have already been the subject of an investigation which commands respect.

---

116. *Rio Ferdinand v MGN* [2011] EWHC 2454 (QB) where adultery by the former captain of England's football team was held to be in the public interest, partly, it seems, because a former captain had been dismissed for his adulterous affair, and because such individuals were role models to young supporters.

117. *Campbell v MGN Ltd* [2004] UKHL 22, [2004] AC 457, [62]. It is inevitable—and not without justification—that the media, in order to 'spice up' a story, add colour in the form of background facts or images. But there are limits, as recognized by the House of Lords: [113] per Lord Hope.

118. It is, of course, ultimately a matter for the court to decide.

6. The urgency of the matter. News is often a perishable commodity.

7. Whether comment was sought from the plaintiff. He may have information others do not possess or have not disclosed. An approach to the plaintiff will not always be necessary.

8. Whether the article contained the gist of the plaintiff's side of the story.

9. The tone of the article. A newspaper can raise queries or call for an investigation. It need not adopt allegations as statements of fact.

10. The circumstances of the publication, including the timing.

This list is not exhaustive...A balancing operation is better carried out by a judge in a reasoned judgment than by a jury. Over time, a valuable corpus of case law will be built up.[119]

These principles might similarly be applied, *mutatis mutandis*, in respect of the publication of personal information. Tugendhat J remarked in the *John Terry* case, that there was 'an uncertainty in the law of misuse of private information (and for that matter the law of confidence). The uncertainty is the extent to which, if at all, the belief of a person threatening to make a publication in the media is relevant on the issue of public interest.'[120]

He added that paragraph 3 of Press Complaints Committee's Code that requires editors to demonstrate that they 'reasonably believed that publication...would be in the public interest' (see later) might be relevant, or even s 32 of the Data Protection Act 1998 which provides that, in the case of the processing of data relating to journalism, literature, and art, the data controller 'reasonably believes that, having regard in particular to the special importance of the public interest in freedom of expression, publication would be in the public interest.'[121] It is indeed possible, he added, that 'the Data Protection Act might well apply to a newspaper publication, and in particular to an online publication. If that Act did apply, it would be anomalous if the public interest defence under s 32 required the court to have regard to the reasonable belief of the journalist, but that the same defence under the general law did not. I cannot decide that any reasonable belief on the part of a journalist or editor would be irrelevant without hearing argument for that proposition, if it is to be advanced.'[122] I consider the application of this statute later.

119. *Reynolds v Times Newspapers* [2001] 2 AC 127, 205.
120. *LNS (John Terry) v Persons Unknown* [2010] EWHC 119 (QB), [2010] EMLR 16, [70].
121. *LNS (John Terry) v Persons Unknown* [2010] EWHC 119 (QB), [2010] EMLR 16, [72]. See text following n 168.
122. *LNS (John Terry) v Persons Unknown* [2010] EWHC 119 (QB), [2010] EMLR 16, [73].

It does not seem unreasonable for courts to enquire whether when defending a breach of an individual's privacy, the media's claim that publication
is in the public interest is merely a mask to conceal their avarice, prurience,
or even malice. Suffice it to say here that while the defendant's motives are
acknowledged as a factor to be considered in determining the genuineness
of an assertion of public interest, the moral dimension does not appear to
weigh as heavily with courts and commentators in privacy cases as it does
in actions for breach of confidence. (See Chapter 2.)

Is the claimant a public figure?

As mentioned earlier, the protection afforded to public figures may be
somewhat reduced. The precise extent turns obviously on the facts of each
case, though there is a tension between the Strasbourg approach in *von Hannover* and the more charitable view expressed in *Campbell*. It is clear that,
though most claimants thus far have been royalty or drawn from the world
of sport, fashion, and entertainment, politicians or high-profile businessmen
are liable to be accorded less protection:

> The free exchange of information and ideas on matters relevant to the or-
> ganisation of the economic, social and political life of the country is crucial to
> any democracy. Without this, it can scarcely be called a democracy at all. This
> includes revealing information about public figures, especially those in elective
> office, which would otherwise be private but is relevant to their participation
> in public life.[123]

The age of the victim is not necessarily a bar to relief.[124]

Balancing the rights

Is it possible to formulate a coherent theory of free speech which is
both sufficiently broad to capture the complexities of the exercise of the

---

123. *Campbell v MGN Ltd* [2004] UKHL 22, [148] per Baroness Hale. See *Rocknroll v News Group
Newspapers Ltd* [2013] EWHC 24 (Ch).
124. In *Spelman v Express Newspapers* [2012] EWHC 355 (QB) the claimant was a 17-year-old. He
had played rugby at international level. Tugendhat J observed that it is 'a condition of partici-
pating in high level sport that the participant gives up control over many aspects of private
life', [69], adding that the 'restriction on what might otherwise be a reasonable expectation of
privacy may well apply to those who aim for the highest level, even if they do not achieve it,

freedom, and sufficiently specific to account for its variable applications? The argument from democracy attracts greater support than the Millian or autonomy-based theories, but all provide at best only the most general guidance in respect of the legitimate controls on the public disclosure of personal information by the media.

An interest-based theory that specifies the particular interests of the parties involved in the disclosure raises numerous difficulties (not unlike the interest-based accounts of privacy). And, while it is useful to distinguish, say, the 'personality' interests involved when private facts are published from the 'reputational' interests affected by defamatory publications or the 'commercial' interests affected by breaches of confidence, this approach fails to explain which species of information warrant protection in the face of the competing claims of free speech.

The US Supreme Court has, in mediating between the two interests, resorted to the process of 'balancing' by which the interest in free speech is weighed against other interests such as national security, public order, and so on. If such interests are found to be 'compelling' or 'substantial', or where there is a 'clear and present danger' that the speech will cause significant harm to the public interest, the Court will uphold the restriction of free speech.

The dynamics of limitation

This is Emerson's phrase. He uses it to describe the proposition that the public interest in the freedom of expression must fit in to a 'more comprehensive scheme of social values and social goals'.[125] So far, I have touched on the inapplicability of certain free speech justifications; I have allowed the right of privacy to escape unscathed. Where there is a genuine conflict between the two values how is privacy to be protected? Or, in other words, why should free speech be subordinated to the protection of personal information? In what circumstances might the absolute protection of free speech be moderated? Emerson suggests three. The first is where the injury is direct and peculiar to the individual, rather than one suffered in common with

or can no longer expect to achieve it', [70]. The claimant was 'a person who is to be regarded as exercising a public function', [72].

125. T Emerson, 'Towards a General Theory of the First Amendment' (1963) 72 Yale Law Journal 877, 881 and, generally, 887–93.

others. The second is when the interest is an intimate and personal one; embracing an area of privacy from which both the state and other individuals should be excluded. The third consideration is whether or not society leaves the burden of protecting the interest to the individual by, for example, recognizing that he or she has a legal cause of action.

In the first two circumstances the harm is likely to be direct and irremediable. Moreover, if the individual has the burden of establishing his or her case, the resources of the state are less likely to be marshalled into a coherent apparatus for the restriction of free speech. He proposes that 'so long as the interest of privacy is genuine, the conditions of recovery clearly defined, and the remedy left to the individual suit, it is most unlikely that the balance will be tipped too far toward restriction of expression.'[126] Even against the background of the First Amendment, Emerson's approach is persuasive.

The public interest—again

Uncovering rational criteria by which to make this controversial judgment presents a perennial challenge. In respect of the misuse of personal information, some of the following considerations would seem to be relevant. To whom was the information given? Is the victim a public figure? Was he or she in a public place? Is the information in the public domain? How was the information acquired? Was it essential for the victim's identity to be revealed? Was the invasion a serious one? What were the publisher's motives in disclosing the information?

In the United States, publishers need only to raise the defence of public interest or newsworthiness for it generally to demolish the protection against the publication of private facts by the media.[127] Thus in *Sidis* the court declared that 'at some point the public interest in obtaining information becomes dominant over the individual's desire for privacy.'[128] The privilege is defined in the *Restatement (Second) of the Law of Torts* as extending to information 'of legitimate concern to the public'—a conclusion which is reached by weighing the competing interests of the public's right to know

---

126. Emerson (n 125), 881 and, generally, 887–93.
127. US courts employ the term 'newsworthiness' synonymously with 'legitimate public interest', 'legitimate public concern', or matters of 'public significance'. See eg *Shulman v Group W Productions, Inc*, 955 P2d 469 (Cal 1998), *passim*.
128. *Sidis v F-R Publishing Corporation*, 113 F2d 806, 809 (2nd Cir 1940). The facts are recounted in the text at n 156.

against the individual's right to keep private facts from the public's gaze. This may be decided by the judge, as a matter of law or, more often, by the jury as a question of fact. The test embodied in the *Restatement*, reads as follows,

> In determining what comprises a matter of legitimate public interest, account must be taken of the customs and conventions of the community; and in the last analysis what is proper becomes a matter of the community mores. The line is to be drawn when the publicity ceases to be the giving of information to which the public is entitled, and becomes a morbid and sensational prying into private lives for its own sake, with which a reasonable member of the public, with decent standards, would say that he had no concern.[129]

The categories of information which are newsworthy have steadily expanded as the courts have become increasingly conscious of the free speech implications of censoring accurate reporting. Sexual matters—understandably—predominate. This is illustrated by two Californian cases. In the first an ex-marine became the subject of intense media interest when he foiled an assassination attempt on President Ford. The *San Francisco Chronicle* revealed that Sipple was a prominent member of the gay community, which indeed was true, but he brought an action under the tort of private facts disclosure because he claimed that he had always kept his homosexuality private from his relatives. The court dismissed his action on two grounds. First, the information was already in the public domain and, secondly, it held that the facts disclosed were newsworthy because the exposé was fuelled by the wish to combat the stereotyping of gays as 'timid, weak and unheroic', and to discuss the potential biases of the President (one newspaper had suggested that the President's reticence in thanking Sipple was on account of the latter's homosexuality).

In the other case, a newspaper article revealed that the first female student body president of a Californian college, Diaz, was a transsexual. The court held that her transsexuality was a private fact and also that, although she was involved in a public controversy (in that she accused the college of misuse of student funds), the disclosure was irrelevant to that issue and, accordingly, not newsworthy. The court emphasized that the purpose of First Amendment protection was 'to keep the public informed so that they may make intelligent decisions on matters important to self-governing people.' It was further explained that 'the fact that she is a transsexual does not adversely

---

129. *Restatement (Second) of the Law of Torts* (Philadelphia, PA: American Law Institute, 1977), para 652B, comment h.

reflect on her honesty or judgment. Nor does the fact that she was the first woman student body president, in itself, warrant that her entire private life be open to public inspection.'

How are these two decisions to be reconciled? The answer may lie in the tenor of the Diaz article. The newspaper argued that the report was intended to portray the 'changing roles of women in society'. But as Elwood points out,[130] it was clear from the tone of the article that the author's objective stopped at the 'stark revelation'.[131] An important feature of both *Diaz* and *Sipple* is that the articles purported to portray alternative lifestyles. As Joseph Raz has argued,

> An important case for the importance of freedom of expression arises out of the fact that public portrayal and expression of forms of life validate the styles of life portrayed, and that censoring expression normally expresses authoritative condemnation not merely of the views or opinions censored but of the whole style of life of which they are a part.[132]

It is therefore arguable that, if the article about Diaz had seriously intended to portray the changing role of women in society, the court would not have censored it.

As suggested earlier, the US test of 'newsworthiness' appears to be needlessly complex. Whether a publication is newsworthy looks like a second-order question which then collapses into a first-order enquiry into the extent to which it is in the public interest. In other words, it is superfluous. Consider, for example, the following judicial attempt to apply the test:

> Newsworthiness—constitutional or common law—is also difficult to define because it may be used as either a descriptive or a normative term...A position at either extreme has unpalatable consequences. If 'newsworthiness' is completely descriptive—if all coverage that sells papers or boosts ratings is deemed newsworthy—it would seem to swallow the publication of private facts tort...At the other extreme, if newsworthiness is viewed as a purely normative

---

130. See JP Elwood, 'Outing, Privacy, and the First Amendment' (1992) 102 Yale Law Journal 747, 759; D Zimmerman, 'Requiem for a Heavyweight: A Farewell to Warren and Brandeis' Privacy Tort' (1983) 68 Cornell Law Review 291 and, generally, *Restatement* (n 129), para 652D, comments d, g.

131. The article ran, 'The students at the College of Alameda will be surprised to learn [that] their student body president, Toni Diaz, is no lady, but is in fact a man whose real name is Antonio. Now I realize, that in these times, such a matter is no big deal, but I suspect his female classmates in PE 97 may wish to make other showering arrangements', Elwood (n 130), 766).

132. J Raz, 'Free Expression and Personal Identification' (1991) 2 Oxford Journal of Legal Studies 303, 310.

concept, the courts could become to an unacceptable degree editors of the news and self-appointed guardians of public taste.[133]

To what extent does the status of the subject of the private-facts disclosure affect the application of the newsworthiness defence?[134] Elwood suggests that it does, and further identifies a dichotomy between 'limited-purpose public figures and general-purpose public figures'.[135] The former, those who have voluntarily injected themselves or been drawn into a particular public controversy, lose their right to privacy in respect of 'the events that made them famous'.[136] Diaz, as the first female student body president, became 'a public figure for some purposes'[137] but not in respect of her sexuality, which, accordingly, she was entitled to keep private.

Celebrities

Our planet is star-struck. The most trivial item of gossip about a celebrity seems to excite huge interest and fascination. News stands are crammed with magazines devoted to the unremitting supply of these ephemeral, mostly trivial, facts. Does US law allow stardom to extinguish privacy? Though the *Restatement* comments that 'there may be some intimate details of her life, such as sexual relations, which even the actress is entitled to keep to herself',[138] the decision in *Ann-Margret v High Society Magazine, Inc* illustrates that this delicacy has not yet been embraced by the courts. In that case, an actress was denied relief in respect of the publication of a nude photograph of her, partly because the photograph was of 'a woman who has occupied the fantasies of many movie-goers' and therefore 'of great interest to many

---

133. *Shulman v Group W Productions, Inc*, 955 P2d 469 (Cal 1998). Werdegar J here draws on 'Comment, The Right of Privacy: Normative-Descriptive Confusion in the Defense of Newsworthiness' (1963) 30 University of Chicago Law Review 722, 725 where the writer asks, 'Is the term "newsworthy" a descriptive predicate, intended to refer to the fact there is widespread public interest? Or is it a value predicate, intended to indicate that the publication is a meritorious contribution and that the public's interest is praiseworthy?' This seems unduly complex. Why not simply cut to the test of public interest, avoiding a second layer of enquiry? As to its precise nature, it is surely the latter. But see E Volokh, 'Freedom of Speech and Information Privacy: The Troubling Implications of a Right to Stop People from Speaking About You' (2000) 52 Stanford Law Review 1049. See Chapter 8.
134. See Chapter 3.
135. Elwood (n 130), 759.
136. Elwood (n 130), 759. See *Restatement* (n 129), para 652D, comment f.
137. *Diaz*, 188 Cal Rptr 762, 772–3 (1983).
138. *Restatement* (n 129), para 652B, comment h.

people'.[139] The chief ground upon which celebrities are denied protection is that they have consented to publicity and, thus, have waived their right to privacy.

Prosser and Keaton enumerate three criteria which must be satisfied to support a finding of implied assumption of risk for *private* figures: the conduct must manifest consent, the risk must be encountered voluntarily, and the risk must be encountered with full knowledge and appreciation.[140] The case law demonstrates that, for private figures, consent must be, at the very least, implied by conduct.[141] Unfortunately, these cases are not followed when the plaintiff is a celebrity. Elwood argues that 'volition' is lacking in many of the cases, for example in *Sidis* where the plaintiff's entry into the public arena was precipitated by his graduation from college at 16 years of age.[142] He contends that if the courts consider a plaintiff's privacy in respect of a certain revelation not to have been waived, they take pains to find that he or she was not a celebrity rather than holding that the newsworthiness test has not been satisfied.[143] There is a need, under general tort law,[144] for the plaintiff to have knowledge not just of the general risk, but of the specific risk that caused his or her harm for waiver to apply. Elwood submits that, accordingly, waiver should never be implied for sex-related disclosures.[145]

Zimmerman asserts that the courts are most reluctant to examine the boundaries between First Amendment protected and unprotected speech.[146] As Justice Powell commented in *Gertz*, the use of a newsworthiness test,

> ...would occasion the additional difficulty of forcing state and federal judges to decide on an ad hoc basis which publications address issues of 'general or public interest' and which do not—to determine, in the words of Marshall J,

139. 498 F Supp 401, 405 (1980).
140. *Prosser and Keaton on Torts*, 5th edn (St Paul, MN: West Publishing Co., 1984), 484–92.
141. Eg *McCabe v Village Voice, Inc,* 550 F Supp 525 (1982) (plaintiff's consent to having his photograph taken for the purposes of the photographer writing a book did not extend to its publication in a weekly newspaper).
142. Elwood (n 130), 761.
143. Elwood (n 130), 761, noting T Gerety, 'Redefining Privacy' (1977) 12 Harvard Civil Rights–Civil Liberties Law Review 233, 295 (who concludes that the Supreme Court's reluctance to find the plaintiff a public figure in *Time, Inc v Firestone*, 424 US 448 (1976): 'derives from the legitimate concern that as to sexual intimacy at least none of the parties in fact intended to waive their rights to privacy').
144. Referring to Prosser (n 140), para 68, p 487.
145. Elwood (n 130), 761. Compare the approach adopted in *Theakston v MGN Ltd* [2002] EWHC 137 (QB) in Chapter 4.
146. Zimmerman (n 130), 353.

'what information is relevant to self-government'. We doubt the wisdom of committing this task to the conscience of judges.[147]

Zimmerman therefore claims that the courts simply accept the judgment of the press as to what is newsworthy.[148] But her suggestion that 'deference to the judgment of the press may actually be the appropriate and principled response to the newsworthiness enquiry'[149] overlooks the reason why the subject is contentious at all. She observes that 'the economic survival of publishers and broadcasters depends upon their ability to provide a product that the public will buy'[150] and argues that marketplace competition breeds into the papers a 'responsiveness to what substantial segments of the population want to know to cope with the society in which they live.'[151] Courts, Zimmerman suggests, simply accept the judgment of the press as to what is newsworthy, adding that 'deference to the judgment of the press may actually be the appropriate and principled response to the newsworthiness enquiry.'[152] But this neglects the reason why the subject is contentious at all. She observes that 'the economic survival of publishers and broadcasters depends upon their ability to provide a product that the public will buy',[153] and argues that marketplace competition breeds into the papers a 'responsiveness to what substantial segments of the population want to know to cope with the society in which they live.'[154]

---

147. 418 US 323, 346 (1974).
148. Zimmerman (n 130), 353, citing eg *Jenkins v Dell Publishing Co*, 251 F2d 447 (3d Cir 1958).
149. Zimmerman (n 130), 353.
150. Zimmerman (n 130), 353.
151. Zimmerman (n 130), 353–4.
152. Zimmerman (n 130), 353–4.
153. Zimmerman (n 130), 353–4. Echoes of Lord Woolf CJ's remark in *A v B plc* [2003] QB 195, [11], where he suggested that the courts should not overlook the fact that unless newspapers publish information in which the public is interested, there will be fewer newspapers, which will not be in the public interest. The Court of Appeal has since distanced itself from this position, stating that Lord Woolf's view is irreconcilable with the decision of the European Court of Human Rights in *von Hannover v Germany* (2005) 40 EHRR 1, which cautioned against equating what is interesting to the public (and hence in the commercial interests of the press to publish) with what may be in the public interest to know: *McKennitt v Ash* [2008] QB 73, [62] per Buxton LJ. Later decisions (eg *Re British Broadcasting Corporation* [2010] 1 AC 145 and *Re Guardian News and Media Ltd* [2010] 2 AC 697) have clarified this question by acknowledging that while the public interest in an economically viable press cannot justify the publication of private information that does not contribute to a debate of general social import, where the information relates to a matter of genuine public interest, such as court proceedings (*Independent News and Media Ltd v A* [2010] 1 WLR 2262) or law reform (*Re Attorney General's Reference (No 3 of 1999)* [2010] 1 AC 145), the commercial viability of the press may be a germane consideration in relation to the extent to which private information may legitimately be published.
154. Zimmerman (n 130), 353–4.

The concept of public interest all too easily camouflages the commercial motives of the media. Worse, it masquerades as the democratic exercise of consumer choice: we get the sensationalism we deserve. Moreover, both forms of cynical 'tabloidism' neglect the consequences for individuals who happen to be public figures who are unfortunate enough to be catapulted into the public eye.

A mores test

To evaluate what is 'highly offensive', the US courts have developed what has been called a mores test. Thus, in *Melvin v Reid*[155] the plaintiff's past as a prostitute and defendant in a sensational murder trial was revealed in a film called *The Red Kimono* which was based on these events. She had, in the eight years since her acquittal, been accepted into 'respectable society', married, and moved in a circle of friends who were ignorant of her past. Her action for the invasion of her privacy caused by the defendant's truthful disclosures was sustained by the California court (which had not hitherto recognized an action for invasion of privacy).

In *Sidis v F-R Publishing Corporation*,[156] on the other hand, the plaintiff, a former child prodigy who, at 11, lectured in mathematics at Harvard, had become a recluse and devoted his time to studying the Okamakammessett Indians and collecting streetcar transfers. The *New Yorker* published an article, 'Where Are They Now? April Fool' written by James Thurber under a pseudonym. Details of Sidis's physical characteristics and mannerisms, the single room in which he lived, and his current activities were revealed. The magazine article acknowledged that Sidis had informed the reporter who had tracked him down for the interview, that he lived in fear of publicity and changed jobs whenever his employer or fellow workers learned of his past. The New York District Court denied his action for invasion of privacy on the ground that it could find no decision 'which held the "right of privacy" to be violated by a newspaper or magazine publishing a correct account of one's life or doings...except under abnormal circumstances which did not exist in the case at bar.'[157] On appeal, the Second Circuit affirmed the dismissal of the privacy action, but appeared to base its decision on a

155. 112 Cal App 285, 297 P 91 (1931).
156. 34 F Supp 19 (SDNY 1938).
157. 34 F Supp 19 (SDNY 1938) at 21.

balancing of the offensiveness of the article with the public or private character of the plaintiff.[158]

In neither case, however, was there a proper attempt to consider the extent to which the information divulged was 'private'. The conceptually vague notions of 'community customs', 'newsworthiness', and the 'offensiveness' of the publication, render these and many other decisions concerning 'public disclosure' unhelpful in an area of considerable constitutional importance. And this is equally true of the efforts by the Supreme Court to fix the boundaries of the First Amendment in respect of publications which affect the plaintiff's privacy. For example, in *Time, Inc v Hill*[159] the Court held that the plaintiff's action for invasion of privacy failed where he (and his family) had been the subject of a substantially false report. The defendant had published a description of a new play adapted from a novel which fictionalized the ordeal suffered by the plaintiff when he and his family were held hostage in their home by a group of escaped prisoners. Adopting the test that it had applied in respect of defamation, the Supreme Court held, by a majority, that unless there was proof of actual malice (ie that the defendant knowingly published an untrue report) the action would fail. Falsity alone did not deprive the defendant of his protection under the First Amendment—if the publication was newsworthy. And, since the 'opening of a new play linked to an actual incident is a matter of public interest', the plaintiff, because he was unable to show malice, failed. Yet it does seem that the decision was not really concerned with the public disclosure of private information whether or not it was even a genuine libel action!

Privacy codes

Section 12(4) of the Human Rights Act provides that a court is required to pay 'particular regard' to 'any relevant privacy code' when considering a matter 'where the proceedings relate to...journalistic, literary or artistic material.' The following is how the three main media codes of practice approach the question of public interest.[160]

---

158. 113 F2d 806 (2d Cir 1940).
159. 385 US 374 (1967).
160. The remedies offered by these bodies are considered in Chapter 7. An admirable analysis of how the three bodies have adjudicated privacy-related complaints—which I cannot pursue here—may be found in Tugendhat and Christie (n 97), 490–512.

Press Complaints Commission

The Press Complaints Commission (PCC) administers a code of practice to which newspapers and magazines agreed to adhere; and to examine complaints from members of the public who claim a breach of the code. The PCC's *Editors' Code of Practice* claims that the 'public interest' is 'impossible to define', yet it provides what is, in effect, a definition of the sorts of matters that fall within the concept, including detecting or exposing crime or serious impropriety, protecting public health and safety, and preventing the public from being misled by an action or statement of an individual or organization. It adds that whenever the public interest is invoked, 'the PCC will require editors to demonstrate fully that they reasonably believed that publication, or journalistic activity undertaken with a view to publication, would be in the public interest and how, and with whom, that was established at the time.' The PCC considers also the extent to which material is already in the public domain, or will become so. Where children under 16 are involved 'editors must demonstrate an exceptional public interest to over-ride the normally paramount interest of the child.'[161]

Ofcom

Unlike newspapers and magazines, in respect of broadcast media, the state exercises control over the licensing of radio and television broadcasters under the Office of Communications Act 2002. Its powers are set out in the Communications Act 2003. Its *Broadcasting Code* provides that 'where broadcasters wish to justify an infringement of privacy as warranted, they should be able to demonstrate why in the particular circumstances of the case, it is warranted. If the reason is that it is in the public interest, then the broadcaster should

---

161. A reformed PCC with so-called 'statutory underpinning' was proposed by the Leveson Inquiry Report (n 90). It excited considerable anxiety among the press and several politicians. The Prime Minister, David Cameron, made a statement in the House of Commons in which he welcomed many of the Inquiry's recommendations, but expressed 'serious concerns and misgivings' about the prospect of any legislation to support the proposed new media self-regulatory body. On 18 March 2013 a new press regulation regime was announced by the Prime Minister to be established by royal charter. He acknowledged, however, that legislation would be required to provide for the award of exemplary damages against newspapers that did not sign up to the regulator, and confirmed that a statute would be passed to require a two-thirds majority of both Houses of Parliament to amend the charter. But, he added, the legislation is 'to protect the royal charter, it is not legislation to recognise the royal charter'. The new system would include 'upfront' apologies from the press to victims of misconduct; fines of up to one million pounds; a self-regulatory body with independent appointments and funding; and a free arbitration service for victims. The draft charter defines a 'relevant publisher' as a newspaper, magazine, or website containing news-related material. See http://www.culture.gov.uk/

be able to demonstrate that the public interest outweighs the right to privacy. Examples of public interest would include revealing or detecting crime, protecting public health or safety, exposing misleading claims made by individuals or organisations or disclosing incompetence that affects the public.' It adds that 'legitimate expectations of privacy will vary according to the place and nature of the information, activity or condition in question, the extent to which it is in the public domain (if at all) and whether the individual concerned is already in the public eye...People under investigation or in the public eye, and their immediate family and friends, retain a right to private life, although private behaviour can raise issues of legitimate public interest.'

The BBC

Its *Editorial Guidelines* provide that the BBC must balance the public interest in freedom of expression with the legitimate expectation of privacy by individuals. Any infringement of a legitimate expectation of privacy in the gathering of material must be justified as proportionate in the particular circumstances of the case. It adds that the Corporation 'must balance the public interest in the full and accurate reporting of stories involving human suffering and distress with an individual's privacy and respect for their human dignity...and justify intrusions into an individual's private life without consent by demonstrating that the intrusion is outweighed by the public interest.' The public interest includes but is not confined to exposing or detecting crime, exposing significantly antisocial behaviour, exposing corruption or injustice, disclosing significant incompetence or negligence, protecting people's health and safety, preventing people from being misled by some statement or action of an individual or organization, and disclosing information that assists the better comprehension of or decision-making about matters of public importance.

Public authorities?

Section 6 of the Human Rights Act 1998 provides that it is unlawful for a 'public authority' to act incompatibly with a Convention right. This phrase is defined in section 6(3) to include 'a court or tribunal'. Are these bodies courts or tribunals? If so, it opens the door for a disappointed complainant to proceed against the regulator under section 7(1) of the Act. The position is uncertain. The House of Lords has exhibited a division on the scope and purport of this provision.[162] But in regard to the exercise of what amount to quasi-judicial powers, the better view would seem to be that all three constitute public authorities.[163]

Data protection and the media

At the core of all data protection legislation—since the guidelines of the Organisation for Economic Co-operation and Development (OECD) in 1980—is the principle that data relating to an identifiable individual should not be collected in the absence of a genuine purpose and the consent of the individual concerned. At a slightly higher level of abstraction, it encapsulates the principle of what the German Federal Constitutional Court has called 'informational self-determination'[164]—a postulate that expresses an important, if inelegant, democratic ideal. Adherence to, or more precisely, enforcement of, this idea (and the associated rights of access and correction) has been mixed in the nearly ninety jurisdictions that have enacted data protection legislation. Most of these statutes draw on the OECD guidelines and those formulated by the Council of Europe in 1980. The European Union 1995 Directive on Data Protection provides a comprehensive framework binding on member states.[165]

There is, however, something of a paradox at the heart of data protection regimes. They all adopt an extravagantly broad concept of 'personal data'. The European Directive itself, although eight explicit references are made to the right to privacy, adopts a broad definition of 'personal data' that extends well beyond questions of privacy. It includes:

[A]ny information relating to an identified or identifiable individual natural person ('data subject'); an identifiable individual is one who can be identified directly or indirectly, in particular by reference to an identification number

---

162. *YL v Birmingham City Council* [2007] UKHL 27, [2008] 1 AC 95.
163. See *R (Ford) v Press Complaints Commission* [2002] EMLR 95; *R (ProLife Alliance) v BBC* [2004] 1 AC 185; *Gaunt v Ofcom* [2010] EWHC 1756 (QB).
164. *Volkszahlungsurteil* (National Census Case) 65 BVerfGE 1, 68–9 (1983), cited in S Simitis, 'Reviewing Privacy in an Information Society' (1987) 135 University of Pennsylvania Law Review 707, 734.
165. The Protection of Individuals with regard to the Processing of Personal Data and on the Free Movement of Such Data Directive, Council Directive 95/46/EC 1995, OJ L 281/31. Recital 9 states that the directive is explicitly concerned with privacy. For a comprehensive account of the Data Protection Act 1998, see R Jay, *Data Protection Law and Practice*, 4th edn (London: Sweet & Maxwell, 2012). Data protection legislation of some kind exists in at least eighty-nine countries with such laws with several more considering the introduction of such laws. 'The most economically significant countries currently missing from the list are the

or to one or more factors specific to his physical, physiological, mental, economic, cultural or social identity.

While this generous definition manifestly incorporates information, the obtaining or disclosure of which would constitute what might properly be called an invasion of privacy, its wide sweep neglects these issues. As argued in Chapter 1, it is principally information that is sensitive or intimate that warrants protection in the name of privacy. But while the European Directive (and the Data Protection Act 1998) neglects this species of information, it does not altogether ignore it. Thus, Article 8 requires member states to prohibit the processing of personal data 'revealing racial or ethnic origin, political opinions, religious or philosophical beliefs, trade union membership, and the processing of data concerning health or sex life.' This restriction is, however, subject to a number of exceptions including: unless domestic legislation specifically provides otherwise, or where the data subject gives his or her explicit consent to such processing. It is also permissible when necessary to protect the rights and duties of the controller in the field of employment law, or to protect the 'vital interests' of the data subject. To this list of 'sensitive personal data', section 2 of the Data Protection Act adds the commission or alleged commission of any offence, or any proceedings for any offence committed or alleged to have been committed, the disposal of such proceedings, or the sentence of any court in such proceedings.

Notwithstanding the fact that data protection regimes extend well beyond the information of an essentially private kind, and their (perhaps inevitable) procedural, rather than substantive, nature,[166] they provide useful signposts to the more effective resolution of the challenges, especially of electronic privacy. The enactment of data protection legislation is driven only partly by altruism. The new information technology disintegrates national borders; international traffic in personal data is a routine feature of commercial life. The protection afforded to personal data in Country A is, in a digital world, rendered nugatory when it is retrieved on a computer in Country B in which there are no controls over its use. Hence, states with data protection laws frequently proscribe the transfer of data to countries that lack them. Indeed, the European Directive explicitly seeks to curtail

USA (private sector), China and Brazil', G Greenleaf, 'Global Data Privacy Laws: 89 Countries, and Accelerating', Queen Mary University of London, School of Law Legal Studies Research Paper No 98/2012.

166. See C Raab and C Bennett, 'The Distribution of Privacy Risks: Who Needs Protection?' (1998) 14 The Information Society 263, 265.

these 'data havens'. Without such legislation, countries risk being shut out of the rapidly expanding information business.

In many respects, the Act, though nowhere does the word appear, is a 'privacy' law. Indeed in *Durant v Financial Services Authority*[167] Buxton LJ declared,

> The guiding principle is that the Act, following Directive 95/46, gives rights to data subjects in order to protect their privacy. That is made plain in recitals (2), (7) and (11) to the Directive, and in particular by recital (10), which tells us that:
>
> > the object of the national laws on the processing of personal data is to protect fundamental rights and freedoms, notably the right to privacy, which is recognised both in Article 8 of the European Convention for the Protection of Human Rights and Fundamental Freedoms and in the general principle of Community law.

The Data Protection Act sets out eight data protection principles in Schedule 1. They include the use limitation, purpose specification, and fair processing principles which are fundamental canons of fair information practice. Together with the principle that personal data shall be collected by means that are fair and lawful, they provide a framework for safeguarding the use and disclosure of such data, but also (in the fair collection principle) for limiting intrusive activities such as the interception of email messages. Personal data may be used or disclosed only for the purposes for which the data were collected or for some directly related purposes, unless the data subject consents. This key precept goes a long way towards regulating the misuse of personal data on the Internet. It requires rejuvenation where it already exists and urgent adoption where it does so only partially (most conspicuously in the United States).

Three aspects of the Data Protection Act are particularly pertinent to the present discussion. First, it is clear that the media are 'data controllers' and therefore subject to the legislative regime's provisions.[168] But, secondly, an

---

167. [2004] FSR 28, [80]. Trenchant criticism of some of the features of the Act, particularly in regard to the narrowness of s 32's exemption, may be found in the written evidence to the Joint Committee on Privacy and Injunctions, *Privacy and Injunctions: Oral and Written Evidence* (2011), at 181–9 by David Erdos of the Data Protection and the Open Society Project.

168. *Douglas v Hello! Ltd* [2003] 3 All ER 996, [230]–[231]. The photographs were held to be 'personal data', and their publication constituted 'processing' of data. A fascinating interpretation of data protection legislation as applied to a 'privacy' complaint relating to the unauthorized taking and publication of photographs of the plaintiff in a public place is *Eastweek Publisher Ltd v Privacy Commissioner of Personal Data* [2000] 1 HKC 692. See R Wacks, 'Privacy and Anonymity' (2000) 30 Hong Kong Law Journal 177; R Wacks, 'Media Intrusion: An Expanded Role for the Privacy Commissioner?' (1999) 29 Hong Kong Law Journal 341.

exemption is specified in section 32 in respect of the 'special purposes' (as defined in s 3) of journalism, literature, and art which extends to a number of the data protection principles as well as sections 7 (right of access), 10 (right to prevent processing that is likely to cause distress or damage), 12 (rights in respect of automated decision-making), and 14(1), (2), and (3) (rectification, blocking, erasure, and destruction of personal data). The exemption applies provided that the processing is undertaken with a view to the publication by any person of any journalistic, literary, or artistic material, and the data controller reasonably believes, first, that having regard in particular to the special importance of the public interest in freedom of expression, publication would be in the public interest and, secondly, that, in all the circumstances, compliance with that provision is incompatible with the special purposes.[169]

The Leveson Inquiry Report proposed that the section 32 exemption be amended to make it available only where: (a) the processing of data is necessary for publication, rather than simply being in fact undertaken with a view to publication; (b) the data controller reasonably believes that the relevant publication would be or is in the public interest, with no special weighting of the balance between the public interest in freedom of expression and in privacy; and (c) objectively, that the likely interference with privacy resulting from the processing of the data is outweighed by the public interest in publication.[170]

Thirdly, Schedule 3 to the Act sets out detailed conditions relating to the processing of sensitive personal data. They include, for example, the

---

169. *Campbell v MGN Ltd* [2003] QB 633 is authority for the proposition that the exemption in s 32 applies before, after, and at the moment of publication. But see n 170.

170. *An Inquiry into the Culture, Practices and Ethics of the Press* (n 90), Part H, ch 5, para 2.59. The Report further recommends that the exemption in s 32 be narrowed in scope, so that it no longer allows for exemption from: (a) the requirement of the first data protection principle to process personal data fairly (except in relation to the provision of information to the data subject under para 2(1)(a) of Part II Schedule 1 to the 1998 Act) and in accordance with statute law; (b) the second data protection principle (personal data to be obtained only for specific purposes and not processed incompatibly with those purposes); (c) the fourth data protection principle (personal data to be accurate and kept up to date); (d) the sixth data protection principle (personal data to be processed in accordance with the rights of individuals under the Act); (e) the eighth data protection principle (restrictions on exporting personal data); and (f) the right of subject access. Section 13, it proposed, should be clarified to ensure that the right to compensation for distress is not restricted to cases of pecuniary loss, but should include compensation for pure distress. The procedural provisions of the Act with special application to journalism in s 32(4) and (5)(b), and ss 44–6 should be repealed: Part H, ch 5, paras 2.45 and 2.59–2.61.

requirement that such processing is necessary to protect the vital interests of the data subject or another person, where consent cannot be given by or on behalf of the data subject, or the data controller cannot reasonably be expected to obtain the consent of the data subject, or to protect the vital interests of another person, in a case where consent by or on behalf of the data subject has been unreasonably withheld. Such processing must be carried out in the course of its legitimate activities by any body or association which is not established or conducted for profit, and exists for political, philosophical, religious, or trade union purposes, with appropriate safeguards for the rights and freedoms of data subjects, relates only to individuals who either are members of the body or association or have regular contact with it in connection with its purposes, and does not involve disclosure of the personal data to a third party without the consent of the data subject. Or where the information contained in the personal data has been made public as a result of steps deliberately taken by the data subject. Other conditions refer to the processing of data relating to legal proceedings and the administration of justice.[171]

The Data Protection Act 1998 and privacy

Despite its limitations, the normative framework of data protection may have a much wider application to the problems of privacy, in general, and

---

171. See the Data Protection (Processing of Sensitive Personal Data) Order 2000. Schedule 2, para 6(1) allows the processing of personal data in general where it is necessary for the purposes of legitimate interests pursued by the data controller or by the third party or parties to whom the data are disclosed, except where the processing is unwarranted in any particular case by reason of prejudice to the rights and freedoms or legitimate interests of the data subject. The provision was considered at first instance in *Douglas v Hello Ltd* [2003] QB 967, [238]; *Campbell v MGN Ltd* [2002] EMLR 617; and *Murray v Express Newspapers plc* [2007] EMLR 22, [76]. Under s 55(1) it is a criminal offence knowingly or recklessly, without the consent of the data controller to (a) obtain or disclose personal data or the information contained in personal data or (b) procure the disclosure to another person of the information contained in personal data, subject to specified defences in s 55(2). It could cover the practice of 'blagging': the obtaining of information by using pretence, a false identity, or false representations. The offence may be committed not merely by data controllers, but by anyone. Section 55(2) expressly provides a defence where in the particular circumstances the obtaining, disclosing, or procuring was justified as being in the public interest. The offence carries a fine of up to £5,000 in the magistrates' court and an unlimited fine in the Crown Court. The Information Commissioner has the power to impose a civil monetary penalty of up to £500,000 for serious breaches of the data protection regime.

those of Internet privacy, in particular.[172] For example, with its focus on the processing of personal data, it may be better able both to anticipate and respond to the threats to online privacy that are generated by the digital revolution. The legislation avoids much of the conceptual confusion of privacy discourse discussed in earlier chapters. The growing international acceptance of this normative framework, as expressed in the European Directive and the legislation of many jurisdictions, may more easily win public support than is presently true, in some respects, of the Human Rights Act.[173]

The data protection principles afford a means of preventing and regulating certain forms of privacy-invading conduct that are currently conducted with impunity, such as snooping in public places and perhaps even the intrusive activities of the media.[174] The strategy of the legislation is largely pre-emptive and preventive, particularly in respect of media intrusion where codes of conduct might be brought under the aegis of the Information Commissioner's Office instead of the contentious jurisdiction and adjudicative purview of media commissions and councils.[175]

---

172. See R Wacks 'What has Data Protection to do with Privacy?' (2000) 6 Privacy Law and Policy Reporter 143–7.
173. In 2012 the European Commission issued a draft European Data Protection Regulation that will supersede the Data Protection Directive. It is an attempt to modernize the legal framework for data protection in the EU to deal with increasingly sophisticated information systems, global information networks, mass information sharing, and the collection of personal data online. Among the amendments to the current directive, are proposals to fortify provisions relating to consent to the processing of data, by requiring explicit rather than implied consent, and the right to object to processing of data, with no requirement to show that use of the data would cause substantial damage or distress. In the present context, Art 80 is especially important; it concerns the processing of personal data and freedom of expression: 'Member States shall provide for exemptions or derogations from the provisions on the general principles in Chapter II, the rights of the data subject in Chapter III ...in Chapter VII for *the processing of personal data carried out solely for journalistic purposes or the purpose of artistic or literary expression in order to reconcile the right to the protection of personal data with the rules governing freedom of expression*' (emphasis added). The explanatory memorandum states that member states should classify activities as 'journalistic' for the purpose of the exemptions and derogations under the Regulation if the object of these activities is the disclosure to the public of information, opinions, or ideas irrespective of the medium which is used to transmit them. They should not be limited to media undertakings and may be undertaken for profit-making or for non-profit-making purposes.
174. The Leveson Inquiry Report recommended that 'consideration should be given to the desirability of including in the Data Protection Act 1998 a provision to the effect that, in considering the exercise of any powers in relation to the media or other publishers, the Information Commissioner's Office should have special regard to the obligation in law to balance the public interest in freedom of expression alongside the public interest in upholding the data protection regime', *An Inquiry into the Culture, Practices and Ethics of the Press* (n 90), Part H, ch 5, para 2.56.
175. Compensation is exigible under s 13 of the Act. See Chapter 7.

The regulatory regime provides an important framework for the formulation of privacy policy by the Information Commissioner who is able
also to monitor and resist the introduction of legislation and practices that
are inimical to the protection of personal information. It also affords an effective means by which consumers may resolve privacy problems without
resorting to expensive and protracted litigation.[176]

On the other hand, the Act in its current form may be inadequate to
deal with a number of privacy issues, such as public disclosure of private
facts by the media, and surveillance and intrusion: the interception of communications plainly requires its own regulatory controls—but it does even
under the conventional approach. The lofty constitutional questions of free
speech and privacy are better contested in the self-consciously legal forum
generated by the ordinary law. As in the case of media regulation, aggrieved
victims may find the administrative remedies they offer inadequate. The Act
safeguards only recorded accessible data which account for only a propor-
tion of the personal data which warrant protection. The numerous exemptions and defences, particularly those permitting collection and transfer of
personal data by law enforcement authorities or justified by considerations
of national security, seriously erode protection, and must be treated with
considerable circumspection.

In a number of respects, however, the Act seems to offer a pragmatic
route out of the labyrinth of privacy law. This is not a retreat from rights,
no entreaty to take the right of privacy less seriously; quite the contrary.[177] But, as I have asserted throughout this book, the concept of privacy,
though the courts have recently contributed to its elucidation, still stands
in need of greater clarity and precision. Much of the responsibility for this
obscurity must be laid at the door of US law. The triumph of the Warren
and Brandeis thesis, whatever its explanation, has generated so expansive a

---

176. The Leveson Inquiry Report recommended that the Information Commissioner's Office
prepare and issue guidance to the public on their individual rights in relation to the obtaining and use by the press of their personal data, and how to exercise those rights. In particular,
it should take immediate steps to publish advice aimed at individuals who are concerned
that their data have or may have been processed by the press unlawfully or otherwise than in
accordance with good practice. In its Annual Report to Parliament under s 52(1) it should
include regular updates on the effectiveness of these measures, and on the culture, practices,
and ethics of the press in relation to the processing of personal data: *An Inquiry into the Culture, Practices and Ethics of the Press* (n 90), Part H, ch 5, paras 2.72 and 2.64.
177. For a defence of the concept of human rights, see R Wacks, 'The End of Human Rights?'
(1992) 24 Hong Kong Law Journal 372.

notion of privacy, common law and constitutional, that it has been almost irredeemably blunted.

An obvious danger of the rhetoric of rights is that it frequently induces complacency, particularly where those rights depend on costly individual enforcement. This is exacerbated when the claimed right is riddled with ambiguity. The data protection approach, with its numerous exemptions and derogations, still leans too far against the protection of personal data, but it nevertheless has the potential to offer a congenial home for the defence of privacy. The Act's fair information practices can provide a rational and sound normative framework for the collection, use, and transfer of personal data. It offers a more pragmatic analysis of the uses to which personal information is actually put, the manner of its collection, and the legitimate expectations of data subjects. These are the questions that are likely to dominate the discussion of privacy in the twenty-first century.

Europe's approach to data protection, which has passed through four phases,[178] is far from perfect and requires regular revision,[179] but it does present a viable, workmanlike infrastructure on which to construct a secure legal framework for the protection of individual privacy. Placing control of personal information at the heart of our deliberations about privacy achieves what the orthodox analysis has conspicuously failed to do: it postulates a presumptive entitlement accorded to all individuals that their personal data may be collected only lawfully or fairly and that once obtained, may not be used, in the absence of the individual's consent, for a purpose other than that for which it was originally given.[180]

Greater appreciation of the Act's value is required. Its regulatory regime cannot and should not *replace* judicial remedies either at common law or where founded upon explicit legislation. Many of the problems that beset the conventional approach cannot be so simply wished away. There is, however, a compelling need to rethink the conceptual underpinnings of privacy if we are to arrest its relentless decline.

---

178. For a lucid account of these developments, see V Mayer-Schonberger, 'Generational Development of Data Protection in Europe' in PE Agre and M Rotenberg (eds), *Technology and Privacy: The New Landscape* (Cambridge, MA: MIT Press, 1997).

179. Article 29 of the European Directive provides for a 'working party on the protection of individuals with regard to the processing of personal data' to consider, inter alia, proposed amendments to the directive.

180. This general principle stands, of course, in need of further elaboration in specific sectoral codes of conduct administered by the data protection authority. But its central premise provides a promising foundation for legislation on wider privacy issues.

Defamation

The tort of defamation, broadly speaking, consists in the publication of a false statement which tends to damage the reputation of another without lawful justification.[181] The line between a claim for the misuse of private information and an action for defamation is sometimes a fuzzy one. Indeed, it will be recalled that among the four 'privacy' torts in US law is included 'publicity which places the defendant in a false light in the public eye'. Whether or not this is properly conceived as a matter of 'privacy', it underlines the association between defamation and privacy.[182] Certainly, the argument is not infrequently heard that an action in defamation provides a means of protecting the claimant's privacy. When a victim of unsolicited publicity looks for relief it is often because the disclosure relates to intimate facts about him or her. But are the interests protected by the 'false light' tort sufficiently distinguishable from those that underpin defamation to justify separate treatment?[183]

The overriding obstacle is the fundamental principle that in defamation truth is a complete defence. This so-called defence of justification provides

181. See generally P Milmo and W Rogers, *Gatley on Libel and Slander*, 11th edn (London: Sweet & Maxwell, 2008). The classic definition of a defamatory statement is to be found in *Parmiter v Coupland* (1840) 6 M & W 105, 108, 151 ER 340, 341–2: 'A publication, without justification or lawful excuse, which is calculated to injure the reputation of another, by exposing him to hatred, contempt, or ridicule ...' Other definitions have been offered over the years, including one that asks whether the words tend to lower the plaintiff in the estimation of right-thinking members of society generally. Or whether they tend to make the plaintiff be shunned and avoided. In *Thornton v Telegraph Media Group* [2010] EWHC 1414 (QB) Tugendhat J sought to screen out trivial claims and to protect the defendant's rights under Art 10 and the principle of proportionality. He preferred an approach that regards as defamatory a statement that substantially affects in an adverse manner the attitude of other people towards the claimant, or has a tendency so to do ([95]).
182. In a number of decisions, the European Court has construed Art 8 to include the right to reputation. See eg *Pfeifer v Austria* App 12556/03 (2007) 48 EHRR 175; *A v Norway* [2009] ECHR 580; *Karakó v Hungary* [2009] ECHR 712; *Petrenco v Moldova* [2010] ECHR 419. The UK Supreme Court followed suit: *Application by Guardian News & Media Ltd, HM Treasury v Ahmed and Others* [2010] UKSC 1, [2010] 2 WLR 325. I consider further this odd interpretation in Chapter 8.
183. In respect of US law, Nimmer claims that the libel standard adopted in *New York Times v Sullivan*, 376 US 254 (1964) was wrongly applied in *Time, Inc v Hill*, 385 US 374 (1967) because the Hill family (the account of whose ordeal was falsely reported) were not defamed by the account of their experience. He suggests that the 'false light' category ought to be dealt with in the same way as 'public disclosure' cases. MB Nimmer, 'The Right to Speak from Times to Time: First Amendment Theory Applied to Libel and Misapplied to Privacy' (1968) 46 California Law Review 935.

a valuable safeguard for freedom of expression. The suggestion is sometimes made that by modifying the defence of justification many of the actions brought to vindicate the plaintiff's loss of 'privacy' might be accommodated within the tort of defamation. The proposal is that in order for the defence to succeed, the defendant ought to be required to show not only that the statement is true, but that its publication is in the public interest, the position which obtains in several Australian and US jurisdictions and in the Roman-Dutch law of Sri Lanka and South Africa. Such a proposal was of course open to Warren and Brandeis to have adopted, though Brandeis might then 'have been marked as a Lorentz, certainly not an Einstein of legal thought'.[184] But since they regarded the principles of the law of defamation as 'radically different' from those underlying the protection of 'privacy', this modification would hardly be consistent with their general thesis. In any event, even if the law of defamation were to be so modified,[185] many actions would still not succeed where the plaintiff's reputation has not, in fact, been affected by the private facts disclosed.

The better view is that the 'false light' category seems to be both redundant (for almost all such cases might equally have been brought for defamation) and only tenuously related to the protection of the plaintiff against aspects of his or her private life being exposed. The Younger Committee recognized that 'placing someone in a false light is an aspect of defamation rather than privacy',[186] and several commentators raise the question 'whether this branch of the tort is not capable of swallowing up and engulfing the whole law of defamation'.[187]

---

184. P Freund, 'Privacy: One Concept or Many?' in JR Pennock and JW Chapman (eds), *Nomos* XIII (New York: Atherton, 1971), 182.

185. The suggestion has been made on several occasions, including as far back as 1843 when a Select Committee of the House of Lords proposed this solution. It was repeated most recently by the *Report of the Committee on the Law of Defamation* (Cmnd 5909, 1975) (Chairman: Mr Justice Faulks), paras 137 ff. Further reform of the law is probable; the Defamation Bill was presented to Parliament on 10 May 2012.

186. *Report of the Committee on Privacy* (Cmnd 5012, 1972) (Chairman: Kenneth Younger), para 70.

187. Prosser (n 140), 813; JW Wade, 'Defamation and the Right of Privacy' (1962) Vanderbilt Law Review 1093; J Skelly Wright, 'Defamation, Privacy and the Public's Right to Know: A National Problem and a New Approach' (1968) 46 Texas Law Review 630; F Davis, 'What Do We Mean By "Right to Privacy"?' (1959) 4 South Dakota Law Review 1; H Kalven, 'Privacy in Tort Law: Were Warren and Brandeis Wrong?' (1966) 31 Law and Contemporary Problems 326. See too FS Haiman, *Speech and Law in a Free Society* (Chicago, IL: University of Chicago Press, 1981), 85–6. In comparing 'defamation' and 'privacy', however, there are several difficulties, not least of which is the fact that these writers share only the most general conceptions of both issues. Eg Davis (at 8) regards the two as 'identical' since they are

It has been said that 'the fundamental difference between a right to privacy and a right to freedom from defamation is that the former directly concerns one's own peace of mind, while the latter concerns primarily one's reputation.'[188] This, however, is not a distinction that has ever been a sharp one, and not only has the jurisdiction of defamation been enlarged, but (more to the point) recovery has been allowed for invasion of privacy in several US decisions where the plaintiff has been depicted in a 'false light' and it is the plaintiff's reputation, rather than his or her 'privacy' that would appear to be affected.

While defamation and the tort of malicious falsehood are obviously concerned with false statements, the falsity or otherwise of the disclosure is irrelevant in an action for public disclosure—or indeed for the misuse of private information.[189] A claimant faced with a true statement by which he or she is embarrassed may obtain relief by bringing an action under the public disclosure tort (provided, it seems, that there is the requisite publicity). In Prosser's view, the tort protects his or her reputation.[190] But this seems mistaken, for the rationale behind the tort of public disclosure is not merely 'to prevent inaccurate portrayal of private life, but to prevent its being depicted at all.'[191] Moreover, even though the disclosure of sensitive information actually portrays the plaintiff in a favourable light, there is no reason why he or she should in principle be barred from recovery. On the other hand, if the statement is false, the tort of 'false light' might have been committed, and here too Prosser, more plausibly, suggests that it is the plaintiff's reputation that is affected. But, since the 'false light' cases appear to be equally actionable in defamation, it is arguable that 'the overlap (between

both concerned largely in protecting the plaintiff's mental feelings. Wade (at 1124) expresses a similar view, but appears to regard disclosure and 'false light' as offending the plaintiff's reputation. Prosser (at 401) and E Bloustein, 'Privacy as an Aspect of Human Dignity: An Answer to Dean Prosser' (1964) 39 New York University Law Review 962, 993, both identify an overlap, but of different interests. If one conceives (as Prosser does) the interest protected by the tort of public disclosure as reputation, the overlap becomes even more substantial.

188. *Themo v New England Newspaper Publishing Co*, 27 NE2d 753, 755 (1940).
189. See eg *P, Q and R v Quigley* [2008] EWHC 1051 (QB); *McKennitt v Ash* [2005] EWHC 2003 (QB), [2006] EMLR 10; *LNS (John Terry) v Persons Unknown* [2010] EWHC 119 (QB), [2010] EMLR 16. The latter decision contains a useful analysis by Tugendhat J of the overlap between defamation and privacy ([96]). See Chapter 8.
190. Prosser (n 89), 398.
191. SD Warren and LD Brandeis, 'The Right to Privacy' (1890) 4 Harvard Law Review 193, 197. For a modern approach to the problem (in which the two causes of action elide) see DJ Solove, *The Future of Reputation: Gossip, Rumor, and Privacy on the Internet* (New Haven, CT: Yale University Press, 2007).

defamation and privacy) might be thought substantial enough to make the approach via privacy superfluous.'[192]

The claimant who proceeds against the publisher of defamatory material normally invites even greater publicity. This may well be the right price to be paid in a society that prizes free speech. But where his or her complaint is that private facts have been disclosed, the salt of a libel action may simply be too much for his or her wound to take.

Circumstances may occasionally arise in which disclosure of private facts carries the defamatory innuendo that the plaintiff consented to its publication. The defendant in *Corelli v Wall*[193] published and sold postcards depicting, without her permission, imaginary events in the plaintiff's life. The court rejected the argument that publication was libellous. She argued also 'that the plaintiff as a private person was entitled to restrain the publication of a portrait of herself which had been made without her authority and which, although professing to be her portrait was totally unlike her.'[194] This could not be supported by any authority. Clearly there must be some defamatory imputation before liability will be imposed. As Greer LJ put it in *Tolley v JS Fry and Sons Ltd*,

> [U]nless a man's photograph, caricature or name be published in such a context that the publication can be said to be defamatory within the law of libel, it cannot be made the subject-matter of complaint by action at law.[195]

In any event, few 'privacy' cases present such facts. In *Kaye v Robertson*[196] (though an argument based on malicious falsehood succeeded in preventing the newspaper from stating that the plaintiff had consented to the intrusion) the court did not regard the publication as defamatory.

---

192. Kalven (n 187), 332:'Practically all the cases (i.e. "false light" cases) ...are covered by the existing remedies of defamation and injurious falsehood and it seems as if the American concept of privacy has been grafted on to these traditional causes of action *ex abundanti cautela*' (G Dworkin, 'The Common Law Protection of Privacy' (1967) 2 University of Tasmania Law Review 418, 426). *Report of the Committee on Privacy* (n 186), para 70; Prosser (n 140), 401; Bloustein (n 187), 993.

193. (1906) 22 TLR 532.

194. Winfield claims the decision cannot be regarded as authority for the view that a plaintiff can never obtain an injunction in an action for libel against a defendant who publishes a bad portrait of him, P Winfield, 'Privacy' (1931) 47 Law Quarterly Review 23, 32.

195. [1930] 1 KB 467, 478. But this goes too far. See *Pollard v Photographic Co* (1888) 40 Ch D 345, discussed in Chapter 3 in the text at n 102.

196. [1991] FSR 62.

The Human Rights Act 1998 poses a number of challenges to the law of defamation.[197] How is the protection of 'private life' in Article 8 to be squared with the defence of justification?[198] And, as a general precept, how is the law of defamation to coexist with Article 10's protection of free speech?[199] The Article does have two important limitations that may assist a publisher found to have defamed a claimant. First, any judgment imposed on the exercise of freedom of expression must be 'prescribed by law'. This condition has been held by the European Court to mean that the law in question must be sufficiently foreseeable and accessible. The Court has not found the common law wanting in this respect.[200] Secondly, an unfavourable defamation judgment must be 'necessary in a democratic society'.[201]

197. Section 6(1) renders it unlawful for public authorities—including courts and tribunals—to act in a way incompatible with Convention rights. Section 12 provides that where a court is considering whether to grant any relief that may affect the exercise of Art 10, it must have particular regard to the importance of that right. Where the material is journalistic, literary, or artistic, the public interest in its publication must be considered. The Defamation Bill of 2012, currently proceeding through Parliament, contains a number of reforms that seek to both simplify and modernize the law, especially of libel.

198. The European Court of Human Rights has, in a number of decisions, held that Art 8 guarantees the right to reputation. See eg *Pfeifer v Austria* App 12556/03 (2007) 48 EHRR 175. This is yet another instance of the unsatisfactorily broad concept of 'private life' that I criticize in Chapter 8. Similar decisions of the European Court are discussed there. According to one commentator, 'It remains unclear how the application of the "ultimate balancing test" will affect the substantive law of defamation, but it appears likely that the established defences, and justification in particular, will have to adapt to claimants' Article 8 rights...Whether that will entail the incorporation of a public benefit test, or simply the introduction of tests of legitimate aim and proportionality, it is too early to say', Richard Parks QC in Tugendhat and Christie (n 97), 333. See now the Supreme Court's judgment in *Flood v Times Newspapers Ltd* [2012] UKSC 11.

199. See M Collins, *The Law of Defamation and the Internet*, 3rd edn (Oxford: Oxford University Press, 2010), Part V.

200. *Sunday Times v United Kingdom* (1979) 2 EHRR 245; *Tolstoy Miloslavsky v United Kingdom* (1995) 20 EHRR 442; *Financial Times v United Kingdom* [2009] ECHR 2065.

201. The Court has construed this condition strictly. It requires evidence of a 'pressing social need' for the restriction: *Zana v Turkey* (1997) 27 EHRR 667, [51]. See *Handyside v United Kingdom* (1976) 1 EHRR 737; *Sunday Times v United Kingdom* (1979) 2 EHRR 245; *Barthold v Germany* (1985) 7 EHRR 383.

6

Media misconduct

While this chapter touches on the prodigious advances in privacy-invading technology, its emphasis is on their use—or potential use—by the media, and the extent to which the law is able to provide protection against these depredations. I do not attempt to provide a comprehensive account of the various sophisticated electronic devices that both threaten privacy and seek to repulse the onslaughts. Nor do the following pages endeavour to describe in any detail the extraordinary developments in social networks such as Facebook and Twitter, and the manner in which the young exhibit a readiness to post considerable amounts of personal information on these websites. The hazards of such data being misused by identity thieves, blackmailers, and sexual predators, or for embarrassing material to be found by current or future employers, raise serious concerns in their own right.

From a media perspective there is a growing practice of journalists looking to these sources for their stories. Even more troubling is the posting of personal information about others without their knowledge or consent, and sites like spokeo.com that provide extensive information about them.[1] The Internet, of course, generates countless questions about the law's capacity to control, or even to limit, the harm inflicted by online malefactors. Some

---

1. For $5.00 per month searches are offered that can retrieve an individual's profiles on social networks, YouTube, blogs, eBay, and so on. 'More than a million people search the Spokeo database each day—making decisions about whether to hire people, grant them credit, or even have sex with them—based on what they read. Often the information is wrong, culled from erroneous or outdated sources and interpreted by imperfect algorithms. Yet the people whose privacy is being invaded may not even realize that Spokeo exists, let alone that it has stigmatized them', L Anderson, *I Know Who You Are and I Saw What You Did: Social Networks and the Death of Privacy* (New York: Free Press, 2012), 10. See generally AM Froomkin, 'The Death of Privacy?' (2000) 52 Stanford Law Review 1461.

of the major threats are described later in this chapter.[2] They may, at first blush, seem tangential to the central concern of this book. What, for example, it could be asked, have RFID (radio frequency identification) codes to do with the media? The same question might have been raised in regard to the voicemail function of mobile telephones. The simple answer is that any of the (increasingly ubiquitous) means by which individual behaviour is susceptible to monitoring provide tempting opportunities for journalistic snooping. No analysis of media freedom can afford to ignore these—and other—potential weapons.

The recent Leveson Inquiry Report into press conduct was emphatically censorious:

> The evidence placed before the Inquiry has demonstrated, beyond any doubt, that there have been far too many occasions over the last decade and more (itself said to have been better than previous decades) when these responsibilities, on which the public so heavily rely, have simply been ignored. There have been too many times when, chasing the story, parts of the press have acted as if its own code, which it wrote, simply did not exist. This has caused real hardship and, on occasion, wreaked havoc with the lives of innocent people whose rights and liberties have been disdained. This is not just the famous but ordinary members of the public, caught up in events (many of them, truly tragic) far larger than they could cope with but made much, much worse by press behaviour that, at times, can only be described as outrageous.[3]

Intrusion

Unlike US law, there is, as yet, no general tort of intrusion recognized by English law. In *Wainwright v Home Office*[4] the House of Lords rejected a complaint by Mrs Wainwright and her son who, when visiting another

---

2. For an early review see R Wacks, 'Privacy in Cyberspace: Personal Information, Free Speech, and the Internet' in P Birks (ed), *Privacy and Loyalty* (Oxford: Clarendon Press, 1997).
3. *An Inquiry into the Culture, Practices and Ethics of the Press* (HC 780, 2012), Executive Summary, para 7, p 4. The Inquiry examined only briefly the subject of the Internet. See Chapter 2.
4. [2003] UKHL 53, [2004] 2 AC 406. I return to this decision later. But see the remarkable judgment of the New Zealand High Court in *C v Holland* [2012] NZHC 2155 which held that 'it is functionally appropriate for the common law to establish a tort equivalent to the North American tort of intrusion upon seclusion', [86]. Whata J took the view that the similarity to the *Hosking v Runting* [2005] 1 NZLR 1 (CA) public disclosure tort 'is sufficiently proximate to enable an intrusion tort to be seen as a logical extension or adjunct to it', ibid. He preferred to look to the North American rather than the English law, attaching particular significance to the Ontario case of *Jones v Tsige*, 2012 ONCA 32. See Chapter 8.

son in prison, were strip-searched in breach of prison rules and suffered humiliation and distress. The invasive search could not give rise to a claim in damages unless it was a tort or a breach of statutory duty. The court held that, while privacy was an important value, the law did not recognize a right of privacy. A claimant who is subjected to an intrusion must therefore look elsewhere for a remedy.

What follows is an outline of some of the major common law and legislative protection available. My hope is to demonstrate the nature and scale of the problem, and to investigate how media intrusion, in particular, might best be curtailed in the face of the increasing fragility of privacy and the growing accessibility and use of digital weapons.

I have also suggested—and I elaborate upon this argument in Chapter 8—that it is only in respect of intrusion that the single test of 'reasonable expectation of privacy' would be appropriate. In the case of disclosure, I contend, that test must be supplemented by an enquiry to verify whether the facts in issue are indeed 'private'. Conflating the two forms of invasion neglects the separate interests of the victims that arise from each act. Furthermore it complicates the balancing of Articles 8 and 10 of the European Convention on Human Rights. It is also worth pointing out that, as I have suggested in Chapter 5, the means by which personal information has been obtained (eg, by surreptitious surveillance) is among the factors to be considered when deciding whether its publication is justifiable in the public interest.[5]

---

5. See *Murray v Express Newspapers plc* [2008] EWCA Civ 446, [2009] Ch 481, [36] per Sir Anthony Clarke MR; *Campbell v MGN Ltd* [2004] UKHL 22, [2004] 2 AC 457, [75] per Lord Hoffmann; *Mosley v News Group Newspapers Ltd* [2008] EWHC 1777 (QB), [2008] EMLR 20, [17] per Eady J. But the method of obtaining the information should not be decisive in the assessment of whether its use was lawful. This seems to have been the approach adopted by the Court of Appeal in *Wood v Commissioner of Police for the Metropolis* [2009] EWCA Civ 414, [39] with which I respectfully disagree, though it here related only to the primary question of whether Art 8 was 'engaged'. It is preferable, even at this preliminary stage of the enquiry, to differentiate between the two issues. The Data Protection Act 1998 provides a degree of protection in respect of the collection of personal data, including sensitive personal data. See Chapter 7. The European Court has decided that the mere taking of a photograph, along with the retention of the negatives, may constitute a breach of Art 8. A newborn in a hospital sterile unit was photographed without his parents' consent. It held that one's image is 'one of the chief attributes of [one's] personality, as it reveals a person's unique characteristics and distinguishes the person from his or her peers', *Reklos v Greece* App 59320/00 (2005) 40 EHRR 1, [40]. It attached importance to the absence of parental consent, the retention of the negatives despite the explicit wishes of the parents to the contrary, the private location where the picture was taken, and the fact that there was no public interest in the newborn. See too *Hachette, Filipacchi Associates v France* App 71111/01 (2009) 49 EHRR 23.

US law prefers a test that includes the offensiveness of the defendant's intrusive act. Its tort of intrusion upon the plaintiff's seclusion or solitude or into his or her private affairs includes the physical intrusion into the plaintiff's premises and eavesdropping (eg, electronic and photographic surveillance, bugging and telephone hacking and tapping). Three requirements must be satisfied: (a) there must be actual prying; (b) the intrusion must offend a reasonable person; and (c) it must be an intrusion into something private. In the words of the gloss of the *Restatement (Second) of the Law of Torts*:

> One who intentionally intrudes, physically or otherwise, upon the solitude or seclusion of another or his private affairs or concerns, is subject to liability to the other for invasion of his privacy, if the intrusion would be highly offensive to a reasonable person.

And its comment reads in part:

> The form of invasion of privacy...does not depend upon any publicity given to the person whose interest is invaded or to his affairs. It consists solely of an intentional interference with his interest in solitude or seclusion, either as to his person or as to his private affairs or concerns, of a kind that would be highly offensive to a reasonable man.[6]

Yet the notion of reasonable expectation of privacy is at the heart of the intrusion tort.[7] In interpreting the Fourth Amendment[8] the US Supreme Court has held that a person has a reasonable expectation of privacy if (a) he, by his conduct, has exhibited an actual (or subjective) expectation of privacy, that is, he has shown that he seeks to preserve something as private, and (b) his subjective expectation of privacy is one that society is prepared to recognize as reasonable, that is, the expectation, viewed objectively, is justifiable under the circumstances.[9] An individual does not have a subjective

---

6. *Restatement (Second) of the Law of Torts* (Philadelphia, PA: American Law Institute, 1977), para 652.
7. In the recent bold decision of the High Court of New Zealand, *C v Holland* [2012] NZHC 2155, the court enumerated the following requirements of the tort of intrusion: (a) an intentional and unauthorized intrusion; (b) into seclusion; (c) involving infringement of a reasonable expectation of privacy; (d) that is highly offensive to a reasonable person, [94]. See Chapter 8.
8. See Chapter 3.
9. *Smith v Maryland*, 442 US 735 (1979). See too *Illinois v Caballes*, 543 US 405 (2005); *Huskey v National Broadcasting Co*, 632 F Supp 1282 (ND Ill 1986); *Sanders v ABC*, 20 Cal4th 907, 85 Cal Rptr2d 909, 978 P2d 67 (1999); *United States v Jones*, 132 S Ct 945 (2012). A US Senate Committee proposed in December 2012 an amendment to the Electronic Communications Privacy Act 1986 which regulates how the government may monitor digital communications. Courts have used

expectation of privacy if he has been put on notice that his activities in a specified area would be watched by others for a legitimate purpose. In US tort law the factors determining the reasonableness of an expectation of privacy include: (a) whether the area is generally accessible to the public; (b) whether the individual has a property interest in the area;[10] (c) whether the individual has taken normal precautions to maintain his privacy; (d) how the area is used; and (e) the general understanding of society that certain areas deserve the most scrupulous protection from intrusion.[11]

The increasing use of electronic surveillance and other forms of intrusion led the Younger Committee to recommend the creation of a tort to deal with surveillance (overt or covert) by means of a technical device. It would comprise the following elements: (a) a technical device; (b) a person who is, or her possessions which are, the object of surveillance; (c) a set of circumstances in which, were it not for the use of the device, that person would be justified in believing that she had protected herself or her possessions from surveillance whether by overhearing or observation; (d) an intention by the user to render those circumstances ineffective as protection against overhearing or observation; and (e) absence of consent by the victim.[12]

The Calcutt Committee defined privacy as 'the right of the individual to be protected against intrusion into his personal life or affairs, or those of his family, by direct physical means or by publication of information.' In *R v Khan* the appellant sought recognition of a right of privacy in respect of private conversations in a private home. Lord Nicholls expressed no view on the existence of the right, but stated that such a right, if it existed, could only do so as part of a larger and wider right of privacy, adding that 'the continuing, widespread concern at the apparent failure of the law to give individuals a reasonable degree of protection from unwarranted intrusion in many situations [was]...well known.'[13]

---

the Act to permit warrantless surveillance of certain kinds of mobile telephone data. The proposed amendment would require the police to obtain a warrant to search email messages regardless of their age. Presently the law allows warrantless searches of email messages that are more than 180 days old.

10. *Rakas v Illinois*, 439 US 128, 153 (1978).
11. *Rakas v Illinois*, 439 US 128, 152–3 (1978); *Oliver v United States*, 466 US 170, 178–83 (1984).
12. *Report of the Committee on Privacy* (Cmnd 5012, (1972)) (Chairman: Kenneth Younger), paras 562–5.
13. *R v Khan* [1997] AC 558, 582H. The European Court of Human Rights has routinely extended the scope of Art 8 to include intrusions such as telephone-tapping and bugging of premises. Yet this interpretation has not been adopted by the English courts. I consider this enigma in Chapter 8.

Intrusion and technology

More than a century ago Warren and Brandeis presciently complained that 'numerous mechanical devices threaten to make good the prediction that "what is whispered in the closet shall be proclaimed from the house-tops".'[14] Their worst nightmares could not have foreseen the ubiquity of Big Brother in our age. 'Low-tech' collection of transactional data in both the public and private sector has become commonplace. In addition to the routine surveillance by CCTV in public places, the monitoring of mobile telephones, the workplace, vehicles, electronic communications, and online activity, have swiftly become widespread in most advanced societies. The concept of privacy in its broadest—and least lucid—sense extends beyond these sorts of intrusions whose principal pursuit is personal information. It includes a diversity of incursions into the private domain, especially by the government, captured in Warren and Brandeis's phrase 'the right to be let alone'. This comprehensive notion, redolent of the celebrated seventeenth-century declaration by Sir Edward Coke that 'a man's house is his castle', embraces a wide range of invasions that encroach not only upon 'spatial' and 'locational' privacy, but also interfere with 'decisional' matters often of a moral character such as abortion, contraception, and sexual preference.

In the case of surveillance, a moment's reflection will reveal some of its many ironies—and difficulties. Its nature—and our reaction to it—are neither straightforward nor obvious. Is 'Big Brother is Watching You' a threat, a statement of fact, or merely mendacious intimidation? Is it the knowledge that I am being observed by, say, a CCTV camera, that violates my privacy? What if the camera is a (now widely available) imitation that convincingly simulates the action of the genuine article: flashing light, probing lens, menacing swing? Nothing is recorded, but I am unaware of its innocence. What is my objection? Or suppose the camera is real, but faulty—and no images are made, stored, or used? My actions have not been monitored, yet subjectively my equanimity has been disturbed. The mere presence of a device that appears to be observing and recording my behaviour is surely tantamount to the reality of my unease. It is, in other words, the *belief* that I am being watched that is my grievance. It is

14. SD Warren and LD Brandeis, 'The Right to Privacy' (1890) 4 Harvard Law Review 193, 195.

immaterial whether I am in fact the subject of surveillance. My objection is therefore not that I am being observed—for I am not—but to the possibility that I may be.

In this respect, being watched by a visible CCTV camera differs from that other indispensable instrument of the spy: the electronic listening device. When my room or office is bugged, or my telephone is tapped, I am by definition usually oblivious to this infringement of my privacy. Yet my ignorance does not, of course, render the practice inoffensive. Unlike the case of the fake or non-functioning camera, however, I *have* been subjected to surveillance: my private conversations have been recorded or intercepted, albeit unconsciously. The same would be true of the surreptitious interception of my correspondence: email or snail mail.

In the former case, no personal information has been captured; in the latter, it has, but I may never know. Both practices are subsumed in the category of 'intrusion', yet each exhibits a distinctive apprehension. Indeed, the more one examines this (neglected) problem, the less cohesive the subject of 'intrusion' becomes. Each activity requires a separate analysis; each entails a discrete set of concerns, though they are united in a general anxiety that one's society may be approaching, or already display features of, the Orwellian horror of relentless scrutiny.

The question is fundamentally one of perception and its consequences. Although my conviction that I am being monitored by CCTV is based on palpable evidence, my unawareness of the interception of my correspondence or conversations is plainly not, the discomfort is similar. In both cases, it is the distasteful recognition that one needs to adjust one's behaviour—on the assumption that one's words or deeds are being monitored. Indeed, the slide towards electronic supervision may fundamentally modify our relationships and our very identity. The increasing use of surveillance in the workplace, for instance, is changing not only the character of that environment, but also the very nature of what we do and how we do it. The knowledge that our activities are, or even may be, monitored undermines our psychological and emotional autonomy. My unawareness explains the paucity of 'intrusion' cases that reach the courts.

More pertinent, in the context of freedom of expression, is the fear that my private communications are anything but, which diminishes that liberty:

> Free conversation is often characterized by exaggeration, obscenity, agreeable falsehoods, and the expression of antisocial desires or views not intended to

be taken seriously. The unedited quality of conversation is essential if it is to preserve its intimate, personal and informal character.[15]

Privacy and freedom of expression are therefore frequently complementary rather than antagonistic rights.[16]

The privacy prognosis

The future of surveillance seems daunting. It promises more sophisticated and alarming intrusions into our private lives, including the greater use of biometrics, and sense-enhanced searches such as satellite monitoring, penetrating walls and clothing, and 'smart dust' devices (minuscule wireless micro-electromechanical sensors—MEMS—that can detect everything from light to vibrations). These so-called 'motes'—as tiny as a grain of sand—would collect data that could be sent via two-way band radio between motes up to 1,000 feet away.

As cyberspace becomes an increasingly perilous domain, we learn daily of new, disquieting assaults on its citizens. This slide towards pervasive surveillance coincides with the mounting fears, expressed well before 11 September 2001, about the disconcerting capacity of the new technology to undermine our freedom. Reports of the fragility of privacy have been sounded for at least a century. But in the last decade they have assumed a more urgent form. And herein lies a paradox. On the one hand, recent advances in the power of computers have been decried as the nemesis of whatever vestiges of our privacy still survive. On the other, the Internet is acclaimed as a Utopia. When clichés contend, it is imprudent to expect sensible resolutions of the problems they embody, but between these two exaggerated claims something resembling the truth probably resides. In respect of the future of privacy at least, there can be little doubt that the legal

---

15. LB Schwartz, 'On Current Proposals to Legalize Wiretapping' (1954) 103 University of Pennsylvania Law Review 157, 162. I draw here on R Wacks, *Privacy: A Very Short Introduction* (Oxford: Oxford University Press, 2010), ch 1. A victim's unawareness of the fact of interception was central to the decision of the US Supreme Court (by 5-4) on 26 February 2013 that Amnesty International and others who challenged warrantless wiretapping lacked standing because, in the words of Justice Alito, their fear of surveillance when foreign terrorists were the target was 'highly speculative,' *Clapper, Director of National Intelligence v Amnesty International USA* 568 US (2013) at 11.

16. See E Barendt, 'Privacy and Freedom of Speech' in AT Kenyon and M Richardson (eds), *New Dimensions in Privacy Law: International and Comparative Perspectives* (Cambridge: Cambridge University Press, 2006); DJ Solove, *The Future of Reputation: Gossip, Rumor, and Privacy on the Internet* (New Haven, CT: Yale University Press, 2007). See Chapter 5.

questions are changing before our eyes. And if, in the flat-footed domain of atoms, we have achieved only limited success in protecting individuals against the depredations of surveillance, how much better the prospects in our brave new binary world?

A world in which our every movement is observed erodes the very freedom that this snooping is often intended to protect. Naturally, we need to ensure that the social costs of the means employed to enhance security do not outweigh the benefits. Thus, one unsurprising consequence of the installation of CCTV in car parks, shopping malls, airports, and other public places is the displacement of crime; offenders simply go somewhere else. And, apart from the doors this intrusion opens to totalitarianism, a surveillance society can easily generate a climate of mistrust and suspicion, a reduction in the respect for law and those who enforce it, and an intensification of prosecution of offences that are susceptible to easy detection and proof.

Other developments have comprehensively altered basic features of the legal landscape. The law has been profoundly affected and challenged by countless other advances in technology. Developments in biotechnology such as cloning, stem cell research, and genetic engineering provoke thorny ethical questions and confront traditional legal concepts. Proposals to introduce identity cards and biometrics have attracted strong objections in several jurisdictions. The nature of criminal trials has been transformed by the use of both DNA and CCTV evidence.[17]

Orwellian supervision already appears to be alive and well in several countries. Britain, for example, boasts more than 4 million CCTV cameras in public places: roughly one for every 14 inhabitants. The United Kingdom also possesses the world's largest DNA database comprising some 5.3 million DNA samples. The temptation to install CCTV cameras by both the public and private sector is not easy to resist. The Data Protection Act 1998 ostensibly controls their use, but such regulation has not proved especially effective. A radical solution, adopted in Denmark, is to prohibit their use, subject to certain exceptions such as in petrol stations. The law in France, the Netherlands, and Sweden is more stringent than in the United Kingdom. These countries adopt a licensing system, and the law requires that warning signs be placed on the periphery of the zone monitored. German law has a similar requirement.

17. See G Laurie, *Genetic Privacy: A Challenge to Medico-Legal Norms* (Cambridge: Cambridge University Press, 2002).

Biometrics

Fingerprints have long been used as a means of linking an individual to a crime, but they also provide a practical method of privacy protection: instead of logging into your computer with a (not always safe) password, an increasing use is being made of fingerprint readers as a considerably more secure entry point. We are likely to see a greater use of fingerprint readers at supermarket checkouts and ATMs. There is no perfect biometric, but the ideal solution is to find a unique personal attribute that is immutable or, at least, unlikely to change over time. A measurement of this characteristic is then employed as a means of identifying the individual in question. Typically, several samples of the biometric are provided by the subject; they are digitized and stored on a database. The biometric may then be used either to identify the subject by matching his or her data against that of a number of other individuals' biometrics, or to validate the identity of a single subject.[18]

The Internet

Online activity is especially vulnerable to attack. The artillery of malicious software (or 'malware') includes viruses, worms, Trojan horses, spyware, 'phishing', 'bots', 'zombies', bugs, and exploits.[19] In late 2012 the British Government proposed its Communications Data Bill that will require

18. In order to counter the threat of terrorism, the future will unquestionably witness an increased use of biometrics. This includes, in particular, a number of measures of human physiography such as fingerprints, aspects of the iris and ear lobes, and DNA. Among the following examples of characteristics on which biometric technologies can be based are one's appearance (supported by still images), eg descriptions used in passports, such as height, weight, colour of skin, hair, and eyes, visible physical markings, gender, race, facial hair, wearing of glasses; natural physiography, eg skull measurements, teeth and skeletal injuries, thumbprint, fingerprint sets, handprints, iris and retinal scans, earlobe capillary patterns, hand geometry, DNA patterns; bio-dynamics, eg the manner in which one's signature is written, statistically analysed voice characteristics, keystroke dynamics, particularly login ID and password; social behaviour (supported by video-film), eg habituated body signals, general voice characteristics, style of speech, visible handicaps; imposed physical characteristics, eg dog-tags, collars, bracelets and anklets, bar codes and other kinds of brands, embedded microchips and transponders. One fear is that in authoritarian countries biometrics may be imposed on the public. Biometrics providers will thrive by selling their technology to repressive governments, and establish a foothold in relatively free countries by seeking soft targets; they may start with animals or with captive populations such as the frail, the poor, the old, prisoners, employees, and so on. I draw here on Roger Clarke's invaluable website: rogerclarke.com.
19. A virus is a block of code that introduces copies of itself into other programs. It normally carries a payload, which may have only nuisance value, though in many cases the consequences

Internet and telephone companies to track, through a 'deep packet inspection' web-monitoring system, the records of every citizen's web and mobile phone use, including social networking sites, without retaining their content, and store them for twelve months. It claimed that the law was a vital operational tool by which criminal gangs could be infiltrated, security threats addressed, and criminal suspects monitored. The Home Office has argued that, as technology develops, the authorities' ability to keep track of suspects has diminished by up to 25 per cent. Clause 1 of the bill confers powers on the Home Secretary to make orders requiring Internet and telephone companies to turn over an individual's communications records to 'relevant public authorities'.

Another means of tracking our computer use is provided by the silent intruders, cookies. These are data that the website servers transmit to the visitor's browser and are stored on his or her computer. They enable the website to recognize the visitor's computer as one with which it has previously interacted, and to remember details of the earlier transaction, including search words, and the amount of time spent reading certain pages. In other words, cookie technology enables a website—by default—furtively to put its own identifier into my PC permanently in order to track my online conduct. And cookies can endure; they may show an extensive list of each website visited during a particular period. Moreover, the text of the cookie file may reveal personal data previously provided. Websites, such as Amazon. com, justify this practice by claiming that it assists and improves the shopping experience by informing customers of books which, on the basis of their browsing behaviour, they might otherwise neglect to buy. But this gives rise to the obvious danger that my identity may be misrepresented by

are serious. In order to evade early detection, viruses may delay the performance of functions other than replication. A worm generates copies of itself over networks without infecting other programs. A Trojan horse is a program that appears to carry out a positive task (and sometimes does so), but is often nasty, eg keystroke recorders embedded in utilities. Spyware is software, often hidden within an email attachment, that secretly harvests data within a device about its user, or applications made by the device. These are passed on to another party. The data may include the user's browsing history, log individual keystrokes (to obtain passwords), monitor user behaviour for consumer marketing purposes (so called 'adware'), or observe the use of copyrighted works. 'Phishing' normally takes the form of an email message that appears to emanate from a trusted institution such as a bank. It seeks to entice the addressee into divulging sensitive data such as a password or credit card details. The messages are normally highly implausible—replete with spelling mistakes and other obvious defects—yet this manifest deceit manages to dupe an extraordinarily high number of recipients. Even apparently innocuous images uploaded to, say, Facebook, may facilitate an invasion of privacy by locating an individual; pictures taken by certain mobile telephones and tablets automatically attach the coordinates of the photograph, unless this function is manually disabled.

concentrating on tangential segments of my surfing or, on the other hand, personal data harvested from a variety of sources may be assembled to create a comprehensive lifestyle profile.

In 2012 the European Union proposed a Data Protection Regulation to protect Internet users from surreptitious tracking and unauthorized use of 'personal data' whose definition is expanded to embrace any information online that can be traced to an individual. Stringent penalties for violations committed by data controllers and stronger enforcement of data protection are included.[20]

Computer hacking

Hackers were once regarded as innocuous 'cyber-snoops' who adhered to a slightly self-indulgent, but quasi-ethical, code that dictated that one ought not to purloin data, but merely report holes in the victim's system. They were, as Lessig puts it, 'a bit more invasive than a security guard, who checks office doors to make sure they are locked...[He] not only checked the locks but let himself in, took a quick peek around, and left a cute (or sarcastic) note saying, in effect, "Hey, stupid, you left your door open".'[21]

While this laid-back culture eventually attracted the interest of law enforcement authorities—who secured legislation against it—the practice continues to produce headaches. According to Simon Church of VeriSign, the online auction sites that criminals use to sell user details are merely the beginning. He anticipates that 'mashup' sites that combine different databases could be converted to criminal use. 'Imagine if a hacker put together information he'd harvested from a travel company's database with Google Maps. He could provide a tech-savvy burglar with the driving directions of how to get to your empty house the minute you go on holiday.'

Identity theft

The appropriation of an individual's personal information to commit fraud or to impersonate him or her is an escalating problem, costing billions of dollars a year. In 2007 a survey by the US Federal Trade Commission found

20. See Chapter 5, n 173.
21. L Lessig, *Code and Other Laws of Cyberspace* (New York: Basic Books, 1999), 194.

that in 2005, a total of 3.7 per cent of survey participants indicated that they had been victims of identity theft. This result suggests that approximately 8.3 million Americans suffered some form of identity theft in that year. Ten per cent of all victims reported out-of-pocket expenses of $1,200 or more. The same percentage spent at least 55 hours resolving their problems. The top 5 per cent of victims spent at least 130 hours. The estimate of total losses from identity theft in the 2006 survey amounted to $15.6 billion.

The practice normally involves at least three persons: the victim, the impostor, and a credit institution that establishes a new account to the impostor in the victim's name. This may include a credit card, utilities service, or even a mortgage. Identity theft assumes a number of forms. Potentially the most harmful comprise credit card fraud (in which an account number is stolen in order to make unauthorized charges), new account fraud (where the impostor initiates an account or 'tradeline' in the victim's name; the offence may be undiscovered until the victim applies for credit), identity cloning (where the impostor masquerades as the victim), and criminal identity theft (in which the impostor, masquerading as the victim, is arrested for some offence, or is fined for a violation of the law). Part of the responsibility must be laid at the door of the financial services industry itself. Its lax security methods in granting credit and facilitating electronic payment subordinate security to convenience.

DNA databases

The growing use of DNA evidence in the detection of crime has generated a need for a database of samples to determine whether an individual's profile matches that of a suspect. The UK DNA database (with its 5.3 million profiles, representing 9 per cent of the population) is the largest anywhere: it includes DNA samples and fingerprints of almost a million suspects who are never prosecuted or who are subsequently acquitted. It is hardly surprising that innocent persons should feel aggrieved by the retention of their genetic information; the potential for misuse is not a trivial matter. This dismal prospect led two such individuals to request that their profiles be expunged following their walking free. Unable to convince the English courts, they appealed to the European Court of Human Rights which, at the end of 2008, unanimously decided that their right to privacy had been violated.

Other jurisdictions tend to destroy a DNA profile when a suspect is acquitted. In Norway and Germany, for example, a sample may be kept permanently only with the approval of a court. In Sweden only the profiles of convicted offenders who have served custodial sentences of more than two years may be retained. The United States permits the FBI to take DNA samples on arrest, but they can be destroyed on request should no charges be laid or if the suspect is acquitted. Among the 40 or so states that have DNA databases, only California permits permanent storage of profiles of individuals charged but then cleared. It has been suggested that, to avoid discrimination against certain sectors of the population (such as black males), everyone's DNA should be collected and held in the database. This drastic proposal is unlikely to attract general support. What is clear, however, is that to maintain the integrity of the system and protect privacy, these vulnerable, sensitive genetic data require strict regulation.

Repulsing the attack

Privacy enhancing technologies (PETs) seek to protect privacy by eliminating or reducing personal data or by preventing unnecessary or undesired processing of personal data without compromising the operation of the data system. Originally they took the form of 'pseudonymization' tools': software that allows individuals to withhold their true identity from operating electronic systems, and only reveal it when absolutely essential. These technologies help to reduce the amount of data collected about an individual. Their efficacy, however, depends largely on the integrity of those who have the power to revoke or nullify the shield of the pseudonym. Unhappily, governments cannot always be trusted.

Instead of pseudonymity, stronger PETs afford the tougher armour of anonymity that denies the ability of governments and corporations to link data with an identified individual. This is normally achieved by a succession of intermediary-operated services. Each intermediary knows the identities of the intermediaries next to it in the chain, but has insufficient information to facilitate the identification of the previous and succeeding intermediaries. It cannot trace the communication to the originator, or forward it to the eventual recipient.

These PETs include anonymous re-mailers, web-surfing measures, and David Chaum's payer-anonymous electronic cash (e-cash) or Digicash which employs a blinding technique that sends randomly encrypted data to my bank which then validates them (through the use of some sort of digital money) and returns the data to my hard disk. Only a serial number is provided: the recipient does not know (and does not need to know) the source of the payment. This process affords an even more powerful safeguard of anonymity. It has considerable potential in electronic copyright management systems (ECMS) with projects such as CITED (Copyright in Transmitted Electronic Documents) and COPICAT, being developed by the European Commission ESPIRIT programme. Full texts of copyrighted works scanned, eg, by the Google Books project are being downloaded and marketed without the owner's consent or royalty being paid. These projects seek technological solutions by which users could be charged for their use of such material. This 'tracking' of users poses an obvious privacy danger: my reading, listening, or viewing habits may be stored and access to them obtained for potentially sinister or harmful purposes. Blind signatures seem to be a relatively simple means by which to anonymize users.

Anonymity is an important democratic value. Even in a pre-electronic age, it facilitates participation in the political process which an individual may otherwise wish to spurn. Indeed, the United States has held that the First Amendment protects the right to anonymous speech. There are numerous reasons why I may wish to conceal my identity behind a pseudonym or achieve anonymity in some other way. On the Internet I may want to be openly anonymous but conduct a conversation with others (with either known or anonymous identities) using an anonymous re-mailer. I may even wish no one to know the identity of the recipient of my email. And I may not want anyone to know to which newsgroups I belong or which websites I have visited.

There are, moreover, obvious personal and political benefits of anonymity for whistleblowers, victims of abuse, and those requiring help of various kinds. Equally, (as always?) such liberties may also shield criminal activities, though the right to anonymous speech would not extend to unlawful speech. Anonymity enjoys a unique relationship with both privacy and free speech. The opportunities for anonymity afforded by the Internet are substantial; we are probably only on the brink of discovering its potential in both spheres. It raises (somewhat disquieting) questions about the very question of who we are: our identity.

The use of strong encryption to protect the security of communications has been met by resistance (notably in the United States and France) and proposals either to prohibit encryption altogether, or, through means such as public key escrow, to preserve the power to intercept messages. The battle has been joined between law enforcers and cryptographers; it is likely to be protracted, especially since enthusiastic would be too meek a word to describe the manner in which the culture of strong encryption has been embraced by ordinary computer users—since Phil Zimmerman's encryption software, PGP ('Pretty Good Privacy') may be generated in less than five minutes, and is freely available on the Internet.

A central feature of modern cryptography is that of the 'public key'. A lock-and-key approach is adopted in respect of telecommunications security. The lock is a public key which a user may transmit to recipients. To unlock the message, the recipient uses a personal encryption code or 'private key'. Public key encryption significantly increases the availability of encryption/identification, for the dual key system allows the encryption key to be made available to potential communicants while keeping the decryption key secret. It permits, for instance, a bank to make its public key available to several customers, without their being able to read each others' encrypted messages.

Technological solutions are especially useful in concealing the identity of the individual. Weak forms of digital identities are already widely used in the form of bank account and social security numbers. They provide only limited protection, for it is a simple matter to match them with the person they represent. The advent of smart cards that generate changing pseudo-identities will facilitate genuine transactional anonymity. 'Blinding' or 'blind signatures' and 'digital signatures' will significantly enhance the protection 'privacy'. A digital signature is a unique 'key' which provides, if anything, stronger authentication than my written signature. A public key system involves two keys: one public, and the other private. The advantage of a public key system is that if you are able to decrypt the message, you know that it could only have been created by the sender. The overriding question is: is my identity *genuinely required* for the act or transaction concerned? It is here that the data protection principles, described in Chapter 7, come into play.

RFID

The technology of radio frequency identification emerged as a means of inventory control to replace barcodes. An RFID system consists of three elements: a minuscule chip on each consumer item (an RFID tag) that stores a unique product identifier; an RFID reader; and a computer system attached to the reader having access to an inventory control database. The database contains extensive product information, including the contents, origin, and manufacturing history of the product. Assigning a tag to a product also discloses its location, rate and place of sale, and, in the case of transport companies, its progress. It has applications in recalling faulty or dangerous merchandise, tracing stolen property, preventing counterfeit, and providing an audit trail to thwart corruption.

The potential of RFID is huge, and it is increasingly being used for 'contactless' payment cards, passports, and the monitoring of luggage, library books, and pets. There is no reason why humans could not be microchipped—like our pets. It could assist the identification of Alzheimer's patients who go astray. Combining RFID and wireless fidelity networks (Wi-fi) could facilitate real-time tracking of objects or people inside a wireless network, such as a hospital. The privacy concern is that the acceptance of these benign applications may initiate less benevolent uses; there are likely to be calls for sex offenders, prisoners, illegal immigrants, and other 'undesirables' to be tagged.

There is also the fear that if RFID data is aggregated with other data (eg, information stored in credit or loyalty cards) to match product data with personal information, this could allow comprehensive personal profiles of consumers to be assembled. Moreover, an increase in the use of RFID in public places and homes and businesses, could portend an enlargement of the surveillance society. For example, my car has an RFID affixed to the windscreen that automatically deducts the toll from my bank account. The fact that it has just passed through the toll station at Pisa may be useful to a party interested in my movements. There is plainly a need for sophisticated PETs here.

The challenges posed by these, and many other, intrusions cannot be overstated. Does the law, in the absence of a tort of intrusion, provide effective protection? The action for breach of confidence (discussed at length in previous chapters) offers victims of media intrusion considerable scope for obtaining a variety of remedies. The other possible routes are summarized below.

Trespass to land

A cause of action will arise when, without justification, the defendant enters on the claimant's land, remains on such land, or places any object upon it. This tort could therefore be used to protect the owner of premises from unjustified invasion of privacy involving physical encroachment upon premises, where, say, a journalist installs a listening device inside the private premises of the claimant,[22] or where the defendant enters upon the claimant's premises to obtain information without the claimant's consent. Thus entry on to premises by a television crew with cameras rolling will constitute trespass unless express or implied licence to enter has been given. But even if the claimant is able to obtain an injunction against trespass, he or she may not succeed in obtaining an injunction against publication of photographs or video taken during the course of the trespass.[23]

The tort protects a person's property and his or her enjoyment of it. It does not protect privacy as such. No trespass is committed when a sketch, photograph, or video is made of someone's property by standing on a public street or on adjoining property: a person does not commit a tort merely by looking.[24] And no injunction will be ordered by a court to prevent a landowner from opening windows which enables him to observe the activities of his neighbours.[25] Nor does a person have a right to prevent another taking a photograph of her even within her own premises. In *Sports and General Press Agency Ltd v 'Our Dogs' Publishing Co Ltd* the court refused to prevent the defendant publishing photographs taken at a dog show by an independent photographer. Horridge J held that 'no one possesses a right of preventing another person photographing him any more than he has a right of preventing another person giving a description of him, provided the description is not libellous or otherwise wrongful.'[26]

In *Bernstein v Skyviews*[27] the defendant took aerial photographs of the plaintiff's house without the latter's consent and then offered the photographs for sale. The court did not grant an injunction restraining the

22. *Sheen v Clegg* [1967] *Daily Telegraph*, 22 June; *Greig v Greig* [1966] VR 376. I am pleased to acknowledge the assistance obtained here and elsewhere from the Report of the Law Reform Commission of Hong Kong, *Civil Liability for Invasion of Privacy* (2004) on whose privacy sub-committee I served from 1989 to 2001.
23. *Kaye v Robertson* [1991] FSR 62; *Service Corporation International plc v Channel Four Television Corporation* [1999] EMLR 83 (HC), 90.
24. *Hickman v Maisey* [1900] 1 QB 752; *Re Penny* (1867) 7 E & B 660. In *Victoria Park Racing and Recreation Grounds Co Ltd v Taylor* (1937) 58 CLR 479, 494, Latham CJ held that the defendant committed no wrong by describing to as wide an audience as he could obtain, what took place on the plaintiff's land.
25. *Turner v Spooner* (1861) 30 LJ Ch 801. In *Tapling v Jones* (1865) 11 HLC 290, 305, it was held that 'invasion of privacy by opening windows' was not a wrong for which the law would give a remedy.
26. [1916] 2 KB 880; affirmed by the Court of Appeal in [1917] 2 KB 125. The landowner may prohibit the taking of photographs on his premises by making it a condition of entry.
27. [1978] QB 479. See R Wacks, 'No Castles in the Air' (1977) 93 Law Quarterly Review 491.

defendant from entering the plaintiff's airspace. It held that a flight several hundred feet above the plaintiff's property did not interfere with his enjoyment of land, nor was the mere taking of a photograph without committing trespass on his land unlawful. Nor will the law assist a claimant who has been subjected to long-distance surveillance, or where an individual who is the victim of eavesdropping with the aid of a parabolic microphone where no wire-tapping or other physical intrusion upon the plaintiff's property takes place. Similarly, no trespass is committed when one's telephone conversation is intercepted—unless it entails physical encroachment upon the plaintiff's land.[28]

A final limitation is that the law of trespass protects only claimants who have a proprietary interest in land. The cause of action is therefore of no avail to guests, lodgers, and hospital patients. The owner of the premises will have an action in trespass, but he or she may be disinclined to launch one. Of course, where the victim is in a public place, the law of trespass is of no use.

Trespass to the person

The main forms of this tort are assault, battery, and false imprisonment. An assault is an overt action, by word or by deed, indicating an immediate intention to commit a battery and with the capacity to carry the threat into action. Battery is actual physical interference with the person of an individual. The merest touching of a person without consent may be actionable. Taking a photograph or shining a light in a person's eyes is not a battery unless done deliberately and it causes injury.[29] False imprisonment is the unauthorized infliction of bodily restraint or confinement. It could assist victims of door-stepping or so-called 'media scrums'.

In *Wainwright v Home Office*[30] the trial judge held that the tort of trespass to the person consisted of wilfully causing a person to do something to himself which infringed his right to privacy. This view was rejected by both the Court of Appeal and the House of Lords.[31]

---

28. *Malone v Commissioner of Police of the Metropolis (No 2)* [1979] 2 All ER 620, 642–4.
29. *Kaye v Robertson and Sport Newspaper Ltd* [1991] FSR 62 (CA).
30. [2001] EWCA Civ 2081, [2002] QB 1334.
31. [2001] EWCA Civ 2081, [2002] QB 1334 (CA), [72]; [2003] UKHL 53; [2004] 2 AC 406 (HL).

Nuisance

The tort of nuisance requires a condition or activity which unduly interferes with the use or enjoyment of land. The interference must continue
for a prolonged period of time. An occupier may have a cause of action in
private nuisance if she is harassed by telephone calls which cause her incon-
venience and annoyance, thereby interfering with the ordinary and reasonable use of the property.[32] Equally, watching and besetting premises may
constitute a private nuisance.[33] However, no cause of action arises in respect
of a single, isolated incident, or if the property suffers no physical injury or
the beneficial use of the property was not interfered with. A person who
takes a photograph of another cannot be liable in nuisance.

Subject to the exception that a person who is in exclusive possession of
land could sue even though he could not prove title to it, a person who
has no interest in the land could not sue in private nuisance. Thus a mere
licensee on the land such as a lodger or member of the householder's family who has no right to exclusive possession has no cause of action. An attempt to extend the protection afforded by this action to mere licensees was
made in *Khorasandjian v Bush*.[34] The Court of Appeal held that harassment
by unwanted telephone calls amounting to interference with the ordinary
and reasonable enjoyment of property which the recipient of the calls had a
right to occupy was actionable as a private nuisance, even though the recipient had no proprietary interest in the property. The decision was, however,
overruled by the House of Lords in *Hunter v Canary Wharf Ltd*.[35]

---

32. *Khorasandjian v Bush* [1993] QB 727.
33. *Hubbard v Pitt* [1976] 1 QB 142.
34. [1993] QB 727, [1993] 3 WLR 476 (CA).
35. [1997] AC 655. Lord Hoffmann pointed out that the development of the common law 'should
    not distort its principles and create anomalies merely as an expedient to fill a gap', 452g. He
    stated: 'If a plaintiff, such as the daughter of the householder in *Khorasandjian v Bush*, is ha-
    rassed by abusive telephone calls, the gravamen of the complaint lies in the harassment which
    is just as much an abuse, or indeed an invasion of her privacy, whether she is pestered in this
    way in her mother's or her husband's house, or she is staying with a friend, or is at her place
    of work, or even in her car with a mobile phone. In truth, what the Court of Appeal appears
    to have been doing was to exploit the law of private nuisance in order to create by the back
    door a tort of harassment which was only partially effective in that it was artificially limited to
    harassment which takes place in her home. I myself do not consider that this is a satisfactory
    manner in which to develop the law, especially when…the step so taken was inconsistent with
    another decision of the Court of Appeal….', 438c.

The action is inadequate to protect individuals against surveillance. A snoop does not seek to interfere with the activities of his victim; on the contrary his desire is for these activities to continue unchanged, in order to observe or record them unobserved. No interference with the use of property occurs where the occupier is unconscious of the intrusion.

Intentional infliction of emotional distress

In *Wilkinson v Downton*[36] the defendant, as a practical joke, told the plaintiff that her husband had been injured whilst returning from a day at the races and was lying in a pub with broken legs. The plaintiff fell seriously ill as a result, and sought damages for, inter alia, mental anguish and for her consequent illness. The jury found that the defendant meant the words to be acted upon, that they were acted upon, and that he knew the words to be false, and a sum of £100 was awarded to compensate the plaintiff for her loss and damage.

Wright J held

> The defendant has...wilfully done an act calculated to cause physical harm to the plaintiff—that is to say, to infringe her legal right to personal safety, and has in fact thereby caused physical harm to her. That proposition without more appears to me to state a good cause of action, there being no justification alleged for the act. This wilful *injuria* is in law malicious, although no malicious purpose to cause the harm which was caused nor any motive of spite is imputed to the defendant.[37]

The decision therefore establishes that doing an act that is calculated to cause physical harm is actionable should physical harm result. The claimant must, of course, show that the defendant's act would cause harm to a person of ordinary firmness, and that the act caused the harm, and is not too remote. Liability will attach even if the act would not affect a person of ordinary sensibilities if the claimant can prove that the defendant was aware of the claimant's susceptibility.[38] As to remoteness, Wright J explicitly recognized that recovery for nervous shock at that time was 'without precedent'.[39]

36. [1897] 2 QB 57.
37. [1897] 2 QB 57, 58–9. See generally NJ Mullany and PR Handford, *Tort Liability for Psychiatric Damage*, 2nd edn (Sydney: Law Book Co, 2006).
38. Eg *Timmermans v Buelow* (1984) 38 CCLT 136.
39. [1897] 2 QB 57, 61. Times have, of course, changed. The Privy Council's decision to refuse to allow recovery for the negligent infliction of nervous shock in *Victorian Railways Commissioner*

Might this action assist a victim of intrusion? How far might the general proposition stated in *Wilkinson* be extended beyond false statements? Also, the meaning of the words 'wilfully done an act calculated to cause physical harm' needs to be ascertained. Finally, other elements of the action require brief examination.

Conduct other than false statements

Judgments following *Wilkinson v Downton* reveal that the broad principle there enunciated is applicable not merely to false statements but to threats,[40] and other conduct.[41] In *Bradley v Wingnut Films Ltd*,[42] for instance, the plaintiff, the holder of an exclusive right to burial in a plot in a certain cemetery, sought an injunction against the defendant film company to prevent the plot being shown as a backdrop to a particular scene of a 'comedy horror' film. The burial plot appeared in the film for a total of only 14 seconds and it was not possible to read the words on the tombstone marking the site. The plaintiff pleaded, inter alia, the intentional infliction of emotional distress as a cause of action having been 'shocked and upset' by the association of the burial site with the film. Although the plaintiff's claim on this ground was rejected (for reasons considered later), Gallen J clearly proceeded on the basis that the film's depiction of the cemetery plot constituted conduct sufficient to found an action under *Wilkinson v Downton*.[43]

The importance of the distinction between false statements and other conduct is that it is far easier to establish the defendant's requisite state of mind for the former than for the latter. In *Bradley* the court specifically adverted to the relative unimportance of the burial plot in the scene in question and considered that the conduct of the defendant could not therefore be taken to have been calculated to produce harm to the plaintiff. Thus, the issue of how the defendant caused the claimant's harm directly affects

v Coultas (1888) 13 App Cas 222 was not followed by the Court of Appeal in *Dulieu v White & Sons* [1901] 2 KB 669.
40. *Khorasandjian v Bush* [1993] 3 WLR 476 and see text at n 59.
41. See FA Trinidade, 'The Intentional Infliction of Purely Mental Distress' (1986) 6 Oxford Journal of Legal Studies 219, 230–1. In *A v B's Trustees* (1906) 13 SLT 830, the plaintiff landlady suffered nervous shock when she came across a lodger who had committed suicide in her bathroom.
42. [1993] 1 NZLR 415.
43. [1993] 1 NZLR 415, 420–2.

the ease with which the claimant can prove that the emotional distress was 'intentionally' inflicted as a matter of law.[44]

The defendant's state of mind

The defendant's act must be wilful; that is to say, either intentional or calculated to cause physical harm. The second requirement is that the defendant's act, in the words of Wright J, be 'so plainly calculated to produce some effect of the kind which was produced that an intention to produce it ought to be imputed.'[45] The ease with which the claimant is able to prove that the defendant's conduct was 'plainly calculated' to cause physical harm depends on the nature of the act. As suggested earlier, this will be more difficult in the case of conduct other than overt, direct statements. But the law will impute intention to cause harm if the defendant intended to carry out an act 'sufficiently likely' to lead to the harm in question.[46] In *Bradley* Gallen J took the view that,

> There is no evidence in this case to suggest that the defendant intended in the ordinary sense of that word, to cause any distress to the plaintiff or his family in filming the sequence under consideration and in context I do not think that the consequences were so foreseeable in terms of the plaintiff's distress bearing in mind the position occupied by the tombstone in the film and its lack of relation to the action, that the damage even if proven could be said to have been intentional.[47]

Though the meaning of the term 'calculated' is far from clear, the boundaries of liability are reasonably plain. 'Calculated' cannot be restricted to *intention*, because in *Wilkinson* itself, the defendant's intention was to play a prank and presumably neither desired the harm nor considered it certain or substantially certain to follow from his statement. Moreover, in order to preserve the distinction between the intentional infliction of physical harm and the corresponding action in negligence, it should not be sufficient for the consequences of the defendant's conduct merely to be reasonably

44. 'As regards the conduct which precipitates the physical harm, it may take any form...What matters is not the kind of conduct but its likely effect on the plaintiff', Mullany and Handford (n 37), 289.
45. *Wilkinson v Downton* [1897] 2 QB 57, 59.
46. *Wainwright v Home Office* [2004] UKHL 53, [2004] 2 AC 406; *Wong v Parkside Health NHS Trust* [2001] EWCA Civ 1721, [2003] 3 All ER 932, [28].
47. [1993] 1 NZLR 415, 422.

foreseen. The defendant must intend, or at least be reckless as to, the consequences.[48]

The nature of the harm

As a matter of principle there is nothing to prevent a claimant recovering under *Wilkinson v Downton* for injury to the person *simpliciter*. In fact, the decisions have generally concerned 'nervous shock'.[49] There is a vital distinction between a transient shock, however severe, which is called 'emotional distress', on the one hand, and the subsequent development of physical symptoms as a result of the initial shock. Only in the latter event is recovery allowed.[50] As Lord Wilberforce has stated, 'nervous shock' is a 'hallowed expression',[51] but modern usage prefers 'recognisable psychiatric illness'.[52] In *Bradley*[53] Gallen J said:

> I accept that on the authorities to which I was referred, it is necessary for the plaintiff to establish something more than a transient reaction, however initially severe. This must translate itself into something physical and have a duration which is more than merely transient.[54]

Despite recent judicial suggestions that the strict requirements of *Downton* be diluted,[55] this has not occurred.

---

48. *Slatter v British Railways Board* (1966) 110 SJ 688 supports the proposition that a negligent act could entail liability under *Wilkinson v Downton*. In *Wong v Parkside Health NHS Trust* [2001] EWCA Civ 1721, [2003] 3 All ER 932, [12], Hale LJ said, 'For the tort to be committed, as with any other action on the case, there has to be actual damage. The damage is physical harm or recognised psychiatric illness. The defendant must have intended to violate the claimant's interest in his freedom from such harm. The conduct complained of has to be such that that degree of harm is sufficiently likely to result that the defendant cannot be heard to say that he did not "mean" it to do so. He is taken to have meant it to do so by the combination of the likelihood of such harm being suffered as the result of his behaviour and his deliberately engaging in that behaviour.'
49. See *Janvier v Sweeney* [1919] 2 KB 316; *Burnett v George* [1992] 1 FLR 525; and *Khorasandjian v Bush* [1993] 3 WLR 476.
50. Lord Ackner stated: 'mere mental suffering, although reasonably foreseeable, if unaccompanied by physical injury, is not a basis for a claim for damages', *Alcock v Chief Constable of South Yorkshire Police* [1992] 1 AC 310, 401.
51. *McCloughlin v O'Brien* [1983] 1 AC 410, 418.
52. *Hinz v Berry* [1970] 2 QB 40, 42 per Lord Denning MR.
53. [1993] 1 NZLR 415.
54. [1993] 1 NZLR 415, 421.
55. Expressed, in particular, by Lord Hoffmann. See *Hunter v Canary Wharf* [1997] AC 655, 707. In *Wainwright v Home Office* [2003] UKHL 53, [2004] 2 AC 406, [44]–[45] however, he said, 'I do not resile from the proposition [stated in *Hunter*, at 707] that the policy considerations which limit the heads of recoverable damage in negligence do not apply equally to torts of intention.

The future of the cause of action

Just when it was thought that *Wilkinson* was moribund, new life was breathed into the cause of action by *Dulieu v White & Sons*,[56] in respect of the *negligent* infliction of nervous shock. As already mentioned, it is not easy to categorize rigidly the varying degrees of foresight into negligence or recklessness, and this has engendered the view that *Wilkinson* should be, and has been, subsumed within the ever-expanding tort of negligence. In *Wilkinson* itself, 'The physical harm was intended only in a limited sense—the acts were intentional, but there was no evidence that the defendant intended the plaintiff to become ill.'[57] The facts of *Wilkinson* certainly fall within current negligence principles, but at the time of the decision recovery upon the basis of mere foreseeability of nervous shock was precluded by the Privy Council's decision in *Victorian Railways Commissioner v Coultas*.[58]

Wilkinson received a shot in the arm from the decision of the Court of Appeal in *Khorasandjian v Bush*.[59] The defendant launched a campaign of harassment against the plaintiff after their relationship broke down. Persistent unsolicited telephone calls were accompanied by threats of violence. The plaintiff was faced with the difficulty that, although the experience caused her considerable stress, she was not suffering from a recognizable psychiatric illness. Acknowledging the fact of her suffering, and that it was not in law sufficient to found an action under *Wilkinson v Downton*, Dillon LJ stated,

> But there is, in my judgment, an obvious risk that the cumulative effect of combined and unrestrained further harassment such as [the plaintiff] has undergone would cause such an illness. The law expects the ordinary person to

If someone actually intends to cause harm by a wrongful act and does so, there is ordinarily no reason why he should not have to pay compensation. But I think that if you adopt such a principle, you have to be very careful about what you mean by intend. In *Wilkinson v Downton* RS Wright J wanted to water down the concept of intention as much as possible. He clearly thought, as the Court of Appeal did afterwards in *Janvier v Sweeney* [1919] 2 KB 316, that the plaintiff should succeed whether the conduct of the defendant was intentional or negligent. But the *Victorian Railway Commissioners* case 13 App Cas 222 prevented him from saying so. So he devised a concept of imputed intention which sailed as close to negligence as he felt he could go. If, on the other hand, one is going to draw a principled distinction which justifies abandoning the rule that damages for mere distress are not recoverable, imputed intention will not do. The defendant must actually have acted in a way which he knew to be unjustifiable and intended to cause harm or at least acted without caring whether he caused harm or not.'

56. [1901] 2 KB 669.
57. AL Goodhart (book review) (1944) 7 Modern Law Review 87, 87–8.
58. (1888) 13 App Cas 222.
59. [1993] 3 WLR 476.

bear the mishaps of life with fortitude and...customary phlegm; but it does not expect ordinary young women to bear indefinitely such a campaign of persecution as that to which the defendant has subjected the plaintiff. Therefore, in my judgment, on the facts of the case and in line with the law as laid down in *Janvier v Sweeney*, the court is entitled to look at the defendant's conduct as a whole and restrain those aspects on a *quia timet* basis also of his campaign of harassment which cannot be strictly classified as threats.[60]

This suggests that the court will protect a claimant in circumstances where there is only a risk, albeit an obvious one, of nervous shock *later* resulting from the cumulative effect of the defendant's conduct.[61] It is possible to reconcile *Khorasandjian* with existing authority; the principle merely being applied to the special concerns of *quia timet* injunctions rather than the usual action for damages. But it is also possible to take the view that the Court of Appeal, in 'practical reality',[62] extended *Wilkinson* to cases of purely emotional distress in situations where an injunction is being sought.[63] This leads inevitably to the possibility of awarding damages for emotional distress under *Wilkinson v Downton*, though it is important to recall the restatement by the House of Lords of the requirement in negligence actions for something more than purely mental distress.[64]

Returning to the question of the desirability of maintaining an action for the intentional infliction of emotional distress distinct from negligence liability, the policy arguments which have led the courts to reject recovery for mental distress in negligence cases are less persuasive when applied to the intentional tort:[65]

There may be good policy reasons for limiting claims for 'nervous shock' arising from *negligent* conduct to harm that can be categorised as genuine psychiatric illness or disorder, based on the fear of opening up the sphere of liability to a potentially vast category of plaintiffs. But where without any legitimate purpose or excuse the defendant intends to inflict mental distress there can

---

60. [1993] 3 WLR 476 at 483.
61. See J Bridgeman and MA Jones, 'Harassing Conduct and Outrageous Acts: A Cause of Action for Intentionally Inflicted Emotional Distress?' (1994) 14 Legal Studies 180, 192–201.
62. Bridgeman and Jones (n 61), 196.
63. In *Burnett v George* [1992] 1 FLR 525, the Court of Appeal, on facts not dissimilar to those in *Khorasandjian*, refused to apply *Wilkinson v Downton*. Sir John Arnold P stated that molestation or interference is not an actionable wrong unless 'there be evidence that the health of the plaintiff is being impaired by [such conduct] calculated to create such impairment, in which case relief would be granted by way of an injunction to the extent that it would be necessary to avoid that impairment of health', 527.
64. *Alcock v Chief Constable of South Yorkshire Police* [1992] 1 AC 310.
65. Bridgeman and Jones (n 61), 196.

be no justification for the law refusing to grant a plaintiff protection from this form of anti-social behaviour.

If this were indeed adopted, the action for the intentional infliction of emotional distress would closely resemble the US tort of 'extreme outrage'.[66] This action ordinarily compensates the plaintiff for 'nervous shock', though the *Restatement* makes it clear that it is not limited to 'bodily harm', and where the conduct is sufficiently extreme and outrageous, recovery may be allowed for emotional distress alone.[67]

Protection against intrusion

The greatest obstacle to the application of *Wilkinson v Downton* is the need to prove that the act in question is calculated to cause physical harm. The plaintiff may, at most, be able to show that the defendant's conduct is negligent, and it is clear that the courts will not allow recovery for mental distress in a negligence action.[68] There is also the possibility, as yet unsupported by authority, that for the intentional tort under *Wilkinson*, the court will be prepared to award damages for purely emotional distress. But what constitutes a meritorious case? Perhaps only where there is distress caused by a *course of conduct* by the defendant or where the mental distress is serious.[69] There are difficulties, however, with both. In the former, isolated instances of extreme behaviour would not be caught by the action. In the latter, limiting recovery to objective states of mind would overlook different subjective reactions of individuals to the same stimulus.

There is merit in the suggestion, albeit in a slightly different context, that,

> ...the very vagueness of the applicability of a molestation tort could be seen as one of its strengths, for the focus is clearly on the actual parties to the action and their relationship. In assessing whether the acts done by the defendant were calculated to cause harm to the plaintiff and whether such harm did, or was likely, to ensue, the defendant's knowledge of his victim will be highly material...Flexibility enables the court to make common-sense judgments based on a determination of when intrusive and unpleasant conduct exceeds

---

66. See *Restatement* (n 6), para 46.
67. *Restatement* (n 6), para 46, comment k.
68. See *Alcock v Chief Constable of South Yorkshire Police* [1992] 1 AC 310.
69. Bridgeman and Jones (n 61), 198–201. The concentration upon *conduct* would be in conformity with the US approach discussed earlier which distinguishes between mere insult and 'extreme and outrageous conduct'. The Protection from Harassment Act 1997 would come into play in such a case. See the following section.

the bounds of what society will tolerate poses a risk of damage to an individual's fundamental right to freedom from injury.[70]

Similar considerations apply to the infliction of emotional distress.

Statutory protection

Several legislative measures provide protection against various forms of media intrusion such as door-stepping and extreme forms of paparazzi pursuits.[71] In particular, the Protection from Harassment Act 1997 creates a number of offences, and offers scope for victims of these activities to recover compensation, indeed there is authority for the Act's specific application to privacy-invading conduct.[72]

Section 1 of the Act prohibits a person from pursuing a 'course of conduct' which amounts to the 'harassment of another' which that person 'knows or ought to know' will amount to harassment of that other.[73] Four conditions must be satisfied. There must have been conduct:

(a) occurring on at least two occasions;
(b) targeted at the claimant;
(c) calculated in an objective sense to cause distress; and
(d) which is objectively judged to be oppressive and unreasonable.[74]

It is plain that conduct that is merely annoying will not suffice.[75]

---

70. M Brazier, 'Personal Injury by Molestation—An Emergent or Established Tort' (1992) Family Law 346, 348.
71. Other legislation that might assist in curtailing the worst excesses of the media include s 5 of the Public Order Act 1986 which creates the offence of 'insulting behaviour' (which was applied to an offender who installed a video camera in a changing room: *Vigon v DPP* [1997] EWHC Admin 947, (1998) 162 JPR 115) and s 67 of the Sexual Offences Act 2003 under which voyeurism is an offence, though it is unlikely to apply to journalists, except perhaps where, say, naked pictures of a model were taken if it were proved that they were for voyeuristic purposes. There are also various interception offences under the Interception of Communications Act 1985 and the Regulation of Investigatory Powers Act 2000.
72. *Hipgrave v Jones* [2004] EWHC 2901 (QB), [21] per Tugendhat J.
73. In *Majrowski v Guy's and St Thomas' NHS Trust* [2005] EWCA Civ 251, [2005] QB 848, [82] May J stated that the conduct in question must be 'calculated, in an objective sense, to cause distress...' He added that 'It has to be conduct which the perpetrator knows or ought to know amounts to harassment, and conduct which a reasonable person would think amounted to harassment.'
74. *Green v DB Group Services (UK) Ltd* [2006] EWHC 1898 (QB), [14].
75. Anxiety, distress, oppressive, unacceptable are among the epithets used by the courts. See eg *Majrowski v Guy's and St Thomas' NHS Trust* [2006] UKHL 34, [2007] 1 AC 224, [30]; *Thomas*

For a defendant who has acted to prevent or detect crime, or whose actions are reasonable, a defence is provided in section 1(3).[76] The Act has been applied in relatively few cases involving media intrusion; the complaint in *Thomas v News Group Newspapers Ltd*,[77] related to publication rather than intrusion. But various activities that have been held to constitute harassment could well be employed by zealous paparazzi.[78] Inevitably Article 10's protection of freedom of expression has been invoked as a defence against harassment by those whose acts seek to expose injustice[79] or vent personal animus.[80]

In *Trimingham v Associated Newspapers Ltd*[81] the complainant's grievance was that the newspaper had, inter alia, published offensive articles about her appearance and sexuality. She claimed damages, including aggravated damages, and an injunction against the newspaper ordering it to refrain from referring to her sexual orientation unless relevant in a particular context distinct from her relationship with a politician and that the newspaper refrain from harassing the claimant. The court, Tugendhat J stated, should ask: (1) was the distress suffered the result of the course of conduct, in the form of speech? (2) If so, ought the defendant to have known that the course of conduct amounted to harassment? (3) If so, has the defendant shown that the pursuit of that course of conduct was reasonable? To both questions (1) and (2) he added, there were secondary questions: namely was the claimant a purely private figure and was she in other respects a person

v News Group Newspapers Ltd [2001] EWCA Civ 1233, [2002] EMLR 4 [30]. In *Conn v Sunderland City Council* [2007] EWCA Civ 1492, [12] the Court of Appeal declared that 'the touchstone for recognising what is not harassment...will be whether the conduct is of such gravity as to justify the sanctions of the criminal law.'

76. See *KD v Chief Constable of Hampshire, John Hull* [2005] EWHC 2550 (QB), [2005] Po LR 253; *Howlett v Holding* [2006] EWHC 41 (QB); *Thomas v News Group Newspapers Ltd* [2001] EWCA Civ 1233, [2002] EMLR 4.

77. [2001] EWCA Civ 1233, [2002] EMLR 4. The Court of Appeal acknowledged that a newspaper could foresee that an article critical of the claimant could constitute harassment since it would lead its readers to address hostile letters to her, occasioning distress.

78. These could include, eg: spying—*Howlett v Holding* [2006] EWHC 41 (QB); *Crawford v CPS* [2008] EWHC 148 (Admin); stalking—*R v Liddle* [1999] 3 All ER 816; *Woolford v DPP*, HC, 9 May 2000; rummaging through an individual's rubbish—*King v DPP* [2001] ACD 7; surreptitious photography—*Crawford v CPS* [2008] EWHC 148 (Admin).

79 *University of Oxford v Broughton* [2008] EWHC 75 (QB); *Heathrow Airport v Garman* [2007] EWHC 1957 (QB).

80. *Howlett v Holding* [2006] EWHC 41 (QB).

81. [2012] EWHC 1296 (QB).

with a personality known to the defendant such that it ought not to have known that the course of conduct amounted to harassment?

In respect of the defence of reasonableness, Tugendhat J decided that in order for the court to comply with section 3 of the Human Rights Act, it must hold that a course of conduct in the form of journalistic speech is reasonable, unless it is so unreasonable that it is necessary (in the sense of a pressing social need) and proportionate to prohibit or sanction the speech in pursuit of one of the aims listed in Article 10(2), including, in particular, the protection of the rights of others under Article 8. The court concluded that the claimant was not a private person by reason of the fact because she worked for a leading politician, and she conducted a sexual relationship with a politician which would result in his leaving his wife. It rejected the argument that the defendant ought to have known that its conduct would be sufficiently distressing to be considered oppressive or amount to harassment. Such a course of conduct might be unreasonable if it interfered with the Article 8 rights of the claimant.[82]

The Internet—again

The Internet poses significant challenges to the enforcement of the law against the publication of personal information by bloggers, Tweeters, and users of social networks such as Facebook.[83] But it is not beyond the ingenuity of the law or technology to find a solution to this, admittedly intractable, problem.[84] The potential for harm is plainly considerably greater than the publication of the same personal information in a local newspaper.

---

82. See *AM v News Group Newspapers Ltd* [2012] EWHC 308 (QB) and *Ting Lan Hong and KLM v Persons Unknown* [2011] EWHC 2995 (QB) which clearly demonstrate the capacity of the Protection from Harassment Act 1997 to restrain journalists and photographers whose conduct amounts to harassment.

83. One suggestion is that legislation ought to require Facebook, MySpace, and other similar social networking sites to have initial privacy settings on newly created accounts to be completely private and accessible only by the person who created them. Users may then decide what and with whom they wish to share their personal information. The current privacy setting default fails to achieve this. Such regulation would ensure that users could assume that all their information is private—unless they decide otherwise.

84. While acknowledging 'that the enforcement of law and regulation online is problematic' (Part C, ch 3, para 7.1), the Leveson Inquiry Report (n 3), pointed out that the Internet Corporation for Assigned Names and Numbers (ICANN) ensured interoperability of the constituent networks, as well as consistent policy on addressing, addresses, and standards; that access to Internet services is regulated in the UK and Europe through telecommunications legislation

Effortlessly and swiftly, intimate details of our lives are disseminated to an enormous audience; and they may remain accessible almost ad infinitum. Why, say, should an injunction be flouted with impunity merely because the medium deployed is a blog or Twitter? The courts have demonstrated a salutary readiness to prevent brazen breaches of its authority. Thus, where a prominent footballer's name was revealed online, notwithstanding an interim injunction against *The Sun* preventing disclosure of his sexual relationship, Eady J refused to vary the terms of the injunction to permit the identification of the claimant. He distinguished his own decision in *Mosley v News Group Newspapers Ltd*[85] on the ground that the intimate video in that case had been seen by hundreds of thousands—even before the application for the order. Here, the disclosure of the footballer's identity occurred after the interim order had been granted.

The learned judge observed that a time might come when the information in question is so widely disseminated that there is nothing left for the law to protect. Nevertheless, he concluded that amending the order would engulf the claimant and his family

> ...in a cruel and destructive media frenzy. Sadly, that may become unavoidable in the society in which we now live but, for the moment, in so far as I

---

as regulated by Ofcom, and that the transmission of content wirelessly through the national radio spectrum network is regulated through the Wireless Telegraphy Act 2006 and has regulatory impacts for access to the Internet through wireless devices other than computers, such as mobile phones (especially smart phones), and other Internet-enabled devices such as tablets. Also, video on demand when made available online is regulated by the Audiovisual Media Services Regulations 2009 and the Audiovisual Media Services Regulations 2010, by the Authority for Television on Demand (ATVOD). And the Internet Watch Foundation (IWF) is a self-regulatory body that works closely with ISPs to ensure that web pages, including those hosted outside the UK, which provide access to potentially criminal content and specifically, images of child abuse, are reported and removed or blocked at source. In the case of Twitter, the Report noted that it had been informed by the website that its rules forbid members from using the service for any unlawful purpose, and any material that is found by the company to contravene that policy can be taken down or removed. Like most social networking sites and publishers of user-generated content, it operates acceptable use policies (AUPs) which set down guidelines for user behaviour on those sites and cover issues such as posting of offensive content and bullying, Part C, ch 3, paras 3.1–7.6.

85. [2008] EWHC 687 (QB). Soon after the claimant's identity was revealed in Parliament by an MP, a further application was made to Tugendhat J to lift the anonymity restriction on the ground that the footballer's name was now readily available. He declined to do so because the object of the injunction was not solely to protect private information, but to prevent intrusion and harassment of the claimant and his family. It was reported that the claimant has launched an action against Twitter Inc to disclose the identities of anonymous account holders alleged to have breached Eady J's injunction by revealing the claimant's identity: *CTB v Twitter, Inc and Persons Unknown* (2012) Case No HQ11XO1814. The Leveson Inquiry did not pursue in any detail the question of online breaches of privacy. See Chapter 2.

am being asked to sanction it, I decline to do so. On the other side…it has
not been suggested that there is *any* legitimate public interest in publishing
the story.

He added,

> It is fairly obvious that wall-to-wall excoriation in national newspapers,
> whether tabloid or 'broadsheet', is likely to be significantly more intrusive
> and distressing for those concerned than the availability of information on
> the Internet or in foreign journals to those, however many, who take the
> trouble to look it up. Moreover, with each exposure of personal informa-
> tion or allegations, whether by way of visual images or verbally, there is a
> new intrusion and occasion for distress or embarrassment. Mr Tomlinson
> argues accordingly that 'the dam has not burst'. For so long as the court is
> in a position to prevent *some* of that intrusion and distress, depending upon
> the individual circumstances, it may be appropriate to maintain that degree
> of protection. The analogy with King Canute to some extent, therefore,
> breaks down.

The enactment of a cause of action along the lines proposed in Chapter 8,
offers a remedy to claimants who are able to identify the publisher, and that
he, she, or it knew or ought to have known that the publication was seriously offensive or objectionable to a reasonable person.

An Internet Service Provider (ISP) who is aware of a posting on its server
and fails to respond to a reasonable request to remove or delete it, may be
held liable as a 'publisher' at common law. This was the case where an ISP
transmitted a defamatory posting to its newsgroup subscribers from the
storage of its news server. The court concluded:

> In my judgment the defendants, whenever they transmit and whenever there
> is transmitted from the storage of their news server a defamatory posting, pub-
> lish that posting to any subscriber to their ISP who accesses the newsgroup
> containing that posting. Thus every time one of the defendants' customers ac-
> cesses [the newsgroup] and sees that posting defamatory of the plaintiff there
> is a publication to that customer.[86]

---

86. *Godfrey v Demon Internet Ltd* [2001] QB 201, 208–9. The ISP was held not to be protected
by the defence in s 1 of the Defamation Act 1996 (which codifies the defence of innocent
dissemination). An ISP would have a defence if it is able to demonstrate that it was not the author, editor, or publisher of the statement in question; that it took reasonable care with regard
to its publication; and it did not know, and had no reason to believe, that what it did caused
or contributed to the publication of the defamatory statement. See too *Loutchansky v Times
Newspapers Ltd (Nos 2–5)* [2002] QB 783; *Harrods Ltd v Dow Jones & Co Inc* [2003] EWHC
1162 (QB). In *Davison v Habeeb* [2011] EWHC 3031 (QB) it was held that Google, as host of

This position is analogous to the owner of a notice board who deliberately refused to remove defamatory matter on premises under his control.[87] A decision in the United States reached the opposite conclusion and held that an ISP was not a 'publisher' of a defamatory email message sent by one its subscribers.[88]

While ISPs collect a certain amount of fairly innocuous information about their users such as their IP addresses, billing information, etc, there is always a risk that they might provide such personal data to the authorities.

blogger.com, was arguably a common law publisher. In *Tamiz v Google* [2012] EWHC 449 (QB), however, the court concluded that Google Inc was not a publisher, notwithstanding the fact that its notice had been drawn to the offending blogs, and it had the technical means to remove them: its role as a platform provider was merely passive. The Electronic Commerce (EC Directive) Regulations 2002 set out the circumstances under which Internet intermediaries are responsible for material not created by them, but which they host, cache, or carry. They distinguish between intermediaries that are mere conduits (reg 17), that cache data (reg 18), and that host data (reg 19). Regulation 19 provides a defence where an ISP does not have actual knowledge of unlawful information or is not aware of facts and circumstances from which it would have been apparent to the service provider that the information hosted was unlawful. Section 1(1) of the Defamation Act 1996 is frequently used by websites as a defence on the ground that they are not the author, editor, or commercial publisher of a statement. Of course, once the defendant becomes aware of a defamatory posting, and declines to remove it, it cannot avail itself of the defence in s 1.

87. *Byrne v Deane* [1937] 1 KB 818.
88. *Lunney v Prodigy Services Co*, 683 NYS2d 557 (AD NY 1998); affirmed 94 NY2d 242 (CA NY 1999). A similar view—in direct contrast to *Godfrey v Demon*—was adopted in *Totalise plc v Motley Fool Ltd* [2001] EMLR 29; *Bunt v Tilley* [2007] 1 WLR 1243; and *Metropolitan International Schools Ltd v Designtechnica Corp* [2009] EMLR 27 (dealing with an online search engine). In *Oriental Press Group Ltd v Fevaworks Solutions Ltd* [2009] HKCU 1556, the Hong Kong Court of First Instance held that Internet intermediaries are publishers only when they become aware of the defamatory material and decide not to remove it from their server, [68]. For a compelling analysis and criticism of the approach in *Bunt v Tilley*, see M Collins, *The Law of Defamation and the Internet*, 3rd edn (Oxford: Oxford University Press, 2010), 112–20. The author contends that intermediaries that host or cache material produced by others 'resemble…public libraries and newsagents, whose liability in defamation law turns on their ability to establish defence. Orthodox analysis favours [their] being treated, for the purpose of defamation law, as publishers of any material hosted or cached by them, even when they did not create it and have no knowledge of its contents', 120. The same logic may be applied where the offending material is personal information in violation of an individual's privacy. Adopting this 'newsagent' analogy, the Supreme Court of Victoria in *Trkulja v Google Inc, LLC & Another (No 5)* [2012] VSC 533, explicitly distinguished *Tamiz v Google*, *Bunt v Tilley*, and *Metropolitan International Schools Ltd v Designtechnica Corp* in rejecting Google's argument that it was not the 'publisher' of defamatory material online since their system was fully automated: there was therefore no human intervention between the request made to the search engine and the publication of the search results. The fact that Google did not monitor how each page was constructed was not determinate of its being a mere platform rather than a publisher. Google's intention to publish arose from the automated program it developed, which generated the defamatory publication. Another relevant factor was that Google was put on notice about the defamatory publication but did not remove the offending articles within a reasonable time.

And even where a security-conscious consumer encrypts such data, the ISP will nevertheless know the IP addresses of both the sender and recipient. An ISP which is an innocent distributor of the offending publication would avoid liability, especially if it had no control over the storage of the posting or is unaware of its presence on the server.

Pursuing paparazzi

An attractive stratagem is to hit the paparazzi where it hurts—in their pockets. By denying them copyright in the images they make or take, the urge both to snoop and publish may be resisted: the fruits of their intrusion will not be theirs to sell.[89] Thus, if the media could re-publish a surreptitiously shot photograph of, say, a film star, without having to pay a fee, the market for such pictures would fall dramatically. The paparazzi could go out of business.

A thin, but rather quaint, line of authority which denies copyright to immoral, deceptive, blasphemous, or defamatory material[90] is unlikely to be invoked given our contemporary laissez-faire mores. It is hard to imagine a court enlarging the scope of turpitude to deny legal protection. In any event, the idea is artificial, unwieldy, and conceptually problematic. If privacy is to be subsumed under copyright, in most cases what the law would be protecting is less the claimant's right of privacy, than his or her right of publicity: the right to control the circumstances under which his or her image may be bought and sold.[91] The attraction of this proprietary approach

---

89. Some years ago an idea under consideration by a group of London lawyers was to propose an amendment to s 85 of the Copyright, Designs and Patents Act 1988 by adding to the list of those who have a right in a commissioned photograph or film, a person who is the subject of an intrusive image. 'Intrusive' would be defined to include the non-consensual depiction of its subjects engaged in lawful activities on private premises. This intriguing suggestion seems to have disappeared without trace. See R Wacks, 'Pursuing Paparazzi: Privacy and Intrusive Photography' (1999) 29 Hong Kong Law Journal 372.

90. *Glyn v Weston Feature Films* [1916] 1 Ch 261, 269–70. The principle is only moribund: in *Stephens v Avery* [1988] 2 WLR 1280, 1284, Browne-Wilkinson V-C said that the law of confidence and copyright would not protect 'matters which have a grossly immoral tendency'. See too *Attorney-General v Guardian Newspapers (No 2)* [1988] 3 WLR 776, 818: Peter Wright's conduct in disclosing confidential information in *Spycatcher* 'reeked of turpitude' and could therefore be copied with impunity; copyright would not attach to it (per Lord Jauncey). See too *Hubbard v Vosper* [1972] 2 QB 84, 101.

91. Copyright may assist a claimant in circumstances where a private letter or family photograph is copied or published. As a general rule, an action for infringement of copyright is actionable only at the suit of the owner of the copyright, eg a photographer, the author of an article, or

to the paparazzi plague is understandable; indeed, property interests were among the midwives at the birth of the right of privacy.[92] And, as described in Chapter 3, the first US judgment to recognize that the common law offered protection to privacy involved what became the tort of appropriation of name and likeness: the use for the defendant's benefit of the plaintiff's identity.[93]

a television or newspaper company. A person whose photograph has been taken by another cannot normally bring an action if the photograph is reproduced or published by that other person without his or her authority. An exception is if the person whose privacy has been invaded has commissioned the photograph and is entitled to the copyright under the terms of the agreement. A person who has commissioned a work may restrain any exploitation of the commissioned work for any purpose against which he or she could reasonably take objection. Where the publication of a photograph constitutes misuse of private information, the copyright of the photograph is typically owned by the publisher. No copyright exists in a person's name, likeness, or image or indeed in information as such. I am free to read a private letter and reproduce its contents in my own words without infringing the copyright of the author. Dissemination of information disclosed in an article would not constitute an infringement if there is no direct quotation. The tort of passing off protects commercial interests, especially business goodwill, rather than privacy. The relevant statute is the Copyright, Designs and Patents Act 1988. Article 10 rights are unlikely to figure here, but see *Douglas v Hello! Ltd* [2008] 1 AC 1 which also touches on the 'right of publicity'.

92. See the discussion of Warren and Brandeis's reliance on *Albert v Strange* in Chapter 3.
93. See the discussion of the judgments of *Pavesich* and *Roberson* in Chapter 3.

7

Remedies

What remedies are available to an individual whose rights under Article 8 of the European Convention on Human Rights have been violated? Where the victim is aware that personal information is about to be published the most effective solution is to seek an interim injunction to prevent such publication. Should publication have already occurred, relief must be sought in a final injunction to thwart further publicity, and/or to seek compensation in the form of damages.[1] Extra-legal remedies are offered by various media regulators such as the Press Complaints Commission (PCC).

This chapter provides a brief outline of each of these routes, with the emphasis on the first—interim injunctions—since they have recently generated considerable controversy.[2]

Injunctions

It will be recalled that section 12 of the Human Rights Act 1998 contains a number of references to remedies that have, as their principal purpose, to assuage fears of the media that Article 8 might stifle free speech.[3]

---

1. Obtaining relief for the misuse of private information does not come cheaply. The figures are alarming. Max Mosley confessed that in his successful action against a newspaper 'the damages were £60,000. The *News of the World* was ordered to pay 82% of my costs, which was £420,000. That is an unusually high percentage. That makes it £480,000. The bill from the solicitors was £510,000...so I was £30,000 out of pocket', Joint Committee on Privacy and Injunctions, *Privacy and Injunctions: Oral and Written Evidence* (2011), 696.

2. Other possible remedies include an account of profits, restitutionary damages, *quantum meruit*, and compensation under s 13 of the Data Protection Act 1998. I consider the last-mentioned briefly later. See *Tugendhat and Christie on the Law of Privacy and the Media*, 2nd edn (M Warby, N Moreham, and I Christie eds) (Oxford: Oxford University Press, 2011), 302–5, 676–81; R Wacks, *Privacy and Press Freedom* (London: Blackstone Press, 1995), ch 6.

3. See Chapter 3. Their purpose, in general, is to signal courts to tread cautiously before granting relief.

Interim injunctions

Prior restraint of the media is always a contentious, highly sensitive matter in any democratic society. Blackstone's powerful pronouncement has been particularly influential in the United States:

> The liberty of the press is indeed essential to the nature of a free state: but this consists in laying no *previous* restraints upon publications, and not in freedom from censure for criminal matter when published. Every freeman has an undoubted right to lay what sentiments he pleases before the public: to forbid this, is to destroy the freedom of the press: but if he publishes what is improper, mischievous, or illegal, he must take the consequence of his own temerity.[4]

In its first encounter with a law imposing prior restraint, the Supreme Court famously declared, 'liberty of the press, historically considered and taken up by the Federal Constitution, has meant, principally although not exclusively, immunity from previous restraints or censorship.'[5] And it has continued resolutely to set its face against any pre-emptive strikes against free speech: 'Any system of prior restraints of expression comes to this Court bearing a heavy presumption against its constitutional validity.'[6]

Nor has the English law discounted Blackstone's authoritative directive. In the words of one judge:

> There is a general principle in our law that the expression of opinion and the conveyance of information will not be restrained by the courts save on pressing grounds. Freedom of expression is as much a sinew of the common law as it is of the European Convention.[7]

The reluctance to restrain publication is at its most compelling when the defendant threatens to publish material that is defamatory of the claimant. Following the 'rule in *Bonnard v Perryman*'[8] courts will not prevent

---

4. William Blackstone, *Commentaries on the Laws of England*, 17th edn (1830), vol 5, Amendment I (Speech and Press), Document 4, Facsimile of the first edition of 1765–1769 (Chicago, IL: University of Chicago Press, 1979).
5. *Near v Minnesota ex rel Olson*, 283 US 697, 716 (1931).
6. *Bantam Books v Sullivan*, 372 US 58, 70 (1963). *New York Times Co v United States* (the 'Pentagon Papers' case), 403 US 713 (1971); *Nebraska Press Association v Stuart*, 427 US 539 (1976). Cf *People v Bryant*, 94 P3d 624 (Colo 2004).
7. *R v Advertising Standards Authority Ltd, ex p Vernons Organisation Ltd* [1992] I WLR 1289, 1293 per Laws J. For equally strong ECtHR antipathy towards prior restraint, see *Observer and Guardian v United Kingdom* App 13585/88 (1991) 14 EHRR 153, 191; *Sunday Times v United Kingdom (No 2)* (1991) 14 EHRR 229, [51]; *Wingrove v United Kingdom* (1996) 24 EHRR 1, [58].
8. [1891] 2 Ch 269 (CA). As to the inappropriateness of the rule's application in breach of confidence cases, see R Wacks, 'Pop Goes Privacy' (1978) 31 Modern Law Review 67. See too *Greene v Associated Newspapers Ltd* [2005] QB 972.

publication of an allegedly defamatory statement unless it is clear that the defence of justification will fail at trial. In respect of the threatened publication of confidential or private facts, however, the rule is plainly out of place for it would defeat the point of a trial of the merits: the cat is out of the bag, or, in the equally colourful simile: 'Confidential information is like an ice cube…Give it to the party who has no refrigerator…and by the time of trial you just have a pool of water.'[9]

The common law confers no power on the courts to award injunctions *contra mundum*, but periodically the courts are faced with circumstances that demand that a restraining order be issued against the world. Such a situation arose in *Venables and Thompson v News Group Newspapers Ltd* in which an injunction was issued to protect the identities and addresses of the killers of James Bulger on their release from imprisonment.[10] It occurred also in a case where the court was persuaded that disclosure of private information would adversely affect the claimant's health.[11]

A so-called 'super injunction' is an interim injunction which restrains a person from (a) publishing information which concerns the applicant and is said to be confidential or private and (b) publicizing or informing others of the existence of the order and the proceedings (the 'super' element of the order).[12] An anonymized injunction is an interim injunction which restrains a person from publishing information which concerns the applicant and is said to be confidential or private where the names of either or both of the parties to the proceedings are not stated.[13]

---

9. *Attorney-General v Newspaper Publishing Ltd* [1988] Ch 333, 358 per Sir John Donaldson. In *Mosley v News Group Newspapers Ltd* [2008] EWHC 687 (QB) Eady J drew the proper distinction between libel and privacy claims, adding that 'once privacy has been infringed, the damage is done and the embarrassment is only augmented by pursuing a court action…Thus, if journalists can successfully avoid the grant of an interlocutory injunction, they can usually relax in the knowledge that intrusive coverage of someone else's sex life will carry no adverse consequences for them…', [230].

10. (2001) 2 WLR 1038.

11. *OPQ v BJM and CJM* [2011] EWHC 1059 (QB). The court's jurisdiction was founded on the European Convention and the Human Rights Act. Eady J held that 'in view of the clear risk of publication in the media, there is unfortunately no other means open to the court of fulfilling its obligation under the Human Rights Act to protect those rights than to grant a *contra mundum* injunction', [26].

12. *Report of the Committee of Super-Injunctions: Super-Injunctions, Anonymised Injunctions and Open Justice* (May 2011), para 2.14

13. *Report of the Committee of Super-Injunctions* (n 12). Concern has been expressed that interim injunctions were maintained for an excessively long, even indefinite, period either because the initial order granting interim relief did not include a return date, or because the claimant failed to pursue the substantive claim to trial. In the latter case, a claimant awarded an interim injunction was satisfied that he or she could not improve on this outcome at trial, and the defendant regarded the interim injunction as resolving the issue since it was not worth

Section 12(3) of the Human Rights Act 1998 provides that an interim injunction is not to be granted unless the court is satisfied that the applicant is likely to establish at trial that publication should not be permitted. As to the degree of likelihood, the House of Lords held in *Cream Holdings Ltd v Banerjee*[14] that the courts should be extremely slow to award such injunctions where the applicant cannot demonstrate that it is 'more likely than not' that at trial he or she will succeed in proving why publication should be restrained.[15]

Prior notification

It does not appear unreasonable to give an individual advance warning that the media propose to publish personal information about him or her. This would avoid the media practice of 'ambushing' a victim: disclosing personal information without allowing the claimant an opportunity to prevent publication through an application for an interim injunction. Damages may be awarded for the infringement, but they come too late. The damage has been done.[16]

proceeding with publication of the invasive story: see *Giggs v News Group Newspapers Ltd* [2012] EWHC 431 (QB).

14. [2005] 1 AC 253.
15. The more stringent test, the House of Lords declared, was to protect freedom of expression. In *LNS (John Terry) v Persons Unknown* [2010] EWHC 119 (QB), Tugendhat J refused to grant an injunction because 'the nub of the applicant's complaint is to protect [LNS's] reputation, in particular with sponsors, and so ...the rule in *Bonnard v Perryman* precludes the grant of an injunction; and ...in any event damages would be an adequate remedy for LNS.' Damages (see further the section entitled 'Damages') have been held in certain cases with a commercial flavour to be the appropriate remedy. In *Shelley Films Ltd v Rex Features Ltd* [1994] EMLR 134, however, the court found that although the core of the plaintiff's complaint was the disclosure of confidential commercial information, an interim injunction was the appropriate remedy under the circumstances. See G Phillipson, 'Max Mosley goes to Strasbourg: Article 8, Claimant Notification and Interim Injunctions' (2009) 1 Journal of Media Law 73. Cf A Scott, 'Prior Notification in Privacy Cases: A Reply to Professor Phillipson' (2010) 2 Journal of Media Law 49.
16. In its report, *Press Standards, Privacy and Libel*, the Culture, Media and Sport Committee (CMS) concluded that a legal or unconditional requirement to pre-notify would be ineffective because of the need for a public interest exception, Second Report of Session 2009–10 (HC 362, 2010). It accepted that while editors did contact subjects prior to publication, in most cases they took a calculated risk not to do so because they knew or suspected that an injunction against them was likely to be obtained. It conceded that 'clearly pre-notification in the form of giving an opportunity to comment is the norm across the industry', and that 'giving subjects of an article the opportunity to comment is often crucial to fair and balanced reporting...' Nevertheless, although it recommended that the *Editors' Code* be amended to reflect the fact that the norm was to pre-notify (subject to a public interest exception), it opposed a legal or unconditional requirement to pre-notify, preferring an encouragement to journalists

This was the essence of the argument that Max Mosley presented to the Strasbourg Court which decided that such a requirement would unduly fetter freedom of expression:

> [T]he Court has consistently emphasised the need to look beyond the facts of the present case and to consider the broader impact of a pre-notification requirement. The limited scope under Article 10 for restrictions on the freedom of the press to publish material which contributes to debate on matters of general public interest must be borne in mind. Thus, having regard to the chilling effect to which a pre-notification requirement risks giving rise, to the significant doubts as to the effectiveness of any pre-notification requirement and to the wide margin of appreciation in this area, the Court is of the view that Article 8 does not require a legally binding pre-notification requirement.[17]

Enforcing such a requirement by the criminal law would be disproportionately Draconian, but where, say, a newspaper intends to publish particularly intimate information, is it irrational to require a forewarning to be given to the individual to whom it relates? Failure to do so might plausibly be penalized by an award of exemplary damages.[18]

The Parliamentary Joint Committee on Privacy and Injunctions while rejecting the case for a statutory requirement to pre-notify nevertheless recommended that

> ...the reformed media regulator's code of practice must include a requirement that journalists should notify the subject of articles that may constitute an intrusion into privacy prior to publication, unless there are compelling reasons not to.[19]

to pre-notify by allowing courts to take into account a failure to do so when assessing damages, as a factor in determining aggravated damages. The PCC's *Editors' Code* provides that: 'there is wide agreement that prior notification...while often desirable, could not and should not be obligatory. It would be impractical, often unnecessary, impossible to achieve and could jeopardise legitimate investigations. Yet at the same time a failure to include relevant sides of the story can lead to inaccuracy and breach of the Code.'

17. *Mosley v United Kingdom* App 48009/08 (10 May 2011), [132]. The media successfully argued that a mandatory duty would have a chilling effect on free speech, and it would, in any event, be difficult to determine the extent of such a duty in view of a public interest exception. It also pointed to the problem of enforcement, and the likelihood that the media would rather pay any fine than comply with the requirement. An application to refer the case to the Grand Chamber was declined on 16 September 2011.

18. I discuss this question later.

19. *Privacy and Injunctions*, Session 2010–12, HL Paper 273 (HC 1443, 27 March 2012), [127]. It remarked that 'claimants seeking a privacy injunction are required by section 12(2) of the Human Rights Act 1998 to notify other parties to the claim of their intention unless there are "compelling reasons" not to notify. It might be considered ironic that such notification is required by the individual, but a newspaper is not required to notify an individual when it

Without argument, the Board proposed by the Leveson Inquiry Report to govern the self-regulatory body is explicitly denied the power to 'prevent publication of any material, by anyone, at any time'.[20] But it should, the Report suggests, be able to offer a service of advice to editors of subscribing publications relating to compliance with the code of conduct, which editors, in their discretion, can deploy in civil proceedings arising out of publication.

The solution may, however, lie elsewhere. It will be recalled that in Chapter 5 I considered the manner in which courts determine whether Article 8 is 'engaged'. I suggested there that, on its own, the test of 'reasonable expectation of privacy' is mistakenly applied to cases of 'publication'. A better approach, I argued, is for the courts to apply a test that looks also to the concept of 'personal information' itself. This would enquire not merely whether a reasonable person would 'expect' the information to be kept private, but also whether the information in question is of such a character that he or she would want to withhold or restrict its use or publication. The latter is another way of saying that its disclosure would offend any reasonable person to whom it relates.

The notion of 'offensiveness' has found little favour with English judges. Indeed, the House of Lords in *Campbell*[21] explicitly eschewed the approach of Gleeson CJ in *Lenah* in which he stated: 'The requirement that disclosure or observation of information or conduct would be *highly offensive to a reasonable person of ordinary sensibilities* is in many circumstances a useful practical test of what is private.'[22] Lord Nicholls regarded this test as stricter than the 'reasonable expectation' test, and he cautioned against its use on

---

intends to publish something about that person's private life', para 124. Another irony is that while, in their evidence to the committee, representatives of the media vehemently opposed a requirement of pre-notification, there was widespread agreement in the press during the BBC debacle in November 2012 that an individual who had been erroneously 'outed' as a child abuser in a television programme, should have been given an opportunity to deny the charge before the broadcast.

20. *An Inquiry into the Culture, Practices and Ethics of the Press* (HC 780, 2012), Part K, ch 7, para 4.38. 'In that way', the Report continues, 'there is potentially the opportunity for the regulatory body, should the need arise, to give reasoned opinions on issues brought to them by editors, or by individuals concerned about potential publication of a matter, that might provide explanation and context and thereby assist the court in any subsequent consideration of the matter', ibid.

21. [2004] 2 AC 457.

22. *Australian Broadcasting Corporation v Lenah Game Meats Pty Ltd* (2001) 185 ALR 1, 13, para 42 (emphasis added).

the ground that it 'brings into account considerations which should more properly be considered at the later stage of proportionality.'[23]

But is this correct? The test of proportionality is *already* applied when the court considers whether to grant an interim injunction. In other words, before issuing an injunction to check publication, a judge will perforce balance the competing rights under Articles 8 and 10. This entails an assessment of whether the public interest in publication (or the extent to which the disclosure contributes to a debate of general interest in a democratic society) is proportionate to the effect it will have on the claimant's right of privacy. Moreover, the five-stage test espoused by the House of Lords, discussed in Chapter 4, involves a dual application of the test of proportionality or what Lord Steyn called 'the ultimate balancing test'.[24]

Applying Gleeson CJ's 'highly offensive' test could provide a mode by which to distinguish potentially serious violations of the claimant's privacy from those that are at the trivial end of the spectrum. The law—preferably in statutory form—would specify that where it is proposed to publish personal information that would be highly offensive to a reasonable person of ordinary sensibilities, a duty is imposed on the prospective publisher to inform the individual to whom the information relates, of the intention to publish. Failure to do so could, as already mentioned, result in exemplary or aggravated damages being awarded against the publisher. This would diminish the curb on freedom of expression, and conform to the spirit of the European Court's 'less restrictive alternative doctrine' that urges states to 'minimize, as far as possible, the interference with…rights, by trying to find alternative solutions and by generally seeking to achieve their aims in the least onerous way as regards human rights.'[25]

What qualifies as 'highly offensive' is not a question that admits of scientific exactitude. But, since it will be largely the media who will be required to ask it, the answer will not be inordinately elusive. Dealing daily, as the media do, with information about individuals, it is not unrealistic to regard

---

23. [2004] 2 AC 457, [21]. Baroness Hale also gave short shrift to the Gleeson test, declaring, 'An objective reasonable expectation test is much simpler and clearer than the test sometimes quoted from the judgment of Gleeson CJ in the High Court of Australia in *Australian Broadcasting Corporation v Lenah Game Meats Pty Ltd*', [135].

24. *Re S (A Child)* [2005] 1 AC 593, [17]. It is sometimes described as 'parallel analysis': *A Local Authority v W* [2006] 1 FLR 1, [53].

25. *Hatton v United Kingdom* (2001) 34 EHRR 1, para 97, quoted by G Letsas, *A Theory of Interpretation of the European Convention on Human Rights* (Oxford: Oxford University Press, 2007), 101.

an editorial judgment of this kind as fairly undemanding. Distinguishing between distressing intimate facts, on the one hand, and 'vapid tittle-tattle',[26] on the other, hardly demands profound philosophical deliberation.

If, in exercising this evaluation in good faith, a prospective publisher concludes that the disclosure would be sufficiently hurtful to the victim, the latter should be informed of the nature, content, and perhaps also, in certain cases, the source of the private information in question. The opportunity is then presented to the claimant to seek an interim injunction which the publisher can, of course, apply to discharge by, for example, demonstrating that publication is in the public interest.

Pre-notification is no panacea, and it is not innocent of its own drawbacks, especially the impact on the media's exercise of freedom of expression. It has also been argued that investigative journalism—which often depends on the element of surprise—might be undermined. But this is to overlook the fact that the information in question is, *ex hypothesi*, personal. Its publication will generally relate to matters whose disclosure rarely serves the public interest. Where, however, notwithstanding the highly offensive nature of the information, a newspaper flouts the pre-notification requirement and decides to publish and be damned, such damnation (in the form of exemplary or aggravated damages) might be worth enduring in the interests of disclosing intimate facts that are claimed to be in the public interest, should a court decide otherwise, or avoided by successfully invoking Article 10.

Final injunction

Should a claimant fear that the risk of publication still exists after success at trial, a final injunction may be awarded. Its terms will normally prevent any future disclosure of the private information in question.[27]

It hardly requires stating that enforcing an injunction in our brave new digital world is a challenge that may be monumentally futile. The facility and velocity with which bloggers, tweeters, and other online commentators spread the word (benignly or otherwise) frustrates the law's efforts to safeguard personal information. Indeed, it is worth asking whether, had Max Mosley been granted a timely 'super injunction' it would have thwarted

---

26. *Jameel v Wall Street Journal* [2006] UKHL 44, [2007] I AC 359, [147] per Baroness Hale.
27. See *Tolstoy v United Kingdom* App 18139/91 (1995) 20 EHRR 442.

sundry bloggers, tweeters, and devotees of YouTube from broadcasting the information. Contempt of court proceedings would be likely to prove difficult. Nor is it a straightforward matter to pursue ISPs, operators of social media networks, or website managers.

'Jigsaw' identification

This practice

> ...involves the separate publication by different entities of different items of information which do not identify the claimant when looked at separately, but do so or risk doing so, when they are put together. Such information therefore does not have to actually identify a claimant. Nor need it be private. The conjunction of publicly available information with the report of proceedings may well lead to 'two and two' being put together.[28]

It represents a serious threat to the authority of the law, especially where a newspaper circumvents an injunction by using anonymous bloggers.[29] The most effective solution is for offenders to be prosecuted for contempt, initiated by the Attorney General or Director of Public Prosecutions or even the court. It is also open to the claimant (whose pocket is sufficiently deep) to pursue proceedings. Where the conduct falls short of contempt, the court has the power to make a costs order against the wrongdoer.

Damages

In a number of cases damages, occasionally substantial, have been awarded for the misuse of private information.[30] This includes claims for pecuniary[31]

---

28. *MNB v News Group Newspapers* [2011] EWHC 528 (QB), [33] per Sharp J. See too *NEJ v Wood* [2011] All ER (D) 218, [11]; *AMM v HXW* [2010] EWHC 2457 (QB); *TSE and ELP v News Group Newspapers* [2011] EWHC 1308 (QB), [33]–[34].
29. *DFT v TFD* [2010] EWHC 2335 (QB), [29].
30. Eg *Campbell v MGN Ltd* [2002] EMLR 30; *Douglas v Hello!* [2003] 3 All ER 996; *McKennitt v Ash* [2006] EMLR 10. Cf *Wainwright v Home Office* [2004] 2 AC 406, [51] per Lord Hoffmann.
31. Thus in *Douglas v Hello!* damages were awarded to *OK!* to compensate the magazine for the lost revenue as a consequence of its competitor, *Hello!*, publishing unauthorized photographs of the celebrity wedding.

and non-pecuniary loss.[32] But compensatory damages may not always be adequate, as Eady J put it in *Mosley v News Group Newspapers Ltd*:[33]

> [I]t is reasonable to suppose that damages for such an infringement may include distress, hurt feelings and loss of dignity. The scale of the distress and indignity in this case is difficult to comprehend. It is probably unprecedented. Apart from distress, there is another factor which probably has to be taken into account of a less tangible nature. It is accepted in recent jurisprudence that a legitimate consideration is that of vindication to mark the infringement of a right…[I]t should be stressed that this is different from vindication of reputation (long recognised as a proper factor in the award of libel damages). It is simply to mark the fact that either the state or a relevant individual has taken away or undermined the right of another—in this case taken away a person's dignity and struck at the core of his personality…As Lord Scott observed in *Ashley*,[34] '…there is no reason why an award of compensatory damages should not also fulfil a vindicatory purpose.'

There was in this case an acknowledgement by the court that 'no amount of damages can fully compensate the Claimant for the damage done. He is hardly exaggerating when he says that his life was ruined. What can be achieved by a monetary award in the circumstances is limited.'[35]

Aggravated damages

Where the defendant has behaved in a high-handed, malicious, insulting, or oppressive manner, the court may go to 'the top of the bracket and [award] as damages the largest sum that could be fairly regarded as compensation.'[36]

---

32. Eg *Lady Archer v Williams* [2003] EMLR 38; *Cornelius v de Taranto* [2001] EMLR 329; *Mosley v News Group Newspapers Ltd* [2008] EMLR 20. Compensation is for injury to feelings, distress, and loss of dignity.
33. [2008] EWHC 1777, [216]. '[I]t has to be accepted that an infringement of privacy cannot ever be effectively compensated by a monetary award. Judges cannot achieve what is, in the nature of things, impossible. That unpalatable fact cannot be mitigated by simply adding a few noughts to the number first thought of', [231].
34. *Ashley v Chief Constable of Sussex* [2008] 2 WLR 975, [21]–[22].
35. *Ashley v Chief Constable of Sussex* [2008] 2 WLR 975, [236].
36. *Mosley v News Group Newspapers Ltd* [2008] EWHC 1777, [222] per Eady J quoting Lord Reid in *Cassell v Broome* [1972] AC 1927. See *Campbell v MGN Ltd* [2002] EMLR 30 where Morland J ordered the newspaper to pay aggravated damages for 'rubbing salt into the claimant's wounds', [161].

Exemplary damages

They are generally perceived to be anomalous in civil cases.[37] In the context of privacy, there is the added possibility of an award generating a chilling effect on free speech. Eady J was concerned that in addition to compensatory damages and injunctive relief, the media should not have to face the 'somewhat unpredictable risk of being fined on a quasi-criminal basis'.[38] Nor was there authority for such an award in actions for breach of confidence or privacy.[39]

Another impediment is the precise status of the cause of action of 'misuse of private information'. Is it a tort? Several judges have answered the question in the affirmative. Indeed, Eady J has queried whether 'it may now be correct to apply the label of tort to this expanded cause of action',[40] adding that 'it can only be a matter for speculation whether a hypothetical future House of Lords would follow Lord Nicholls's classification of invasion of privacy as a tort and having done so would regard it as a wrong to which exemplary damages should now be extended.'[41]

Eady J concluded that, in the context of balancing of rights enshrined in Articles 8 and 10, the courts were required to deploy the tools of necessity and proportionality. And he questioned whether the remedy of exemplary damages was either necessary or proportionate in relation to the protection provided in Article 8 as balanced against Article 10.[42]

---

37. See *Rookes v Barnard* [1964] AC 1129 for the two categories under which exemplary damages might be awarded. Since they may be awarded in defamation cases, it is difficult to see why the same reasoning ought not to apply to serious cases of misuse of private information.

38. *Mosley v News Group Newspapers Ltd* [2008] EWHC 687 (QB), [173].

39. *Kuddus v Chief Constable of Leicestershire Constabulary* [2002] AC 122. See *Report on Aggravated, Exemplary and Restitutional Damages* (Law Com No 247, 1997).

40. If it is indeed a tort, exemplary damages would be available. According to Eady J in *Mosley*, the term was being 'used advisedly to convey the message that infringements of privacy should now be regarded as an independent tort by any limitations deriving from its equitable origins', [182]. See N Witzleb, 'Justifying Gain-based Remedies for Invasions of Privacy' (2009) Oxford Journal of Legal Studies 1.

41. *Mosley v News Group Newspapers Ltd* [2008] EWHC 687 (QB), [184]. The Leveson Inquiry Report proposes that exemplary damages (re-named 'punitive damages') be available for actions for breach of privacy, breach of confidence, and similar media torts, *An Inquiry into the Culture, Practices and Ethics of the Press*, HC 780 (2012), Part J, Chapter 3, para 5.12. Part of the rationale for this recommendation is to provide an incentive to publishers to join the proposed voluntary independent regulatory system: Membership and good practice would be relevant.

42. [194]. Exemplary damages in cases involving the media were criticized as 'draconian' by Lord Lester in the House of Lords on 11 January 2013. It was reported on 21 February 2013 that an opinion by three senior counsel concluded that the Leveson proposal was in breach of Art 10 of the ECHR. 'To punish the press for what others may do without punishment is inconsistent with the special importance that domestic and Strasbourg jurisprudence attach to freedom of the press,' the opinion is reported as asserting, adding that it could have a 'chilling effect' on free speech, *The Times*, 21 February 2013.

Data Protection Act 1998

As described in Chapter 5, the Act is applicable to the media in a number of respects. It also provides, in section 13, for compensation for damage caused by the contravention by a data controller of any requirement of the Act.[43] An individual who can prove to have suffered financial or physical damage, or damage and distress, as the consequence of a breach of the Act, and the data controller is unable to establish that it has taken such care as in all the circumstances was reasonably required to comply with the Act, may be awarded compensation.[44] Compensation for distress alone is exigible only where the violation relates to the processing of personal data for 'special purposes' which normally means artistic, literary, or journalistic purposes.

How might this affect the media? To obtain compensation under section 13, a claimant must prove that the information is published, and that the defendant data controller has failed to comply with the Act. Nevertheless,

> [I]t is easy to see that if a media organization has published something about a data subject that is false it may well have an uphill struggle to establish that this was not a result of some shortcomings in its attempted compliance with the Act. Innocent mistakes are likely to be forgiven, but a failure of systems or practices is likely in many cases to make out liability.[45]

The data controller is deprived of the defences in defamation such as qualified privilege. Its liability turns solely on its failure to exercise reasonable care to comply with the Act.[46]

---

43. Article 23 of the EU directive provides for compensation for damage suffered by anyone as a consequence of a data breach. This would include distress. Since s 13 restricts compensation to distress only where there is pecuniary loss (see *Johnson v Medical Defence Union* [2007] EWCA Civ 262, [74]), it is arguable that the section may be vulnerable to challenge under the Human Rights Act 1998. There is an additional anomaly: s 55 provides that the Information Commissioner may impose fines of up to £500,000 where data breaches cause distress or damage. The Leveson Inquiry Report recommended that it 'should be made clear that the right to compensation for distress conferred by section 13 of the Data Protection Act 1998 is not restricted to cases of pecuniary loss, but should include compensation for pure distress', Part H, ch 5, para 2.62.
44. But see *Douglas v Hello! Ltd* [2003] 3 All ER 996 and *Murray v Express Newspapers plc* [2007] EMLR 22, where it was doubted that the damage and distress suffered by the claimants could reasonably be regarded as arising from a contravention of the Act as required by s 13. See too *Lord Ashcroft v (1) Attorney-General and (2) Department for International Development* [2002] EWHC 1122 (QB).
45. Tugendhat and Christie (n 2), 304.
46. The precise status of the remedy (eg, whether it has created a new tort, or what the quantum of damages is) is uncertain. See *Quinton v Peirce* [2009] EWHC 912 (QB); *Smeaton v Equifax plc* [2012] EWHC 2322 (QB), [2012] BPIR 888.

Privacy codes

Section 12(4) of the Human Rights Act provides that a court is required to pay 'particular regard' to 'any relevant privacy code' when considering a matter 'where the proceedings relate to …journalistic, literary or artistic material.' Here I shall consider briefly the extent to which the three principal codes of practice provide remedies for breaches of their privacy provisions: the PCC, the Office of Communications (Ofcom), and the BBC.[47] Their relevance to the question of 'public interest' was considered in Chapter 5.

Press Complaints Commission

The Commission was established in 1991 to administer a code of practice by which newspapers and magazines agreed to abide; and to deal with complaints from members of the public who claim a breach of the code. In 2010, the PCC received over 7,000 complaints. In 2011 the Commission ruled on or successfully mediated 1,687 cases (accounting for about 2,300 complaints). The most frequent cause of complaint is inaccurate or misleading reporting.[48]

In regard to privacy, the *Editors' Code* provides:

i) Everyone is entitled to respect for his or her private and family life, home, health and correspondence, including digital communications.

ii) Editors will be expected to justify intrusions into any individual's private life without consent.

---

47. Section 32 of the Data Protection Act 1998 provides an exemption from several parts of the Act where personal data are processed for 'special purposes'—where the processing is undertaken with a view to the publication by any person of any journalistic, literary, or artistic material. The data controller must reasonably believe that, having regard in particular to the special importance of the public interest in freedom of expression, publication would be in the public interest, and the data controller reasonably believes that, in all the circumstances, compliance with that provision is incompatible with the special purposes. In determining the reasonableness of a newspaper's belief that publication would be in the public interest, regard may be had to its compliance with any relevant code of practice. These include the PCC Code of Conduct, the BBC Producers' Guidelines, and the Ofcom Code. The Leveson Inquiry Report proposed restricting the availability to newspapers of the defence in s 32. See Chapter 5.
48. This summary is based on the PCC's evidence to the Parliamentary Joint Committee on Privacy and Injunctions (n 1), 504 ff. A comprehensive statement of the Commission's powers and procedures, as well as a detailed account of its adjudications in respect of complaints relating to 'privacy', instances of its 'proactive approaches', advice provided to editors, and other examples of its work may be found there. The Committee's conclusions are published as *Privacy and Injunctions* (n 19).

Account will be taken of the complainant's own public disclosures of information.

iii) It is unacceptable to photograph individuals in private places without their consent.

Note—Private places are public or private property where there is a reasonable expectation of privacy.

The following are among its 'sanctions': negotiation of an agreed remedy; publication of a critical adjudication in the offending publication, which may be followed by public criticism of a title by its chairman; a letter of admonishment from the chairman to the editor; follow-up from the PCC to ensure that changes are made to avoid a repetition, and to establish what steps have been taken against those responsible for serious breaches of the code; and formal referral of the editor to his or her publisher. In 2010, 182 complaints raised a possible breach of one of the code's privacy clauses.

The Leveson Inquiry Report recommended that the Board should have the power to impose 'appropriate and proportionate sanctions' (including fines up to 1 per cent of turnover, with a maximum of £1 million), on any subscriber responsible for serious or systemic breaches of the standards code or governance requirements of the body. The sanctions should include the power to require publication of corrections, if a breach relates to accuracy, or apologies if a breach relates to other provisions of the code.[49]

The PCC has been subjected to considerable criticism over the years, centred largely on its 'lack of teeth'.[50] It routinely attracts epithets such as 'useless' and 'pointless'. The Prime Minister has said, 'The PCC has failed. In this

49. *An Inquiry into the Culture, Practices and Ethics of the Press* (n 20), Part K, ch 7, para 4.38.
50. In 1977 I published an article in the *New Statesman* in which I rather haughtily described the (then) Press Council as an 'otiose, toothless watchdog' (R Wacks, 'Privacy and the Press', *New Statesman*, 29 April 1977, p 554). I called its adjudications 'terse, often unreasoned and conflicting' providing 'little guidance to either editor or individual on the legitimate bounds of press disclosures'. Its chairman, Sir Hartley Shawcross (as he then was), took grave offence and responded with an acerbic letter, pronouncing my article 'otiose and toothless', defending the council, and asserting that public figures who 'seek to cultivate public support or even become public idols must accept that the public may be properly concerned to know about aspects of their lives which they themselves might prefer to protect from public appraisal, possibly because they do not feel that these aspects would enhance the kind of reception which they seek to cultivate', Letter, *New Statesman*, 6 May 1977, p 600. My rejoinder was published the following week, *New Statesman*, 13 May 1977. The Shawcross standpoint was adopted in a number of the council's decisions. Several of its early adjudications are discussed in R Wacks, *The Protection of Privacy* (London: Sweet & Maxwell, 1980), 57–61 and 89–94. See too L Blom-Cooper and L Pruitt, 'Privacy Jurisprudence of the Press Complaints Commission' (1994) 23 Anglo-American Law Review 133. A higher degree of subtlety is evident in more recent rulings of the PCC. See *Privacy and Injunctions: Oral and Written Evidence* (n 1), 504 ff.

case [telephone hacking] it was absent, ineffective and lacking in rigour. It lacks public confidence. We need a new system entirely.'[51] In its evidence to the Joint Committee on Privacy and Injunctions, the group, Lawyers for Media Standards, stated:

> Unfortunately, the common perception of the PCC is that it is a toothless tiger in thrall to its paymasters, the press; the prospects of it improving its public image and reputation in its current form are remote.[52]

The Committee concluded,

> The Press Complaints Commission was not equipped to deal with systemic and illegal invasions of privacy. A strong, independent media regulator is essential to balance the competing rights of privacy and freedom of expression.[53]

The Leveson Inquiry Report is scathing in its appraisal of the performance, powers, and credibility of the PCC, and recommended sweeping changes to its constitution. It justified the new regime of media self-regulation on three grounds:

> First, it would enshrine, for the first time, a legal duty on the Government to protect the freedom of the press. Second, it would provide an independent process to recognise the new self-regulatory body and reassure the public that the basic requirements of independence and effectiveness were met and continue to be met[54]...Third, by recognising the new body, it would validate its standards code and the arbitral system sufficient to justify the benefits in law that would flow to those who subscribed; these could relate to data protection and the approach of the court to various issues concerning acceptable practice, in addition to costs consequences if appropriate alternative dispute resolution is available.[55]

---

51. *The Guardian* (Greenslade blog), 8 July 2011.
52. *Privacy and Injunctions: Oral and Written Evidence* (n 1), 325. In its report, *Press Standards, Privacy and Libel* (n 16), the CMS recommended that the PCC be accorded the power to fine newspapers for serious breaches of its code.
53. *Privacy and Injunctions: Oral and Written Evidence* (n 1), Executive Summary. Its view was that, 'The most important step towards improving protection of privacy is to provide for enhanced regulation of the media. We conclude that the Press Complaints Commission lacked the power, sanctions or independence necessary to be truly effective. The new regulator should be demonstrably independent of the industry and of government. It should be cost-free to complainants and should have access to a wider range of sanctions, including the power to fine and more power to require apologies to be published. Sanctions should be developed to ensure that all major news publishers, including digital publishers, come under its jurisdiction', ibid. This critique foreshadowed that of the Leveson Inquiry Report. See earlier.
54. The Report recommends this function would be discharged by Ofcom. See later.
55. *An Inquiry into the Culture, Practices and Ethics of the Press* (n 20), Part K, ch 7, para 6.23.

A major weakness is that membership of the body is voluntary and not all newspapers are members.[56] Nor can it act pre-emptively to restrain publication or impose any financial sanctions. Despite these (and several other) shortcomings, a complaint to the PCC has the benefits of economy, speed, and accessibility. Nor is a complainant prevented from seeking a legal remedy after the PCC has issued its adjudication. Since the Human Rights Act 1998 became law, the PCC has achieved a significant measure of judicial recognition.[57]

Ofcom

Several of the features of the PCC mentioned earlier apply also to Ofcom.[58] The major difference is that, unlike newspapers, in respect of broadcast media, the state exercises control over the licensing of radio and television broadcasters. Its *Broadcasting Code* is more comprehensive than the PCC's code, and, in regard to privacy, Section 8 provides guidance as to the circumstances when infringements of privacy may be 'warranted', the 'legitimate expectations' of individuals, and the limits of surreptitious recording.

A broadcaster who breaches the code may be referred to the Content Sanctions Committee which may impose any of a number of penalties including a fine of up to £250,000 or 5 per cent of the broadcaster's 'qualifying revenue', requiring the offending item to be re-edited, not to repeat it, or to broadcast a correction or a summary of the findings against it. A serious breach may result in its licence being truncated or revoked.[59]

---

56. The Leveson Inquiry Report recommends incentives to encourage newspapers to join the proposed new regulatory body. They include a 'kite mark for use by members to establish a recognised brand of trusted journalism' (Part K, ch 4, para 5.41) and an amendment to the rules of civil procedure to require a court, when considering the appropriate order for costs, to take into account the availability of an arbitral system set up by an independent regulator itself recognized by law, Part J, ch 3, para 6.9.

57. Eg in *Douglas v Hello!* [2001] QB 967, 994, [94]–[95]; *A v B plc* [2002] 3 WLR 542, [11]; *Mills v News Group Newspapers Ltd* [2001] 1 EMLR 41; *Mosley v News Group Newspapers Ltd* [2008] EWHC 687 (QB), [31]; *X and Y v Persons Unknown* [2007] EMLR 10, [49], [51]; *McKennitt v Ash* [2006] EMLR 10, [94].

58. The body was created by the Office of Communications Act 2002. Its powers are to be found in the Communications Act 2003.

59. Revocation of a broadcaster's licence has occurred only twice, for infractions unrelated to privacy. The BBC is exempt from the penalty of licence revocation.

The BBC

The extensive *Editorial Guidelines* contain several stipulations about privacy which, it declares it 'respects...and does not infringe...without good reason, wherever in the world it is operating.' It has a separate code of practice that sets out the procedure for dealing with complaints. The Editorial Complaints Unit deals with serious complaints about breaches of the BBC's editorial standards in connection with specific programmes or items of content. If complainants are not satisfied by its finding an appeal may be made to the Editorial Standards Committee of the BBC Trust. Where the Editorial Complaints Unit identifies a serious breach of the guidelines, its finding is normally published on the BBC complaints website. It may also require the BBC to broadcast an apology or correction.

8

Problems and prospects

The quest continues. Developments in the law, spawned principally by the Human Rights Act 1998 and the reception of the European Convention on Human Rights, have been striking. Yet the right of privacy still occupies a preternatural position. Like its former habitat—an adventitious offshoot of breach of confidence—it now dwells under the shadow of Article 8's amorphous concept of 'private life'. Its conceptual independence remains elusive.

Before the advent of the Human Rights Act 1998, I wrote:

> A statutory cause of action for the public disclosure of private facts (subject, of course, to the accepted defences) is the best way forward. But if Parliament is unwilling to grasp the nettle, the courts must. The combined force of three recent developments provide ample support for initiative in an appropriate case: the expanding equitable remedy for breach of confidence, the revived tort of inflicting emotional distress, and the growing influence of the international recognition of 'privacy', especially the jurisprudence of the European Convention on Human Rights. With these weapons to hand, the campaign demands only modest judicial heroism.[1]

The nettle appears to have been grasped, and, as previous chapters reveal, a sophisticated jurisprudence has heroically emerged under which equilibrium is struck between the protection of private information (carved out of Art 8's protection of 'private life') and Article 10's defence of freedom of expression. But the courts perform this taxing feat by invoking the excessively broad principles applied in judgments of the European Court. This process, I suggest later, affords inadequate guidance to both the public and the media. Lucid legislation is the cure for this affliction.

---

1. R Wacks, *Privacy and Press Freedom* (London: Blackstone Press, 1995), 173.

My appraisal of the current law in this final chapter would be futile if
the ten gripes adumbrated here do not contribute, even slightly, to the
improved protection of both privacy and free speech. They are offered in
the hope that they are both practical and constructive. In the Appendix
I presumptuously propose a draft bill designed to protect the individual
against both intrusion into seclusion and unwanted publication of personal
information.

Ten qualms and quibbles

1. What is 'private life'?

The trouble appears early in Act One. It long predates the arrival of Strasbourg in our courts. Indeed, the curtain was barely up when the plot took
a needless turn. The American authors of the drama, Warren and Brandeis
ruined the show by introducing to their otherwise compelling production a
superfluous feature: the 'right to be let alone'.[2] Despite numerous attempts,
I am unable to comprehend their unnecessary—and detrimental—reliance
on Cooley's phrase as a foundation for the protection of privacy. Not only
was Cooley, in his 1888 treatise on the law of tort, describing a right to
be free from physical assault or threats of violence,[3] but the distinguished
lawyers had successfully established the case for the recognition of a new
tort that was wholly unrelated to physical assault. Indeed, their—entirely
convincing—historical argument which lay at the heart of their article was
the very converse: the common law, they argued, had developed *from* the
protection of the physical person and corporeal property to the protection
of the individual's '[t]houghts, emotions and sensations'.[4]

The tragedy is that, in spite of their thesis that 'solitude and privacy have
become more essential to the individual; but modern enterprise and invention have, through invasion upon his privacy, subjected him to mental pain
and distress, far greater than could be inflicted by mere bodily injury'[5] they
opened the door to the expansive 'right to be let alone' that has contributed

---

2. See Chapter 1.
3. 'The right to one's person may be said to be a right of complete immunity: to be let alone', TM
   Cooley, *Treatise of the Law of Torts,* 2nd edn (Chicago, IL: Callaghan, 1888), 29.
4. Cooley (n 3), 195.
5. SD Warren and LD Brandeis, 'The Right to Privacy' (1890) 4 Harvard Law Review 193, 196.

to the conceptual disarray that continues to afflict the legal protection of privacy, especially in the United States, and poses a similar threat to the English law under the aegis of the European Convention on Human Rights.

The concept of 'private life' is exasperatingly broad. What could conceivably lie outside it? My 'private life' is, to all intents and purposes, my existence, my being. It is true that, despite this amorphous expression, the European Court has occasionally ruled against an applicant,[6] yet the scope of the provision is as indeterminate as the 'right to be let alone'. I suggested in Chapter 1 that to inflate rights is to devalue them.

Nor, it should be recalled, does Article 8 protect 'privacy' *stricto sensu*. In fact, if it protects 'privacy' at all, it protects the right to '*respect*' for privacy.[7] From a legal standpoint, its purview is unbearably capacious. The European Court has construed it to include 'physical and psychological integrity',[8] protection of one's environment,[9] identity,[10] and personal autonomy.[11] This conceptual indeterminacy resembles the exasperating imprecision of the 'right to be let alone'. And the protection of the 'right to respect for…private and family life, [and]…home' plainly opens the door to an alarming range of activities.

The reach of Article 8 thus extends well beyond the protection of privacy, let alone (in my preferred formula) personal information. Hence, to refer to only one example to add to those mentioned in Chapter 1, the Court has, in a number of decisions, held that Article 8 guarantees the right to reputation. Its reasoning in one case was that the applicant's right to respect for private and family life had been infringed by the state's failure to protect his reputation.[12] Of course, Article 10 provides explicit protection for an individual's reputation.[13] But the court has adopted the position that notwithstanding this, Article 8 may be engaged where the allegations against the applicant are 'of such a seriously offensive nature…[that they have] an inevitable direct

---

6. In *Botta v Italy* App 21439/93 (1998) 26 EHRR 241, the Court rejected a claim that the failure to provide disabled persons with adequate physical access to a beach violated Art 8.

7. See *M v Secretary of State for Work and Pensions* [2006] 2 AC 91, [83] per Lord Walker; *R (Gillan) v Commissioner of Police for the Metropolis* [2006] 2 AC 307, [28] per Lord Bingham.

8. *YF v Turkey* App 24209/94 (2004) 39 EHRR 34, [33]; *Pretty v United Kingdom* App 2346/02 (2002) 35 EHRR 1, [61].

9. *Hatton v United Kingdom* App 36022/97 (2003) 37 EHRR 28, [119], including the right to sleep: see Chapter 1.

10. *Pretty v United Kingdom* App 2346/02 (2002) 35 EHRR 1, [61].

11. *Goodwin v United Kingdom* App 28957/95 (2002) 35 EHRR 523, [90].

12. *Pfeifer v Austria* App 12556/03 (2007) 48 EHRR 175. A similar conclusion was reached by the Court in *A v Norway* [2009] ECHR 580.

13. See Chapter 4.

effect on the applicant's private life.'[14] This munificent construction of Article 8 is yet further confirmation of its disconcerting compass.[15] One can only hope that the English courts exercise restraint, and attempt to confine the operation of this Article to prudent limits.[16]

Both privacy and freedom of expression are better protected when their formulation is more modest, less ambiguous, and incoherent.[17] Privacy deserves recognition in its own right. A violation of privacy is sufficiently distinguishable from an attack on an individual's reputation to warrant clear

14. *Karakó v Hungary* [2009] ECHR 712. See too *Petrenco v Moldova* [2010] ECHR 419.
15. This comprehensive construction of Art 8 has been described by a distinguished British human rights lawyer as 'an intellectually devious reading of the Convention'. He claims that 'in 1950 an attempt was specifically made to insert "reputation" as a privacy right, and it was roundly defeated. To bring it back through the subterfuge of "judicial interpretation" has damaged respect for the European Court of Human Rights', G Robertson QC, 'Why We Need a British Bill of Rights', *Standpoint*, January/February 2010. See too G Robertson and A Nicol, *Media Law*, 5th edn (London: Sweet & Maxwell, 2008), 66–70. Another bountiful interpretation of Art 8 was recently accepted by the Court of Appeal in *T, R (on the application of) v Chief Constable of Greater Manchester and others* [2013] EWCA Civ 25 which held that the provision extended to the disclosure of a spent criminal conviction, notwithstanding that such information 'is public by virtue of the simple fact that convictions are made and sentences are imposed in public. But as the conviction recedes into the past, it becomes part of the individual's private life …[T]he disclosure of historic information about convictions or cautions can lead to a person's exclusion from employment, and can therefore adversely affect his or her ability to develop relations with others: this too involves an interference with the right to respect for private life. Excluding a person from employment in his chosen field is liable to affect his ability to develop relationships with others, and the problems that this creates as regards the possibility of earning a living can have serious repercussions on the enjoyment of his private life.' [31]. The fact that the applicant received warnings from the police in connection with two stolen bicycles was, the court held, '*sensitive information* about himself which he wished to keep to himself…(which) …was properly to be regarded as an aspect of his private life.' [32]. (Emphasis added). While the court—rightly—sought to limit the scope of the exemptions of the Rehabilitation of Offenders Act 1974 to the disclosure of spent offences that are directly relevant to the purpose for which they are required, the quoted dictum strains the meaning of 'sensitive information'—and compounds the confusion spawned by the application of Art 8 to the protection of privacy.
16. It will be recalled that Prosser regards 'reputation' as an interest protected by the tort of public disclosure of private facts. I suggest, in Chapter 5, that, while this is true of the tort of 'false light' (and, hence, my argument that it is effectively indistinguishable from defamation), it is mistaken in the case of public disclosure.
17. Is Art 10's protection of freedom of expression (that may be overridden only by subsidiary rights, such as the right to reputation—when necessary in a democratic society) an adequate safeguard when an applicant's defamation suit springs from Art 8? Does the inclusion of 'reputation' in this Article undermine the free speech protections written into the defamation defences, especially justification and fair comment? This seems a neglected—and troubling—question. Reference (sadly, without comment) to the inclusion of defamation under Art 8's wing is made by Lord Phillips in *Flood v Times Newspapers Ltd* [2012] UKSC 11, [44]: 'the Strasbourg Court has recently recognised that reputation falls within the ambit of the protection afforded by article 8—see *Cumpana and Mazare v Romania* (2004) 41 EHRR 200 (GC) at para 91 and *Pfeifer v Austria* (2007) 48 EHRR 175 at paras 33 and 35.'

separation. 'The mental injuries suffered by a privacy plaintiff' in the words of one commentator, 'stem from exposure of the private self to public view. The mental injuries suffered by a defamation victim, by contrast, arise as a consequence of the damage to reputation, either real or perceived. Thus, both torts provide redress for "wounded feelings," but the *source* of the harm differs substantially.'[18] Moreover, while there is an obvious overlap between the two wrongs, in the case of defamation 'the injuries result from real or imagined harm to reputation, an objectively determinable interest. In privacy actions the injuries arise solely from public exposure of private facts.'[19]

2. What is 'private information'?

This is an unacceptably neglected matter. That neither Prosser nor the US courts sought explicitly to define what is 'private' seems to be, in part, a consequence of the perspective, which is also adopted by Warren and Brandeis—and now—unhappily—by the English courts, deploying the language of the ECHR, that conceives of the right of privacy in disappointingly nebulous terms. In the former case, it treats privacy as equivalent to the obscure 'right to be let alone' or, in the latter, as bound up with the vague concept of 'private life' which, as the European Court itself concedes, 'is a broad term not susceptible to exhaustive definition':

> It covers the physical and psychological integrity of a person. It can sometimes embrace aspects of an individual's physical and social identity. Elements such as, for example, gender identification, name and sexual orientation and sexual life fall within the personal sphere protected by Article 8. Article 8 also protects a right to personal development, and the right to establish and develop relationships with other human beings and the outside world. Although no previous case has established as such any right to self-determination as being contained in Article 8 of the Convention, the Court considers that the notion of personal autonomy is an important principle underlying the interpretation of its guarantees.[20]

---

18. Note, 'Defamation and Privacy' (1976) Duke Law Journal 1016. Both wrongs—at least in the analysis of privacy advanced in this book—do share an important element: they are both concerned with information.

19. Note (n 18), 1034. See Tugendhat J's analysis of the 'limited classes of cases that the law of privacy gives rise to an overlap with the law of defamation' in *LNS (John Terry) v Persons Unknown* [2010] EWHC 119 (QB), [2010] EMLR 16, [96].

20. *Pretty v United Kingdom* [2002] 35 EHRR 1, [2002] ECHR 427, [61].

This fuzziness is unhelpful; it obscures the critical question of what constitutes the class of information that is susceptible to legal protection. If privacy is believed to express a general right of this kind, the need to declare in advance the precise circumstances in which it is invaded is less important than if the starting point is some conception of private or personal information. But it is an unsatisfactory statement of precisely what both the individual and the media need to know.[21]

Lord Nicholls's widely cited caveat in *Campbell v MGN Ltd*, though it purports to circumscribe the concept of 'private life', relates only to the application of the test of 'reasonable expectation of privacy'. It does not attempt to identify what species of *private information* are worthy of protection:

> Accordingly, in deciding what was the ambit of an individual's 'private life' in particular circumstances courts need to be on guard against using as a touchstone a test which brings into account considerations which should more properly be considered at the later stage of proportionality. Essentially the touchstone of private life is whether in respect of the disclosed facts the person in question had a reasonable expectation of privacy.

In Chapter 7 I questioned the correctness of this test in cases of misuse of private information. The thrust of my argument was that the test of proportionality is *already* applied when the court considers whether to grant an interim injunction. In other words, before, say, issuing an injunction to prevent publication, a court will necessarily attempt to balance the rival rights in Articles 8 and 10. This requires an appraisal of whether the public interest in publication (or the extent to which the disclosure contributes to a debate of general interest in a democratic society) is proportionate to its effect on

---

21. Nevertheless, in seeking to draw the boundaries between 'private' and 'public', the US courts have, in effect, formulated a relatively clear test of what information may be protected. In so doing, they have appealed to what is *reasonable in the circumstances*. Thus, in the case of 'intrusion' it has been held that there is no cause of action where, eg, the plaintiff is photographed in a public place: *Gill v Hearst Publishing Co*, 40 Cal2d 224, 253 P2d 441 (1953). And in the case of 'public disclosure', it has been held that the plaintiff cannot complain where publicity is given to matters of public record such as his or her date of birth or marriage: *Meetze v Associated Press*, 230 SC 330, 95 SE2d 606 (1956). A limiting factor in both torts is that the intrusion or disclosure is offensive and objectionable to a reasonable man of ordinary sensibilities. In the latter case, it is clear that the law applies 'something in the nature of a "mores test" under which there will be liability only for publicity given to those things which the customs and ordinary views of the community would regard as highly objectionable', WL Prosser, 'Privacy' (1960) 48 California Law Review 383, 397; *Restatement (Second) of the Law of Torts* (Philadelphia, PA: American Law Institute, 1977), para 652D, comment h. The test was first suggested in *Sidis v F-R Publishing Corporation*, 34 F Supp 19 (SDNY 1938).

the claimant's right of privacy. Besides, the five-stage test adopted by the House of Lords, discussed in Chapter 4, entails a dual application of the test of proportionality or what Lord Steyn called 'the ultimate balancing test'.[22] I suggested there that the application of Gleeson CJ's 'highly offensive' test might offer a workmanlike method by which to differentiate between potentially serious violations of the claimant's privacy and those that are at the insignificant end of the continuum. This is an issue that is closely related to the following matter.

3. Why a 'reasonable expectation of privacy'?

In Chapter 7 I criticized at some length the application of this test to cases of misuse of private information. Albeit only a preliminary assessment by which to determine whether Article 8 is 'engaged', it is a crucial hurdle that a claimant must clear if the court is to proceed to a consideration of the publication in question. Moreover, as with the determination of what information is considered 'private' (discussed earlier), its significance lies in the proper balancing of privacy and media freedom. Consider the following pronouncement by the House of Lords:

> Miss Campbell's 'public lies' precluded her from claiming protection...When talking to the media Miss Campbell went out of her way to say that, unlike many fashion models, she did not take drugs. By repeatedly making these assertions in public Miss Campbell could no longer have a reasonable expectation that this aspect of her life should be private. Public disclosure that, contrary to her assertions, she did in fact take drugs and had a serious drug problem for which she was being treated *was not disclosure of private information*.[23]

This captures the error at the heart of the 'reasonable expectation' test. To find that this 'was not disclosure of private information' is, with respect, mistaken. It was indeed private information, the publication of which the supermodel reasonably wished to control. This is the essence of my criticism of the 'reasonable expectation' test, and my proposal of an alternative analysis based on the individual's right to prohibit or restrict intimate facts.[24]

22. *Re S (A Child)* [2005] 1 AC 593, [17]. It is sometimes described as 'parallel analysis': *A Local Authority v W* [2006] 1 FLR 1, [53].
23. *Campbell v MGN Ltd* [2004] UKHL 22, [24], per Lord Nicholls (emphasis added).
24. Lord Hope was content to regard certain information as 'obviously private' without explaining why: 'If the information is obviously private, the situation will be one where the person to whom it relates can reasonably expect his privacy to be respected. So there is normally no need to go on and ask whether it would be highly offensive for it to be published', [96]. This

'Privacy', as one commentator has correctly observed, 'is ultimately about our power to choose our audience. When privacy is invaded, we are compelled to have an audience we do not want...If every private statement on a public subject may be forcibly disclosed because it contributes to public debate, then privacy is a dead letter.'[25]

The 'reasonable expectation of privacy' test, I attempted to demonstrate in Chapter 7, is—on its own—unsuited to judge complaints of misuse of private information. This is because it concerns the *use, disclosure, or publication* of private facts to which the individual is prepared to consent. It is a question of *control* over the distribution or circulation of personal details. This standard is appropriate in cases of intrusion: where an individual's solitude or seclusion is intruded upon, the question is whether, in all the circumstances, he or she had a reasonable expectation of privacy. This provides an objective measure to evaluate the extent to which the claimant is entitled to believe that his or her privacy is safe. It therefore scrutinizes the *circumstances* rather than merely the *information* that may warrant protection.

---

approach provides almost no reliable guidance either to those who publish or who seek to prevent publication. A similar reluctance to expound the criteria by which 'private information' are to be identified is evident in *Murray v Express Newspapers plc* [2009] 1 Ch 481 (CA), [36] where the court preferred to switch the enquiry to the 'reasonable expectation of privacy' test, which 'takes account of all the circumstances of the case. They include the attributes of the claimant, the nature of the activity in which the claimant was engaged, the place at which it was happening, the nature and purpose of the intrusion, the absence of consent and whether it was known or could be inferred, the effect on the claimant and the circumstances in which and the purposes for which the information came into the hands of the publisher', per Sir Anthony Clarke MR. See too *Lord Browne of Madingley v Associated Newspapers Ltd* [2008] 1 QB 103 (CA), [33]–[36]. In *Rocknroll v News Group Newspapers Ltd* [2013] EWHC 24 (Ch), the court considered the effect publication of photographs of the semi-nude claimant would have on the children of the actress Kate Winslet, whom the claimant had recently married. There is, Briggs J held, 'real reason to think that a grave risk would arise as to Miss Winslet's children being subjected to teasing or ridicule at school about the behaviour of their newly acquired step-father, within a short period after his arrival within their family, and that such teasing or ridicule could be seriously damaging to the caring relationship which, on the evidence, the claimant is seeking to establish with them', [36]. Regrettably, the 'reasonable expectation' test makes an unwelcome—but seemingly mandatory—appearance in the judgment.

25. P Gewitz, 'Privacy and Free Speech' (2001) Supreme Court Review 139, 155, commenting on the Supreme Court's majority decision in *Bartnicki v Vopper*, 532 US 514 (2001) which held the defendant radio station not liable for broadcasting a taped conversation of a trade union official discussing with members a possible strike, even though the conversation had been illegally intercepted because the defendant did not itself acquire the tape unlawfully. The Court seems to have incorporated the common law concept of 'newsworthiness' into constitutional law. See RA Smolla, 'Information as Contraband: The First Amendment and Liability for Trafficking in Speech' (2002) Northwestern University Law Review 1099. Cf DJ Solove, 'The Virtues of Knowing Less: Justifying Privacy Protections against Disclosure' (2003) 53 Duke Law Journal 967, 987; *Boehner v McDermott*, 484 F3d 573 (DC Cir 2007).

I have instead proposed an approach, in respect of wrongful publication, that seeks to ascertain what *specific interests* of the individual the law ought to protect. At the heart of the right of privacy is the interest every individual has in thwarting those in pursuit of personal or sensitive information. The concept of 'private life' in Article 8 has facilitated the judicial protection of 'private facts' against unauthorized disclosure. But the core of the analysis should be to decide whether the facts sought to be protected are genuinely private, thereby also affording greater protection to freedom of expression, since trivial or innocuous information would fall outside the law's aegis. A focus on the type of private information, rather than the circumstances that may give rise to a reasonable expectation of privacy, would convey a less equivocal statement—to both public and publisher—about the boundary between privacy and free speech.

4. Why no distinction between intrusion and disclosure?

The failure conceptually to differentiate the two forms of invasion, both discounts the particular interests of victims inherent in the two kinds of abuse, and unnecessarily obscures the balancing act between Articles 8 and 10 in cases of disclosure or misuse. The distinction is between *expectation* in the case of intrusion, and *desire* in the case of publication. They are frequently closely connected, but not always. A film star may abjure a furtive photograph, yet permit its publication. Even if she objects to both, however, the wrongfulness of the intrusion turns on her reasonable expectation of privacy, while, in the case of any subsequent publication, the violation should be judged in accordance with her right to control the use or misuse of her image.[26]

---

26. There are a handful of decisions in which a severance is espoused. In *Wood v Commissioner of Police for the Metropolis* Laws LJ distinguished between 'the fact or threat of publication in the media, and…the snapping of the shutter', [2010] EMLR 1 (CA), [33]. A dichotomy of this kind was adopted also in *Theakston v MGN Ltd* [2002] EMLR 22, where the court drew a distinction between the intrusion into the claimant's sexual activities (which it did not protect), on the one hand, and the publication of photographs of him in a brothel (which it did), on the other. Moreover, in the leading authority, to which the courts routinely defer, *von Hannover v Germany* App 59320/00 (2005) 40 EHRR 1, the European Court applied the 'reasonable expectation of privacy' test to the intrusive activities of the media, not to the publication of the material so obtained. And it followed its earlier decision in *Halford v United Kingdom* (1997) EHRR 523.

5. What about 'intrusion'?

It is difficult to discern the basis upon which the House of Lords in *Campbell v MGN Ltd*[27] made the analytical move from Article 8's protection of 'private life' to a recognition of the right to 'privacy'—even if it is restricted to the misuse of private information. If 'privacy' is protected by Article 8—and the judgment bristles with sweeping pronouncements of its significance—why is 'intrusion' excluded? Surely the normally criminal acts such as bugging, tapping, and hacking are no less worthy of protection than the publication of private facts. Did the court feel bound by its (correct) decision in *Wainwright v Home Office*[28] that 'there is no general tort of invasion of privacy' but (erroneous) view that strip-searches were an example of intrusion? Or was it simply that it confined its judgment to the complaint before the court: the *publication* of personal information? Moreover, the European Court has not hesitated to incorporate intrusion under the wing of Article 8. Furthermore, it has counselled that 'private life' should not be construed restrictively.[29]

The use of covert audio and video recording equipment, it held in *Khan v United Kingdom*,[30] may amount to an interference with an individual's right to private life. This aspect of the decision is not cited (perhaps understandably) in *Campbell* or (less so) in *Wainwright*. Why not? The European Court has, however, found that monitoring an individual in a public place by the use of photographic equipment without recording such data does not, as such, give rise to an interference with the individual's private life, but the *recording* of the data and the systematic or permanent nature of the record may generate such considerations.[31] This view does not appear to have cut ice with the English courts.

---

27. [2004] 2 AC 457.
28. [2003] 3 WLR 1137, [43].
29. *Amann v Switzerland* App 27798/95 (2000) 30 EHRR 843, [65]–[70].
30. App 35394/97 (2001) 31 EHRR 45.
31. *Perry v United Kingdom* App 63737/00 (2004) 39 EHRR 37, [38]. The European Court has found numerous cases of 'intrusion' to be a breach of Art 8: *Wood v United Kingdom* App 23414/02, 16 November 2004; *Khan v United Kingdom* App 35394/97 (2001) 31 EHRR 45; *Allan v United Kingdom* App 48539/99 (2003) 36 EHRR 12 (bugging); *Halford v United Kingdom* App 20605/92 (1997) 24 EHRR 523; *Amman v Switzerland* App 27798/95 (2000) 30 EHRR 843; *Huvig v France* App 11105/84 (1990) 12 EHRR 528; *Doerga v Netherlands* App 50210 (2005) 41 EHRR 4 (telephone-tapping); *Allan v United Kingdom*, above, *Peck v United Kingdom* App 44647/98 (2003) 36 EHRR 719; *Perry v United Kingdom*, above (unauthorized or unwarranted videoing); *Wainwright v United Kingdom* App 12350/04 (2007) 44 EHRR 40 (intimate body searches). It is worth noting that in several of these judgments, the European Court has (rightly) applied the 'reasonable expectation of privacy' test.

This reluctance did not impede the High Court of New Zealand from recently recognizing a tort of intrusion.[32] The plaintiff was an occupant in a house owned by her boyfriend and Holland who surreptitiously installed a recording device in the roof cavity above the shower and toilet. He videoed her while she was showering. When she discovered the videos she was understandably deeply distressed. Holland accepted that he had invaded her privacy, but argued that his act did not fall within the legal protection of privacy. The court held otherwise. It ruled that invasion of privacy of this type, without publicity or the prospect of publicity, was indeed an actionable tort in New Zealand. Whata J took the view that the similarity to the tort of public disclosure as formulated in *Hosking v Runting*[33] 'is sufficiently proximate to enable an intrusion tort to be seen as a logical extension or adjunct to it.'[34] Interestingly, he explicitly eschewed English jurisprudence, and looked to North America in support of his decision.

A Canadian court recently reached a similar conclusion in a case in which, over a period of some four years, the defendant had used her workplace computer to access personal information of a co-worker. During that time the defendant was in a relationship with the plaintiff's former husband. The court decided that Ontario recognized a cause of action in tort for intrusion.[35]

6. Where is the 'misuse'?

As mentioned earlier, the English courts have—curiously—resisted recognition of a cause of action for intrusion committed by a variety of (normally criminal) acts such as surreptitious photography, electronic surveillance, telephone interception, and the like. This is in spite of the liberal terms of Article 8 which offer a congenial home for such violations. The tort of misuse of private information obviously requires evidence of *misuse* which, in practice, signifies *publication* of such information: 'the right to control the *dissemination* of information about one's private life...'[36] Nevertheless, there are a number of *obiter dicta* that imply that the clandestine recording

---

32. *C v Holland* [2012] NZHC 2155. I am grateful to Michelle Ainsworth for alerting me to this decision.
33. [2005] 1 NZLR 1 (CA).
34. [2012] NZHC 2155, [86].
35. *Jones v Tsige* [2012] ONCA 32. Considerable reliance was placed on this decision by Whata J in *C v Holland* [2012] NZHC 2155.
36. *Campbell v MGN Ltd* [2004] 2 AC 457, [51] per Lord Hoffmann.

of private matters does 'engage' Article 8,[37] that the mere taking of a photograph of a child[38] or an adult in a public place[39] might fall within the
category of 'misuse'. These pronouncements are either (uncharacteristic)
judicial lapses or subtle, possibly even subconscious, acknowledgements of
the present anomaly!

7. What are the requirements of liability?

Does the cause of action have a lucid or coherent 'profile'?[40] It is not clear
whether it is a tort, though a number of dicta suggest that it might be.[41] Its
status may well have consequences in respect, for example, of jurisdiction
and available remedies. Another problem arises in regard to how courts address Article 8. There is a tendency to accept that once Article 8 is 'engaged',
the question of its breach is assumed. More disturbingly, it is rare to find
any mention of the wide publicity that ought to be a criterion (as it is in
the US tort of public disclosure of private facts). This error is not confined
to judges; it is to be found in the literature where breach of confidence is
(properly) championed as an effective remedy for disclosures of personal

37. *Mosley v News Group Newspapers Ltd* [2009] EMLR 20, [104]. The court stated that it was 'fairly
obvious that the clandestine recording of sexual activity on private property must be taken to
engage Article 8', per Eady J.
38. *Murray v Express Newspapers plc* [2008] EWCA Civ 446, [2008] 3 WLR 1360. 'It may well
be that the mere taking of a photograph of a child in a public place when out with his or
her parents, whether they are famous or not, would not engage article 8 of the Convention.
However, as we see it, it all depends upon the circumstances', [17] per Sir Anthony Clarke
MR. Why the doubt? Article 8, as interpreted, cannot engage Art 10. At first instance, Patten J
allowed intrusion (the taking of the children's photographs) and their publication to elide. But
this was perhaps understandable since the two acts are plainly related, but it does confuse the
matter, [2007] EWHC 1908 (Ch), [17].
39. *Wood v Commissioner of Police of the Metropolis* [2010] EMLR 1 (CA). Laws LJ states that 'ordinarily the taking of photographs in a public street involves no element of interference with
anyone's private life', [31]. But why 'ordinarily'? Surely 'never'. To be fair, he subsequently adds:
'It might be thought that if (as I would hold) the mere taking of the pictures does not engage
Article 8(1), there follows a wholly separate question: whether their retention and intended
use might do so', [39].
40. This apprehension is reminiscent of Kalven's dissatisfaction with Warren and Brandeis's tort of
public disclosure. He complained that it 'has no legal profile. We do not know what constitutes
a prima facie case, we do not know on what basis damages are to be measured, we do not
know whether the basis of liability is limited to intentional invasions or includes also negligent
invasions and even strict liability', H Kalven, 'Privacy in Tort Law: Were Warren and Brandeis
Wrong?' (1966) 31 Law and Contemporary Problems 326, 333.
41. In *McKennitt v Ash* [2008] 1 QB 73, [11]: Arts 8 and 10 are 'the very content of the domestic
tort that the English law has to enforce', per Buxton LJ. *Campbell v MGN Ltd* [2004] 2 AC
457, [14]: 'the essence of the tort is better encapsulated now as misuse of private information',
per Lord Nicholls.

information—but without the need for extensive dissemination.[42] Disclosure to a single individual may satisfy the requirements of breach of confidence, or indeed of defamation but, as I attempted to show in Chapters 3 and 4, substantial circulation of private facts is central to the tort. Where the claimant's confidential information has been widely circulated, breach of confidence may, of course, serve as a surrogate form of privacy protection, as in the cases involving personal information discussed in Chapter 3.

8. What is the 'public interest'?

Deliberations about the 'public interest' inexorably raise two apprehensions: how, and by whom, it is to be defined. The first concern is often one of despair that the concept is incapable of definition. The second asks whether it is best suited to legislative, judicial, or regulatory resolution. But the argument is in both respects specious and misconceived.[43] I consider each in turn.

Definition

Typical of this kind of unease is the approach adopted by the British Government's consideration in the draft Defamation Bill of a statutory definition of 'public interest' in respect of the so-called 'Reynolds defence of responsible journalism'. In rejecting the proposal, the Consultation Paper asserted:

> We believe that this is a concept which is well-established in the English common law and that in view of the very wide range of matters which are of public interest and the sensitivity of this to factual circumstances, attempting to define it in statute would be fraught with problems. Such problems include

---

42. This is not, of course, a scientific calculation. See *Restatement* (n 21), para 652D, comment a. As *American Jurisprudence* notes: 'While an actionable disclosure is generally one made only to a large number of people, it cannot be said that disclosure of embarrassing private facts to a comparatively small number of people will automatically be insufficient to constitute a public disclosure. There is no magic formula or "body count" that can be given to permit counsel to determine with certainty whether the number of persons to whom private facts have been disclosed will be sufficient in any particular case to satisfy the public disclosure requirement. The concept of public disclosure is not subject to precise or rigid formulae but is flexible, and the facts and circumstances of a particular case must be taken into consideration in determining whether the disclosure was sufficiently public so as to be actionable.' See 62A *Am Jur* 2d, Privacy, § 95.

43. Though a central issue, very few media defendants in the English courts raise a public interest argument; even fewer such defendants support this defence with plausible evidence. Trials on the merits are extremely rare.

the risk of missing matters which are of public interest resulting in too narrow a defence and the risk of this proving a magnet for satellite litigation adding to costs in relation to libel proceedings.[44]

Similar apprehension is echoed by the Joint Committee on Privacy and Injunctions:

> We conclude that a privacy statute would not clarify the law. The concepts of privacy and the public interest are not set in stone, and evolve over time. We conclude that the current approach, where judges balance the evidence and make a judgment on a case-by-case basis, provides the best mechanism for balancing article 8 and article 10 rights.[45]

And the Leveson Inquiry Report followed suit:

> I take the same view in respect of a statutory definition of the concept of the public interest. Depending on the circumstances, different situations will invoke different aspects of the public interest and the relevant considerations will be fact sensitive and of variable significance. As time passes and different social culture and customs develop, so the test will have to adjust. Whereas a regulator should be able to identify the public interest in the context of the press (as the Editors' Code of Conduct seeks to do), the ability to adapt is important. Again, in line with the view expressed by the Joint Committee on Privacy and Injunctions, I endorse the view that the incremental approach of the courts to this concept is to be preferred and I do not recommend a statutory definition.[46]

But this difficulty is grossly exaggerated; there is no need for translucent precision here, nor is it possible. The very concept of 'public interest'—either normative or descriptive—is unavoidably protean. A descriptive test looks to 'social mores', and is likely to prove 'self-defeating or at least self-eroding'.[47] Warren and Brandeis allowed an exception for 'matters of public and general interest'. They acknowledged that individuals 'with whose affairs the community has no legitimate concern' would enjoy protection from unwanted publicity. Only public officials or those who exercise official functions were excluded, but only in respect of information 'bearing upon any act done by [them] in a public or quasi public capacity'.[48] Their normative justification was twofold: such persons were worthy of public scrutiny, and because

---

44. Ministry of Justice, *Draft Defamation Bill Consultation* (CP3/11 March 2011), para 13.
45. *Privacy and Injunctions*, Session 2010–12, HL Paper 273 (HC 1443, 27 March 2012), para 50.
46. *An Inquiry into the Culture, Practices and Ethics of the Press* (HC 780, 2012), Part J, ch 3, para 4.3.
47. DA Anderson, 'The Failure of American Privacy Law' in BS Markesinis (ed), *Protecting Privacy* —*The Clifford Chance Lectures Volume Four* (Oxford: Oxford University Press, 1999), 149–50.
48. Warren and Brandeis (n 5), 216.

they voluntarily subject themselves to public attention. This approach had a double purpose: the elevation of dissolute public predilections, and the protection of privacy.

It will be recalled that in order to evaluate what is 'highly offensive', the US courts have developed what has been called a 'mores test'.[49] The *Restatement (Second) of the Law of Torts* describes the test as follows:

> In determining what is a matter of legitimate public interest, account must be taken of the customs and conventions of the community; and in the last analysis what is proper becomes a matter of the community mores. The line is to be drawn when the publicity ceases to be the giving of information to which the public is entitled, and becomes a morbid and sensational prying into private lives for its own sake, with which a reasonable member of the public, with decent standards, would say that he had no concern. The limitations, in other words, are those of common decency, having due regard to the freedom of the press and its reasonable leeway to choose what it will tell the public, but also due regard to the feelings of the individual and the harm that will be done to him by the exposure.[50]

A descriptive or empirical approach of this kind is likely to transform social norms into community expectation. If the law protects what is socially accepted as private, the public conception of 'private facts' is formed by what is in fact made public; and the more privacy is invaded the less privacy is protected. Thus, with an increase in the public appetite for titillating gossip anxiety about privacy declines: publications hitherto regarded as seriously offensive will ultimately become socially acceptable.[51]

But a normative test is only slightly less problematic. It casts as moral guardians those charged with assessing the merits of a publication. Neither test therefore satisfies the requirement of neutrality, or at least objectivity.[52] An element of normativity, however, seems unavoidable when the

---

49. See Chapter 5, and the account of *Melvin v Reid*, 112 Cal App 285, 297 P 91 (1931), and *Sidis v F-R Publishing Corporation*, 34 F Supp 19 (SDNY 1938).

50. *Restatement* (n 21), para 652D, comment h.

51. *Restatement* (n 21), para 652D, comment h. 'For most of the past half-century, courts have resolved the tension between privacy and press freedoms by deferring heavily to journalists in determining newsworthiness. Partly out of First Amendment concerns and partly out of a sense of their own limited competence, judges have regularly declined to second guess journalists' editorial decisions', A Gajda, 'Judging Journalism: The Turn toward Privacy and Judicial Regulation of the Press' (2009) 97 California Law Review 1039, 1041.

52. The limitations of both a descriptive and a normative test, in respect of the US criterion of newsworthiness, are recognized by the California Supreme Court in *Shulman v Group W Productions, Inc*, 955 P2d 469 (Cal 1998). The court concluded that neither position is acceptable, suggesting a need to strike a balance between them. See Chapter 5. For an extraordinary US judgment—in respect of both its descriptive notion of newsworthiness, and its bizarre concept

boundaries of media freedom are drawn. So, for example, the European Court of Human Rights in *von Hannover v Germany* applied the principle of whether publication would contribute to a 'debate of general interest':[53] Article 8 of the ECHR requires that publication achieve some legitimate social purpose, such as the prevention of a crime, or would be acceptable under any of the other categories specified in Article 8(2) as grounds for derogating from the right to privacy;[54] and whether, in the words of the Press Complaints Commission's (PCC's) *Editors' Code of Practice*, publication would prevent 'the public from being misled by an action or statement of an individual or organisation.'[55]

Who decides?

This preoccupation, though it continues to generate an impassioned debate, is ultimately hollow. If, as I suggest later, any practical or prudent attempt to 'define' the public interest would take the form of a guide or list of pointers, the question is not of major significance. Even if the test is statutorily prescribed, the courts would still be required to apply and interpret its provisions and—according to section 12 (4)(b) of the Human Rights Act 1998—a court must have particular regard to freedom of expression and, where the proceedings relate to journalistic, literary, or artistic material, to any relevant privacy code. In a sense, therefore, should legislation incorporate (as it must) guidance to the factors relevant to an evaluation of the public interest, all three institutions are involved.

The objection to any statutory formulation of the public interest, however, stems instead from a dread of codification that may curtail media freedom.

---

of 'public figure'—see *Fraley v Facebook* (2011) No 11-CV-01726-LHK, 2011 WL 6303898 (ND Cal 2011) in which a court in the Northern District of California held that Facebook users could be regarded as 'public figures' to their friends and that their 'likes' were newsworthy merely because they had been disseminated on social networks where they were known. Could this approach signal a future which sees the online application of the principle of *volenti non fit iniuria*? See *Rocknroll v News Group Newspapers Ltd* [2013] EWHC 24 (Ch) where photographs of the partially naked claimant were posted on Facebook and the copyright subsequently assigned to the newspaper whose attempt to publish it was successfully prevented, the court holding that the claimant, recently married to the actress Kate Winslet, was neither a public figure nor was there a public interest in the publication of the images.

53. (2005) 40 EHRR 1. See Chapter 5.
54. 'There shall be no interference by a public authority with the exercise of this right except such as is in accordance with the law and is necessary in a democratic society in the interests of national security, public safety or the economic well-being of the country, for the prevention of disorder or crime, for the protection of health or morals, or for the protection of the rights and freedoms of others.'
55. *CTB v News Group Newspapers Ltd* [2011] EWHC 1232 (QB), [25].

This is misguided for at least three reasons. First, it presupposes a Draconian statement of the conception. This is highly improbable especially in view of section 12 of the Human Rights Act. Secondly, it postulates a narrow articulation of the principle. But it does not follow that the legislation would adopt this approach; the method proposed later envisages a series of indicators rather than a single criterion. Thirdly, it overlooks the fact that it would fall to a court to interpret its provisions which, moreover, is obliged by section 12 to consult codes devised by the media themselves.

Any assessment of whether publication of private facts is in the public interest, whatever the source of the guidelines, or the setting in which they are adjudicated—statute, judge, or media regulator—ought to turn on a range of factors, rather than a single monolithic benchmark. They would include criteria such as whether the claimant was a public figure, how the information was acquired, the defendant's motive, the gravity of the invasion, and so on.[56] And, as suggested in the bill in the Appendix, the media would be protected by a presumption that a publication is in the public interest if it was disseminated in pursuit of a number of interests, including the prevention, detection, or investigation of crime, the prevention of unlawful or seriously improper conduct, establishing whether the claimant was able to discharge his or her public or professional obligations, or whether the claimant was fit for any public office or profession held or carried on by him or her, or which he or she sought to hold or carry on professional responsibilities, and so on.[57]

Media disquiet (assuming it to be genuine) appears to be based on the assumption that any statutory guide as to what comprises 'public interest' would take the form of an exhaustive and hence 'chilling' formula. The source of this mistaken supposition is difficult to uncover. Adopting a general list of criteria, as earlier—or indeed, along the lines of the PCC's *Editor's Code*—offers a workmanlike (and reassuring) resolution to the matter.[58]

---

56. A suggested inventory of queries is set out in Chapter 5, and is incorporated in the draft legislation in the Appendix. See too R Wacks, *The Protection of Privacy* (London: Sweet & Maxwell, 1980), 98–106, Wacks (n 1), 105–12.
57. See clause 3(2) of my proposed Protection of Privacy Bill in the Appendix.
58. The Leveson Inquiry Report recommended that the code should 'take into account the importance of freedom of speech, the interests of the public (including the public interest in detecting or exposing crime or serious impropriety, protecting public health and safety and preventing the public from being seriously misled) and the rights of individuals. Specifically, it must cover standards providing for: (a) conduct, especially in relation to the treatment of other people in the process of obtaining material; (b) appropriate respect for privacy where there is no sufficient public interest justification for breach; and (c) accuracy, and the need to avoid

9. Why the dissolution of the action for breach of confidence?

Since the implementation of the Human Rights Act in 2000, judges have been presiding over the dilution of the divide between the related, but often distinct, concepts of 'privacy' and 'confidence'. This might simply be a consequence of the flurry of actions pursued under Article 8. In Chapter 4 I argued for the preservation of the doctrinal separation between the two causes of action. It is important to recognize that cases arise in which the root of the claimant's grievance is that confidential information imparted in a relationship of confidence has been wrongfully disclosed. There is not necessarily a misuse of private information.[59]

In *McKennitt v Ash*,[60] it will be remembered, the former friend of the Canadian folk singer published a book which the singer sought to restrain. And in *Lord Browne of Madingley v Associated Newspaper Ltd*[61] the Chief Executive Officer of BP complained of a breach of confidence by a newspaper which wished to publish details of his homosexual relationship with a Mr Chavalier and any information relating to the relationship that he had acquired in the course of the relationship. The claimants in both cases were successful, but the Court of Appeal applied the 'reasonable expectation of privacy' test to each. The confidential nature of the relationship—and its breach by the defendants—appears to have had no bearing on the decisions.

It did, on the other hand, in a judgment involving the Prince of Wales, copies of whose private journals were made available to a newspaper, in

---

misrepresentation', *An Inquiry into the Culture, Practices and Ethics of the Press* (n 46), Part K, ch 7, para 4.23.

59. Where widespread publication is threatened or has occurred, the requirements of breach of confidence are normally satisfied, though, as argued earlier, an action for misuse of private information ought to *require* wide publicity. Posting confidential information on a website will not necessarily annihilate its confidentiality. It depends on the extent of the dissemination: 'general availability of material upon the internet would mean that it would be likely to lose its confidential character. However, equally, there is guidance and observations that very limited dissemination and only partial dissemination, perhaps in some remote or expert site that is not generally available to the public without a great deal of effort, may not result in such a loss of confidentiality', *Barclays Bank plc v Guardian News and Media Ltd* [2009] EWHC 591 (QB), [22] per Blake J. The offending disclosure had appeared on the newspaper's website for no more than about five hours; the injunction was therefore continued since the confidential character of the information remained intact. See too *Attorney General v Greater Manchester Newspapers Ltd* [2001] EWHC QB 451; *Aegis Defence Services Ltd v Stoner* [2006] EWHC 1515 (Ch).
60. [2006] EWCA Civ 1714, [2008] QB 73. See Chapter 5.
61. [2007] EWCA Civ 295, [2008] QB 103.

breach of contract, by an employee.[62] Among the Prince's personal impressions were disparaging descriptions of a banquet attended by the President of China marking the handover of Hong Kong to the People's Republic. The publication of and comments on extracts by the newspaper were made shortly after a state visit to Britain by the Chinese President during which he held a dinner to which Prince Charles declined an invitation.

Lord Phillips CJ acknowledged:

> This action is not concerned, however, with a claim for breach of privacy that involves an extension of the old law of breach of confidence. There is an issue in this case as to whether the information disclosed was private so as to engage Article 8 and there is an obvious overlap between this question and the question of whether the information was capable of being the subject of a duty of confidence under the old law. Assuming that it was, there are in this action all the elements of a claim for breach of confidence under that law. The information was disclosed in breach of a well recognised relationship of confidence, that which exists between master and servant. Furthermore, the disclosure was in breach of an express contractual duty of confidentiality. The Newspaper was aware that the journals were disclosed in breach of confidence.[63]

Stressing the public interest in the observance of the obligation of confidence, he accepted that, under the new order, the question was whether that duty imposed a disproportionate fetter on Article 10's protection of freedom of expression. The learned judge concluded that

> [A] significant element to be weighed in the balance is the importance in a democratic society of upholding duties of confidence that are created between individuals. It is not enough to justify publication that the information in question is a matter of public interest...[T]he test to be applied when considering whether it is necessary to restrict freedom of expression in order to prevent disclosure of information received in confidence is not simply whether the information is a matter of public interest but whether, in all the circumstances, it is in the public interest that the duty of confidence should be breached. The court will need to consider whether, having regard to the nature of the information and all the relevant circumstances, it is legitimate for the owner of the information to seek to keep it confidential or whether it is in the public interest that the information should be made public.[64]

The court was in no doubt that the Prince's journals were both confidential and private, and found in his favour. The continuing utility—and

62. *Associated Newspapers Ltd v HRH Prince of Wales* [2006] EWCA Civ 1776.
63. *Associated Newspapers Ltd v HRH Prince of Wales* [2006] EWCA Civ 1776 at [28].
64. *Associated Newspapers Ltd v HRH Prince of Wales* [2006] EWCA Civ 1776 at [67]–[68].

conceptual integrity—of the remedy for breach of confidence should not, under the new order, be allowed to expire.

10. Is media self-regulation adequate?

In Chapter 7, after examining the various bodies that are charged with regulating the media, I concluded that, while their guidelines are constructive and valuable, their powers and complaints procedure fail to afford satisfactory protection to victims of media malpractice.[65] Even a beefed up media self-regulatory body, as proposed in the Leveson Inquiry Report, with enhanced powers, independence, funding, and statutory support, while it may be able efficaciously to handle victims' complaints and impose sanctions, is unlikely to have the facility to develop a coherent or consistent body of principle that affords guidance to the media and the public. Reconciling privacy and free speech is too important a constitutional enterprise to be left to a random process that lacks a doctrine of binding precedent.[66]

Conclusion

As I argued in Chapter 4, a superior approach to the protection of privacy is to identify the specific interests of the individual that the law should secure. I have recommended an analysis that identifies the nucleus of the right of privacy as the safeguarding of private facts. Within Article 8's concept of 'private life' the courts have, of course, fashioned a remedy for the misuse of private information. But uncertainty lingers. Greater precision is required in respect of both the conception of 'private information' and the 'public interest'. In the case of the latter, there is a conspicuous need for clear, authoritative guidelines as to what sort of publications are incorporated within this otherwise nebulous notion. A statute is the best option.

---

65. At my last count, twenty-two jurisdictions have voluntary (ie, non-state-supported) press councils or similar bodies. Statutory bodies exist in fifteen jurisdictions, while six have councils that receive some state support. The Leveson Inquiry Report includes a useful review of press regulation in China, France, Germany, the Netherlands, Scandinavia, and the United States. See Part K, ch 2.

66. The PCC, according to the Leveson Inquiry Report, 'operates a principle of abiding by precedent, looking to previous decisions for guidance when deciding cases and seeking to keep decisions consistent. Key decisions are collated in the Editors' Codebook, an amplified version of the Editors' Code of Practice. A decision in one case would determine or at least influence the approach taken by the PCC in a similar case in future', Part J, Chapter 4, para 3.23. This is a far cry from the principle of *stare decisis*.

There are two typical responses to a legislative solution. The first claims that it represents political interference with free speech. This is unpersuasive; it could apply equally to any statute that touched on public order, defamation, obscenity, contempt of court, blasphemy, copyright, hate speech, and so on.

The second contention is that a privacy statute would, in the words of the Joint Committee on Privacy and Injunctions, 'risk becoming outdated quickly, would not allow for flexibility on a case-by-case basis and would lead to even more litigation over its interpretation.'[67] In support of this argument, the committee makes the following (implausible) assertions:[68] 'Any law that sought to define what is private would, in order to remain compliant with the European Convention on Human Rights, also have to set out that the right to privacy is balanced against the right to freedom of expression (and, potentially, other rights)'. Where precisely is the problem? It adds: 'There would then be pressure to spell out in more detail those rights and to define the public interest.' Why? The allegation continues: 'There is a risk that definitions will not keep pace with developments in society.' This assertion presumes, as already pointed out, a detailed, comprehensive statute. In any event, surely this is a feature of any legislation. Next it claims: 'There is danger that any list will be treated as exhaustive, and so fail to cover information which should be protected as private.' Not if the statute explicitly states that the list is not exhaustive. The committee adds: 'Any list that purports to be exhaustive will imply that anything not in the list should not be covered.' Why should it do so if the draftsman states otherwise? And the committee concludes: 'There would no doubt be litigation over the interpretation of the new provisions.' No doubt?

To repeat, this analysis presumes that legislation would be formulated in elaborate, intricate terms. It is certainly not what I propose, as will be seen from my draft bill in the Appendix. But, of course, even a highly detailed, comprehensive statute is not immune to amendment and updating.

Before the advent of the Human Rights Act 1998, at least, it was not uncommon for English judges to manifest a reluctance to 'make law' in this field, and to express the view that the right to privacy 'has so long been

---

67. *Privacy and Injunctions* (n 45), para 37. The Leveson Inquiry Report explicitly endorses this view: 'It does not appear that legislative intervention will do other than generate further litigation as attempts are made to discover the extent to which the new framework matches the developing law', Part J, ch 3, para 4.2.
68. *Privacy and Injunctions* (n 45), para 37.

disregarded here that it can be recognised only by the legislature.'[69] The case for legislation adumbrated in these pages rests on a different premise. I have sought to show that the increasing complexity of the challenge faced by the courts in mediating between privacy and free speech renders the subject a perfect candidate for the creation of a statutory tort.

The bill proposed in the Appendix—an amateurish attempt at legislative drafting—is intended as a possible prototype which stands in need of refinement and, of course, improvement. It does not affect to be equipped for instant enactment! I have resisted the temptation to offer a gloss or elucidation of its clauses; I hope that their meaning and rationale, aided by the analysis above and in earlier chapters, speak for themselves. Nor do I consider here some of the procedural and technical questions that such a statute would need to address. So, for example, I have left open the matter of whether any of the existing causes of action (under the Human Rights Act,[70] the Data Protection Act 1998, the action for breach of confidence, and so on) should be abolished.[71] And, I disregard the subject of court-ordered apologies, quantum of damages, and any limitation period.

69. *Kaye v Robertson* [1991] FSR 62, 71 per Legatt LJ. Similar sentiments were expressed at 66 per Glidewell LJ and 70 per Bingham LJ. See too *Malone v Metropolitan Police Commissioner* [1979] Ch 344, 372–81, at 372 per Sir Robert Megarry V-C: 'It seems to me that where Parliament has abstained from legislating on a point that is plainly suitable for legislation, it is indeed difficult for the court to lay down new rules of common law or equity that will carry out the Crown's treaty obligations, or to discover for the first time that such rules have always existed.' More recently in *Secretary of State for the Home Department v Wainwright* [2001] EWCA Civ 2081, 94, Buxton LJ declared: 'It is thus for Parliament to remove, if it thinks fit, the barrier to the recognition of a tort of breach of privacy…'

70. Of course, if enacted, a statute such as this would fall to be interpreted, as s 3(1) of the Human Rights Act 1998 requires, in a manner that conforms with the ECHR: 'So far as it is possible to do so, primary and subordinate legislation must be read and given effect in a way which is compatible with the Convention rights.' This should not give rise to any difficulties in respect of the rights protected under Arts 8 and 10 with which it is entirely consistent. In fact following this course is no more than 'purposive interpretation', see J van Zyl Smit, 'The New Purposive Approach to Statutes: HRA Section 3 after *Ghaidan v Godin-Mendoza*' (2007) 70 Modern Law Review 294.

71. In recommending a federal privacy statute, the Australian Law Reform Commission proposed that 'any action at common law for invasion of a person's privacy should be abolished', *For Your Information: Australian Privacy Law and Practice* (Report 108, May 2008), recommendations 74–6. In its report, the New South Wales Law Reform Commission proposed a privacy statute, suggesting that it would be 'undesirable for the common law to develop a tort of invasion of privacy if the statutory cause of action that we propose is enacted. The cause of action that we propose not only involves a more sophisticated balancing of privacy and other interests than may occur through a tortious action at common law, but also incorporates a more flexible remedial pattern. Further, a common law action could seriously undermine the statutory cause of action, for example, by evading the limits on the amount of compensation that can be awarded for non economic loss or by countenancing awards of exemplary or aggravated damages', *Invasion of Privacy* (Report 120, 2009), para 8.1.

Conclusion

There is no silver bullet. Enactment tomorrow of a privacy statute would generate new problems for the judicial construction of victims' rights against unsolicited invasions of privacy. The media would continue to be tested daily (with more concentrated minds) as to whether stories are in the public interest:

> How far is the sexual deviancy of family doctor of legitimate interest to his patients? How far is a schoolteacher's adherence to Satanism of legitimate interest to parents? Is there a public interest in revealing the true behaviour of pop stars or sportsmen, who may serve as role models to thousands of adolescents? If a Member of Parliament has an affair and is deceiving either his family or his mistress, is the public interest served by allowing voters to know, so that they may form a view about his stewardship of office?[72]

Nothing will make these questions disappear. The real issue is whether, as appears to be the case, the interests of the individual are invariably to be sacrificed at the altar of an often contrived 'public interest'? It goes without saying that the law ought to be a last resort. Non-legal regulatory forms of mediation will, in many cases, satisfy a claimant's grievance against an offending publication. Nor should the inculcation of appropriate, privacy-respecting norms, especially online, be neglected. Sensitivity to hurtful exposures of intimate information posted on social networks and blogs must become a vital element of moral responsibility. Schools should ensure that pupils appreciate the perils of impetuous, malevolent, and petulant posting—including those that disclose individuals' own intimate details which (they ought to be warned) are permanent and effortlessly re-broadcast by third parties, including, of course, the media.[73] The 'architecture' of the

---

72. C Munro, 'Press Freedom—How the Beast was Tamed' (1991) 54 Modern Law Review 104, 107. Professor Munro describes these as 'formidable difficulties' (ibid).
73. 'The press—or anyone else—can access huge amounts of personal material themselves and through others. A reporter can legitimately find personal information published on the internet or source recorded audio/video from members of the public. Equally, a reporter can illegitimately access private material or illicitly record personal moments or private phone calls. The papers can then publish as much of this material as they like—in text, audio, or video—online. Or anyone else can publish this information, on a website, on a blog, on a social networking site like Facebook, on Twitter, on a wiki. The information can then ripple rapidly outwards across the net', Fifth submission of the Media and Standards Trust: 'Privacy: Submission to the Joint Committee on Privacy and Injunctions' November 2011, pp 7–8 quoted in *An Inquiry into the Culture, Practices and Ethics of the Press* (n 46), Part F, ch 6, para 2.77.

Web can significantly enhance privacy.[74] Default settings of social media need to be clearly and visibly set in favour of privacy.[75]

The Internet has radically changed not only how we communicate, educate, transact, and present ourselves; it is a habitat in which many of us increasingly dwell—voluntarily or inescapably—in which our very identity may be transformed and distorted. Potential employers, at the click of a mouse, can uncover details of an applicant that may be obsolete, erroneous, or irrelevant. The potential for the misuse of sensitive information has grown exponentially. Yet, despite this metamorphosis, we need to recall what has *not* changed. The values that we cherish in a free society including, of course, privacy and the freedom of the media, are simultaneously enhanced and endangered by the digital revolution. It is these values, though their survival is sustained by social norms, that occasionally require the sustenance and defence of the law.

In view of the post-Leveson brouhaha engendered by the proposed 'legislative underpinning' of an enhanced media regulatory body, it might seem foolhardy to advance a statutory resolution to the intractable question of reconciling privacy and media freedom.[76] Why wade into the choppy waters of legislation when, if left alone, the courts will continue their interpretive

---

74. See L Lessig, *Code and Other Laws of Cyberspace* (New York: Basic Books, 1999); JR Reidenberg, 'Lex Informatica: The Formulation of Information Policy Rules Through Technology' (1998) 76 Texas Law Review 553.

75. In December 2012 Facebook announced a new—visible—control called 'Privacy Shortcuts' that will permit users to change who has access to their 'stuff', and who can contact them through the website. It includes a one-click means by which to block a particular individual.

76. Reassuringly, I am not alone in urging a legislative solution. Law reform bodies in a number of jurisdictions including, eg, in Australia have proposed state and federal legislation. See, eg, New South Wales Law Reform Commission, *Protecting Privacy in New South Wales* (Report 127, 2010); Australian Law Reform Commission (n 71); New Zealand Law Commission, *Review of the Law of Privacy* (4 stages: 2006–11); Law Reform Commission of Hong Kong, *Privacy and Media Intrusion* (2004); *Civil Liability for Invasion of Privacy* (2004); *Privacy: The Regulation of Covert Surveillance* (2006). The New South Wales Law Reform Commission expressed the view that 'tampering with existing causes of action or developing specific torts would not provide a satisfactory basis for the ongoing development of the law of privacy in a climate of dynamic societal and technological change. Recognising the inherent value of privacy does provide such a basis. It also fills any gaps that manifest themselves in privacy protection. The statutory cause of action that we propose achieves both of these aims', para 4.14. The distinguished former Justice of the Australian High Court, The Hon Michael Kirby, has long supported this course of action. See M Kirby, 'Publication Privacy: Action at Last?' (2012) 17 Media and Arts Law Review 202. See too R Wacks, 'Michael Kirby: Privacy Pioneer' (2012) 17 Media and Arts Law Review 216. I agree with Michael Kirby's paradox that, in the absence of legislative action, the common law could well outstrip the protection that a privacy statute would contain. This is not an unmixed blessing, for a comprehensive privacy statute would specify detailed defences that safeguard, above all, free speech. Incremental judicial balancing is far less satisfactory: it is necessarily slow, and dependent on the serendipity of litigation.

pursuit of solutions to the problem? To this legitimate question, there are two answers. First, my intention is not to control or curtail the activities of the media, but to suggest reasonable measures better to protect the privacy of victims of intrusion or unsolicited publication of personal information. Unlike the contentious Levesonian plan, this legislation is mainly in the shape of elucidation and assistance—rather than regulation and supervision.

Secondly, as I have sought to demonstrate in this book, the current law, under the disconcerting sway of the Human Rights Act 1998, and particularly Article 8's bloated abstractions, provides inadequate guidance both to the individual and to the media in regard to their respective rights and obligations in this elemental sphere of democratic freedom.

Appendix

Protection of Privacy Bill[1]

1. This bill—which is based largely upon several of the recommendations of the Law Reform Commission of Hong Kong's report, *Civil Liability for Invasion of Privacy* (2004)—benefited from the perceptive comments of Professor Megan Richardson for which I am most grateful, but who bears no responsibility for its remaining shortcomings. The Law Reform Commission and its privacy sub-committee (on both of which I was privileged to serve) have been particularly active in this area. See its related reports, *Reform of the Law Relating to the Protection of Personal Data* (1994), *Regulating the Interception of Communications* (1996), *Privacy and Media Intrusion* (1999), *Stalking* (2000), and *Privacy: The Regulation of Covert Surveillance* (2006). All are available on the Law Reform Commission's web site.

A
BILL
TO
Protect the right of privacy.

BE IT ENACTED by the Queen's most Excellent Majesty, by and with the advice and consent of the Lords Spiritual and Temporal, and Commons, in this present Parliament assembled, and by the authority of the same, as follows:—

1 Personal information

'Personal information' means those facts, communications, or opinions which relate to an individual and which it would be reasonable to expect him or her to regard as intimate or sensitive and therefore to want to withhold, or at least to restrict, their collection, use or publication.

2 Intrusion

(1) Any person who intentionally intrudes, physically or otherwise, upon the solitude or seclusion of another or into his or her private affairs or concerns in circumstances where that other has a reasonable expectation of privacy should be liable in tort, provided that the intrusion is highly offensive to a reasonable person of ordinary sensibilities.

Reasonable expectation of privacy

(2) A court shall take into account the following factors when determining whether the claimant had a reasonable expectation of privacy at the time of the alleged intrusion—
   (a) the place where the intrusion occurred (for example, whether the claimant is at home, in office premises or in a public place, and whether or not the place is open to public view from a place accessible to the public, or whether or not the conversation is audible to passers-by);

(b) the object and occasion of the intrusion (for example, whether it interferes with the intimate or private life of the claimant); and

(c) the means of intrusion employed and the nature of any device used (for example, whether the intrusion is effected by means of a high-technology sense-enhancing device, or by mere observation or natural hearing).

Highly offensive

(3) A court shall take into account the following factors when determining whether an intrusion was highly offensive to a reasonable person—

(a) the extent and duration of the intrusion;

(b) the means by which the intrusion was conducted;

(c) the type of information obtained or sought to be obtained by means of the intrusion;

(d) whether the claimant could reasonably expect to be free from such conduct in the location where it was carried out;

(e) whether the claimant has taken any steps which would indicate to a reasonable person the claimant's desire that the defendant not engage in the intrusive conduct.

Defences

(4) The following are defences to an action for intrusion—

(a) the claimant expressly or by implication authorised or consented to the intrusion;

(b) the act or conduct in question was authorised by or under any enactment or rule of law;

(c) the intrusion has been authorised by or under any enactment or rule of law;

(d) the act or conduct constituting the intrusion was necessary for and proportionate to—

(i)   the protection of the person or property of the defendant or another;

(ii) the prevention, detection or investigation of crime;

(iii) the prevention, preclusion or redress of unlawful or seriously improper conduct;

(iv) the protection of national security.

3 Public disclosure of personal information

(1) Any person who gives publicity to a matter concerning the private life of another should be liable in tort provided that the publicity is of a kind that would be highly offensive to a reasonable person of ordinary sensibilities and he or she knows or ought to know in all the circumstances that the publicity would be highly offensive to such a person.

Highly offensive

(2) A court shall take into account the following factors when determining whether the publicity would be highly offensive to a reasonable person—

(a) whether the facts, communications or opinions, pertaining to an individual are particularly sensitive or intimate;

(b) whether the defendant used unlawful or intrusive means to obtain the facts, communications or opinions;

(c) the manner of publication;

(d) the extent of the dissemination;

(e) the degree of harm to the claimant's legitimate interests; and

(f) the motive of the defendant.

Defences

(1) The following are defences to an action for public disclosure—

(a) the claimant has expressly or by implication authorised or consented to the publication;

(b) the publicity has been authorised by or under any enactment or rule of law;

(c) the publicity would have been privileged had the action been for defamation;

(d) the publication was in the public interest.

4 Public interest

(1) A court shall take into account the following factors when determining whether the publicity was in the public interest—
   (a) To whom was the information given?
   (b) Is the claimant a 'public figure'?
   (c) Was the claimant in a public place?
   (d) Is the information in the public domain?
   (e) How was the information acquired?
   (f) What was the defendant's motive?
   (g) Was it essential for the claimant's identity to be revealed?

(2) The publication should be presumed to be in the public interest if it was necessary for—
   (a) the prevention, detection or investigation of crime;
   (b) the prevention of unlawful or seriously improper conduct;
   (c) establishing whether the claimant was able to discharge his or her public or professional obligations;
   (d) establishing whether the claimant was fit for any public office or profession held or carried on by him or her, or which he or she sought to hold or carry on professional responsibilities;
   (e) the prevention of the public being materially misled by a public statement made by the claimant;
   (f) the protection of public health or safety;
   (g) the protection of national security; and was proportionate to the legitimate aims pursued by the defendant.

(3) The claimant should not be precluded from obtaining relief by reason merely of the fact that the matter to which the defendant has allegedly given publicity—
   (a) could be found in a register to which the public or a section of the public had access;
   (b) has been disclosed by the claimant to his or her family members, friends or other individuals;
   (c) has been disclosed or published by a third party without the consent of the claimant;
   (d) has been posted on the Internet by a third party without the consent of the claimant; or

(e) related to an event which occurred in a place visible or accessible to the public.

5 Remedies

(1) In an action for intrusion or public disclosure of personal information a court may—

(a) award damages, including, where appropriate, exemplary damages;

(b) grant an injunction if it shall appear just and convenient;

(c) order the defendant to account to the claimant for any profits which he or she has made by reason or in consequence of the intrusion or unwarranted publicity, or order the defendant to destroy or deliver up to the claimant any articles or documents containing information about the claimant which have come into the possession of the defendant by reason or in consequence of the intrusion or, as the case may be, which have resulted in the defendant being held liable to the claimant for public disclosure of personal information.

(2) Damages shall include injury to feelings.

(3) In awarding damages a court shall have regard to all the circumstances of the case, including—

(a) the effect of the intrusion or disclosure of personal information on the health, welfare, social, business or financial position of the claimant or his or her family;

(b) any distress, annoyance, embarrassment or humiliation suffered by the claimant or his or her family; and

(c) the conduct of the claimant and the defendant both before and after the intrusion or disclosure, including publicity for, and the adequacy and manner of, any apology or offer of amends made by the defendant.

6 Hearing

(1) A hearing in an action for intrusion or disclosure may be held in private if publicity would defeat the object of the hearing.

(2) The court may order that the identity of any party or witness shall not be disclosed if it considers non-disclosure necessary in order to protect the interests of that party or witness.

7 Living individuals

(1) Actions for intrusion or unwarranted publicity should be limited to living individuals and the person to whom any right of action should accrue is the individual whose right of privacy is threatened or has been infringed.

(2) On the death of the complainant or defendant, the cause of action should survive for the benefit of the claimant's estate or, as the case may be, against the defendant's estate.

8 Operators of websites

(1) This section applies where an action for disclosure of personal information is brought against the operator of a website in respect of a statement posted on the website.

(2) It is a defence for the operator to show that it was not the operator who posted the statement on the website.

(3) The defence is defeated if the claimant shows that—
   (a) it was not possible for the claimant to identify the person who posted the statement;
   (b) the claimant gave the operator a notice of complaint in relation to the statement; and
   (c) the operator failed to respond to the notice of complaint.

(4) For the purposes of subsection (3)(a), it is possible for a claimant to 'identify' a person only if the claimant has sufficient information to bring proceedings against the person.

9 Order for removal of publication from website

(1) Where a court gives judgment for the claimant in an action for defamation the court may order the operator of a website on which the publication of personal information is posted to remove the statement.

(2) Subsection (1) does not affect the power of the court apart from that subsection.

Index

284